A·N·N·U·A·L E·D·I·T·I·O·N·S

Early Childhood Education

Twentieth Edition

EDITORS

Karen Menke Paciorek
Eastern Michigan University

Karen Menke Paciorek is a professor of early childhood education at Eastern Michigan University. Her degrees in early childhood education include a B.A. from the University of Pittsburgh, an M.A. from George Washington University, and a Ph.D. from Peabody College of Vanderbilt University. She is the coeditor, with Joyce Huth Munro, of *Sources: Notable Selections in Early Childhood Education* (Dushkin/McGraw-Hill Publishers). She has served as president of the Michigan Association for the Education of Young Children and is the current chair of the Michigan Early Childhood Education Consortium. She presents at local, state, and national conferences on curriculum planning, guiding behavior, preparing the learning environment, and working with families.

Joyce Huth Munro

Joyce Huth Munro is visiting professor at Francis Marion University in Florence, South Carolina. She is an editor for a teaching cases series and coeditor (with Karen Menke Paciorek) of *Sources: Notable Selections in Early Childhood Education.* At regional and national conferences, she presents seminars on innovative methods of teacher education and curriculum design. Dr. Munro holds an M.Ed. from the University of South Carolina and a Ph.D. from Peabody College at Vanderbilt University.

Dushkin/McGraw Hill
Sluice Dock, Guilford, Connecticut 06437

Visit us on the Internet
http://www.dushkin.com/annualeditions/

Credits

1. Perspectives
Unit photo—© 1999 by CLEO Freelance Photography.
2. Child Development and Families
Unit photo—Courtesy of Gina Mulqueen.
3. Care and Educational Practices
Unit photo—© 1999 by CLEO Freelance Photography.
4. Guiding and Supporting Young Children
Unit photo—© 1999 by CLEO Freelance Photography.
5. Curricular Issues
Unit photo—Dushkin/McGraw-Hill photo by Pamela Carley.
6. Trends
Unit photo—© 1999 by PhotoDisc.

Copyright

Cataloging in Publication Data
Main entry under title: Annual Editions: Early childhood education. 1999/2000.
    1. Education, Preschool—Periodicals. 2. Child development—Periodicals. 3. Child rearing—United States—Periodicals. I. Paciorek, Karen Menke, *comp.;* Munro, Joyce Huth, *comp.* II. Title: Early childhood education.
ISBN 0-07-039784-8   372.21'05   77-640114   ISSN: 0272-4456

Twentieth Edition

Cover image © 1999 PhotoDisc, Inc.

Printed in the United States of America   1234567890BAHBAH5432109   Printed on Recycled Paper

Members of the Advisory Board are instrumental in the final selection of articles for each edition of ANNUAL EDITIONS. Their review of articles for content, level, currency, and appropriateness provides critical direction to the editor and staff. We think that you will find their careful consideration well reflected in this volume.

Editors/Advisory Board

Staff

To the Reader

In publishing ANNUAL EDITIONS we recognize the enormous role played by the magazines, newspapers, and journals of the public press in providing current, first-rate educational information in a broad spectrum of interest areas. Many of these articles are appropriate for students, researchers, and professionals seeking accurate, current material to help bridge the gap between principles and theories and the real world. These articles, however, become more useful for study when those of lasting value are carefully collected, organized, indexed, and reproduced in a low-cost format, which provides easy and permanent access when the material is needed. That is the role played by ANNUAL EDITIONS.

New to ANNUAL EDITIONS is the inclusion of related World Wide Web sites. These sites have been selected by our editorial staff to represent some of the best resources found on the World Wide Web today. Through our carefully developed topic guide, we have linked these Web resources to the articles covered in this ANNUAL EDITIONS reader. We think that you will find this volume useful, and we hope that you will take a moment to visit us on the Web at *http://www.dushkin.com* to tell us what you think.

Early childhood education is an interdisciplinary field that includes child development, family issues, educational practices, behavior guidance, and curriculum. *Annual Editions: Early Childhood Education 99/00* brings you the latest information in the field from a wide variety of recent journals, newspapers, and magazines. In selecting articles for this first edition of the new millennium we were careful to provide you with a well-balanced look at the issues and concerns facing teachers, families, society, and children. There are four themes found in readings chosen for this twentieth edition of *Annual Editions: Early Childhood Education.* They are: (1) the recent release of key findings on how the brain develops, (2) the importance of long-term effects of quality preschool experiences, (3) activities for children with special needs, and (4) the knowledge possessed by infants at birth and how those abilities can best be fostered and honed for later success.

We continue to find more articles that are relevant for our readers in popular magazines. For this we are pleased, for it indicates that the field of early childhood education has made an impact on the economy, lifestyle, education, and behavioral patterns of the general public. As much as we would like to include more of these articles, however, we realize that we cannot forget the advanced student or seasoned professional who looks to *Annual Editions: Early Childhood Education* for a complete summary of current trends and issues. Therefore, in this edition we have included a few articles appropriate for the non-beginning-level reader. While we recognize that we cannot provide articles equally suited for all readers, we do want to include a sample of the many high-quality research articles available for the early childhood professional. In most cases what is included is an edited version of the complete article. The reader is directed to the journal for the full text.

Continuing in this edition of *Annual Editions: Early Childhood Education* are selected *World Wide Web* sites that can be used to further explore topics addressed in the articles. These sites will be cross-referenced by number in the *topic guide.*

Given the wide range of topics it includes, *Annual Editions: Early Childhood Education 99/00* may be used with several groups: undergraduate or graduate students studying early childhood education, professionals pursuing further development, or parents seeking to improve their skills.

The selection of readings for this edition has been a cooperative effort between the two editors. We meet each year with members of our advisory board, who share with us in the selection process. The production and editorial staff of Dushkin/McGraw-Hill ably support and coordinate our efforts.

To the instructor or reader interested in the history of early childhood care and education programs throughout the years, we invite you to review our latest book, also published by Dushkin/McGraw-Hill. *Sources: Notable Selections in Early Childhood Education, 2nd ed.* (1999) is a collection of numerous writings of enduring historical value by influential people in the field. All of the selections are primary sources that allow you to experience firsthand the thoughts and views of these important educators. The instructor interested in using both *Sources* and *Annual Editions* may contact the editors for a list of compatible articles from the two books.

We are grateful to readers who have corresponded with us about the selection and organization of previous editions. Your comments and articles for consideration are welcomed and will serve to modify future volumes. Please take the time to fill out and return the postage-paid *article rating form* on the last page. You may also contact either one of us online at: *ted_paciorek@online. emich.edu or jhmunro@aol.com.*

We look forward to hearing from you.

Karen Menke Paciorek

Joyce Huth Munro
Editors

Contents

UNIT 1

Perspectives

Six selections consider
both the national and
international development
of early childhood education.

The concepts in bold italics are developed in the article. For further expansion please refer to the Topic Guide and the Index.

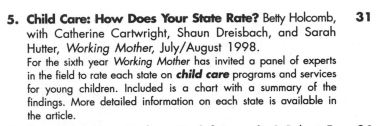

UNIT 2

Child Development and Families

Six selections consider the effects of family life on the growing child and the importance of parent education.

The concepts in bold italics are developed in the article. For further expansion please refer to the Topic Guide and the Index.

UNIT 3

Care and Educational Practices

Eight selections examine
various educational programs,
assess the effectiveness of some
teaching methods, and consider
some of the problems faced by
students with special needs.

The concepts in bold italics are developed in the article. For further expansion please refer to the Topic Guide and the Index.

The concepts in bold italics are developed in the article. For further expansion please refer to the Topic Guide and the Index.

The concepts in bold italics are developed in the article. For further expansion please refer to the Topic Guide and the Index.

The concepts in bold italics are developed in the article. For further expansion please refer to the Topic Guide and the Index.

UNIT 6

Trends

Three selections consider the present and future of early childhood education.

The concepts in bold italics are developed in the article. For further expansion please refer to the Topic Guide and the Index.

This topic guide suggests how the selections and World Wide Web sites found in the next section of this book relate to topics of traditional concern to students and professionals involved with the study of early childhood education. It is useful for locating interrelated articles and Web sites for reading and research. The guide is arranged alphabetically according to topic.

The relevant Web sites, which are numbered and annotated on pages 4 and 5, are easily identified by the Web icon (◎) under the topic articles. By linking the articles and the Web sites by topic, this ANNUAL EDITIONS reader becomes a powerful learning and research tool.

TOPIC AREA	TREATED IN	TOPIC AREA	TREATED IN
Abuse	24. Creating a Community of Learning for Homeless Children ◎ *17, 19, 20, 21*		31. Beginning to Implement the Reggio Philosphy 32. Supporting Math Thinking ◎ *14, 15, 16, 18, 22, 23, 24, 25, 27, 28*
Advocacy	1. Preschoolers' Education 3. Highlights of the Quality 2000 Initiative 4. Child Shall Lead Us ◎ *3, 7, 17, 19, 20, 21, 32, 33*	**Developmentally Appropriate Practice**	15. Simply Sensational Spaces 18. From Philosophy to Practice 19. Together Is Better 26. Why Curriculum Matters 29. Learning to Read and Write 30. NAEYC Position Statement 35. Let's Be Real! ◎ *13, 16, 17, 20, 32*
Assessment	13. It May Cause Anxiety, but Day Care Can Benefit Kids 28. Challenging Movement Experiences 33. Documenting Children's Learning ◎ *10, 11, 15, 16, 25, 29, 30, 33*	**Discipline**	22. Beyond Discipline to Guidance 23. Teaching Peace Concepts 25. Fostering Intrinsic Motivation ◎ *13, 14, 15, 16, 17, 18, 20*
Brain Development	2. New Brain Development Research 7. Fetal Psychology 10. Baby Talk ◎ *12, 13*	**Diversity**	1. Preschoolers' Education 4. Child Shall Lead Us 6. Can Education Reduce Social Inequity? 12. Education of Hispanics 21. Challenges to Family ◎ *11*
Child Care: Full Day/Half Day	5. Child Care 6. Can Education Reduce Social Inequity? 13. It May Cause Anxiety, but Day Care Can Benefit Kids 14. Meeting Basic Needs 21. Challenges to Family ◎ *3, 5, 17*	**Divorce**	4. Child Shall Lead Us 34. Tomorrow's Child ◎ *21*
Child Development	2. New Brain Development Research 7. Fetal Psychology 8. Children's Prenatal Exposure 9. Bundle of Emotions 10. Baby Talk 11. Boys Will Be Boys 12. Education of Hispanics 24. Creating a Community of Learning for Homeless Children ◎ *10, 12, 13, 19, 21*	**Emergent Literacy**	10. Baby Talk 29. Learning to Read and Write ◎ *22*
		Emotional Development	8. Children's Prenatal Exposure 9. Bundle of Emotions 15. Simply Sensational Spaces 17. Don't Shut Fathers Out ◎ *10, 12*
Collaboration	3. Highlights of the Quality 2000 Initiative 4. Child Shall Lead Us 20. Inclusion of Young Children 24. Creating a Community of Learning for Homeless Children ◎ *3, 7, 17, 19, 21*	**Families**	4. Child Shall Lead Us 11. Boys Will Be Boys 13. It May Cause Anxiety, but Day Care Can Benefit Kids 17. Don't Shut Fathers Out 18. From Philosophy to Practice 21. Challenges to Family 24. Creating a Community of Learning for Homeless Children 34. Tomorrow's Child ◎ *3, 7, 9, 21*
Constructivist Practice	31. Beginning to Implement the Reggio Philosophy 32. Supporting Math Thinking ◎ *18, 22, 24, 31, 32, 33*	**Guiding Behavior**	22. Beyond Discipline to Guidance 23. Teaching Peace Concepts 25. Fostering Intrinsic Motivation ◎ *14, 15, 16, 17, 18*
Curriculum	26. Why Curriculum Matters 27. Fostering Creativity 28. Challenging Movement Experiences 29. Learning to Read and Write 30. NAEYC Position Statement	**Health and Safety**	8. Children's Prenatal Exposure 14. Meeting Basic Needs ◎ *10, 13, 17, 19*

◉ AE: Early Childhood Education

The following World Wide Web sites have been carefully researched and selected to support the articles found in this reader. If you are interested in learning more about specific topics found in this book, these Web sites are a good place to start. The sites are cross-referenced by number and appear in the topic guide on the previous two pages. Also, you can link to these Web sites through our DUSHKIN ONLINE support site at http://www.dushkin.com/online/.

The following sites were available at the time of publication. Visit our Web site—we update DUSHKIN ONLINE regularly to reflect any changes.

General Sources

1. Educational Resources Information Center
http://www.accesseric.org:81
This invaluable site provides links to all ERIC sites: clearinghouses, support components, and publishers of ERIC materials. You can search the massive ERIC database, find out what is new in early childhood education at *http://ericps. ed.uiuc.edu/ericece.html*, and ask questions about ERIC.

2. National Association for the Education of Young Children
http://www.naeyc.org
The NAEYC Web site is a valuable tool for anyone working with young children. Also see the National Education Association site: *http://ww.nea.org*.

3. National Parent Information Network/ERIC
http://npin.org
This clearinghouse of elementary, early childhood, and urban education data has information for parents and for people who work with parents.

4. U.S. Department of Education
http://www.ed.gov/pubs/TeachersGuide/
Government goals, projects, grants, and other educational programs are listed here as well as many links to teacher services and resources.

Perspectives

5. Child Care Directory: Careguide
http://www.careguide.net
Find licensed/registered childcare by state, city, region, or age of child at this site. Site contains providers' pages, parents' pages and many links.

6. Goals 2000: A Progress Report
http://www.ed.gov/pubs/goals/progrpt/index.html
Open this site to survey a progress report by the U.S. Department of Education on the Goals 2000 reform initiative. It provides a sense of educators' future goals.

7. Poverty in America Research Index
http://www.mindspring.com/~nexweb21/povindex.htm
Open this page to find definitions and tables related to poverty and poverty areas. The site provides answers to FAQs, facts about poverty, and discussion of poverty myths vs. realities. Welfare reform is also addressed.

Child Development and Families

8. Early Childhood Education Online
http://www.ume.maine.edu/cofed/eceol/welcome.shtml
This site gives information on developmental guidelines, presents issues in the field, gives tips for observation and assessment, and information on advocacy.

9. Global SchoolNet Foundation
http://www.gsn.org
Access this site for multicultural education information. The site includes news for teachers, students, and parents as well as chat rooms, links to educational resources, programs, and contests and competitions.

10. The National Academy for Child Development
http://www.nacd.org
The NACD, an international organization, is dedicated to helping children and adults reach their full potential. Its home page presents links to various programs, research, and resources into such topics as learning disabilities, ADD/ADHD, brain injuries, autism, accelerated and gifted, and other similar topic areas.

11. World Education Exchange/Hamline University
http://www.hamline.edu/~kjmaier/
This site, which aims for "educational collaboration," takes you around the world to examine virtual classrooms, trends, policy, and infrastructure development. It leads to information about school reform, multiculturalism, technology in education, and much more.

12. Zero to Three
http://www.zerotothree.org
Find here developmental information on the first 3 years of life: an excellent site for both parent and professional.

Care and Educational Practices

13. American Academy of Pediatrics (AAP)
http://www.aap.org
AAP provides information for physical, mental, and social health for infants, children, adolescents, and young adults.

14. Canada's Schoolnet Staff Room
http://www.schoolnet.ca/home/e/
Here is a resource and link site for anyone involved in education, including special-needs educators, teachers, parents, volunteers, and administrators.

15. Classroom Connect
http://www.classroom.net
A major Web site for K–12 teachers and students, this site provides links to schools, teachers, and resources online. It includes discussion of the use of technology in the classroom.

16. ERIC Clearinghouse on Disabilities and Gifted Education
http://www.cec.sped.org/gifted/gt-faqs.htm
Information on identifying and teaching gifted children, attention deficit disorders, and other topics in gifted education may be accessed at this site.

17. National Resource Center for Health and Safety in Child Care
http://nrc.uchsc.edu
Search through this site's extensive links to find information on health and safety in child care. Health and safety tips are provided, as are other child-care information resources. In addition, national U.S. health and safety performance standards are reproduced here.

18. Online Innovation Institute
http://oii.org

A collaborative project among Internet-using educators, proponents of systemic reform, content-area experts, and teachers who desire professional growth, this site provides a learning environment for integrating the Internet into educators' individual teaching styles.

Guiding and Supporting Young Children

19. Child Welfare League of America (CWLA)
http://www.cwla.org

The CWLA is the United States' oldest and largest organization devoted entirely to the well-being of vulnerable children and their families. Its Web site provides links to information about issues related to morality and values in education.

20. Early Intervention Solutions (EIS)
http://www.earlyintervention.com

EIS presents this site to address concerns about child stress and reinforcement. It suggests ways to deal with negative behaviors that may result from stress and anxiety among children.

21. National Network for Family Resiliency
http://www.nnfr.org

This organization's home page will lead you to a number of resource areas of interest in learning about resiliency, including General Family Resiliency, Violence Prevention, and Family Economics.

Curricular Issues

22. California Reading Initiative
http://www.sdcoe.k12.ca.us/score/promising/ prreading/prreadin.html

The California Reading Initiative site provides valuable insight into topics related to emergent literacy. Many resources for teachers and staff developers are provided.

23. Education Week on the Web
http://www.edweek.org

At this *Education Week* home page, you will be able to open archives, read special reports, keep up on current events, look at job opportunities, and access a variety of articles of relevance in educational psychology. A great deal of material is helpful in learning and instruction.

24. Kathy Schrock's Guide for Educators
http://www.discoveryschool.com/schrockguide/

This is a classified list of sites on the Internet found to be useful for enhancing curriculum and teacher professional growth. It is updated daily.

25. Phi Delta Kappa
http://www.pdkintl.org

This important organization publishes articles about all facets of education. By clicking on the links in this site, for example, you can check out the journal's online archive, which has resources such as articles having to do with assessment.

26. Reggio Emilia
http://ericps.ed.uiuc.edu/eece/reggio.html

Through ERIC, you can link to publications related to the Reggio Emilia Approach and to resources, videos, and contact information.

27. Teachers Helping Teachers
http://www.pacificnet.net/~mandel/

Basic teaching tips, new teaching-methodology ideas, and forums for teachers to share their experiences are provided on this Web site. Download software and participate in chat sessions. It features educational resources on the Web, with new ones added each week.

28. Verio Pittsburgh
http://pittsburgh.verio.net

This site contains Web sites for educators and covers a wide range of topics dealing with K–12 resources and curricula. Its links will prove useful for examining issues ranging from curricular concerns to teaching values.

Trends

29. Awesome Library for Teachers
http://www.neat-schoolhouse.org/teacher.html

Open this page for links and access to teacher information on everything from educational assessment to general child development topics.

30. Carfax
http://www.carfax.co.uk/subjeduc.htm

Look through this index for links to education publications such as *Journal of Beliefs and Values, Educational Philosophy and Theory,* and *Assessment in Education.* The site also provides links to articles and research that will prove helpful in assessment.

31. EdWeb/Andy Carvin
http://edweb.cnidr.org

The purpose of EdWeb is to explore the worlds of educational reform and information technology. Access educational resources around the world, learn about trends in education policy and information infrastructure development, and examine success stories of computers in the classroom.

32. National Institute on the Education of At-Risk Students
http://www.ed.gov/offices/OERI/At-Risk/

The At-Risk Institute supports a range of research and development activities designed to improve the education of students at risk of educational failure due to limited English proficiency, race, geographic location, or economic disadvantage. Access numerous links and summaries of the Institute's work at this site.

33. Prospects: The Congressionally Mandated Study of Educational Growth and Opportunity
http://www.ed.gov/pubs/Prospects/index.html

This report analyzes cross-sectional data on language-minority and LEP students in the United States and outlines what actions are needed to improve their educational performance. Family and economic situations are addressed. Information on related reports and sites is provided.

We highly recommend that you review our Web site for expanded information and our other product lines. We are continually updating and adding links to our Web site in order to offer you the most usable and useful information that will support and expand the value of your Annual Editions. You can reach us at: *http://www.dushkin.com/annualeditions/.*

www.dushkin.com/online/

Unit Selections

1. **Preschoolers' Education Takes Center Stage,** Linda Jacobson
2. **New Brain Development Research—A Wonderful Window of Opportunity to Build Public Support for Early Childhood Education!** Julee J. Newberger
3. **Highlights of the Quality 2000 Initiative: Not by Chance,** Sharon L. Kagan and Michelle J. Neuman
4. **A Child Shall Lead Us,** Marian Wright Edelman
5. **Child Care: How Does Your State Rate?** Betty Holcomb, with Catherine Cartwright, Shaun Dreisbach, and Sarah Hutter
6. **Can Education Reduce Social Inequity?** Robert E. Slavin

Key Points to Consider

❖ How can quality preschool programs benefit children?

❖ What should be done to capitalize on the window of opportunity in early care and education?

❖ What steps should be taken to ensure all children have a fair start for a lifetime of learning?

❖ What are the key goals of the Quality 2000 Initiative? How can they best be attained?

❖ What states are doing the most to provide quality care and education experiences for all of their children?

 **Links**   **www.dushkin.com/online/**

5. **Child Care Directory: Careguide**
   http://www.careguide.net
6. **Goals 2000: A Progress Report**
   http://www.ed.gov/pubs/goals/progrpt/index.html
7. **Poverty in America Research Index**
   http://www.mindspring.com/~nexweb21/povindex.htm

These sites are annotated on pages 4 and 5.

The wide dissemination of research on how a baby's brain develops has afforded early childhood educators many opportunities to educate the general public about the importance of quality early childhood experiences. The information that scientists are gathering supports brain development activity during prenatal development as well as during the early years of a child's life. This has brought significant attention to the field of early childhood care and education. As recently as 15 years ago it was believed that brain structure and capacity were set at birth. We now know that the types of early experiences a child has, the frequency with which they occur, and with whom they happen can determine a child's future learning capacity. John Locke's proposal back in the 1600s that young children are born with what he called "tabula rasa," or with a blank slate, certainly has been disproven. Each year scientists are obtaining more information on the abilities of newborns to hear, smell, see, and make decisions.

We begin this twentieth edition of *Annual Editions: Early Childhood Education* with an article on the increased interest in early childhood education found in many states throughout the country. Governors and state legislators, as well as local school board members, are putting increased funding and effort into providing high-quality early childhood programs for the young children of their state or district. The key factor that will determine the success of these programs will be the availability of well-prepared and adequately compensated early childhood professionals who view their job as a profession and are ready to step into the many job openings that are anticipated. Early childhood programs are only as good as the staff who care for and educate children on a day-to-day basis.

An article on brain development research follows. For professionals in the field, now is the time to capitalize on the interest and resources available. It is our responsibility to provide stimulating envi-ronments in which young children best learn. We must be responsive to each child and provide many opportunities for language, music, and literature to be heard on a daily basis. We can educate parents as to their responsibility in providing an appropriate

environment that allows the brain to develop to its full capacity.

With many political leaders talking of welfare reform, the key message to remember is this: Welfare reform will work only if child care works. Most people on welfare are children, and most of the adults on welfare are the mothers of those children. The recent welfare reform and the push to have mothers in the workforce will only be successful if the mothers have affordable, quality, and regulated or licensed child care for their children. Families who receive reimbursements so small that they can pay only for low-quality, unstimulating care will not be contributing members of the workforce.

Many welfare reform proponents want to skimp on the funding available for quality child care to make their reforms work. This is unwise. Quality early care and education should be the cornerstone of successful welfare reform. Once again we have included information from the 1998 Children's Defense Fund Yearbook on the State of America's Children. In this selection, "A Child Shall Lead Us," CDF founder and president Marian Wright Edelman asks some tough questions about our national priorities. We encourage readers to reflect and to discuss their thoughts with others after reading this selection.

For the reader interested in public policy and advocacy, we encourage you to read the complete article from *Working Mother* on how each state rates in the area of child care. We have only included the chart and rating system, but the full text provides a paragraph description of the important programs and initiatives in each of the 50 states as well as the District of Columbia.

The final article in this unit examines school reform. The inequities that exist in school funding are creating a class system in our schools. The rich districts are getting richer due to the fact that they can receive as much as twice the funding as the poorer districts based on property values in their community. The poor districts are getting poorer as they pay for more out-of-pocket expenses for security and remedial programs.

Preschoolers' Education Takes Center Stage

By Linda Jacobson

Last October's White House conference on child care was meant to spark a national conversation about the needs of young children.

And it has. Throughout the country, state spending on preschool is growing. Efforts to improve child care are under way. And never before has there been such interest in how babies grow and develop.

The question now is whether policymakers intend to make a long-term financial commitment to an age group that for generations has been served through a mixture of public and private programs, or simply stayed at home until starting kindergarten.

"Now we're having a political discussion," said Faith Wohl, the executive director of the Child Care Action Campaign, a New York City advocacy group. "But I think the jury is still out on what we're going to have when all the talking stops."

With a handful of states moving toward universal access to preschool, the debate is also broadening from how to provide services to low-income children to how to design programs that are appropriate for children from a variety of backgrounds.

Academics or Convenience?

Some observers wonder whether state leaders are truly concerned about children's readiness for school or are merely trying to appeal to their constituents by proposing convenient programs that many middle-class parents can already afford.

Expanded programs for preschoolers also place higher demands on early-childhood teachers, who often don't have the professional training that may be called for.

With most states' economies strong, spending on early-childhood programs has been rising, according to a 50-state National Governors' Association survey released in December.

In addition, a separate study from the Children's Defense Fund, a Washington-based advocacy group, found 21 states last year had bolstered funding for programs that serve preschool-age children.

At the federal level, it's still uncertain if Congress will support more spending on child care this year. But what the government is doing is spending money on large research projects that will ultimately provide more information about the kinds of programs that best serve children in their earliest years.

"There is a fair amount of money flowing in terms of basic research and applied research," said Robert Pianta, an education professor at the University of Virginia in Charlottesville.

In the fall, the U.S. Department of Education will begin following 23,000 kindergartners in 1,000 schools. The study will continue until the children complete 5th grade. And in cooperation with the U.S. Department of Health and Human Services, the Education Department will begin a long-term study of 11,000 babies born in 2000.

'Broad Social Investment'

Margretta Fairweather, who works for the New York state education department, calls Aug. 20, 1997, the day her life changed. That's the day the state's new universal prekindergarten program became law.

"It's the most challenging thing that anyone has done around here in a long time," said Ms. Fairweather, the leader of the department's child, family, and community-services team.

The state plans to spend $500 million over the next four years to implement the program, which will eventually be open to any 4-year-old, regardless of family income. First to offer it in the fall will be 124 districts, with the rest that want to provide the program phased in over time.

The California education department just last month issued a report that rec-

ommends universal preschool for all 3- and 4-year-olds in the state within the next 10 years. The 53-member task force that wrote the report said that such a program would essentially "add two full grade levels of children to the public education system," at a cost of $5 billion a year. The committee also recommended spending $500 million in the next state budget to get the program rolling.

Kathy Lewis, a deputy superintendent in the department, acknowledges that there's a huge gap between that figure and the $25 million Gov. Pete Wilson, a Republican, wants to spend to expand preschool programs for poor children. But she thinks the timing is right to spend money up-front to curtail teenage pregnancy, crime, and other problems down the line.

"People are starting to understand that prevention, while it might be expensive, is going to save us money in the long run," she said.

New Jersey, meanwhile, is spending $288 million this year to provide a half-day of preschool for 4-year-olds and full-day kindergarten in 125 of the most disadvantaged districts. Within those districts, the programs are open to any child.

The same is true in Connecticut, where a new program for 3- and 4-year-olds is serving roughly 3,500 children in 25 districts. But in that state, the program is free only to families on public assistance. A sliding-fee scale is used for families with higher incomes.

In Georgia, the first state to use a first-come, first-served approach to preschool, enrollment this coming fall will surpass 61,000 4-year-olds.

"The bottom line for me is that it is wonderful to have situations where kids are not separated by income," said Gina Adams, a senior program associate at the Children's Defense Fund. "It's useful to have people understand that this is a broad social investment. This is investing in all of our kids."

Ms. Adams, however, stresses that publicly financed programs should still focus on reaching children whose parents cannot afford private preschool.

Public Schools' Role?

At the heart of this growing emphasis on preschool are questions about the role of public schools in serving children before kindergarten.

Nowhere was that more apparent than in Vermont earlier this year when a state lawmaker introduced legislation that would have required all schools to offer programs for 3- and 4-year-olds.

"We passed an equal-opportunity-education law, and my feeling was that unless all children had adequate pre-school training, it wouldn't be equal," said Rep. William Suchmann, a Republican.

Lawmakers there decided to review the current state of preschool programs.

In addition to New Jersey's prekindergarten program, which is part of the state's new school funding law, a recommendation pending before the state supreme court could heap even more responsibility on the state for the education of preschoolers.

In *Abbott* v. *Burke,* the decades-old case about ensuring a thorough and efficient education for all students, a judge is recommending that the state add all-day preschool for 3- and 4-year-olds in 28 largely urban districts. Attorney General Peter Verniero has argued that this plan would exceed the state's constitutional obligations. A decision by the high court is expected soon.

Clearly, a ruling in favor of the plan would take the state's involvement to a new level.

"As soon as you fund [preschool] through the school aid formula, that makes it more formal," said Allan R. Odden, a school finance expert at the University of Wisconsin-Madison and a consultant in the New Jersey case.

Whether preschool programs could become the subject of future legal challenges over equity is still up in the air, he added.

For the most part, efforts to expand early-childhood programs are far less drastic. While most people agree that schools play an important role in serving younger children, few are arguing that they should carry the burden alone.

Most proposals to expand preschool call for services to be offered in a variety of places, including private child-care centers, home-based programs, and public school classrooms. Even churches are receiving state funds to run nonreligious programs.

But some observers warn that such collaboration will inevitably invite more government regulation of private providers.

No Inoculation

While educators, particularly those at the elementary level, strongly support early-childhood education, they don't want the additional responsibility if it isn't accompanied by additional money.

"We have nothing against these partnerships, but we don't want the money to come from existing education funding," said Sally McConnell, the director of government relations for the National Association of Elementary School Principals.

Some have suggested that the growing sense of urgency about early intervention—and the belief that it will pay off later in terms of higher achievement, lower teenage-pregnancy rates, and less juvenile crime—will lead some lawmakers to neglect older populations of children.

Jack Berckemeyer, the director of member and affiliate services for the Columbus, Ohio-based National Middle School Association, said he believes it's wise for states to focus on the early years. But prevention, he said, doesn't address the immediate issues facing older students.

"When it comes to middle school education, we know it's our last, best chance to really mold and influence who they are going to be," he said. "We can't wait until we get a whole new batch of kids."

Mr. Pianta of the University of Virginia added that it's wrong to view early-childhood education as a silver bullet. "It's not inoculation, like if kids get this dose of resources that that is going to take care of them," he said.

And even some child advocates, who are obviously welcoming the swell of support for preschoolers, are also concerned that the needs of even younger children, particularly infants, are getting overlooked. Research has shown that infants are more likely than older children to be in poor-quality child-care settings.

Some observers disagree with the basic premise that governments should be in the business of creating preschool programs, regardless of whom they serve.

"If the schools are already failing, why would you expand their role?" said Darcy Olsen, an entitlements-policy analyst at the Cato Institute, a Washington think tank. "Besides, there's no consensus on what these kids need."

Richard C. Seder, from the Los Angeles-based Reason Public Policy Institute, added that while early-childhood programs have been shown to benefit poor youngsters, it's unclear whether they do anything for children from wealthier homes.

"To subsidize middle- and upper-income families is almost crazy," said Mr. Seder, the director of education studies at the institute, a free-market think tank.

Campaign Watching

With the number of preschool programs growing, it's not surprising that another conversation is intensifying—the one about what all these youngsters should be learning and who is going to teach it to them.

Since the national education goals, were unveiled in 1990, numerous efforts have sought to spell out the skills that children need to be "ready" for school—the first of the goals.

Adding to the mix is the comprehensive reading report the National Research Council released last month. It places a heavy emphasis on the importance of literacy development during the preschool years.

The report also recommends more training for early-childhood professionals in the fundamental literacy activities that prepare children for reading.

Focusing on young children is clearly a politically popular stand to take. But evidence that governors are taking the issue seriously lies in the fact that several have established new positions or assigned members of their staffs to work specifically on children's issues. Others have appointed entire committees.

Gov. Roy Romer of Colorado, a Democrat, helped initiate the trend in 1987 with his First Impressions program, which now has nine people who work exclusively on early-childhood policy and programs.

And earlier this year, Democratic Gov. Paul E. Patton of Kentucky created an office for early-childhood development, which will study and coordinate existing efforts in the state to serve young children.

One change that could slow this momentum is that the governors who have led in this area, including Mr. Romer, his fellow Democrats Lawton Chiles of Florida and Zell Miller of Georgia, and Republican George V. Voinovich of Ohio, are finishing up their final terms this year.

"The destiny of child care is in the states," said the Child Care Action Campaign's Ms. Wohl. In the approaching election season, "it will be interesting to see who campaigns on this issue, to see how the conversation translates to the polls."

New Brain Development Research—A Wonderful Window of Opportunity to Build Public Support for Early Childhood Education!

Julee J. Newberger

More than 20 years of brain development research is finally making news. Articles have appeared recently in *Time* (see Nash 1997), *Working Mother* (see Jabs 1996), *The Chicago Tribune*, *Newsweek* (see Begley 1996), and *The Washington Post*. A special edition of *Newsweek* focusing on learning in the early years is on the newsstands this spring in conjunction with the April 28, ABC-TV special "I Am Your Child." Receiving unprecedented attention, they kick off a massive three-year campaign to engage the public. What is the significance of this new research on the brain, and what does it mean for early childhood professionals?

New brain-imaging technologies have enabled scientists to investigate how the brain develops and works. Stimulated in part by growing concern about the overall well-being of children in America, the findings affirm what many parents and caregivers have known for years: (1) good prenatal care, (2) warm and loving attachments between young children and adults, and (3) positive, age-appropriate stimulation from the time of birth really do make a difference in children's development for a lifetime.

In addition to giving us a glimpse of the complex activity that occurs in the brain during infancy, the new research tools have stimulated dialogue between scientists and educators. In June 1996 Families and Work In-

> Just as experts agree that we have only begun to understand the complexities of the growing brain, so we have only begun to bridge the gap between neuroscience and education. The question for early childhood professionals is, How can we take advantage of the public interest that these stories and events have sparked to build support for high-quality early childhood education?

stitute sponsored a conference, "Brain Development in Young Children: New Frontiers for Research, Policy, and Practice," at the University of Chicago (see Families and Work Institute 1996). Convening professionals from the media, human services, business, and public policy, the conference explored how knowledge about the brain can

Julee J. Newberger, M.F.A., is a communications specialist in the NAEYC public affairs division. She is the primary author of "Early Years Are Learning Years" news releases.

From *Young Children*, May 1997, pp. 4-9. © 1997 by the National Association for the Education of Young Children. Reprinted by permission.

inform our efforts to make better beginnings for children and families. One month later, a workshop sponsored by the Education Commission of the States and the Charles A. Dana Foundation brought together 74 neuroscientists, cognitive psychologists, and education researchers and practitioners to foster communication and bridge a "historical communications gap" (ECS 1996). Similar events have followed, such as President Clinton's White House Conference on Early Childhood Development and Learning on April 17, 1997.

Just as experts agree that we have only begun to understand the complexities of the growing brain, so we have only begun to bridge the gap between neuroscience and education. The question for early childhood professionals is, How can we take advantage of the public interest that these stories and events have sparked to build support for high-quality early childhood education?

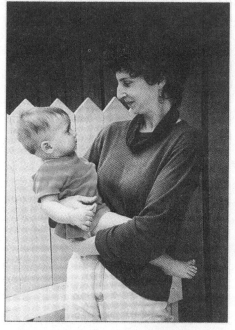

© The Growth Program

Many parents and caregivers have understood intuitively that warm, everyday interaction—cuddling infants closely or singing to toddlers—actually helps prepare children for the learning they will do throughout life. More and more we begin to understand the biological reasons behind this.

What we know about how children learn

Although the scientists of all varieties who have been researching biology-versus-environment issues for much of this century have long agreed that both are enormously important influences on growth and development, only about 20 years ago neuroscientists believed that the genes we are born with determine the structure of our brains. They held that this fixed structure determines the way we develop and interact with the world. But recent brain research, enabled by new technologies, disproves this notion. Heredity may determine the basic number of neurons (brain cells) children are born with, and their initial arrangement, but this is merely a framework. A child's environment has enormous impact on how the circuits of the brain will be laid. Nature and nurture together—not nature or nurture alone—determine the outcome of our lives.

Beginning even before birth, the kind of nourishment and care a child receives affects not only the "wiring" of her brain but also the qualities of her experiences beyond the first few years of life. Many parents and caregivers have understood intuitively that warm, everyday interaction—cuddling infants closely or singing to toddlers—actually helps prepare children for learning throughout life. More and more we begin to understand the biological reasons behind this.

When a child is born, the brain produces trillions more neurons and synapses (connections between the brain cells) than she will ultimately need. Positive interactions with caring adults stimulate a child's brain profoundly, causing synapses to grow and existing connections to be strengthened. Those synapses in a child's brain that are used tend to become permanent fixtures; those that are not used tend to be eliminated. If a child receives little stimulation early on, synapses will not sprout or develop, and the brain will make fewer connections. Therefore, a child's experiences during the first few days, months, and years may be more decisive than scientists once believed.

We now know that during the early years the brain has the greatest capacity for change. Neural plasticity, the brain's ability to adapt with experience, confirms that early stimulation sets the stage for how children will continue to learn and interact with others throughout life.

Neural plasticity: The brain's ability to adapt

Particularly during the first three years of life, brain connections develop quickly in response to outside stimulation. A child's experiences—good or bad—influence the wiring of his brain and the connections in his nervous system. Thus, when we snuggle a baby or talk to him in a singsong, undulating rhythm, we are contributing to the growth of his brain. How do we know this?

Particularly during the first three years of life, brain connections develop quickly in response to outside stimulation. Thus, when we snuggle a baby or talk to him in a singsong, undulating rhythm, we are contributing to the growth of his brain.

Recent research examining one of the body's "stress-sensitive" systems demonstrates how outside experiences shape a child's developing brain (Gunnar et al. 1996). One stress-sensitive system in particular is activated when children are faced with physical or emotional trauma. Activation of this system produces a steroid hormone called *cortisol*. High levels of cortisol cause the death of brain cells and a reduction in connections between the cells in certain areas of the brain. Research in adults who have experienced chronic or intense activation of the system that produces cortisol shows shrinkage of a certain brain region that is important in learning and memory. Clearly, a link exists between physical or emotional trauma and long-term impairments to learning and development.

But nature has provided a way of buffering the negative effects of these stress systems in the brain: strong attachments between children and their parents or caregivers. Studies measuring the levels of cortisol in children's saliva showed that those who received warm and responsive care were able to turn off this stress-sensitive response more quickly and efficiently. Babies with strong emotional bonds to their caregivers showed consistently lower levels of cortisol in their brains.

While positive, nurturing experiences can help brighten a child's future, negative experiences can do the opposite. Children who are emotionally neglected or abandoned early in life not only are more likely to have difficulty in learning but also may have more trouble experiencing empathy, attachment, and emotional expression in general. An excess of cortisol in the brain is linked to impaired cognitive ability and difficulty in responding appropriately or productively in stressful situations. Healthy relationships during the early years help children create a framework for interactions with others throughout life.

Windows of opportunity

Studies have increased our understanding of "windows of opportunity" or critical periods in children's lives when specific types of learning take place. For instance, scientists have determined that the neurons for vi-

sion begin sending messages back and forth rapidly at two to four months of age, peaking in intensity at eight months. It is no coincidence that babies begin to take notice of the world during this period. A well-known experiment conducted in the 1970s prompted research on the window of opportunity in development of vision in children. The original study demonstrated that sewing shut one eye of a newborn kitten caused the kitten's brain to be "rewired." Because no synapses were created in the brain to allow the kitten to see with the eye that had been closed, the kitten was blind in that eye even

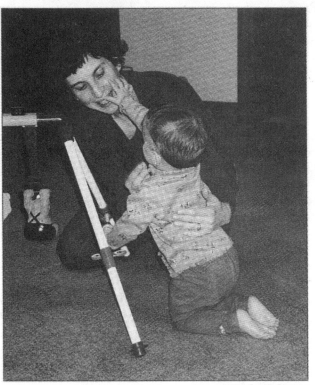

© The Growth Program

Studies make one thing clear: Talking to an infant increases the number of words she will recognize and eventually come to understand. She also will learn better when spoken to in brief phrases, preferably in singsong tones.

after scientists reopened it. The results could not be repeated in adult cats, whose brains were already wired for sight in both eyes. We now know that by the age of two these synapses in the human brain have matured as well. The window of opportunity for vision has already closed.

Scientists believe that language is acquired most easily during the first decade of life. Infants under six months respond with equal interest to the sounds of all languages, but they soon develop "perceptual maps" that direct them toward the sounds of the language they hear most frequently and away from the sounds of other languages. They start by forming connections for specific vowel sounds they hear repeatedly. The circuits in children's brains then become wired for those sounds that are significant in their own language, diminishing their ability to discern

sounds that are not. As a result, the brains of babies in Japan, for example, begin to develop differently than those of babies in the United States. These perceptual maps eventually account for regional accents—and the increasing difficulty in acquiring new languages as we grow older.

Studies well-known to early childhood educators make one thing clear: Talking to an infant increases the number of words she will recognize and eventually come to understand. She also will learn better when spoken to in brief phrases, preferably in singsong tones. Researchers report that infants whose parents and caregivers frequently speak to them recognize far more words later on than do infants whose parents are less vocal or less engaged. An infant's repeated exposure to words clearly helps her brain build neural circuitry that

Children who are emotionally neglected or abandoned early in life not only are more likely to have difficulty in learning but also may have more trouble experiencing empathy, attachment, and emotional expression in general. An excess of cortisol in the brain is linked to impaired cognitive ability and difficulty in responding appropriately or productively in stressful situations.

will enable her to learn more words later on. For infants, individual attention and responsive, sensitive care-giving are critical for later language and intellectual development.

Many reports on brain research point to the implications for the introduction of second-language learning during the early years (ECS 1996). We now know that if children are to learn to speak a second language like a native, they should be introduced to the language by age ten. Mastering an additional language is still possible after this point, but the window of opportunity for easy acquisition is gone.

Research does not suggest drilling children in alphabet songs from different languages or using flash cards to promote rote memorization of letters and numbers. Rather, it reinforces the principles of developmentally appropriate practice. Children learn any language best in the context of meaningful, day-to-day interactions with adults or other children who speak the language.

More windows of opportunity in children's learning may exist. Studies show that the most effective time to begin music lessons, for instance, is between the ages of three and ten. Few professional musicians began later in life. Music also seems to be linked to spatial orientation, so providing a child with the opportunity to play an instrument and using basic music education to spark her interest may do more than help her become musically inclined. With such knowledge, scientists and educators can work together to create the best plans for developing the whole child during the early years of life.

Implications for early care and education programs

Now that scientific research has reinforced what many already knew about early childhood education, what impact will this knowledge have on programs and centers across the country? We know that enriched home and school environments can help make the most of children's mental capacities. We also know that when we bring an understanding of child development to our interactions with children, we can meet their developmental needs more than just adequately. Parents and the general public, having children's best interests in mind, may raise issues about early education practices. Here are some questions that are likely to arise.

1. Should new parents put off employment and stay at home?

The relationship between secure attachment and healthy brain development makes this a reasonable question, although working parents should not be blamed for any and every developmental obstacle their children encounter. At a time when 55% of women provide about half or more of their families' income, decisions as to whether parents should put off employment remain a personal, family matter (Families and Work Institute 1996). Research shows that the best scenario for children and families if child care is used involves high-quality parenting and access to high-quality, affordable child care and early education that enhances—not disrupts—attachments between parents and children. Flexible workplace policies can help accommodate and support modern family life.

2. Is it too late for children to develop cognitive skills after the early years?

While scientists have found that the early years may be even more important than anticipated, human development continues throughout the life span. It may not be as easy to acquire a second language at the age of fifty, but learning new skills is always possible. A meaningful context and the desire to develop new skills make learning more likely at any age.

The significance of this new research, according to Harry Chugani (1997) of Wayne State University, is for all of us to "be aware and take advantage of these critical periods nature has provided us with." Chugani says, "We must create innovations to make learning fun." Parents and educators should focus on ways to take advantage of windows of opportunity that remain open.

Research does not suggest drilling children in alphabet songs from different languages or using flash cards to promote rote memorization of letters and numbers. Rather, it reinforces the principles of developmentally appropriate practice. Children learn any language best in the context of meaningful, day-to-day interactions with adults or other children who speak the language.

3. To take advantage of the early years of learning, should I invest more in toys and new products for my child?

New developments in research may prompt manufacturers to market products that claim to make the most of children's learning potential. Remember that scientific evidence does not change the fundamental principles of developmentally appropriate practice. In fact, research supports the theory that learning must take place in a meaningful context and in an environment of love and support. A developing brain doesn't know the difference between an inexpensive set of measuring cups and a pricey set of stackables purchased at a toy store.

The key to fostering early childhood learning is understanding that there will be a range in the amount of stimulation children are comfortable with and can tolerate. Before children can move on to new skills, they must have time to practice and master those they have already learned. Parents or caregivers who push children too fast or too hard can do as much damage as those who do not challenge children at all. Chugani recommends, "Be rigorous, but be aware of early signs of overload" (1997). Continue to respect the child as a human being and use common sense in determining when he enjoys what he is learning and when he is resistant.

Bridging the gaps

The ECS workshop on neuroscience and education outlined the following conflicts between research and current education practice (ECS 1996):
• While we know that development of children's capacity to learn is crucial in the first few years of life, children during these years receive the least attention from the educational world.
• Interactive environments enhance development, but many children are in child care programs today with staff who are underpaid, lack training in early childhood and brain development, and may be responsible for too many children.
• Although some adverse effects can be reversed or prevented for much less than it costs to provide special services later on, our educational system waits for children

to fall behind, then places them in special education programs at high costs to states.

In light of this research, shouldn't parents have more options to stay home with children during the years in which this critical learning takes place? Parental leave policies must be put on the table for discussion. And what about new welfare reform policies that push single mothers into the workforce without guaranteeing high-quality child care to promote children's optimum development and learning? The concerns raised and the dialogue generated at this workshop and other conferences may be timely in preventing more children from growing up without the benefit of the kind of education that early childhood professionals, utilizing years of research and practice, can provide.

Where we go from here

The Families and Work Institute conference on brain development offered the following recommendations for parents, caregivers, policymakers, and the public to institute policies and practices that improve the day-to-day experiences of all young children and families.

First, do no harm.

• Allow parents to fulfill their all-important role in providing and arranging sensitive, predictable care for their children.
• Work to reform policies that prevent parents from forming strong, secure attachments with their infants in the first months of life.
• Mount intensive efforts to improve the quality of child care and early education so that families can be sure their

Parents or caregivers who push children too fast or too hard can do as much damage as those who do not challenge children at all.

> **While we know that development of children's capacity to learn is crucial in the first few years of life, children during these years receive the least attention from the educational world.**

young children's learning and emotional development are being fostered while parents are at work.

Prevention is best, but when a child needs help, intervene quickly and intensively.

• Ensure consistent and responsive care to help cushion children against the stresses of everyday life.
• Provide timely, intensive, sustained assistance to help children recover from serious trauma or overcome developmental problems.

Promote healthy development and learning for every child.

• Be aware that missed opportunities to promote healthy development. may result later on in more expensive and less effective attempts at remediation.
• Support ongoing efforts to enhance the cognitive, emotional, and social development of children and adults in every phase of the life cycle.

Improve health and protection by providing health care coverage for expectant and new parents and their young children.

• Medical care, including preventive health screening, well-baby care, timely immunization, and attention to children's emotional and physical development, is cost-effective and provides a foundation for lifetime development.

Promote responsible parenthood by expanding proven approaches.

• Identify parent education and family support programs that promote the healthy development of children, improve the well-being of parents, and are cost-effective.

Safeguard children in early care and education from harm and promote their learning and development.

• Ensure that children will learn and thrive by improving the quality of early childhood programs and centers.

Enable communities to have the flexibility and resources they need to mobilize on behalf of young children and their families.

• Bring together leaders from business, media, community organizations, and religious institutions to develop goals and strategies for achieving the kind of community that supports all children and families.

❧

Increased public awareness prompted by news-breaking reports on brain research may represent a window of opportunity in the early childhood field. With plans to make further links between science and education, early childhood professionals and advocates may find increased support for our cause—public understanding and support for child care that guarantees proper nutrition, well-planned physical environments, and developmentally appropriate practices to ensure the most promising future for all young children and families. The window of opportunity is open and the time for action is now.

References

Begley, S. 1996. I am your child. *Newsweek,* 19 February, 55–61.

Chugari, H. 1997. Personal communication, 21 March.

ECS (Education Commission of the States). 1996. *Bridging the gap between neuroscience and education: Summary of the workshop co-sponsored by Education Commission of the States and the Charles A. Dana Foundation.* Denver: Author.

Families and Work Institute. 1996, Rethinking the brain: New insights into early development. Executive summary of the Conference on Brain Development in Young Children: New frontiers for Research, Policy, and Practice. University of Chicago, June.

Gunnar, M. R., L. Brodersen, K. Krueger, & R. Rigatuso. 1996. Dampening of behavioral and adrenocortical reactivity during early infancy: Normative changes and individual differences. *Child Development* 67 (3): 877–89.

Jabs, C. 1996. Your baby's brain power. *Working Mother,* November, 24–28.

Nash, M. 1997. Fertile Minds. *Time,* 3 February, 48–56.

Highlights of the Quality 2000 Initiative:

Not by Chance

Sharon L. Kagan and Michelle J. Neuman

Sharon L. Kagan, Ed.D., *senior associate at Yale University's Bush Center in Child Development and Social Policy in New Haven, Connecticut, is recognized nationally and internationally for her work related to the care and education of young children and their families and investigation of issues, including policy development, family support, early childhood pedagogy, strategies for collaboration and service integration, and evaluation of social programs.*

Michelle J. Neuman *was recently a research assistant at the Yale Bush Center in Child Development and Social Policy. Her research has focused on issues related to children and families, including early care and education policy, family support, children's transitions to school, school readiness, and French family policy.*

The quality crisis in early care and education

Each day 13 million children spend time in early care and education centers or family child care homes. This should be heartening given that quality early care and education contributes to the healthy cognitive, social, and emotional development of all young children (CQ&O Study Team 1995) and in particular children from low-income families (Schweinhart, Barnes, & Weikart 1993; Barnett 1995; Gomby et al. 1995; Phillips 1995; Yoshikawa 1995). Yet we know that the quality of a majority of these settings does not optimize children's healthy development; in fact, many settings seriously jeopardize it (Galinsky et al. 1994; CQ&O Study Team 1995).

We well understand many of the reasons for low quality: underfinanced services, poorly compensated teachers, precarious turnover rates, inadequate and inconsistent regulation and enforcement, fragmented training and delivery mechanisms—the litany goes on. We understand less well how to alter the situation and what it would *really* take to reverse the pattern of neglect and provide quality early care and education to all young children.

The Quality 2000 initiative

For the past four years, hundreds of experts in early childhood education and allied fields have been examining these very questions under the auspices of an inventive initiative, Quality 2000: Advancing Early Care and Education. The primary goal of this initiative is that by the year 2010, high-quality early care and education programs will be available and accessible to all children from birth to age five whose parents choose to enroll them. Funded by the Carnegie Corporation of New York, with supportive funding from the David and Lucile Packard, W.K. Kellogg, A.L. Mailman Family, and Ewing Marion Kauffman foundations, the initiative carried out its work through a series of commissioned papers, cross-national literature reviews, task forces, and working groups. Informed by national and international research, the fruit of that work, *Not by Chance: Creating an Early Care and Education System for America's Children,* offers a comprehensive, long-range vision for the field.

The vision is not about adding more services or disparate programs to what exists, although additional funds and services are essential to the vision. Rather, consisting of eight recommendations, the vision sets forth new patterns of thinking and pathways for action. Some of the recommendations seem familiar; others may

From *Young Children,* September 1997, pp. 54-62. © 1997 by the National Association for the Education of Young Children. Reprinted by permission.

sound bold, if not audacious. However they are interpreted, the recommendations are not modest or quick fixes; they will take time and energy to accomplish. That is why we set them in the context of the year 2010, not the year 2000 as the project's name suggests.

Recommendations for eight essential functions

The Quality 2000 recommendations are broad and represent eight essential functions or areas where action to improve quality is needed; each recommendation is accompanied by suggested strategies to be tailored to fit individual community needs. Finally, the recommendations, although individualized to reflect each of the eight essential functions, need to be read in the aggregate—as a set of linked ideas.

1. Program quality

Imagine a time when we expect and support quality in all family child care and center-based programs (Head Start, for-profit and nonprofit child care centers, prekindergartens, nursery schools), allowing staff flexibility in using state-of-the-art strategies, technologies, and resources creatively and cost effectively.

To address the quality crisis, early care and education programs need the flexibility to explore and implement fresh ideas and strategies—strategies that consider changing demographic and technological realities as well as strategies that focus on the total program and individual classrooms or settings.

STRATEGIES

Promote cultural sensitivity and cultural pluralism. Children, staff, and families need opportunities to better understand and express their own cultural values and beliefs and to learn about other cultures (Derman-Sparks & the A.B.C. Task Force 1989; Phillips 1994; Phillips & Crowell 1994; Chang, Pulido-Tobiassen, & Muckelroy 1996). Staff should be trained to promote cultural sensitivity and cultural pluralism, and where possible, staff should come from the communities they serve. Children should be encouraged to cherish diversity.

Encourage pedagogical inventiveness in family child care and centers. Quality may result from a variety of strategies, including working with children in mixed-age groups (Katz, Evangelou, & Hartman 1990) and working inventively with families, grouping children in new ways, and considering ways of adapting child-staff ratios to capitalize on staff abilities to meet preschoolers' needs.

Focus on improving the overall organizational climate. The organizational climate of the total early care and education program—not only classrooms—must be considered as we create positive environments for all staff, parents, and families. Such environments should focus on the program as a learning organization ready to experiment, adapt, and grow.

Increase the number of accredited programs. Research indicates that accreditation—a voluntary process of self-assessment—significantly raises program quality. Because accredited centers provide higher quality services than nonaccredited programs (Bredekamp & Glowacki 1995; Bloom 1996; Whitebook, Sakai, & Howes 1997) and because the process promotes professionalism in the field, concerted efforts must be made to significantly increase the numbers of accredited programs.

Link programs to networks, supportive services, or other community resources. Linking early care and education programs with other services, especially resource-and-referral agencies, can help address unmet needs, expedite service delivery, minimize duplication of services, ensure smooth transitions for children, and help parents navigate through the social services maze (NACCRRA 1996). In addition, by creating family child care systems or networks, family child care providers can reduce their isolation and be more effectively linked to each other and community services.

2. Results for children

Imagine a time when clear results and expectations are specified and used to guide individual planning for all three- and four-year-old children, based on all domains of development (social/emotional, physical/motor, cognitive, language) and approaches to learning.

Traditionally, researchers have focused on inputs (e.g., child-staff ratios, group size, staff training and education) and on the manner in which services are delivered (e.g., the nature of adult-child interactions) (Hofferth & Chaplin 1994). Recently, however, there has been mounting interest in gauging quality in terms of the results that programs or interventions produce for preschool-age children and their families (Schorr 1994; CCSSO 1995). A focus on results for three- and four-year-olds can assist teachers with pedagogical planning and improvement as well as for purposes of evaluation and accountability. By defining desired goals and results, practitioners who work with young children can plan and tailor their activities to foster individual children's development. In addition, specified goals and results can provide programs with the feedback they need to evaluate their effectiveness and identify areas for improvement. Results also can be used to help assess the overall status of young children in communities, states, and the nation (Schorr 1994). With this information in hand, parents, practitioners, and the public can hold decisionmakers at all levels accountable for investing in early care and education (Kagan, Rosenkoetter, & Cohen 1997).

STRATEGIES

Identify appropriate results. To move toward a results-focused approach and to safeguard children from the misuses of results, parents, practitioners, policymakers, and the public need to come together to define results and expectations for three- and four-year-old children, taking into consideration the child, family, and community conditions that promote healthy development. In particular, results should be considered from the perspective of children—across programs and over time. Results should be specified at the local, state, and national levels, increasing the customization and specificity at each level.

Develop appropriate strategies and instruments. Developmentally appropriate and culturally sensitive instruments should be developed to evaluate progress toward the achievement of specified results in all domains of development. These strategies should include capturing children's development via portfolios and other documentation of children's work.

Share results effectively, ensuring safeguards for children. Demonstration projects, evaluation, and basic research will expand the knowledge base of what helps children achieve positive results. This information needs to be shared in ways that increase public understanding of the connection among child results, effective services, and the expenditure of public funds, not in ways that may label or stigmatize children. Guidelines for the effective use of results should be developed.

3. Parent and family engagement

Imagine a time when parents of young children are actively involved in their children's programs and when programs provide diverse opportunities for such involvement. Imagine a time when parents have the user-friendly information and support they need to be effective consumers in choosing programs for their children. Imagine a time when employers provide policies that enable parents to become involved in their children's early learning and education.

Research shows that parent and family engagement in early care and education programs improves re-sults for children, increasing the likelihood of children's success and achievement and decreasing the likelihood of negative outcomes, both in school and later in life (Bronfenbrenner 1974; Bronson, Pierson, & Tivnan 1984; Powell 1989).

STRATEGIES

Support parents as partners in early care and education programs. By focusing on developing regular communication among practitioners and parents (Weissbourd 1987), parents can be more effectively engaged as equals, with valuable information and resources. To that end, programs can offer multiple activities to involve parents (Henderson, Marburger, & Ooms 1986; Epstein 1995), taking into consideration how parent's interests, needs, and work and family responsibilities may influence their participation. Parents also should be engaged in governance opportunities (Kagan 1994).

Support parents as effective consumers. Parents can benefit from objective information about programs so they can make educated decisions that will promote their children's early development and learning. Well-funded resource-and-referral agencies, along with other parenting education efforts, can assist parents in learning about and evaluating their early care and education options. Such efforts must acknowledge and respect parents' diverse backgrounds, cultures, and needs.

Increase the family-friendliness of workplaces. Parents need support from their employers so they can fulfill their roles as partners in their children's programs, as effective consumers of early care and education services, and as productive employees (Staines & Galinsky 1991; Galinsky, Bond, & Friedman 1993). Employers should consider offering significantly greater employee benefits, at a minimum providing time for parents to find a program and monitor and participate in their children's early care and education. Corporations should offer parents the choice of working part-time, paid sick days to care for sick children, and job-protected paid maternity and parental leave.

4. Staff credentialing

Imagine a time when all individuals working with children in early care and education programs have—or are actively in the process of obtaining—credentials related to the position they hold or seek. Imagine a time when all staff are encouraged to pursue ongoing training and education—a course of lifelong learning.

Because individuals who work with children in early care and education programs have a major impact on children's early development and learning experiences, their credentialing/licensing is critical. Licensing individual early childhood educators has many benefits. Licensing

• holds promise for increasing the compensation of staff,

• increases professionalization in the field,

• promotes the creation and coordination of quality training and education as well as career mobility, and

• helps prevent harm to children and ensure the quality of programs (APHA & AAP 1992).

The model for individual licensing can be found in Western European nations and Japan, which require significantly more training and education of practitioners and a more coordinated and sequenced training delivery system (Pritchard 1996). Structures to support licensing individuals are well established in many other occupations in the United States, including helping professionals (e.g., social workers, registered and licensed practical nurses, teachers), technical professionals (e.g., architects, engineers), tradespeople (e.g., electricians), and even service workers (e.g., cosmetologists) (Mitchell 1996).

Individual licenses should be distinct from, but complementary to, facility licenses. They should specify the preparatory and ongoing train-

An Approach to Licensing Individuals:
Requirements for Early Care and Education Staff

Administrator license

For center directors and directors of family child care support services,

- at least a bachelor's or master's degree in early childhood education or child development from an accredited institution, including at least 15 credits in early childhood administration
- certification in pediatric first aid
- demonstration of competency in management and in working with children and families

Educator license

For center teachers and public school teachers of children ages three and four,

- at least an associate's or bachelor's degree in early childhood education or child development from an accredited institution
- practicum with the age of children with whom individuals would work
- certification in pediatric first aid
- demonstration of competency in working with children and families

Associate educator license

For lead providers in large family child care homes and assistant teachers in centers,

- at least a Child Development Associate (CDA) credential, the revised National Association for Family Child Care (NAFCC) accreditation or equivalent—meaning at least 120 clock hours of formal education in child development/early childhood education and the demonstration of competency in working with children and families
- practicum with the age group with which individuals would work
- certification in pediatric first aid

Entry-level position requirement

For aides in centers and in large family child care homes and for family child care providers in small family child care homes,

- interest in and aptitude for working with children and families
- commitment to participating in ongoing training leading to licensure

---

ing that staff need to work with children in a variety of roles. While there are many approaches to individual licensing, Quality 2000 offers one that calls for a series of three licenses for early care and education workers (see "An Approach to Licensing Individuals" chart).

STRATEGIES

Create early childhood administrator licenses. All center directors and directors of family child care support services would be required to have early childhood administrator licenses. To obtain this license, an individual would need at least a bachelor's or master's degree in early childhood education or child development from an accredited institution, including at least 15 credits in early childhood administration, certification in first aid, and demonstrated competency in management and in working with children and families.

Create early childhood educator licenses. All teachers in centers would be required to have early childhood educator licenses. Teachers of three- and four-year-old children in public schools would have the option of obtaining public school teacher certification/licenses or the early childhood educator license. To obtain the early childhood educator license, individuals would need to have at least an associate's or bachelor's de-gree in early childhood education or child development from an accredited institution; have practicum experience with the age group with which they would work; be certified in pediatric first aid; and pass a competency-based assessment in working with children and families.

Create early childhood associate educator licenses. All assistant teachers in centers, as well as lead providers in large family child care homes, would be required to have early childhood associate educator licenses. To obtain the license, an individual working in a center would need to have a Child Development Associate (CDA) credential or the equivalent; an individual working in a family child care home would need to have a CDA, the revised National Association for Family Child Care (NAFCC) accreditation, or equivalent certification. Each of these certifications requires at least 120 clock hours of formal education in early childhood development and education and the demonstration of the competencies needed to work with young children and their families. Assistant teachers and lead providers also would need to have practicum experience with the age group with which they would work and certification in pediatric first aid.

Maintain access to entry-level positions. Individuals who do not have training or education in child development or early childhood education, but who have an interest in and aptitude for working with young children and families and a commitment to seeking training in the field, would have access to entry-level jobs as aides in child care centers and in large-group family child care homes or as providers in small family child care homes. These individuals would be considered an integral part of the profession as long as they are actively pursuing training to achieve licensure as early childhood associate educator or educator.

5. Staff training and preparation

Imagine a time when all training for early childhood positions is child and family focused, reflecting and respecting cultural and linguistic diversity. Imagine a time when all approved training bears credit, leads to increased credentials and compensation, and equips individuals for diverse and advanced roles.

The quality of the credentials just discussed is contingent upon the quality of the training individuals receive. All training and education sequences should, at a minimum, address the CDA competency areas (establishing and maintaining a safe, healthy learning environment; advancing physical and intellectual competence; supporting social and emotional development and provid-

ing positive guidance; establishing positive and productive relationships with families; ensuring a well-run, purposeful program that is responsive to participant needs; and maintaining a commitment to professionalism [Council for Early Childhood Professional Recognition 1992]). More preservice and inservice training, particularly at intermediate and advanced levels, needs to be developed and made available to practitioners in the following areas (Morgan et al. 1993): engaging and supporting families; developing cultural competency; observing and assessing children; working with mixed-age groups and larger groups, and team teaching; working with infants and toddlers; working with children with special needs; promoting ethics; working across human service disciplines; and developing management and leadership skills.

STRATEGIES

Revise and develop staff training/preparation curricula and sequences. Revamping the content of and opportunities for practitioner training/preparation will necessitate the participation of many stakeholders. State licensing boards for early care and education should require staff to have appropriate ranges of skills to earn and maintain licenses, including appropriate preparatory and ongoing course work. Colleges and community organizations that educate and train early care and education staff should revise and develop curricula and sequences to address the broad-based knowledge (early childhood pedagogy and content from allied disciplines) and skills that practitioners need to be competent in today's early care and education programs.

Promote the development of leaders and managers. To promote the development of leaders and managers at the local, state, and national levels, program administrators with strong leadership potential should be supported through fellowships and training and mentoring oppor-

tunities. Such mentoring programs are an effective strategy to support staff as they acquire knowledge and skills and to enhance the professional development of more skilled and experienced mentor-teachers (Whitebook, Hnatiuk, & Bellm 1994; Breunig & Bellm 1996).

6. Program licensing

Imagine a time when all early care and education programs are licensed, without any legal exemptions. Imagine a time when facility licensing procedures are streamlined and enforced to ensure that all programs promote children's safety, health, and development. Imagine a time when incentives exist for programs to continually enhance their facilities.

Research demonstrates that about 40% of center-based programs—including many part-day, school-based, and church-based programs (Adams 1990)—and as many as 80 to 90% of family child care providers (Willer et al. 1991) are legally exempt from regulation despite the fact that states with more stringent regulation yield higher quality programs (CQ&O Study Team 1995).

STRATEGIES

Eliminate exemptions. All programs available to the general public should be required to meet basic safeguards that protect children's well-being and foster equity in the early care and education field; there should be no legal exemptions. For example, programs should not be legally exempt from facility regulations because of their size, hours of operation, location, or auspices.

Streamline facility licensing. State facility licensing should be streamlined to focus on essential safeguards of safety, health, and development and to complement the system of individual licensing described earlier (U.S. ACIR 1994; Gormley 1995; Gwen Morgan, personal communication, 22 March 1996). Standards for staffing levels should allow programs the flexibility to group children and organize staff in ways that maximize quality.

Enforce requirements. To fully promote children's safety, health, and development, states must not only eliminate exemptions and streamline regulations but also enforce requirements. Licensing agencies must have the appropriate resources to carry out enforcement functions. State monitoring and enforcement systems should employ positive, incentive-based strategies to enable programs to meet licensing requirements. State licensing systems also should provide incentives for programs to invest in facility enhancement to increase capacity for meeting the increasing demand for early care and education services.

Develop national licensing guidelines. Although the main responsibility for the development and issue of facility licensing requirements should remain at the state level, national licensing guidelines should be developed to promote regulatory consistency across the country.

7. Funding and financing

Imagine a time when young children's early care and education is funded by the public and private sectors at per-child levels commensurate with funding for elementary-age children and when 10% of the funds are set aside for professional and staff development, enhanced compensation, parent information and engagement, program accreditation, resource-and-referral services, evaluation, research, planning, and licensing and facility enhancement.

Adequate funding is essential to ensuring that all children have access to quality early care and education services and that their parents have choice in selecting services. The costs must be shared by the public at large, parents (according to income), employers, government, and community organizations. While parents need access to and choice of quality early care and education services, they also need the option of caring for their own very young children; therefore, paid parental leave for parents of very

young children should be provided. These efforts to increase investment necessitate additional research and planning.

STRATEGIES

Estimate the actual cost of a quality early care and education system. The field needs to estimate the actual cost of mounting and sustaining a comprehensive quality early care and education system. In making such estimates, early care and education professionals need to work closely with funding and financing experts, using cost-calculation approaches that other fields have found useful. Such an analysis also should estimate the revenues that the early care and education system would generate in both the short and long term. Longer-term cost-benefit accounting should be used to determine the extended benefits of a quality early care and education system, benefits that include savings in special education, corrections, public assistance, and other social services.

Identify several revenue-generation mechanisms. Several revenue-generation options for funding for a comprehensive early care and education system—including increased staff compensation—need to be considered and implemented. Some possible mechanisms include establishing individual and corporate income taxes, federal payroll taxes, and new sales or excise taxes; expanding the populations eligible to receive the school aid formula; cutting other government expenditures to raise some of the needed funds; and procuring funds as part of a larger revenue-generation package designed to support a range of social services that families need. None of these approaches are easy to sell to the public or policymakers, but each would help improve the amount of funding available to support early care and education.

Develop model approaches for distributing funds to parents. State-level agencies may be best suited for

administering funds to parents. Mechanisms to distribute funds to parents should promote parent choice, such as vouchers, direct payments to programs of parents' choice, and/or tax credits. Parents should receive assistance in paying for early care and education programs based on a sliding scale linked to parents' income. (As family income increases over time, public assistance for early care and education would decrease proportionately but not be completely cut off [Stangler 1995]).

Create a targeted, coordinated funding initiative. Scholarship and knowledge of how to generate increased revenues for the development of a comprehensive early care and education system is emerging but remains piecemeal and embryonic. Focused research is needed to carry out the analyses mentioned above. Therefore, it will be necessary to create a targeted, coordinated initiative focused on funding a quality early care and education system.

8. Governance structures

Imagine a time when early care and education is governed rationally. Imagine a time when mechanisms (councils, boards) are established or built upon in every community and state to carry out planning, governance, and accountability roles in early care and education.

To increase coordination, efficiency, and continuity of services for young children and their families, it is critical to establish a rational governance system. Quality 2000 recommends establishing governance entities in every state and locality—to be called State Early Care and Education Board and Local Early Care and Education Board, respectively. Where these governing boards or coordinating councils already exist, the State or Local Early Care and Education Board could be built from the existing body or created in collaboration with it.

STRATEGIES

Establish state boards. State boards should be responsible for ensuring quality and achieving agreed-upon results for children. They should engage in planning, collecting, and analyzing data; defining eligibility and subsidy levels and parental-leave conditions; and determining how to allocate funds to parents. They would also develop state standards for results to align with national goals. As with other governance entities, state boards would facilitate collaboration, service integration, and comprehensive services delivery. State boards would be composed of appointed or elected board members, including equal numbers of parents/consumers; practitioners; community and state leaders, including clergy; and municipal or government agency representatives.

Establish local boards. Local boards would have responsibility for both the governance and the coordination of early care and education for children birth to age five. They could be geographically aligned with school districts, but would be distinct entities. Like their state counterparts, they should be composed of a broad-based group of appointed or elected board members who would be responsible for developing performance benchmarks for child results, taking into consideration local strengths, needs, priorities, and resources. Local boards would involve consumers and citizens in comprehensive needs assessment and planning.

Support effective federal governance. To support these efforts, the federal government will need to provide mandates and incentives to these boards. In addition, the federal government will guide states as they develop standards and communities as they develop benchmarks to meet state standards and national goals. The federal government also will collect national data, provide funding for evaluating demonstration efforts, and offer technical assistance to states and localities. Their well-

being, and the nation's, simply cannot be left to chance.

The quality of daily life for millions of American children and families depends on how the United States solves—or fails to solve—the quality crisis in early care and education. Quality 2000 and the *Not by Chance* report address this crisis by recommending that the nation make a planned, significant, and immediate advance to improve quality and to create a system of services. It is the hope of those involved in the Quality 2000 initiative that the ideas put forth in these recommendations will provoke discussion, advance our collective thinking, and spark bold, new action on behalf of our nation's children. Their well-being, and the nation's, simply cannot be left to chance.

References

Adams, G. 1990. *Who knows how safe? The status of state efforts to ensure quality child care.* Washington, DC: Children's Defense Fund.

APHA (American Public Health Association), & AAP (American Academy of Pediatrics). 1992. *Caring for our children: National health and safety performance standards—Guidelines for out-of-home child care programs.* Washington, DC: APHA.

Barnett, W.S. 1995. Long-term effects of early childhood programs on cognitive and school outcomes. *The Future of Children* 5 (3): 25–50.

Bloom, P.J. 1996. The quality of work life in early childhood programs: Does accreditation make a difference? In *NAEYC accreditation: A decade of learning and the years ahead,* eds. S. Bredekamp & B.A. Willer, 13–24. Washington, DC: NAEYC.

Bredekamp, S., & S. Glowacki. 1995. The first decade of NAEYC accreditation: Growth and impact on the field. Paper prepared for an invitational conference sponsored by the Robert McCormick Tribune Foundation and NAEYC, 18–20 September, Wheaton, Illinois.

Breunig, G.S., & D. Bellm. 1996. *Early childhood mentoring programs: A survey of community initiatives.* Washington, DC: National Center for the Early Childhood Work Force.

Brofenbrenner, U. 1974. *A report on longitudinal evaluations of preschool programs, Vol. 2: Is early intervention effective?* Washington, DC: Office of Child Development, U.S. Department of Health, Education, and Welfare.

Bronson, M.B., D.E. Pierson, & T. Tivnan. 1984. The effects of early education on children's competence in elementary school. *Evaluation Review* 8: 615–29.

Chang, H.N., D. Pulido-Tobiassen, & A. Muckelroy. 1996. *Looking in, looking out: Redefining care and early education in a di-*verse society. San Francisco: California Tomorrow.

CCSSO (Council of Chief State School Officers). 1995. *Moving toward accountability for results: A look at ten states' efforts.* Washington, DC: Author.

Council for Early Childhood Professional Recognition. 1992. *Child Development Associate assessment system and competency standards.* Washington, DC: Author.

CQ&O (Cost, Quality, & Outcomes) Study Team. 1995. *Cost, quality, and child outcomes in child care centers.* Denver: Department of Economics, University of Colorado at Denver.

Derman-Sparks, L., & the A.B.C. Task Force. 1989. *Anti-bias curriculum: Tools for empowering young children.* Washington, DC: NAEYC.

Epstein, J.L. 1995. School/family/community partnerships: Caring for the children we share. *Phi Delta Kappan* (May): 701–12.

Galinsky, E., J.T. Bond, & D.E. Friedman. 1993. *The changing workforce: Highlights of the National Study.* New York: Families and Work Institute.

Galinsky, E., C. Howes, S. Kontos, & M. Shinn. 1994. *The study of children in family child care and relative care.* New York: Families and Work Institute.

Gomby, D.S., M.B. Larner, C.S. Stevenson, E.M. Lewit, & R.E. Behrman. 1995. Long-term outcomes of early childhood programs: Analysis and recommendations. *The Future of Children* 5 (3): 6–24.

Gormley, W.T. 1995. *Everybody's children: Child care as a public problem.* Washington, DC: Brookings Institution.

Henderson, A.T., C.L. Marburger, & T. Ooms. 1986. *Beyond the bake sale: An educator's guide to working with parents.* Columbia, MD: National Committee for Citizens in Education.

Hofferth, S.L., & D. Chaplin. 1994. *Child care quality versus availability: Do we have to trade one for the other?* Washington, DC: Urban Institute Press.

Kagan, S.L. 1994. *Defining America's commitments to parents and families. An historical-conceptual perspective.* Kansas City, MO: Ewing Marion Kauffman Foundation.

Kagan, S.L., S. Rosenkoetter, & N.E. Cohen, eds. 1997. *Considering child-based outcomes for young children: Definitions, desirability, feasibility, and next steps.* New Haven, CT: Bush Center in Child Development and Social Policy, Yale University.

Katz, L.G., D. Evangelou, & J.A. Hartman. 1990. *The case for mixed-age grouping in early education.* Washington, DC: NAEYC.

Mitchell, A. 1996. Licensing: Lessons from other occupations. In *Reinventing early care and education: A vision for a quality system,* eds. S.L. Kagan & N.E. Cohen, 101–123. San Francisco: Jossey-Bass.

Morgan, G., S.L. Azer, J.B. Costley, A. Genser, I.F. Goodman, J. Lombardi, & B. McGimsey. 1993. *Making a career of it: The state of the states report on career development in early care and education.* Boston: Center for Career Development in Early Care and Education, Wheelock College.

NACCRRA (National Association of Child Care Resource and Referral Agencies). 1996. *Creating and facilitating health linkages: The role of child care resource and referral.* Washington, DC: Author.

Phillips, C.B. 1994. The movement of African-American children through sociocultural contexts: A case of conflict resolution. In *Diversity and developmentally appropriate practices: Challenges for early childhood education*, eds. B.L. Mallory & R.S. New, 137–54. New York: Teachers College Press.

Phillips, D.A., ed. 1995. *Child care for low-income families: Summary of two workshops.* Washington, DC: National Academy Press.

Phillips, D.A., & N.A. Crowell, eds. 1994. *Cultural diversity in early education: Results of a workshop.* Washington, DC: National Academy Press.

Powell, D.R. 1989. *Families and early childhood programs.* Washington, DC: NAEYC.

Pritchard, E. 1996. Training and professional development: International approaches. In *Reinventing early care and education: A vision for a quality system*, eds. S.L. Kagan & N.E. Cohen, 124–41. San Francisco: Jossey-Bass.

Schorr, L.B. 1994. The case for shifting to results-based accountability. In *Making a difference: Moving to outcome-based accountability for comprehensive service reforms*, eds. N. Young, S. Gardner, S. Coley, L. Schorr, & C. Bruner, 13–28. Falls Church, VA: National Center for Service Integration.

Schweinhart, L.J., H.V. Barnes, & D.P. Weikart, with W.S. Barnett, & A.S. Epstein. 1993. *Significant benefits: The High/Scope Perry Preschool Study through age 27.* Ypsilanti, MI: High/Scope Press.

Staines, G.L., & E. Galinsky. 1991. *Parental leave and productivity: The supervisor's view.* New York: Families and Work Institute.

Stangler, G. 1995. Lifeboats vs. safety nets: Who rides . . . who swims? In *Dollars and sense: Diverse perspectives on block grants and the Personal Responsibility Act*, 67–72. Washington, DC: The Finance Project and Institute for Educational Leadership.

U.S. ACIR (Advisory Commission on Intergovernmental Relations). 1994. *Child care: The need for federal-state-local coordination.* Washington, DC: Author.

Weissbourd, B. 1987. A brief history of family support programs. In *America's family support programs*, eds. S.L. Kagan, D.R. Powell, B. Weissbourd, & E.F. Zigler, 38–56. New Haven, CT: Yale University Press.

Whitebook, M., P. Hnatiuk, & D. Bellm: 1994. *Mentoring in early care and education: Refining an emerging career path.* Washington, DC: National Center for the Early Childhood Work Force.

Whitebook, M., L. Sakai, &, C. Howes. 1997. *NAEYC accreditation as a strategy for improving child care quality, executive summary.* Washington, DC: National Center for the Early Childhood Work Force.

Willer, B., ed. 1990. *Reaching the full cost of quality in early childhood programs.* Washington, DC: NAEYC.

Willer, B., S. Hofferth, E. Kiskar, P. Divine-Hawkins, E. Farquhar, & F. Glantz. 1991. *The demand and supply of child care in 1990: Joint findings from the National Child Care Survey 1990 and a profile of child care settings.* Washington, DC: NAEYC.

Yoshikawa, H. 1995. Long-term effects of early childhood programs on social outcomes and delinquency. *The Future of Children* 5 (3): 51–75.

A Child Shall Lead Us

America is great because America is good, and if America ever ceases to be good, America will cease to be great.

Alexis de Tocqueville

Capitalism forgets that life is social, and the kingdom of brotherhood is found neither in the thesis of communism nor the antithesis of capitalism but in a higher synthesis. It is found in a higher synthesis that combines the truth of both. ... It means ultimately coming to see that the problem of racism, the problem of economic exploitation, and the problem of war are all tied together! These are the triple evils that are interrelated."

Dr. Martin Luther King Jr.
Where Do We Go from Here:
Chaos or Community?

You shall not pervert the justice due to your poor.

Exodus 23:6

America appears to be riding high on the cusp of the 21st century and third millennium. Wall Street is booming. Excess, Russell Baker says, has become a way of life for the very rich. In what may be the ultimate in corporate hubris, Miller Brewing Company has applied for a trademark or been recently registered as the "official sponsor of the Millennium" according to *Harper's Magazine*. Corporate CEOs, who earned 41 times as much as their workers made in 1960, made 185 times as much as their workers in 1995. The average CEO in 1995 earned more every two days than the average worker earned in a whole year. Fortune 500 CEOs averaged $7.8 million each in total compensation. This exceeds the average salaries of 226 school teachers a year.

The rosy view of American prosperity at the top hides deep and dangerous moral, economic, age, and racial fault lines lurking beneath the surface. Unless we heed and correct them, they will destroy America's fundamental ideals of justice and equal opportunity, family and community stability, economic productivity, and moral legitimacy as the democratic standard bearer in the next era.

In the 25 years since the Children's Defense Fund began, great progress has been made in improving children's lives in many areas. Millions of children with disabilities have a right to education; millions of poor children have received a Head Start, health care, immunizations, better child care, and permanent adoptive homes. But shamefully high child poverty rates persist, and children are the poorest group of Americans. The gap between America's poor and rich has grown into a chasm, the wages of young families with children have eroded, and many middle class families are treading economic water.

Since 1989 the poorest fifth of families have lost $587 each and the richest 5 percent have gained $29,533 each. We have five times more billionaires but 4 million more poor children. While millions of stock options helped quintuple the earnings of corporate CEOs between 1980 and 1995, those same employers threw millions of children out of health insurance plans at their parents' workplaces, and parental wages stagnated.

More than 11 million children are uninsured, 90 percent of whom have working parents. More parents worked longer hours and more families

From *The State of America's Children Yearbook, 1998*, pp. xi-xix. © 1998 by the Children's Defense Fund. Reprinted by permission.

sent a second or only parent into the labor force to meet family necessities. But for millions of families, work did not pay a family-supporting wage, and a minimum wage no longer prevents poverty. Sixty-nine percent of poor children live in working families. Ending welfare as we know it will not help them. Ending poverty as we know it will. Sustained economic investment in rebuilding our communities and in stable jobs with decent wages, quality affordable child care, and health insurance must become top American priorities.

Six years of economic expansion with low inflation and a soaring stock market have not filtered down to 36.5 million poor people, including 14.5 million children. In 1996 the number of *very* poor people who live below half the poverty line (a mere $8,018 for a family of four) increased, while the current income of households in the top 5 percent increased by $12,500. Today more than one in five children is growing up poor and one in 11 is growing up extremely poor. This is shameful and unnecessary.

If we are truly concerned about preventing welfare, teen pregnancy, youth violence, school dropouts, and crime, then we need to start first by preventing child poverty and ensuring every child a fair start in life. The moral, human, and economic costs of permitting 14.5 million children to be poor are too high.

■ A baby born poor is less likely to survive to its first birthday than a baby born to an unwed mother, a high school dropout, or a mother who smoked during pregnancy.

■ Poverty is a greater risk to children's overall health status than is living in a single-parent family.

■ Poor children face greater risk of stunted growth, anemia, repeated years of schooling, lower test scores, and less education, as well as lower wages and lower earnings in their adult years.

■ Poverty puts children at a greater risk of falling behind in school than does living in a single-parent home or being born to teenage parents.

Dr. Laura D'Andrea Tyson, former chair of the President's Council of Economic Advisors, says, "Policies to reduce the poverty rate among children—which typically remains higher in the United States than in any other advanced industrial countries—must be a fundamental part of our efforts to build a healthy economy for the 21st cen-

tury." Nobel laureate in economics Robert M. Solow of the Massachusetts Institute of Technology states, "In optimistic moments, I like to believe that most Americans would want to lift children out of poverty even if it cost something. It is hard to blame little children for the problems that surround them now and will damage their future health, ability, and learning capacity. Doing nothing about it seems both immoral and unintelligent."

All segments of society pay the costs of child poverty and would share the gains if child poverty were eliminated. America's labor force is projected to lose as much as $130 billion in future productive capacity for every year 14.5 million American children continue to live in poverty. These costs will spill over to employers and consumers, making it harder for businesses to expand technology, train workers, or produce a full range of high-quality products. Additional costs will be borne by schools, hospitals, and taxpayers and by our criminal justice system. Poor children held back in school require special education and tutoring, experience a lifetime of heightened medical problems and reliance on social service, and fail to earn and contribute as much in taxes.[*]

When legitimate avenues of employment are closed, poor youths and adults turn to illegitimate ones, especially the lethal underground economy of drugs and crime fueled by out-of-control gun trafficking. Since 1970 America's prison population has increased more than fivefold at an annual taxpayer tab exceeding $20 billion. Almost one in three young Black and one in 15 young White males between ages 20 to 29 are under some type of correctional control (incarceration, probation, or parole). Two-thirds of state prison inmates in 1991 had not completed high school and one-third had annual incomes under $5,000. Joseph Califano, head of Columbia University's National Center on Addiction and Substance Abuse, reports that if present trends persist, one of every 20 Americans born in 1997 will spend some time in jail, including one of every 11 men and one of every four Black men.

Is this America's dream for its children and itself? Can an $8.7 trillion American economy not afford decent jobs, quality child care, education, and health care for all its children?

---

[*] These and other findings are detailed in a CDF report by Arloc Sherman, *Poverty Matters: The Cost of Child Poverty in America.*

What Kind of Ancestors Will We Be?
What Is America's Legacy?

It is time for every American to see and excise the moral tumors of child neglect, violence, poverty, and racism eating away the core of our national soul. What kind of billboard are we for democracy or capitalism—in a world where more than 3 billion people live on less than $2 per day and 200 million children suffer malnutrition every year—when millions of American children are hungry, homeless, neglected, abused, and dying from diseases we have the money and power but not the decency to prevent?

How will we lead a world where 5 of 6 billion citizens are not White, when young Black and Latino males see no jobs, hope, or future choices beyond prison and death? How do we fill our privileged children—who, like many poor children, are longing for a sense of purpose things cannot meet—with spiritual anchors and worthwhile goals? Will our children have something besides drugs and booze and cigarettes and rollicking good times to turn to when life's rough seas batter their souls?

How will they remember us as parents and leaders? Will they remember the jets, second mansions, and multiple nannies, or will they remember how often we watched their games and plays and concerts and were home to soothe over a bad nightmare? Will their memory books be chock-full of expensive toys and designer clothes, or of regular mealtimes, shared conversation, family games, prayer, and worship? Are they able to get our attention in the small daily ways that matter and say I love you, or only through desperate screams of violence, gangs, guns, sexual promiscuity, and substance abuse?

Does what we do every day really matter for anyone besides ourselves and our immediate family? Is our example one we would like our children to emulate and pass on to our grandchildren and the children of the world? Will we leave them a country and Earth more just, virtuous, and safe than we inherited? What messages do our lives convey about the brotherhood and sisterhood of humanity?

How will each of us add to or subtract from America's moral bank account when the God of the universe asks for an accounting? Will God care how many times our excessive nuclear stockpiles can blow up humankind? Will God be proud that we sell more weapons to other nations than any other country, which

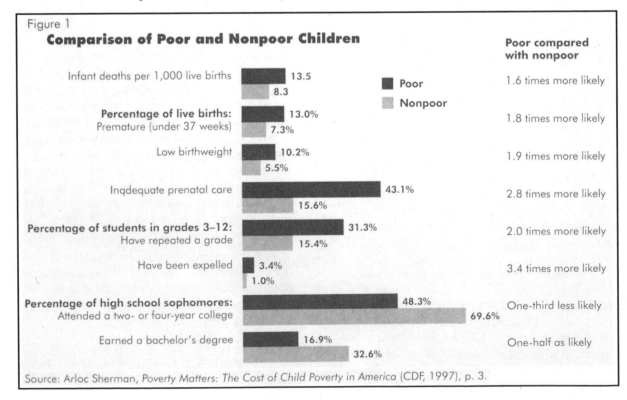

Figure 1

Comparison of Poor and Nonpoor Children

Poor compared with nonpoor

	Poor	Nonpoor	
Infant deaths per 1,000 live births	13.5	8.3	1.6 times more likely
Percentage of live births: Premature (under 37 weeks)	13.0%	7.3%	1.8 times more likely
Low birthweight	10.2%	5.5%	1.9 times more likely
Inqdequate prenatal care	43.1%	15.6%	2.8 times more likely
Percentage of students in grades 3–12: Have repeated a grade	31.3%	15.4%	2.0 times more likely
Have been expelled	3.4%	1.0%	3.4 times more likely
Percentage of high school sophomores: Attended a two- or four-year college	48.3%	69.6%	One-third less likely
Earned a bachelor's degree	16.9%	32.6%	One-half as likely

Source: Arloc Sherman, *Poverty Matters: The Cost of Child Poverty in America* (CDF, 1997), p. 3.

Table 1   **Poor Outcomes for Poor Children**

Outcome	Poor children's higher risk relative to nonpoor children
Health	
Death in childhood	1.5 to 3 times more likely
Stunted growth	2.7 times more likely
Iron deficiency in preschool years	3 to 4 times more likely
Partial or complete deafness	1.5 to 2 times more likely
Partial or complete blindness	1.2 to 1.8 times more likely
Serious physical or mental disabilities	About 2 times more likely
Fatal accidental injuries	2 to 3 times more likely
Pneumonia	1.6 times more likely
Education	
Average IQ score at age 5	9 points lower
Average achievement scores at age 3 and above	11 to 25 percentiles lower
Learning disabilities	1.3 times more likely
Placement in special education	2 or 3 percentage points more likely
Below-usual grade for child's age	2 percentage points more likely for each year of childhood spent in poverty
Dropping out between ages 16 and 24	2 times more likely than middle-income youths; 11 times more likely than wealthy youths

Source: Arloc Sherman, *Poverty Matters: The Cost of Child Poverty in America* (CDF, 1997), p. 4.

---

fuel wars all over the globe that kill mostly women and children? Will God ask how many billionaires and millionaires we created with the land and water and talents God blessed us with and praise us for developing the cleverest ads to sell tobacco's deadly poisons to our children? Will God agree that a child's life in Bangladesh is less precious than one in Bangor, Maine, as America's tobacco industry markets its deadly wares to developing nations? Or will God ask did we feed the hungry, heal the sick, visit the prisoner, protect the widow, orphan, and stranger? How will America answer? How will you and I answer? How will we teach our children to answer as citizens of the richest nation on earth blessed with the opportunity to abolish want and disease?

America's children will make or break America's greatness and future. One in four current Americans is a child. Children are the future tense of our humanity. Its quality will depend largely upon our present-tense care of them. The Rev. Dr. Gardner Taylor, the dean of American preachers, says:

> If we do not bequeath to them something worth calling life, then we cannot expect of them any lives that are worthwhile.... Might it be that this land with all of its richness, with all of its opportunity for true greatness, its opportunity to present itself before the world as what a nation ought to be,

might now be sowing the seeds of its very destruction in abandonment of its children?

I believe so. That is why the Children's Defense Fund has been struggling for 25 years to plant seeds for a massive moral movement to Leave No Child Behind and to ensure every child of every race born in every place in America a healthy, fair, safe, and moral start in life and a successful passage to adulthood, with the help of caring families and communities.

Children are life, power, hope, and the chance for renewal and immortality. Children will carry on our families, communities, institutions, and values. How then do we honestly examine and transform the values and priorities of the wealthiest nation in history, which lets its children be the poorest group of Americans and lets a child be killed by guns every hour and a half? How do we reverse the prevailing political calculus that would rather pay three times more to lock children up *after* they get into trouble than to give them incentives to stay in school and out of trouble, through good afterschool and summer programs, jobs, and service opportunities? How do we make it easier rather than harder for parents to balance work and family responsibilities and to get the community and financial support they need to carry out the most important role in America?

Key Facts About American Children

1 in 2	preschoolers has a mother in the labor force.
1 in 2	will live in a single-parent family at some point in childhood.
1 in 2	never completes a single year of college.
1 in 3	is born to unmarried parents.
1 in 3	will be poor at some point in childhood.
1 in 3	is a year or more behind in school.
1 in 4	is born poor.
1 in 4	is born to a mother who did not graduate from high school.
1 in 4	lives with only one parent.
1 in 5	is poor now.
1 in 5	lives in a family receiving food stamps.
1 in 5	is born to a mother who received no prenatal care in the first three months of pregnancy.
1 in 6	has a foreign-born mother.
1 in 7	has no health insurance.
1 in 7	lives with a working relative but is poor nonetheless.
1 in 8	never graduates from high school.
1 in 8	is born to a teenage mother.
1 in 11	lives at less than half the poverty level.
1 in 12	has a disability.
1 in 13	is born at low birthweight.
1 in 24	is born to a mother who received late or no prenatal care.
1 in 25	lives with neither parent.
1 in 132	dies before age 1.
1 in 680	is killed by gunfire before age 20.

Five Questions All American Citizens Should Ask Ourselves and Our Political Leaders About National Priorities

As a Democrat, as a Christian, as a southern Baptist, as someone who fundamentally believes in the words of the Bible... I [do not] believe that God's response to the poor is to treat them as though they are the least priority, almost as though they are a nuisance to be dealt with.... With all due respect to the Christian Coalition, where does it say in the Scriptures that the character of God is to give more to those who have and less to those who have not?... If there is one thing evident in the Scriptures, it is that God gives priority to the poor.

U.S. Representative Glenn Poshard
Democrat, Illinois 19th district
Speech to the House of Representatives

No one may claim the name Christian and be comfortable in the face of hunger, hopelessness, insecurity, and the injustice found in this country and around the world.... Every economic decision and institution must be judged in light of whether it protects or undermines the dignity of the human person.

National Conference of Catholic Bishops
Pastoral Letter on the Economy

The time has come for an all-out world war against poverty. The rich nations must use their vast resources of wealth to develop the underdeveloped, school the unschooled and feed the unfed. The well-off and the secure have too often become indifferent and oblivious to the poverty and deprivation in their midst. The poor in our countries have been shut out of our minds, and driven from the mainstream of our societies, because we have allowed them to become invisible. Ultimately, a great nation is a compassionate nation. No individual or nation can be great if it does not have a concern for "the least of these."

Dr. Martin Luther King Jr.
Where Do We Go from Here:
Chaos or Community?

1. **Why is our nation continuing to spend $265 billion a year, $5.1 billion a week, $727 million a day, and $30 million an hour on "National Defense" in a post-Cold War era with no towering external enemies?** Our military budget exceeds the total military expenditures of the 12 next-largest spenders—including Russia, France, Great Britain, Germany, and China—combined. Congress gave the Pentagon $9 billion more than it requested in 1996, while cutting $54 billion from child nutrition programs for poor and legal immigrant children and families. The military plans to purchase three new tactical fighter systems that will cost $355 billion—systems the U.S. General Accounting Office says we don't need and can't afford—at a time when millions of struggling parents left behind in the global economy need better-paying jobs and millions of children need health care, quality child care, education, and housing.

As President Dwight Eisenhower reminded us in 1953, "Every gun that is made, every warship launched, every rocket fired signifies . . . a theft from those who hunger and are not fed, those who are cold and not clothed. This world in arms is not spending money alone. It is spending the sweat of its laborers, the genius of its scientists, and the hopes of its children."

■ Every 14 hours we spend more on the military than we do annually on programs to prevent and treat child abuse.

■ Every 29 hours we spend more on the military than we do annually on summer jobs for unemployed youths.

■ Every six days we spend more on the military than we do annually on the Child Care and Development Block Grant for child care for low-income working parents.

■ Every six days we spend more on the military than we do annually on Head Start, which still serves only one in three eligible children.

■ Every 11 days we spend more on the military than we do annually on Title I compensatory education for disadvantaged children.

It takes only a few nuclear weapons to blow up humankind. America spends tens of billions of dollars to maintain a nuclear overkill "advantage" at a time when irresponsible leaders and gangsters seek access to inadequately secured nuclear weapon stockpiles and a cheap computer chip can accidentally launch a nuclear war. "Can't we do better than condone a world in which nuclear weapons are accepted as

Key Facts About Poor Children

3 in 5	are White.
1 in 3	lives in suburban America.
1 in 3	lives in a family with married parents.
2 in 3	live in a working family.

commonplace?" asks retired General George Lee Butler, former head of the Strategic Air Command. "The elimination of nuclear weapons," Butler states, "is called utopia by people who forget that for so many decades the end of the Cold War was considered utopia."

As we near the close of a 20th century marked by dazzling scientific and technological progress, but also the bloodiest century in history, we all need to reassess the meaning of power and of life. More than 109 million human beings lost their lives in wars during this century, and far more civilians than soldiers died due to military conflicts. We must heed General Omar Bradley's warning on Armistice Day in 1948:

> We have grasped the mystery of the atom and rejected the Sermon on the Mount. . . . Ours is a world of nuclear giants and ethical infants. We know more about war than we know about peace, more about killing than we know about living. The way to win an atomic war is to make certain it never starts. And the way to make sure it never starts is to abolish the dangerous costly nuclear stockpiles which imprison humankind.

2. **Why, with over 200 million guns in circulation already killing a child every hour and a half, does our country manufacture or import a new gun every eight seconds?** American children under age 15 are 12 times more likely to die from gunfire than children in 25 other industrialized nations combined. Virtually all violent youth crime is gun-driven. Yet many politicians seek to return to the barbaric practice of locking up children (the majority of whom are neither violent nor repeat offenders) in adult jails instead of locking up the adults who sold or gave them the guns. Why seek to protect guns rather than protect children from guns?

When the polio virus killed 2,700 children and adults in its peak year—seven a day—we declared a national emergency. Why don't we declare a national emergency to stop the deadly gun virus that kills almost twice as many children—5,285 a year, 14 a day—in their homes,

Moments in America for Children

Every 9 seconds	a child drops out of school
Every 10 seconds	a child is reported abused or neglected.
Every 15 seconds	a child is arrested.
Every 25 seconds	a child is born to an unmarried mother.
Every 32 seconds	a child sees his or her parents divorce.
Every 36 seconds	a child is born into poverty.
Every 36 seconds	a child is born to a mother who did not graduate from high school.
Every minute	a child is born to a teen mother.
Every 2 minutes	a child is born at low birthweight.
Every 3 minutes	a child is born to a mother who received late or no prenatal care.
Every 3 minutes	a child is arrested for drug abuse.
Every 4 minutes	a child is arrested for an alcohol-related offense.
Every 5 minutes	a child is arrested for a violent crime.
Every 18 minutes	an infant dies.
Every 23 minutes	a child is wounded by gunfire.
Every 100 minutes	a child is killed by gunfire.
Every 4 hours	a child commits suicide.

neighborhoods, schools, and parks? It is ironic that the world's leading military power stands by as White militia gangs and Black, Latino, Asian, and White street gangs stockpile arsenals that endanger all citizens.

3. **How much do we truly value children and families when we don't put our money and our respect behind our words?** Is a child care worker who earns $6.12 an hour, $12,058 a year, and receives no benefits 182 times less valuable to America's future than the average professional basketball player who earns $2.2 million a year, or 162 times less valuable than the average HMO head who made $1.95 million in 1996? Is she only one-fourth as important to America's well-being as an advertising manager for a tobacco brand who makes $23.32 an hour? Most states require 1,500 hours of training to become a manicurist or hair stylist, but more than 30 states do not require a single hour of training for child care workers.

What family values dictate a public policy in many states that pays more to nonrelatives than to relatives to care for children whose parents cannot nurture and protect them? Why are we willing to spend $10,000 a year to place a child in a foster home and much more to place a child in an institution *after* the family fails but refuse to invest $4,500 in job creation, child care, and income supplements for poor parents? Why does an average welfare payment of $365 a month to a poor family undermine personal responsibility when billions in "subsidies and incentives"—euphemisms for government welfare for the nonpoor and powerful—do not?

4. **Why should every 66-year-old in the United States be guaranteed health coverage and not every 6-year-old or 16-year-old?** Is one life more valuable than the other? Why should a child in one state have a chance to live and grow up healthy and not a child in another state? Why should our leaders decide it is acceptable to provide health insurance to *every other child*? And why are some of our political leaders and powerful lawyers so eager to protect a tobacco industry that saps 420,000 lives a year, $50 billion in direct health costs, and entices nearly 2 million children to smoke and shorten their lives? Former Surgeon General C. Everett Koop and former Food and Drug Administration head David Kessler propose a $2 a pack tobacco tax to deter teen smoking. That money not only could save millions of young lives by preventing them from smoking but also fund millions of children's hopes and dreams. A $2 tobacco tax would yield more than $100 billion dollars. That is enough to end childhood poverty, fund child care for working families, and ensure every child the healthy start that the tobacco industry has done so much to destroy.

5. **Why is the United States, save Somalia (which lacks a legally constituted government to act), alone among nations in failing to ratify the Convention on the Rights of the Child?** All the other nations of the world are willing to commit to the convention's goals of ending illegal child labor, sexual exploitation, violent abuse of, and capital punishment for children. Why do we refuse to pledge to make reasonable efforts to give all of our nation's children the adequate health care, food, shelter, and education that should be every child's birthright? ...

CHILD CARE:
HOW DOES YOUR STATE RATE?

by Betty Holcomb with Catherine Cartwright, Shaun Dreisbach and Sarah Hutter

The child care story this year was mixed, but with many bright spots. The continuing flow of federal money into state coffers, combined with a strong economy, led to many new initiatives from coast to coast.

Most notably, caregiver pay became a new priority in many states. "The biggest problem in child care is making up the gap between what parents can afford to pay and what it costs to keep skilled teachers on the job," says Marcy Whitebook of the Center for the Child Care Workforce. "Caregivers currently take up the slack, working for low pay and with virtually no benefits. Even teachers with bachelor's degrees and years of experience average below $20,000 a year." This is a key concern for working parents since poor pay leads to high turnover among child care workers, robbing both children and their families of stable care. On average, child care workers leave the field at an astonishing annual rate of nearly 40 percent.

But this year, in an effort to address the problem, many states raised the rates they pay for child care. California, one of our 10 Best, pushed ahead with its model mentoring program, which rewards experienced teachers with higher pay when they train newcomers to the field. Six others—Colorado, Florida, Georgia, Illinois, New York and North Carolina—now have an incentive program called T.E.A.C.H. for caregivers who take courses in child development.

Equally important, nearly a dozen states have begun to pay higher rates to centers that are accredited by the National Association for the Education of Young Children (NAEYC). That's a key barometer of quality, since NAEYC standards are higher than any state's licensing requirements. Even better, several states have begun to adopt easy-to understand rankings for centers that meet the new standards. New Mexico, for example, started ranking centers as "gold," "silver" or "bronze," and Florida has launched a "gold seal" program, so parents will get an immediate reading on the quality of care in an individual program. "I'm very excited about this. It's really the first time that there's been solid consumer information about child care," says Wheelock College's Gwen Morgan, one of the nation's leading experts on child care.

As this one-of-a-kind, state-by-state report shows, many states have launched or greatly expanded other promising programs, most notably prekindergarten programs in Connecticut, Massachusetts, New York and New Jersey. Tennessee established a modest pilot prekindergarten program.

But our reporting also turned up serious problems. Many, many states still have long waiting lists for families who need help paying for care. The Children's Defense Fund has found, in fact, that the vast majority of states simply cannot serve all the working families who need child care. In Iowa, about 90,000 families qualify for assistance paying for child care, but only 11,000 get help. In Virginia, 6,000 families were on the waiting list for state-subsidized care as of January 1998.

That situation, of course, leaves parents with harrowing choices. One Florida mother, who works full time, says that she is forced to choose between groceries and child care. "I work a full-time job, but after I pay taxes and insurance I bring home $230 a week," she says. "That leaves me $110 a week to care for my children."

Such stories are now accruing from families across the country, as child care advocates gather evidence to make a case for better child care and lobby Congress to pass new child care proposals. President Clinton advocates adding $21 billion to the nation's child care budget over the next five years, and powerful politicians at both ends of the political spectrum champion child care bills. "We hope that we'll see some action this summer on child care," says Helen Blank of the Children's Defense Fund. "Clearly, families need more help paying for care." . . .

First appeared in *Working Mother,* July/August 1998, pp. 22-23, 31-33. Written by B. Holcomb, C. Cartwright, S. Dreisbach, and S. Hutter. © 1998 by MacDonald Communications Corporation. Reprinted by permission.

STATE   QUALITY   SAFETY

STATE	Rating	Accredited Centers	Accredited FCC	Ratios Infants	Ratios Toddlers	Ratios Pre-K	Group Size	Training Centers	Training FCC	Pay	Rating	Adult Supervision	Regulated FCC	Playground Centers	Playground FCC	Hand-Washing Centers	Hand-Washing FCC	Inspections Centers	Inspections FCC
ALABAMA	**	44	8	6	8	12	GOOD	0	0		**	POOR	1+	-	-	POOR	POOR	1X2YR	1X2YR
ALASKA	**	12	13	5	6	10	NONE	0	0		**	MEDIOCRE	5+	+	+	GOOD	GOOD	NONE	NONE
ARIZONA	**	144	4	5	8	13	NONE	0	NR		**	POOR	5+	-	-	FAIR	FAIR	1XYR	2XYR
ARKANSAS	**	43	21	6	12	12	NONE	0	0		**	POOR	6+	-	-	FAIR	POOR	3XYR	3XYR
CALIFORNIA	***	520	138	4	12	12	NONE	12C	0	+	****	MEDIOCRE	2+	+	-	FAIR	FAIR	1XYR	RARE
COLORADO	***	124	4	5	7	10	MEDIOCRE	0	12H	+	***	MEDIOCRE	2+	+	-	GOOD	POOR	VARIES	VARIES
CONNECTICUT	****	267	9	4	4	10	GOOD	0	0		****	GOOD	1+	+	-	POOR	POOR	1X2YR	RARE
DELAWARE	***	20	31	4	10	12	NONE	60H	15H		***	MEDIOCRE	1+	-	-	GOOD	GOOD	1XYR	1XYR
DIST. OF COLUMBIA	***	36	12	4	4	8	MEDIOCRE	9C	0		****	GOOD	1+	+	+	GOOD	GOOD	1-3XYR	1-3XYR
FLORIDA	**	381	98	4	11	15	NONE	30H	3H	+	**	POOR	2+	+	-	FAIR	POOR	2XYR	2XYR
GEORGIA	**	137	4	6	10	15	POOR	10H	0	+	**	POOR	3+	+	+	FAIR	POOR	1XYR	RARE
HAWAII	****	40	2	4	8	12	GOOD	BA	0		****	MEDIOCRE	3	+	-	GOOD	NR	NONE	NONE
IDAHO	*	12	3	6	12	12	NONE	0	NR		*	POOR	13+	-	-	GOOD	GOOD	NONE	NONE
ILLINOIS	***	294	93	4	8	10	MEDIOCRE	6C	0	+	***	MEDIOCRE	4	+	-	GOOD	GOOD	1XYR	1XYR
INDIANA	***	64	25	4	5	10	MEDIOCRE	0	0		**	GOOD	6+	-	-	GOOD	POOR	3XYR	3XYR
IOWA	***	157	5	4	6	8	NONE	0	NR		**	GOOD	7	-	-	FAIR	POOR	RARE	RARE
KANSAS	***	48	3	3	7	12	MEDIOCRE	12C	0		***	GOOD	1+	-	-	GOOD	GOOD	1XYR	1XYR
KENTUCKY	**	126	10	5	10	12	MEDIOCRE	0	6H		**	POOR	4+	-	-	FAIR	FAIR	1XYR	1XYR
LOUISIANA	*	54		6	12	14	POOR	0	NR		*	POOR	7	+	-	GOOD	POOR	1XYR	NONE
MAINE	***	12	4	4	5	10	POOR	0	6H		***	GOOD	3+	+	+	FAIR	FAIR	1XYR	1XYR
MARYLAND	****	68	1	3	6	10	MEDIOCRE	6C	9H		****	GOOD	1+	+	+	GOOD	GOOD	1XYR	1X2YR
MASSACHUSETTS	****	461	2	3	4	10	MEDIOCRE	SOME	0	+	****	GOOD	1+	+	+	GOOD	GOOD	1X2YR	RARE
MICHIGAN	***	114	20	4	4	10	NONE	0	0		***	GOOD	1+	-	-	GOOD	POOR	1X2YR	RARE
MINNESOTA	****	203	94	4	7	10	MEDIOCRE	16C	6H	+	****	GOOD	5+	-	-	FAIR	FAIR	1X2YR	1X2YR
MISSISSIPPI	*	27		5	12	14	MEDIOCRE	0	0		*	POOR	6+	+	+	FAIR	NR	1XYR	1XYR
MISSOURI	***	40	7	4	8	10	MEDIOCRE	0	0		**	MEDIOCRE	5+	+	+	FAIR	FAIR	1XYR	1XYR
MONTANA	**	10	1	4	8	8	NONE	8H	0		**	MEDIOCRE	3+	-	-	POOR	POOR	1XYR	RARE
NEBRASKA	***	18	8	4	6	10	NONE	0	12H		**	GOOD	4+	+	-	FAIR	FAIR	1X2YR	1X2YR
NEVADA	**	9	3	6	10	13	NONE	3H	3H		**	POOR	5+	+	+	FAIR	FAIR	2XYR	2XYR
NEW HAMPSHIRE	**	30		4	6	8	MEDIOCRE	72H	0		***	GOOD	4+	+	+	GOOD	GOOD	1XYR	1XYR
NEW JERSEY	***	140	10	4	7	10	POOR	15C	NR		**	MEDIOCRE	6+	-	-	GOOD	GOOD	1XYR	RARE
NEW MEXICO	**	41	3	6	10	12	NONE	0	0	+	**	POOR	5+	+	-	GOOD	GOOD	2XYR	2XYR
NEW YORK	***	264	83	4	5	7	MEDIOCRE	0	0	+	***	GOOD	3+	-	-	GOOD	GOOD	1X2YR	RARE
NORTH CAROLINA	**	113	37	5	10	15	MEDIOCRE	0	0	+	**	POOR	3+	-	-	GOOD	POOR	1XYR	RARE
NORTH DAKOTA	**	8	3	4	5	7	NONE	0	0	+	**	GOOD	6	-	-	FAIR	FAIR	2XYR	1X2YR
OHIO	**	185	5	5	7	12	MEDIOCRE	0	NR		**	MEDIOCRE	7	+	+	FAIR	FAIR	2XYR	2XYR
OKLAHOMA	**	44	4	4	8	12	MEDIOCRE	0	0		***	MEDIOCRE	1+	+	-	GOOD	GOOD	3XYR	3XYR
OREGON	**	37	3	4	4	10	GOOD	0	0		**	GOOD	4+	-	-	GOOD	POOR	2XYR	NONE
PENNSYLVANIA	***	147	24	4	6	10	GOOD	0	0		***	GOOD	4+	+	+	FAIR	FAIR	NONE	RARE
RHODE ISLAND	***	17	6	4	6	9	GOOD	BA	0		**	MEDIOCRE	4+	+	-	GOOD	POOR	2XYR	RARE
SOUTH CAROLINA	**	51	1	6	10	13	NONE	0	0		**	POOR	2+	+	-	GOOD	POOR	2XYR	NONE
SOUTH DAKOTA	**	3		5	5	10	POOR	0	NR		*	MEDIOCRE	13	-	-	FAIR	FAIR	1XYR	1XYR
TENNESSEE	**	103	11	5	8	12	MEDIOCRE	0	0		**	MEDIOCRE	5+	+	-	FAIR	FAIR	1XYR	1XYR
TEXAS	**	377	72	4	13	17	POOR	8H	0		**	POOR	4+	-	-	GOOD	GOOD	1-3XYR	RARE
UTAH	***	12		4	7	12	POOR	0	2H		**	MEDIOCRE	NR	+	+	GOOD	POOR	2XYR	1XYR
VERMONT	****	31	3	4	5	10	MEDIOCRE	3C	0		***	GOOD	3+	+	-	GOOD	FAIR	2XYR	NONE
VIRGINIA	**	184	10	4	10	10	NONE	0	0		**	MEDIOCRE	6+	+	-	GOOD	FAIR	1XYR	1XYR
WASHINGTON	***	110	42	4	7	10	MEDIOCRE	0	0	+	****	GOOD	2+	+	-	GOOD	POOR	NONE	NONE
WEST VIRGINIA	**	8		4	8	10	NONE	0	NR		**	MEDIOCRE	4	-	-	GOOD	FAIR	NONE	NONE
WISCONSIN	***	163	16	4	6	10	MEDIOCRE	SOME	40H	+	***	GOOD	4+	+	-	GOOD	GOOD	1XYR	1XYR
WYOMING	**	35	9	5	8	10	NONE	0	0		**	MEDIOCRE	3+	-	-	FAIR	FAIR	1XYR	1XYR

For an explanation of these abbreviations, see "Key to the Ratings."

AVAILABILITY   COMMITMENT

Rating	Tax Breaks	R&R	Public Pre-K	Pay Rate	Rating	Comments
**	F	-	N	OK	**	Alabama lawmakers failed to approve better standards.
**		-	Y	OK	**	Alaska made some slight improvements in quality this year.
**	F	-	Y	POOR	**	Governor Jane Dee Hull launched a new program to improve care in Arizona.
**	C+	-	Y	OK	***	Arkansas officials still make only a marginal commitment to child care.
****	F	+	Y	OK	****	California approved major new funding for school-age child care.
****	C	+	Y	NA	****	Colorado, a model state, is giving new attention to off-hours care.
****	F		Y	POOR	****	A brand-new prekindergarten initiative helps Connecticut keep its place in the top 10.
***	C	-	Y	POOR	***	Delaware is devoting new resources to inspections.
**	C+	-	Y	NA	**	The District of Columbia continues to struggle to meet the needs of its tiniest citizens.
***		+	Y	OK	****	Florida's Governor Lawton Chiles continues to introduce important new initiatives.
***	F	+	Y	POOR	***	Prekindergarten and school-age care are the only truly bright spots in Georgia.
****	B+		Y	POOR	****	Hawaii's budget shortfalls have slowed action in this visionary state.
*	C-		N	POOR	*	Idaho remains woefully behind most other states.
***	F		Y	NA	***	Illinois made a huge new investment in child care this year.
***	F		N	OK	***	School-age care got more attention in Indiana this year.
**	B	-	Y	OK	**	Governor Terry Branstad launched a program to improve the quality of care in Iowa.
**	C	+	N	POOR	**	Kansas has made progress in upgrading quality of care.
***	C	-	Y	NA	***	Governor Paul Patton held a high-profile conference on child care that should lead to positive change in Kentucky.
*	C		Y	POOR	*	Louisiana retains its low standards.
**	C	-	Y	POOR	**	Maine officials improved oversight of family child care this year.
****	C-	+	Y	OK	****	Maryland's resource and referral system continues to shine.
****	C-	+	Y	POOR	****	Prekindergarten and school-age programs got a big lift this year in Massachusetts.
***	F	+	Y	OK	***	Michigan legislators launched a new caregiver training program.
****	A-	+	Y	OK	****	Minnesota expanded care, but took a step backward on standards.
*	F	-	N	POOR	*	Mississippi took some tiny steps to improve caregiver training and safety in child care.
**	F	-	N	POOR	***	Governor Mel Carnahan of Missouri proposed a big new initiative to expand and improve child care.
*	C-	+	N	OK	**	Some action was taken to improve caregiver training in Montana.
***	C	-	N	POOR	**	Nebraska took no major action on child care this year.
*		-	N	OK	*	Nevada lawmakers slightly improved the quality of child care.
**		+	Y	POOR	*	New Hampshire officials approved modest improvements in caregiver training.
***	F	-	Y	POOR	***	New Jersey's prekindergarten program grew this year.
*	C+	-	N	OK	*	New Mexico officials continue to promote a bold new way for parents to learn about child care quality.
***	B	+	Y	POOR	***	Prekindergarten was the big news in New York.
****	C+	+	Y	NA	****	Governor Jim Hunt continues to spearhead positive change on child care across North Carolina.
*	F		N	POOR	*	Caregiver training in North Dakota was improved this year.
****	B	+	Y	POOR	****	Ohio continues to expand the supply of care across the state.
**	C		Y	NA	**	Oklahoma officials approved several new programs to address quality issues.
***	B	+	Y	POOR	****	Governor John Kitzhaber of Oregon was forced to veto a bill that would have improved oversight of family child care.
***	F	-	Y	POOR	***	Pennsylvania boosted its child care spending and launched a new initiative for caregiver training.
****			Y	POOR	***	The tiny state of Rhode Island continues to be innovative and committed to improving child care.
**	C	-	Y	POOR	**	South Carolina lawmakers dragged their feet on improving infant care.
**		-	N	OK	**	Governor William Janklow of South Dakota put a spotlight on school-age care via a state-sponsored conference.
**		+	Y	POOR	***	A tragedy precipitated proposals to improve child care policies in Tennessee.
***		-	Y	NA	**	Texas has a large prekindergarten program, but low standards.
**	F	+	N	OK	**	Utah legislators took a step backward and deregulated family child care.
***		+	Y	POOR	****	Vermont officials approved new background checks for caregivers.
**	C-	-	Y	OK	**	Virginia's commitment to child care is seriously eroding.
****		+	Y	POOR	****	Lawmakers in Washington continue to make child care a priority, with a new fund to both expand and improve child care.
***	F	-	Y	POOR	***	West Virginia officials approved new spending in the past year to serve more children.
****	F	+	Y	OK	***	Wisconsin tripled its child care spending, but some money goes to untrained caregivers.
**		-	N	OK	**	The picture is mixed in Wyoming, with the governor lacking a strong commitment.

KEY TO THE RATINGS

We consulted our panel of experts to evaluate the states in four areas, as reported in the chart on the previous two pages. The highest rating a state could get in each category is five stars(*****), but no state has yet to achieve that high a score.

QUALITY

Accredited centers: Indicates the number of child care centers in the state that have been accredited by the National Association for the Education of Young Children (NAEYC), the nation's preeminent organization of early-childhood educators. To gain accreditation, a center must apply to NAEYC, be inspected and meet standards in a wide range of areas, including teacher training, proper adult supervision and a curriculum that encourages a child's healthy intellectual and emotional development. An accredited program is especially valuable in a state with poor standards for adult supervision and caregiver training—parents can rest easier knowing such a center meets the standards of this professional organization.

Accredited family child care (FCC): Indicates the number of family child care providers that meet standards set by the National Association for Family Child Care (NAFCC), the nation's leading organization for family child care providers. Family child care is offered in private homes, and in most cases, operates in a casual, even underground fashion. As our report shows, many states exempt family child care providers from all licensing requirements, including basic health and safety measures, even when they are caring for four or five children besides their own. This association has worked hard to bring standards of safety and professionalism to such care. Caregivers accredited by NAFCC must pass muster in measures of safety and health, as well as be observed as respectful and responsive to children and have activities appropriate to children's ages.

Child-to-adult ratios: Kids need plenty of attention to thrive in child care. We report the maximum number of children one adult can care for, age by age. We used data collected by Wheelock College on standards for nine-month-olds, two-year-olds and three-year-olds. For comparison, experts recommend the following: 3 to 4 infants • 4 to 6 toddlers • 7 to 10 preschoolers.

Group size: Studies show that kids do better in smaller groups, with less noise and distraction. States that follow guidelines suggested by NAEYC are rated "Good." Those that set some limits are ranked either "Mediocre" or "Poor." Those with no standards are simply reported as "None."

Caregiver training: This is an important quality indictor, according to the latest research. Child care workers who are educated about child development tend to be more sensitive and responsive to children's needs and more adept at handling behavior problems. Wheelock College, one of the nation's leading institutions of early education, provided us with a state-by-state analysis of how much education caregivers must have before they start work in a child care center or open up a family child care home. We report the training as either "hours" (H) or "college credits" (C). In practical terms, three college credits (the equivalent of one college course) works out to about 45 hours of training. "NR" indicates not regulated.

Caregiver pay: Caregivers' compensation is increasingly recognized as a predictor of quality care, since low pay contributes to turnover among child care staff. A plus sign (+) indicates

that the state has an initiative to address this issue. *No state could receive the highest rating in this category without meeting NAEYC standards for child-to-adult ratios and group size and requiring at least some workers in child care centers to have some college credits in child development.*

SAFETY

Adult supervision: Limiting the number of children one adult may care for (see "Quality" section above) not only boosts the quality of a program but also helps keep kids safe. Studies show that good child-to-adult ratios help to limit injuries in child care. Therefore, we take such ratios into account in ranking a state on safety as well as quality. A "Good" rating means the state licensing standards meet or are very close to NAEYC standards; "Mediocre" means the state's standards allow for only modest supervision; "Poor" means the state has such low standards that it would be hard for any caregiver to assure a child's safety if she takes in the maximum number of kids the state allows.

Size at which family child care is regulated: The number here indicates how many children a caregiver may take into a private home before she is required to be registered or licensed and therefore meet basic health and safety rules. A plus sign (+) indicates she may take in additional children, under certain circumstances. She may, for example, be able to take in more kids if some are related to her.

Playground surfaces: This factor is important because kids suffer so many injuries from falls onto hard surfaces. States got a plus sign (+) when they require an energy-absorbing surface that prevents injuries on outdoor play areas under climbers and other equipment. States that do not require such surfaces received a minus (–). (In this report, we focus only on rules for outdoor equipment, but parents should check indoor play areas as well.)

Hand-washing: The simple act of washing hands before preparing food and after diaper changes, toileting and wiping noses can go a long way toward preventing the spread of infectious disease in child care settings. States were rated "Good" if they require caregivers to wash their hands at all these key times; "Fair" if they leave out nose-wiping or if they don't specify exact times; and "Poor" if they do not require hand-washing.

Inspections: This figure reports the frequency of unannounced inspections conducted by the state. "Rare" indicates that such inspections occur less than every two years.

To get the highest rating in this category, a state had to have good supervision, require that family child care providers meet health and safety standards once they care for three children and have good standards on immunizations, playground surfaces and hand-washing.

AVAILABILITY

Tax breaks: States that have a personal income tax were ranked by the National Women's Law Center on the value of their child care tax credits to working families. The higher the grade, the grater the financial benefit. The 16 states that have income taxes but no such tax breaks got an "F." The states with no personal income tax received no grade. Rhode Island

and Vermont also received no grades, since their tax credits are so closely tied to federal tax credits.

Resource & Referral (R&R): Child care resource & referral agencies often play a key role in making child care available to parents. All track the supply of child care in their communities and refer parents to openings. Some also provide counseling on how to evaluate that care. The National Association of Child Care Resource and Referral Agencies has provided us with information about whether there is a statewide network of R&Rs. A plus sign (+) indicates the network has funding and staff; a minus (–) indicates the network operates without government funding or staff.

Public pre-K: "Y" indicates that there is a state-funded pre-kindergarten program. "N" indicates there is none.

Pay rate: The rate the state pays child care programs for state-subsidized children affects child care across the state. Lower rates mean that fewer people are willing to care for kids; higher rates encourage more people to join the field. Here, "OK" in-dicates the state pays at a rate of at least 75 percent of the market rate for child care in 1996 or 1997. "Poor" indicates the state's official rate is less than that. "NA" means that the state has not determined a market rate recently. This information was provided by the Children's Defense Fund.

To get the highest rating in this category, a state had to do well in these four categories and also be contributing state funds to initiatives to expand its supply of child care.

COMMITMENT

In this category, we looked at the actions taken by state officials to improve and expand child care from current levels.

To get the highest rating in this category, the governor and/or state lawmakers had to make child care a high priority on the state agenda by pushing for policies to improve its quality and expand its supply. . . .

Can EDUCATION Reduce Social Inequity?

Students in many U.S. schools have achieved unparalleled success
through research-based programs like the Abecedarian Project,
Success for All, and Reading Recovery. The equity gap does not have to exist.

Robert E. Slavin

There is a crisis of equity in U.S. schools. Once thought of as the most equalizing institution in our society, public schools play as much of a role in magnifying differences between children from wealthy and impoverished backgrounds and between children of different ethnic backgrounds as they do in overcoming these differences.

The equity gap relates both to the opportunities children are provided and to the outcomes they achieve. Regarding opportunities, children from lower-class homes start off at a disadvantage, with less access to prenatal and early health care, quality day care as infants, quality early childhood programs, and other supports that most children from middle-class homes take for granted. The school system often compounds these inequities. In most states, the amount of money spent on education is strongly influenced by local property values. As a result, children who live in low-wealth inner cities or rural areas are likely to receive much less in per-pupil funding than are children in wealthy suburbs. In most states, the

difference in per-pupil funding between the highest-spending districts (95th percentile) and the lowest-spending (5th percentile) is a ratio of from 1.5:1 to 2:1.

For example, in 1990, high-spending districts in Pennsylvania spent $7,058 per pupil, compared to $3,794 for low-spending districts. The difference was $5,457 to $3,910 in Florida, $4,557 to $2,803 in Missouri, and $6,078 to $3,879 in Oregon (Riddle and White 1993). A difference of even $1,000, a typical difference between an inner city and its surroundings suburbs, translates into $25,000 per class per year for a class of 25 students or a half-million dollars for a typical elementary school of 500 children. Of course, even equal dollars would not be equal in impact; schools serving many children in poverty also have to cope with higher needs for special education services, security guards, and other services not needed in wealthier jurisdictions.

This degree of inequity is unique in the industrialized world. All major trading partners of the United at least *equalize* funding for all children, but

in most cases they provide *additional* funding for poor or minority children. In the Netherlands, for example, a funding formula provides 25 percent more funding for each lower-class Dutch child in a school and 90 percent more funding for each minority child. European observers of our schools are aghast to discover that our system does exactly the opposite.

In outcomes, American students vary substantially according to social class and ethnicity. For example, on the 1994 National Assessment of Educational Progress (NAEP) (Campbell et al. 1996), 71 percent of white 4th graders scored at or above the *basic* level in reading. Only 31 percent of African-American and 36 percent of Latino students scored that well. These differences correspond closely with differences in social class. Among 4th graders whose parents graduated from college, 70 percent were reading at or above the basic level. This drops to 54 percent for children of high school graduates and 32 percent for children of high school dropouts. Among children whose homes had magazines, newspapers, en-

From *Educational Leadership*, Vol. 55, No. 4, December 1997/January 1998, pp. 6-10. Reprinted with permission of the Association for Supervision and Curriculum Development.

cyclopedias, and at least 25 books, about 70 percent scored at or above basic; among those without these resources, fewer than half scored this well. Differences in mathematics, writing, and science are similar. Further, performance differences increase as students get older.

In some ways, the equity gap has been diminishing. Since the first NAEP assessments in 1971, the difference between African-American and white students in NAEP reading and other measures has been cut in half. Differences in Scholastic Assessment Test (SAT) scores have also been dropping. Dropout rates for African-American students have diminished substantially over the past 20 years, although those for Latino students remain very high. Most of the gains

---

We cannot have a just or peaceful society if major segments of it see little hope for their children.

---

made by *minority* students, however, took place during the 1970s, when major improvements in the education of African-American students were taking place in the South. Since 1980, the gap has slightly increased, with a particularly disturbing drop in the reading performance of African-American and Latino 4th graders in 1994.

The Equity Gap Is Unacceptable and Unnecessary

The differences in academic performance among children from different social class and ethnic backgrounds are unacceptably large, and they are not diminishing rapidly enough. These differences underlie many of the most polarizing issues in the United States, from affirmative action to immigration policies. Their conse-

quences are getting progressively worse, as the income gap between well-educated and poorly educated workers is increasing. We cannot have a just or peaceful society if major segments of it see little hope for their children.

There will always be achievement differences, on average, among groups of students. No one realistically expects that the children of high school dropouts and those of college graduates will ever perform at exactly the same levels. Yet these gaps are far greater than they need to be. In particular, differences among ethnic groups are unacceptably high and completely unnecessary. Some portion of these differences results from socioeconomic differences among different ethnic groups, over which the schools have no control. Nevertheless, schools can have a powerful impact on the educational success of all children and can greatly increase the achievement of disadvantaged and minority children. As educators, we cannot wait for U.S. society to solve its problems of racism and economic inequity. We can and must take action now to prepare all children to achieve their full potential.

How Can We Reduce the Equity Gap?

The only way to decrease the equity gap in academic performance is to greatly increase the achievement and school success of disadvantaged and minority students. If we could place a high floor under the achievement of all children, regardless of social background, we would substantially reduce inequalities. Imagine, for example, that we could ensure that every American 4th grader were reading at or above the basic level on

---

Imagine how different U.S. schools and society would be if every child entering 5th grade had 5th grade reading and math skills.

NAEP, as President Clinton has proposed. This would be enormously beneficial for *millions* of white, middle-class students, of course, but it would have a far more dramatic effect on disadvantaged and minority children, as a group. Imagine how different U.S. schools and society would be if every child entering 5th grade had 5th grade reading and math skills.

No single policy or program can ensure the school success of every child, but a combination of approaches can. Research in education is increasingly identifying the kinds of approaches we could use if we decided as a society to end the poor academic performance of so many of our children.

1. Begin to think of all children as being at promise. The first requirement for a policy designed to ensure the school success of all children is to change the mindset of educators and policymakers. As my colleague Wade Boykin (1996) puts it, we need to move away from seeing children as being *at risk* toward seeing them as being *at promise*. We identify and build on cultural and personal strengths, and accept nothing less than outstanding performance. Rather than thinking in terms of remediation or compensation, we insist on high-quality instruction sensitive to students' needs from the beginning of their time in school and respond immediately and intensively if children start to fall behind.

2. Start early. As a rule, children enter preschool or kindergarten highly motivated, bright-eyed and bushy-tailed, fully confident in their abilities to learn. Schools can build on this energy and enthusiasm and thereby ensure children a good start in elementary school. Research on Head Start and other programs for 3- and 4-year-olds finds consistent and powerful impacts of high-quality early childhood programs on the cognitive performance of young children (McKey et al. 1985; Berrueta-Clement et al. 1984). Researchers debate long-term effects of preschool experiences; clearly, no one-year or two-year program will ensure the success of every child (see Karweit 1994). But there is no question that quality early childhood programs can greatly enhance children's preparation for elementary school; it's just up to the school to take advantage of this preparation.

One extraordinary study shows how much early intervention can contribute to the success of children who are placed at risk. The Abecedarian Project provided the children of low-income African-American parents in North Carolina with intensive services

at risk if we stop the process of falling behind before it begins.

3. *Overdetermine success—work on many fronts at once.* Children who are placed at risk by their life circumstances can fail for many reasons. Effective schooling, therefore, anticipates all the ways children might fail and then plans how each will be prevented or quickly and effectively dealt with. Wade Boykin (1996) calls this "overdetermining success"— being *overprepared* to ensure the success of every child.

An example of over-determining success is our own Success for All program (Slavin et al. 1996). It provides elementary schools, mostly high-poverty schoolwide Title I schools, with an array of programs and services intended to ensure that children

full year ahead at the end of 5th grade. That difference is maintained into middle school (Slavin et al. 1996). In nearly every study, the students who gain the most are those who are most at risk: low achievers, special education students, and speakers of languages other than English (a Spanish bilingual version of the program has been particularly successful). Special education referrals are typically cut in half or, in one study, cut to a quarter of what they had been before (Smith et al. 1994).

One study of Success for All found that the program eliminated an achievement gap between African-American and white students. This study (Ross et al. 1997) compared integrated Success for All and control schools in Ft. Wayne, Indiana. At pretest, African-American and white students showed large differences on reading scores. At post-test, these differences remained in the control schools, but in the Success for All schools they had essentially disappeared, because African-American students made substantial gains.

We can make a substantial difference in the school success of children placed at risk if we stop the process of falling behind before it begins.

---

from infancy to age 8. The project included high-quality infant care, preschool, kindergarten, and school-age programs; support to parents; and other services. In comparison to matched controls, the children in the Abecedarian Project scored substantially higher on measures of IQ, reading, and mathematics, at ages 8, 12, and 15. By age 15, Abecedarian children were half as likely to have been assigned to special education or to have been retained (Campbell and Ramey 1995).

The Abecedarian Project is too expensive under current conditions to replicate widely, but it clearly establishes the principle that nothing is inevitable about the failure of so many at-risk children.

These results and those from other early intervention programs that continue into the early elementary grades (Karweit 1994) demonstrate that we can make a substantial difference in the school success of children placed

begin with success in preschool and then remain successful throughout the elementary grades. The program emphasizes research-based materials and instructional approaches from prekindergarten to 6th grade, with extensive professional development, follow-up, and assessment to be sure that all students are on track. If children begin to fall behind in reading, teachers or paraprofessionals may give them one-to-one tutoring until the children are able to progress on their own with their classmates. A family support program engages parents in their children's learning and solves such nonacademic problems as truancy, behavior problems, or the need for eyeglasses.

Research on Success for All in 12 school districts in the United States has shown consistent positive effects of the program. On average, Success for All children read almost three months ahead of matched controls at the end of 1st grade. and more than a

Other programs also demonstrate that if we want to place a high floor under the achievement of all children, we can do it. One widely known example is Reading Recovery, which provides one-to-one tutoring to 1st graders who are falling behind in reading. Studies of Reading Recovery find consistent positive effects of the program on student reading achievement (Lyons et al. 1993).

Reading Recovery and Success for All are expensive, of course, but large numbers of schools have shifted resources to fund them. As of fall 1997, Success for All is in 750 schools, and Reading Recovery is in more than 6,000. But consider: What does "expensive" mean? Imagine that all high-poverty schools received the funding typical in suburban schools. Every school could afford Success for All, Reading Recovery, high-quality preschool programs, and much more.

At present, schools and districts fund these programs primarily through Title I; but high-poverty, underfunded schools face very difficult choices in the use of these funds. All high-poverty schools should be able to provide effective programs for their students, even if these programs are costly.

Are We Willing to Do What It Takes?

The research on the Abecedarian Project, Success for All, Reading Recovery, and other programs demonstrates that if we, as a society, decided to substantially reduce the equity gap, we could do so. We could decrease the gap between middle-class and disadvantaged children—not by taking away from the middle class but by building a high floor under the achievement level of all children, of all backgrounds. Simply by giving high-poverty schools the resources typical of suburban schools, and focusing these new resources on proven, replicable programs and practices, we could make profound changes in the achievement gaps that so bedevil our educational system and our society.

Certainly we need more research and more development to understand how to transform large numbers of schools and to solve remaining tough problems. But we already know enough to take action. So many children are suffering, and we know how to help them. How can we justify doing less?

References

Berrueta-Clement, J.R., L.J. Schweinhart, W.S. Barnett, A.S. Epstein, and D.P. Weikart. (1984). *Changed Lives.* Ypsilanti, Mich.: High/Scope.

Boykin, A.W. (April 10, 1996). "A Talent Development Approach to School Reform." Paper presented at the annual meeting of the American Educational Research Association, New York.

Campbell, F.A., and C.T. Ramey. (1995). "Cognitive and School Outcomes for High-risk African-American Students at Middle Adolescence: Positive Effects of Early Intervention." *American Educational Research Journal* 32: 743–772.

Campbell, J.R., P.L. Donahue, C.M. Reese, and G.W. Phillips. (1996). *NAEP 1994 Reading Report Card for the Nation and the States.* Washington, D.C.: National Center for Education Statistics, U.S. Department of Education.

Karweit, N.L. (1994). "Can Preschool Alone Prevent Early Reading Failure?" In *Preventing Early School Failure,* edited by R.E. Slavin, N.L. Karweit, and B.A. Wasik. Boston: Allyn and Bacon.

Lyons, C.A., G.S. Pinnell, and D.E. DeFord. (1993). *Partners in Learning: Teachers and Children in Reading Recovery.* New York: Teachers College Press.

McKey, R., L. Condelli, H. Ganson, B. Barrett, C. McConkey, and M. Plantz. (1985). *The Impact of Head Start on Children, Families, and Communities.* Washington, D.C.: CSR, Inc.

Riddle, W., and L. White. (1993). *Variations in Expenditures per Pupil among Local Educational Agencies Within the States.* Washington, D.C.: Congressional Research Service.

Ross, S.M., L.J. Smith, and J.P. Casey. (1997). "Preventing Early School Failure: Impacts of Success for All on Standardized Test Outcomes, Minority Group Performance, and School Effectiveness." *Journal of Education for Students Placed at Risk* 2, 1: 29–53.

Slavin, R.E., N.A. Madden, L.J. Dolan, and B.A. Wasik. (1996). *Every Child, Every School: Success for All.* Thousand Oaks, Calif.: Corwin.

Smith, L.J., S.M. Ross, and J.P. Casey. (1994). *Special Education Analyses for Success for All in Four Cities.* Memphis. Tenn.: University of Memphis, Center for Research in Educational Policy.

Robert E. Slavin is Codirector of the Center for Research on the Education of Students Placed At Risk (CRESPAR), 3505 N. Charles St., Baltimore, MD 21218-2498 (e-mail: rslavin@inet.ed.gov). Web site (http://scov.csos.jhu.edu/crespar/CReSPaR.html).

Unit 2

Key Points to Consider

❖ Why is it important for teachers and caregivers to know about major changes affecting young children and their families?

❖ Discuss how parents and caregivers can take advantage of the stages of emotional development of infants.

❖ What are some of the negative effects of prenatal drug exposure on an infant? How can parents and teachers minimize these conditions?

❖ How can the cultural values emphasized in each family help children to develop a sense of who they are and to assist them in learning?

❖ What behavioral characteristics are unique to boys? What positive qualities exists as a result of boys' behaviors?

❖ How do early experiences affect language development? Describe an optimal environment for learning language.

 **Links** | **www.dushkin.com/online/**

These sites are annotated on pages 4 and 5.

Startling information about brain development has been released that has brought on a flurry of speculation about the best ways to prepare children for a lifetime of learning. The information now in the hands of pediatric neurobiologists indicates that the types of experiences that children have before to the age of 10 can affect their future capacity to learn. Early experiences, once thought to be useless, now have been found to help support the developing neurons in a child's brain. These neurons, which make successful and complete connections when a child is young, will be used in the future to work complicated mathematical problems, learn a second language, or play a musical instrument.

Knowledge of the way a child's brain develops led the writers of the Carnegie Corporation Starting Points Report to conclude, "How children function from the preschool years all the way through adolescence, and even adulthood, hinges in large part on their experiences before the age of three." What we now know about language development, emotional development, and cognitive development is vastly different from what was known 5 years ago. It is imperative that educators remain up-to-date and well aware of best practices as a result of current research.

We cannot separate the child from his or her family or home environment. Therefore, for professionals in early childhood education, much of what is done involves the child's family. Families come in many different arrangements, and the more familiar teachers and caregivers are with the people whom the child sees on a regular basis, the easier communication with those individuals will be. Professionals who are aware of the enormously varied life circumstances that children and parents experience today are mindful not to offer a magic formula, quick remedies, or simplistic solutions to complicated, long-standing problems. Instead, parents appreciate a sense that they are respected and given up-to-date, objective information about their child. Collaborative efforts to build bridges between home and school allow for maximized learning for all children.

Early childhood educators are often the first professionals to interact with children who were exposed to drugs before birth. Phyllis Mayfield and Keith Chapman provide specific guidelines for those educators as well as suggestions for family-centered intervention programs.

Participating in a game of mousie, an adult walked her fingers up 18-month-old Margaret's legs and trunk and tickled her under the chin while saying, "mousie, mousie, mousie, etc." Margaret walked around the room for a few minutes then found 10-year-old Clay lying on the floor. She went over to him and moved her hand up his body while saying, "mou, mou, mou." The very beginning

stages of learning one's language are both fascinating and exciting to observe, as emphasized by Shannon Brownlee in "Baby Talk." Adults who are active participants in the language-learning process can be key supporters to children in this challenging task. Parents of boys have long been told that their boys are more aggressive and not as easy to control as girls. In "Boys Will Be Boys," authors Barbara Kantrowitz and Claudia Kalb provide guidance to parents and educators who are often at a loss when it comes to controlling the energy and exuberance that boys often bring to the learning situation. The recent attention to boys' development includes looking at their behavior. The day-to-day challenges can be draining for many parents and teachers. One parent reported that she is worried that her years of telling her son to "keep yourself in check, C. B.," or to "calm down," will greatly curtail his energy, creativity, and zest for life and learning that have been such a major part of who he is as a person. Just what is the best way to handle all of that energy? Teachers have come to expect the same behavior from girls and boys, and we now know that the two behave very differently.

Child Development and Families

FETAL PSYCHOLOGY

Behaviorally speaking, there's little difference between a newborn baby and a 32-week-old fetus. A new wave of research suggests that the fetus can feel, dream, even enjoy *The Cat in the Hat*. The abortion debate may never be the same.

By Janet L. Hopson

The scene never fails to give goose bumps: the baby, just seconds old and still dewy from the womb, is lifted into the arms of its exhausted but blissful parents. They gaze adoringly as their new child stretches and squirms, scrunches its mouth and opens its eyes. To anyone watching this tender vignette, the message is unmistakable. Birth is the beginning of it all, ground zero, the moment from which the clock starts ticking. Not so, declares Janet DiPietro. Birth may be a grand occasion, says the Johns Hopkins University psychologist, but "it is a trivial event in development. Nothing neurologically interesting happens."

Armed with highly sensitive and sophisticated monitoring gear, DiPietro and other researchers today are discovering that the real action starts weeks earlier. At 32 weeks of gestation—two months before a baby is considered fully prepared for the world, or "at term"—a fetus is behaving almost exactly as a newborn. And it continues to do so for the next 12 weeks.

As if overturning the common conception of infancy weren't enough, scientists are creating a startling new picture of intelligent life in the womb. Among the revelations:

• By nine weeks, a developing fetus can hiccup and react to loud noises. By the end of the second trimester it can hear.

• Just as adults do, the fetus experiences the rapid eye movement (REM) sleep of dreams.

• The fetus savors its mother's meals, first picking up the food tastes of a culture in the womb.

A fetus spends hours in the rapid eye movement sleep of dreams.

Reprinted with permission from *Psychology Today*, September/October 1998, pp. 44-48, 76. © 1998 by Sussex Publishers, Inc.

• Among other mental feats, the fetus can distinguish between the voice of Mom and that of a stranger, and respond to a familiar story read to it.

• Even a premature baby is aware, feels, responds, and adapts to its environment.

• Just because the fetus is responsive to certain stimuli doesn't mean that it should be the target of efforts to enhance development. Sensory stimulation of the fetus can in fact lead to bizarre patterns of adaptation later on.

The roots of human behavior, researchers now know, begin to develop early—just weeks after conception, in fact. Well before a woman typically knows she is pregnant, her embryo's brain has already begun to bulge. By five weeks, the organ that looks like a lumpy inchworm has already embarked on the most spectacular feat of human development: the creation of the deeply creased and convoluted cerebral cortex, the part of the brain that will eventually allow the growing person to move, think, speak, plan, and create in a human way.

At nine weeks, the embryo's ballooning brain allows it to bend its body, hiccup, and react to loud sounds. At week ten, it moves its arms, "breathes" amniotic fluid in and out, opens its jaw, and stretches. Before the first trimester is over, it yawns, sucks, and swallows as well as feels and smells. By the end of the second trimester, it can hear; toward the end of pregnancy, it can see.

FETAL ALERTNESS

Scientists who follow the fetus' daily life find that it spends most of its time not exercising these new abilities but sleeping. At 32 weeks, it drowses 90 to 95% of the day. Some of these hours are spent in deep sleep, some in REM sleep, and some in an indeterminate state, a product of the fetus' immature brain that is different from sleep in a baby, child, or adult. During REM sleep, the fetus' eyes move back and forth just as an adult's eyes do, and many researchers believe that it is dreaming. DiPietro speculates that fetuses dream about what they know—the sensations they feel in the womb.

Closer to birth, the fetus sleeps 85 to 90% of the time, the same as a newborn. Between its frequent naps, the fetus seems to have "something like an awake alert period," according to developmental psychologist William Fifer, Ph.D., who with his Columbia University colleagues is monitoring these sleep and wakefulness cycles in order to identify patterns of normal and abnormal brain development, including potential predictors of

sudden infant death syndrome. Says Fifer, "We are, in effect, asking the fetus: 'Are you paying attention? Is your nervous system behaving in the appropriate way?' "

FETAL MOVEMENT

Awake or asleep, the human fetus moves 50 times or more each hour, flexing and extending its body, moving its head, face, and limbs and exploring its warm wet compartment by touch. Heidelise Als, Ph.D., a developmental psychologist at Harvard Medical School, is fascinated by the amount of tactile stimulation a fetus gives itself. "It touches a hand to the face, one hand to the other hand, clasps its feet, touches its foot to its leg, its hand to its umbilical cord," she reports.

Als believes there is a mismatch between the environment given to preemies in hospitals and the environment they would have had in the womb. She has been working for years to change the care given to preemies so that they can curl up, bring their knees together, and touch things with their hands as they would have for weeks in the womb.

Along with such common movements, DiPietro has also noted some odder fetal activities, including "licking the uterine wall and literally walking around the womb by pushing off with its feet." Laterborns may have more room in the womb for such maneuvers than first babies. After the initial pregnancy, a woman's uterus is bigger and the umbilical cord longer, allowing more freedom of movement. "Second and subsequent children may develop more motor experience in utero and so may become more active infants," DiPietro speculates.

Fetuses react sharply to their mother's actions. "When we're watching the fetus on ultrasound and the mother starts to laugh, we can see the fetus, floating upside down in the womb, bounce up and down on its head, bum-bum-bum, like it's bouncing on a trampoline," says DiPietro. "When mothers watch this on the screen, they laugh harder, and the fetus goes up and down even faster. We've wondered whether this is why people grow up liking roller coasters."

FETAL TASTE

Why people grow up liking hot chilies or spicy curries may also have something to do with the fetal environment. By 13 to 15 weeks a fetus' taste buds already look like a mature adult's, and doctors know that the amniotic

By 15 weeks, a fetus has an adult's taste buds and may be able to savor its mother's meals.

fluid that surrounds it can smell strongly of curry, cumin, garlic, onion and other essences from a mother's diet. Whether fetuses can taste these flavors isn't yet known, but scientists have found that a 33-week-old preemie will suck harder on a sweetened nipple than on a plain rubber one.

"During the last trimester, the fetus is swallowing up to a liter a day" of amniotic fluid, notes Julie Mennella, Ph.D., a biopsychologist at the Monell Chemical Senses Center in Philadelphia. She thinks the fluid may act as a "flavor bridge" to breast milk, which also carries food flavors from the mother's diet.

FETAL HEARING

Whether or not a fetus can taste, there's little question that it can hear. A very premature baby entering the world at 24 to 25 weeks responds to the sounds around it, observes Als, so its auditory apparatus must already have been functioning in the womb. Many pregnant women report a fetal jerk or sudden kick just after a door slams or a car backfires.

Even without such intrusions, the womb is not a silent place. Researchers who have inserted a hydrophone into the uterus of a pregnant woman have picked up a noise level "akin to the background noise in an apartment," according to DiPietro. Sounds include the whooshing of blood in the mother's vessels, the gurgling and rumbling of her stomach and intestines, as well as the tones of her voice filtered through tissues, bones, and fluid, and the voices of other people coming through the amniotic wall. Fifer has found that fetal heart rate slows when the mother is speaking, suggesting that the fetus not only hears and recognizes the sound, but is calmed by it.

FETAL VISION

Vision is the last sense to develop. A very premature infant can see light and shape; researchers presume that a fetus has the same ability. Just as the womb isn't completely quiet, it isn't utterly dark, either. Says Fifer: "There may be just enough visual stimulation filtered through the mother's tissues that a fetus can respond when the mother is in bright light," such as when she is sunbathing.

Japanese scientists have even reported a distinct fetal reaction to flashes of light shined on the mother's belly. However, other researchers warn that exposing fetuses (or premature infants) to bright light before they are ready can be dangerous. In fact, Harvard's Als believes that retinal damage in premature infants, which has long been ascribed to high concentrations of oxygen, may actually be due to overexposure to light at the wrong time in development.

A six-month fetus, born about 14 weeks too early, has a brain that is neither prepared for nor expecting signals from the eyes to be transmitted into the brain's visual cortex, and from there into the executive-branch frontal lobes, where information is integrated. When the fetus is forced to see too much too soon, says Als, the accelerated stimulation may lead to aberrations of brain development.

FETAL LEARNING

Along with the ability to feel, see, and hear comes the capacity to learn and remember. These activities can be rudimentary, automatic, even biochemical. For example, a fetus, after an initial reaction of alarm, eventually stops responding to a repeated loud noise. The fetus displays the same kind of primitive learning, known as habituation, in response to its mother's voice, Fifer has found.

But the fetus has shown itself capable of far more. In the 1980s, psychology professor Anthony James DeCasper, Ph.D., and colleagues at the University of North Carolina at Greensboro, devised a feeding contraption that allows a baby to suck faster to hear one set of sounds through headphones and to suck slower to hear a different set. With this technique, DeCasper discovered that within hours of birth, a baby already prefers its mother's voice to a stranger's, suggesting it must have learned and remembered the voice, albeit not necessarily consciously, from its last months in the womb. More recently, he's found that a newborn prefers a story read to it repeatedly in the womb—in this case, *The Cat in the Hat*—over a new story introduced soon after birth.

DeCasper and others have uncovered more mental feats. Newborns can not only distinguish their mother from a stranger speaking, but would rather hear Mom's voice, especially the way it sounds filtered through amniotic fluid rather than through air. They're xenophobes, too: they prefer to hear Mom speaking in her native language than to hear her or someone else speaking in a foreign tongue.

By monitoring changes in fetal heart rate, psychologist Jean-Pierre Lecanuet, Ph.D., and his colleagues in Paris have found that fetuses can even tell strangers' voices apart. They also seem to like certain stories more than others. The fetal heartbeat will slow down when a familiar French fairy tale such as *"La Poulette"* ("The Chick") or *"Le Petit Crapaud"* ("The Little Toad"), is read near the mother's belly. When the same reader delivers another unfamiliar story, the fetal heartbeat stays steady.

The fetus is likely responding to the cadence of voices and stories, not their actual words, observes Fifer, but the conclusion is the same: the fetus can listen, learn, and remember at some level, and, as with most babies and children, it likes the comfort and reassurance of the familiar.

A fetus prefers hearing Mom's voice over a stranger's—speaking in her native, not a foreign tongue—and being read aloud familiar tales rather than new stories.

FETAL PERSONALITY

It's no secret that babies are born with distinct differences and patterns of activity that suggest individual temperament. Just when and how the behavioral traits originate in the womb is now the subject of intense scrutiny.

In the first formal study of fetal temperament in 1996, DiPietro and her colleagues recorded the heart rate and movements of 31 fetuses six times before birth and compared them to readings taken twice after birth. (They've since extended their study to include 100 more fetuses.) Their findings: fetuses that are very active in the womb tend to be more irritable infants. Those with irregular sleep/wake patterns in the womb sleep more poorly as young infants. And fetuses with high heart rates become unpredictable, inactive babies.

"Behavior doesn't begin at birth," declares DiPietro. "It begins before and develops in predictable ways." One of the most important influences on development is the fetal environment. As Harvard's Als observes, "The fetus gets an enormous amount of 'hormonal bathing' through the mother, so its chronobiological rhythms are influenced by the mother's sleep/wake cycles, her eating patterns, her movements."

The hormones a mother puts out in response to stress also appear critical. DiPietro finds that highly pressured mothers-to-be tend to have more active fetuses—and more irritable infants. "The most stressed are working pregnant women," says DiPietro. "These days, women tend to work up to the day they deliver, even though the implications for pregnancy aren't entirely clear yet. That's our cultural norm, but I think it's insane."

Als agrees that working can be an enormous stress, but emphasizes that pregnancy hormones help to buffer both mother and fetus. Individual reactions to stress also matter. "The pregnant woman who chooses to work is a different woman already from the one who chooses not to work," she explains.

She's also different from the woman who has no choice but to work. DiPietro's studies show that the fetuses of poor women are distinct neurobehaviorally—less active, with a less variable heart rate—from the fetuses of middle-class women. Yet "poor women rate themselves as less stressed than do working middle-class women," she notes. DiPietro suspects that inadequate nutrition and exposure to pollutants may significantly affect the fetuses of poor women.

Stress, diet, and toxins may combine to have a harmful effect on intelligence. A recent study by biostatistician Bernie Devlin, Ph.D., of the University of Pittsburgh, suggests that genes may have less impact on IQ than previously thought and that the environment of the womb may account for much more. "Our old notion of nature influencing the fetus before birth and nurture after birth needs an update," DiPietro insists. "There is an antenatal environment, too, that is provided by the mother."

Parents-to-be who want to further their unborn child's mental development should start by assuring that the antenatal environment is well-nourished, low-stress, drug-free. Various authors and "experts" also have suggested poking the fetus at regular intervals, speaking to it through a paper tube or "pregaphone," piping in classical music, even flashing lights at the mother's abdomen.

Does such stimulation work? More importantly: Is it safe? Some who use these methods swear their children are smarter, more verbally and musically inclined, more physically coordinated and socially adept than average. Scientists, however, are skeptical.

"There has been no defended research anywhere that shows any enduring effect from these stimulations," asserts Fifer. "Since no one can even say for certain when a fetus is awake, poking them or sticking speakers on the mother's abdomen may be changing their natural sleep patterns. No one would consider poking or prodding a newborn baby in her bassinet or putting a speaker next to her ear, so why would you do such a thing with a fetus?"

Als is more emphatic: "My bet is that poking, shaking, or otherwise deliberately stimulating the fetus might alter its developmental sequence, and anything that affects the development of the brain comes at a cost."

Gently talking to the fetus, however, seems to pose little risk. Fifer suggests that this kind of activity may help parents as much as the fetus. "Thinking about your fetus, talking to it, having your spouse talk to it, will all help prepare you for this new creature that's going to jump into your life and turn it upside down," he says—once it finally makes its anti-climactic entrance.

How does substance abuse by pregnant women affect their children? Knowing about the impact of children's prenatal exposure to drugs can help caregivers work more effectively with children and their families.

Children's Prenatal Exposure to Drugs: Implications for Early Childhood Educators

Phyllis K. Mayfield and J. Keith Chapman

Pregnant women who use or abuse alcohol, tobacco, and illicit substances endanger not only their own lives and well-being, but their unborn children as well. The dramatic increase in the use of cigarettes by teenagers and the abuse of illicit substances such as crack-cocaine by pregnant women in the United States are among the issues that remain of public concern.

Women who use drugs rarely use only one. Illegal substances such as cocaine and marijuana are typically combined with cigarettes and/or alcohol. Polydrug use makes it difficult to determine the extent, duration, or the direct effects of a specific type of substance on fetal development (Kronstadt, 1991). Along with the effects of continued use of well-known drugs and addictive narcotics, such as phencyclidine (PCP) and heroin, educators and related professionals must address the needs of these families and their children as they develop from infancy into adulthood.

Effects of Drug Use During Pregnancy

Early Impact on Development

Research findings on the potential harmful impact of legal drugs such as cigarettes and alcohol on the fetus are relatively consistent. Isolating the specific and unique

> **The unique needs of families with children who were exposed prenatally to drugs necessitate a comprehensive, interdisciplinary family-centered approach.**

effects of common illicit drugs has proven to be more difficult. Although cocaine, crack-cocaine, marijuana, and heroin are the most common illicit substances used by childbearing women (Feig, 1990; GAO, 1990), no drug-specific syndrome or distinct developmental profile correlated with illicit substance exposure has been identified. There are however, several indicators of the effects of these substances on unborn and newborn children.

Phyllis K. Mayfield, Ph.D., is Early Childhood Program Specialist at Shelby County Public Schools, Alabaster, Alabama.

J. Keith Chapman, Ph.D., is Assistant Professor, College of Education, programs in Special Education, at The University of Alabama, Tuscaloosa.

From *Dimensions of Early Childhood*, Summer/Fall 1998, pp. 20-22. © 1998 by the Southern Early Childhood Association (SECA), Little Rock, AR. Reprinted by permission.

What Is the Extent of Women's Drug Use?

- Each year, between 100,000 to 375,000 women in the United States give birth to infants prenatally exposed to drugs (GAO, 1990).

- Approximately 15% of women from 15 to 44 years of age use illicit drugs (National Institute on Drug Abuse [NIDA], 1991).

- Overall, the prevalence of cocaine use in this country is declining, but women of childbearing age continue to use cocaine at high rates (NIDA, 1991).

- An estimated 4.8 million women of childbearing age use some form of illicit substance(s) during any given month (Khalsa & Gfroerer, 1991).

- Each year, approximately 10 to 45% of women giving birth use cocaine during their pregnancy (Mentis & Lundgren, 1995).

- About 15% of women use alcohol or some type of drug(s) during pregnancy, and these patterns of substance abuse cross all socio-economic boundaries (Chasnoff, Landress, & Barrett, 1990).

- An increase in the number of infants exposed to drugs is anticipated (Office of the Inspector General, 1990).

- One conservative estimate is that each year 11% of all live births in this country are prenatally exposed to some form(s) of legalized and/or illicit substances (Tyler, 1992).

- Approximately 34 million women of childbearing age consume alcoholic beverages. More than 18 million are cigarette smokers. More than 6 million use an illicit drug, of which 44% have tried marijuana, and 14% have tried cocaine at least once (NIDA, 1991).

Drugs such as cocaine, marijuana, and PCP may cause a reduction in the flow of blood and vital nutrients to the developing infant, resulting in intrauterine growth retardation. This can lead to spontaneous abortion, abruptio placentae, premature labor, fetal cerebral infraction, and stillbirth (Feig, 1990).

Medical researchers have documented a high incidence of premature birth, low birth weight and shorter length, abnormal head circumference, intracranial hemorrhage, heart rate abnormalities, and occasional congenital anomalies (Chasnoff, Griffith, Freier, & Murray, 1992; Lutiger, Graham, Einarson, & Koren, 1991; van de Bor, Walthes, & Sims, 1990). By the time infants are 6 months old, their brain measurements are similar to those of infants who were not exposed to drugs in utero, but concerns remain as to the drugs' effects on mental functioning, such as memory in later childhood.

Furthermore, drug-exposed infants may exhibit initial abnormal behavioral patterns such as extreme irritability, irregular sleep and wake cycles, tremors, gaze aversion,

limited coping skills during child and caregiver separation, and poor feeding routines (Eisen et al., 1991; Neuspiel & Hamel, 1991; Odom-Winn & Dunagan, 1991).

Effects on Later Development

Researchers are also interested in the relationships among prenatal drug exposure, postnatal development, and long-term outcomes (Chasnoff, Griffith, Freier, & Murray, 1992; Hawley, Halle, Drasin, & Thomas, 1995; Phelps & Cox, 1993). The imprint of prenatal substance exposure may persist into toddlerhood and beyond.

Knowledge about short- and long-term effects of exposure to crack-cocaine is only beginning to emerge. Most children who have experienced substance exposure have normal intellectual abilities but less capacity to modulate and control their own behavior and less task persistence than nonexposed peers (Griffith, 1992).

Many children who are drug-exposed exhibit behavior difficulty, impulsivity, and moodiness which may be directly related to central nervous system damage (Odom-Winn & Dunagan, 1991). This damage may lead to learning difficulties as the child matures (Tyler, 1992; Wright, 1994).

The GAO (1990) predicted that between 42 to 52% of children prenatally exposed to drugs will require special education. The report also found that 25% of children prenatally exposed to drugs exhibit some type of developmental delay, and that 40% experienced neurologic dysfunction that may affect their ability to relate to others in the classroom setting.

Among the findings about prenatal drug exposure that persist into childhood are these:

- Young children may exhibit delays in cognition, language (especially in the decoding of receptive information), adaptive behavior, and fine motor development, which may extend into diverse long-

Table 1. Teachers may find these behavioral and learning characteristics in children prenatally exposed to drugs

Behavioral Characteristics	Learning Characteristics
Behavioral extremes	Inconsistent problem-solving
Difficulty with relationships	Language delays
Easily overstimulated	Lack of concentration
Increased testing of limits	Fine motor difficulty
Difficulty with transitions	Reduced visual attention
Adverse to touch	Random and less imaginative play
Little remorse for hurting others	Memory difficulty
Less sense of a conscience	Difficulty with visual cues
Excessive fidgeting	Less understanding of cause and effect

term learning and behavior problems (GAO, 1990; Griffith, 1992; Trad, 1992; Williams & Howard, 1993; Wright, 1994).

- Children's communication skills may be affected (Angelilli et al., 1994; Griffith, Azuma, & Chasnoff, 1994; Johnson, Seikel, Madison, Foose, & Rinard, 1997).
- Children showed significant delays in verbal reasoning skills over time (Griffith et al., 1994).
- Children with histories of prenatal polydrug exposure were at risk for language delays and deficits (Johnson et al., 1997).
- In a follow-up study from 1995, children with polydrug exposure that included cocaine were at risk for speech-language, cognitive, and behavioral deficits (Rivers & Hedrick, 1998).
- Abnormal behavioral features in social interaction, organizing play, achievement of goals, and following through with task to successful completion have been observed (Rivers & Hedrick, 1998).

Table 1 summarizes behavioral and learning characteristics identified through research (Chasnoff et al., 1992; GAO, 1990; Trad, 1992; Tyler, 1992).

Guidelines for Early Childhood Educators

Current knowledge about the long-term effects of substance exposure on children's school performance is limited. However, the projected increase in the numbers of children prenatally exposed to drugs makes it clear that effective interventions for these children and their families will require a coordinated effort by many different disciplines and agencies.

Screenings, and thorough assessments as indicated, are essential to assure that children's placements are appropriate and that the best education practices are implemented to address each child's strengths and special needs (Wolery, Strain, & Bailey, 1992). Some children may be eligible for special services to assist them in compensating for their developmental difficulties. Many are likely to benefit from enrollment in inclusive environments.

Classroom Recommendations

The most effective teaching strategies, such as those considered here, demonstrate respect for children's cultures and individual learning styles, and incorporate the most recent knowledge about how to support children's learning. In general, the fields o[f] early children and special education are moving away from rigid, behavioristic approaches, and toward more integrated, responsive teaching methods (see Thompson, 1998).

Among the early proposals for working with children who have been exposed prenatally to drugs was Bellisimo's (1990) classroom teaching model. This model

General intervention guidelines for early childhood settings that include children with prenatal drug exposure

Structure the learning environment

- Establish supportive home-school relationships and encourage family participation whenever possible
- Set up small designated learning areas rather than a large open area
- Organize the environment and define boundaries
- Use area signs or drawings to help children associate specific behaviors, activities, and materials with a particular space
- Rotate materials; do not put everything out at once
- Limit the number of classroom rules, and keep them positive
- Make daily routines as predictable as possible, and limit interruptions
- Keep adult-child ratios low

Encourage teacher-child interactions

- Address children by name and make eye contact or touch children before making a verbal request if these are appropriate in their cultures
- Focus children's attention by limiting distractions and providing engaging activities
- Praise verbally and specifically rather than with just hugs or smiles
- Encourage decision making by providing daily opportunities for choices, and talk about consequences of choices
- Structure and limit the number and length of transitions, prepare children for transitions with verbal cues and role playing
- Encourage attachments and respect
- Provide role models and direct instruction if needed for appropriate classroom behaviors such as sharing, greeting, and thanking
- Encourage communication, and respond to all attempts to verbalize
- Urge children to verbally express their wants and needs

Plan engaging activities

- Structure, model, and guide appropriate play activities; provide individual instruction to support play behaviors, such as how to join a group or welcome another child
- Initiate opportunities for children to engage in parallel and small-group play
- Implement a developmentally appropriate, integrated curriculum
- Promote active participation in group activities

Infants exposed to drugs prenatally are at greatest risk when other environmental risk factors are present.

recommended environments that are predictable, with established routines; are characterized by self-directed exploration; are sensitive to transitional periods; and have a small teacher-pupil ratio designed to enhance positive attachments to caregivers.

Most children are not likely to need a separate curriculum or methodology (Shores, 1991; Kinnison, Sluder, & Cates, 1995). Instead, these authors suggest that children who were exposed to drugs prenatally will benefit from the use of professional educational practices, with emphasis placed on long-term expectations and predictable routines, individualized teaching strategies, reteaching of concepts, concrete activities, and modeling.

Family-Centered Intervention

Education and social service agencies must be well prepared to work with families and children who were, and may still be, abusing drugs. Most research studies show that infants exposed to drugs prenatally are at greatest risk when other environmental risk factors are present, such as:

- poverty
- parents or caregivers who have not completed high school
- one-parent households
- multiple foster-care placements of children or their teen parents
- more than four people in a family
- discrimination due to ethnicity or language

The unique needs of families with children who were exposed prenatally to drugs necessitate a comprehensive, interdisciplinary family-centered approach which sees the family in holistic terms as a diverse and heterogeneous group who are at increased risk for an array of developmental, behavioral, and societal challenges (Chapman, Mayfield, Cook, & Chissom, 1995). Service providers can assist these families in identifying their concerns, priorities, and resources.

The GAO (1990) found that tremendous diversity exists among county, state, and federal agencies in attempting to identify and serve these children and families. Families with children who were exposed to drugs prenatally are most likely to realize their full potential when allied professionals develop and implement a formal referral and assessment process, offer family-centered educational programs, provide consistent and coordinated multiple agency involvement, and increase public awareness about the opportunities and challenges in working with these young children.

Key elements of family-centered services

- Services must fit the family rather than making the family fit the services
- Families are usually the constant in children's lives, while professionals come and go
- Parent-professional collaboration is essential in all decision making
- Unbiased information about child and family care must be shared with families
- Policies must meet the emotional and financial needs of families
- Family individuality must be respected
- Parent-to-parent support must be facilitated
- Services must be flexible and accessible

(adapted from Bailey, Buysse, Edmondson, & Smith, 1992)

References

Angelilli, M. L., Fischer, H., Delaney-Black, V., Rubinstein, M., Ager, J. W., & Sokol, R. J. (1994). History of in-utero cocaine exposure in language-delayed children. *Clinical Pediatrics, 33*(9), 514–516.

Bailey, D. B., Buysse, V., Edmondson. R., & Smith, T. M. (1992). Creating family-centered services in early intervention: Perceptions of professionals in four states. *Exceptional Children, 58,* 298–309.

Bellisimo, Y. (1990, January). Crack babies: The school's new high-risk students. *Thrust,* pp. 23–26.

Chapman, J. K., Mayfield, P. K., Cook, M. J., & Chissom, B. S. (1995). Service patterns and educational experiences among two groups who work with young children prenatally exposed to cocaine: A study across four states. *Infant-Toddler Intervention: The Transdisciplinary Journal, 5,* 31–50.

Chasnoff, I. J., Griffith, D. R., Freier, C., & Murray, J. (1992). Cocaine/polydrug use in pregnancy: Two-year follow-up. *Pediatrics, 89,* 284–289.

Chasnoff, I. J., Landress, H. J., & Barrett, M. E. (1990). The prevalence of illicit drug or alcohol use during pregnancy and discrepancies in mandatory reporting in Pinellas County, Florida. *The New England Journal of Medicine, 322*(17), 1202–1206.

Eisen, L. M., Field, T. M., Bandstra, E. S., Roberts, J., Morrow, C., Larson, S., & Steele, B. M. (1991). Perinatal cocaine effects on neonatal stress behavior and performance on the Brazelton Scale. *Pediatrics, 88,* 477–480.

Feig, L. (1990). *Drug-exposed infants and children: Service needs and policy questions.* Washington, DC: U.S. Department of Health and Human Services. Office of Social Services, Division of Children and Youth Policy.

General Accounting Office (GAO). (1990). *Drug-exposed infants: A generation at risk.* Washington, DC: U.S. Department of Health and Human Services.

Griffith, D. R. (1992, September). Prenatal exposure to cocaine and other drugs: Developmental and educational prognoses. *Phi Delta Kappan,* 30–34.

Griffith, D. R., Azuma, S. D., & Chasnoff, I. J. (1994). Three-year outcome of children exposed prenatally to drugs. *Journal of the American Academy of Child and Adolescent Psychiatry, 33*(1), 20–27.

Hawley, T. L., Halle, T. G., Drasin, R. E., & Thomas, N. G. (1995). Children of addicted mothers: Effects of the "crack epidemic" on the caregiving environment and the development of preschoolers. *American Journal of Orthopsychiatry, 65*(3), 364–379.

Johnson, J. M., Seikel, J. A., Madison, C., Foose, S. M., & Rinard, K. D. (1997). Standardized test performance of children with a history of prenatal exposure to multiple drugs/cocaine. *Journal of Communication Disorders, 30*, 45–73.

Khalsa, J. H., & Gfroerer, J. (1991). Epidemiology and health consequences of drug abuse among pregnant women. *Seminars in Perinatology, 15*, 265–270.

Kinnison, L. R., Sluder, L. C., & Cates, D. (1995). Prenatal drug exposure: Implications for teachers of young children. *Day Care and Early Education, 22*(30), 35–37.

Kronstadt, D. (1991, Spring). Complex developmental issues of prenatal drug exposure. *The Future of Children*, 36–49.

Lutiger, B., Graham, K., Einarson, T., & Koren, G. (1991). Relationship between gestational cocaine use and pregnancy outcome: A meta-analysis. *Teratology, 44*, 405–414.

Mentis, M., & Lundgren, K. (1995). Effects of prenatal exposure to cocaine and associated risk factors on language development. *Journal of Speech and Hearing Research, 38*, 1303–1318.

National Institute on Drug Abuse (NIDA). (1991). *National household survey of drug abuse for 1990*. Bethesda, MD: Author.

Neuspiel, D. R., & Hamel, S. C. (1991). Cocaine and infant behavior. *Developmental and Behavioral Pediatrics, 12*, 55–64.

Odom-Winn, D., & Dunagan, D. (1991). *Crack kids in school: What to do and how to do it*. Freeport, NY: Educational Activities.

Office of the Inspector General. (1990). *Crack babies*. Washington, DC: U. S. Department of Health and Human Services.

Phelps, L., & Cox, D. (1993). Children with prenatal cocaine exposure: Resilient or handicapped? *School Psychology Review, 22*(4), 710–724.

Rivers, K. O., & Hedrick, D. L. (1998). A follow-up study of language and behavioral concerns of children prenatally exposed to drugs. *Infant Toddler Intervention: The Trans-disciplinary Journal, 8*(1), 29–51.

Shores, E. F. (1991). *Prenatal cocaine exposure: The South looks for answers*. Little Rock, AR: Southern Early Childhood Association.

Thompson, S. H. (1998, January). Working with children of substance-abusing parents. *Young Children, 53*(1), 34–37.

Trad, P. V. (1992). Toddlers with prenatal cocaine exposure: Diagnostic peer groups Part II. *Infant-Toddler Intervention: The Transdisciplinary Journal, 2*, 285–305.

Tyler, R. (1992). Prenatal drug exposure: An overview of associated problems and intervention strategies. *Phi Delta Kappan*, 705–708.

Van de Bor, M., Walthes, F. J., & Sims, M. E. (1990). Increased cerebral bloodflow velocity in infants of mothers who abuse cocaine. *Pediatrics, 85*, 733–736.

Williams, B. F., & Howard, V. F. (1993). Children exposed to cocaine: Characteristics and implications for research and intervention. *Journal of Early Intervention, 17*, 61–72.

Wolery, M., Strain, P.S., & Bailey, D. B., Jr. (1992). Reaching potentials of children with special needs. In S. Bredekamp & T. Rosegrant (Eds.), *Reaching potentials: Appropriate curriculum and assessment for young children, Vol. 1*. Washington, DC: National Association for the Education of Young Children.

Wright, R. (1994). Drugged out. *Texas Monthly, 20*(11), 150–154.

YOUR CHILD'S EMOTIONS

A Bundle of Emotions

Whether by smiling or screaming, crying or cuddling, babies find ways early on to tell us how they feel. Good behavior comes along later. What to watch and listen for:

• A Repertoire of Cries

All babies cry, and usually for good reason. Before they learn to talk, crying is one way to express their needs and send out signals of distress. Examples of three typical cries, and differences in volumes, pitch and rhythm:

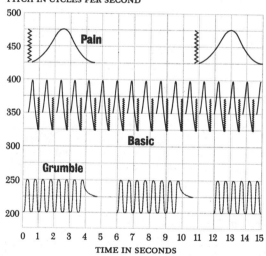

PITCH IN CYCLES PER SECOND

Pain A cry of pain or distress usually begins with an inward gasp followed by a long pause until the next painful scream. Soothe the baby by rocking or with music.

Basic A basic cry rises and falls rhythmically, broken up with a breath and a pause. The child may cry this way when demanding food or attention.

Grumble A grumble cry is the first attempt at communication. It has a lower pitch and volume, often sounding whimpery and whiny. It is a signal that the child may be getting restless. Move the child to a different environment and provide new stimulation.

• Toys and Games for Curious Tots

Children love playtime, especially when parents or siblings join in the fun. Look for educational toys and games that encourage development:

1–3 months old Mobiles, unbreakable mirrors and activity centers attached to crib, rattles, stuffed toys with black and white patterns, music boxes, large colorful rings.

4–6 months old Beach balls, chunky bracelets, building blocks, squeaky toys, paper streamers, books made of cloth or vinyl, playing peekaboo or come-and-get-me with others.

7–9 months old Stuffed animals, balls, nesting cylinders, pop-up toys, large dolls and puppets, bath toys, performing "so big" or pat-a-cake.

10–12 months old Push-and-pull toys like miniature cars, ordinary household objects like empty egg cartons and large spoons, stacked rings on a spindle, playing simple ball games.

13–15 months old Toy telephones, acrobatics, pushing a carriage or toy horse, playing with cups and clothespins.

16–18 months old Sandbox, simple musical instruments like a drum or tambourine, large colored beads, jack-in-the-boxes, blowing bubbles.

19–21 months old Rocking horse, toys to take apart and fit back together, small rubber balls, digging toys, large crayons, kiddie cars, water games, easy jigsaw puzzles, making mud pies, playing tag or hide-and-seek.

22–24 months old Kiddie lawn mowers and kitchen sets for make-believe play, modeling clay, construction sets, action toys like trains, telephones, dump trucks and fire engines, old magazines, baskets, tubes and containers with lids.

2–3 years Beginner tricycle, mini-trampoline, roller skates or Rollerblades, dolls and accessories like strollers and baby bottles, dress-up clothes, coloring books, easel, crayons and markers, music, kiddie cassette player, swing sets, books, finger paint, mini basketball hoop, woodworking bench, kiddie swimming pool.

0–2 months old

1 month old
Behavior Alert to stimuli like loud sounds and bright patterns. Quiets to holding and cuddling.
Interaction Child may recognize parent's voice or make eye-to-eye contact.
Tips Spend special time with siblings who may feel abandoned or jealous.

2 months old
Emotions Cries to show distress or pain, coos when happy or excited.
Tips If leaving child with a sitter, choose someone both you and the baby know, like a grandparent or close friend. Keep a list of emergency numbers handy.

3–8 months old

3 months old
Behavior Smiles often to others or while sleeping.
Interaction May cry differently when mother leaves the room than with other people. Begins to sort out who's who in his life. May prefer certain people.

4 months old
Behavior Laughs while playing and may cry if playtime is interrupted. May still act passively, taking in whatever toy or face comes near.
Emotions Showing curiosity when inspecting rattle and dependency when wanting to be held. Moods may change rapidly.
Interaction Tries to get parent's attention by banging rattle or crying.

5 months old
Behavior Child may become more assertive as he learns to reach for objects.
Emotions Shows anger when someone tries to take away his toy. May begin to handle stresses better because of maturing nervous system.
Tips Set clear rules if sibling tries to hurt baby. Give child responsibilities as big brother or sister.

6 months old
Interaction May fear strangers. Responds positively to other children.
Tips When baby repeatedly puts an object in his mouth that he should not, gently pull his arm away, say no and distract with another activity.

7 months old
Behavior May test parents' authority by refusing to follow their directions.
Emotions Shows humor and laughs at funny expressions or positions.
Interaction May give familiar people hugs and kisses. May raise his arms to be picked up.

8 months old
Behavior Smiles at, pats or even kisses his mirror image. May distinguish between baby and image.
Interaction May reject being alone or confined in a crib or playpen. May fear being separated from parents as he learns to crawl. Buries head in parent's shoulder when meeting new people.

🌐 Circles of Friends

A baby's first friends are his parents, and interaction with them prepares the child for future relationships in larger social circles:

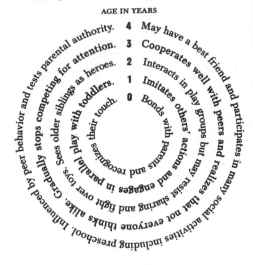

AGE IN YEARS

4 May have a best friend and participates in many social activities including preschool. Influenced by peer behavior and tests parental authority.

3 Cooperates well with peers and realizes that not everyone thinks alike. Gradually stops competing for attention.

2 Interacts in play groups but may resist sharing and fight over toys. Sees older siblings as heroes.

1 Imitates others' actions and engages in parallel play with toddlers.

0 Bonds with parents and recognizes their touch.

9–16 months old

9 months old
Interaction May perform tricks like "so big" and peekaboo for familiar people. May repeat act if applauded. Near the end of the first year, child may learn to assess moods and imitate them. If baby sees someone crying, he may cry too.

10 months old
Emotions Shows twinges of jealousy. May cry or whimper when sibling is at center of attention.
Interaction Starts to become aware of social approval and disapproval.

11 months old
Behavior May use a security blanket for comfort in strange places.
Interaction May assert himself among siblings. Likes to imitate gestures and sounds.

12 months old
Tips Try not to fuss when leaving child at home. Allow time for him to adjust to sitter. Distract baby with another activity and give a quick good-night kiss. Crying will probably stop after parents depart.

13 months old
Behavior Laughs when chased. May become more demanding and seek constant attention.
Emotions After the first year, personality begins to emerge. May be an explorer, a tease, a showoff.

14 months old
Behavior Child may turn more aggressive as she learns to walk. May throw objects in anger.
Interaction May enjoy playing alone, but still likes to act for an audience (Toys and Games for Curious Tots).
Tips Time to baby-proof your house.

15 months old
Emotions May communicate feelings with a clear intent or purpose.
Interaction By midyear, some babies may recognize when familiar people are missing. May offer toys to others but will quickly want them back.

16 months old
Behavior Instead of using words, child flings arms or moves away to say no.
Interaction May hit parents in anger.

17-24 months old

17 months old
Interaction May respond correctly to what parents say. If scolded, child cries; if praised, she smiles.
Tips Some toddlers shy away from others. Give child time to adapt to new situations and hold her hand.

18 months old
Behavior Frustration may trigger tantrums. At this age, child acts on impulse due to limited understanding of good and bad, rules and warnings.
Interaction Communicates desire for closeness by plopping on parent's lap. Still has no sense of sharing with others.

19 months old
Behavior Enjoys getting out of the house and exploring new environments.
Interaction Some children will play among others in a group. May engage in parallel play.
Tips Praise will motivate child to obey the simple rules set. Give precedence to rules that

keep her safe, as well as ones that prohibit hitting and kicking.

20 months old
Behavior During pretend play, child acts out what happens around her.
Emotions May fear thunder, lightning, big animals and the dark. Install night light if sleep is consistently disrupted.
Interaction Slowly warms to a new babysitter, but may still cling to mother around people she was comfortable with earlier.

21 months old
Emotions May sympathize with other people or recognize their feelings. Expresses love for parents by hugging and smiling.
Interaction Still possessive of toys but may give up objects that belong to someone else.

22 months old
Interaction Cooperates with others. Language development facilitates communication. Engages in parallel play with toddlers, often back to back.

Tips To build self-reliance, encourage child to separate from parents for short periods of time.

23 months old
Emotions May fear rejection and become frustrated with new activities.
Interaction May be willing to play alone. Likes to follow siblings and imitate their actions.
Tips Try to give siblings some privacy and designate a special time to spend with them.

24 months old
Behavior May become manipulative and bossy. Learns rules through trial and error.
Emotions Able to explain feelings and desires using gestures and simple phrases. Trusts adults.
Interaction Plays well with older children. May hand toy to another child. Imitates others through pretend play. May show signs of jealousy or revert to babyish actions when a new sibling arrives.

2–3 years old

25–29 months old
Behavior Sees the world almost exclusively through his needs. Assumes everyone thinks and acts like him. May throw tantrum when angry or frustrated.
Emotions May have frequent mood swings. May pout or feel guilty when scolded. Learns how to express sadness or stress.
Interaction May pull away from familiar children or adults. Siblings take on a greater role in daily life. May enjoy play groups; the concept of "friend" evolves.
Tips Do not give child an audience during a tirade. Try not to scream back or dwell on the tantrum after it's finished.

30–36 months old
Behavior Toddler slowly begins to realize what's acceptable and what's not. May find it difficult to concentrate on new tasks.
Interaction Child may be conscious of being a member of a family. May show pity or sympathy to familiar people. Sharing parent's attention with siblings can be difficult. Insists on being at the center of play and may dislike sharing limelight with peers. May be ready for nursery school, which can create separation anxiety. In nursery school, child learns to follow rules, to cooperate with others and to spend a few hours away from home.

Tips Encourage child to act responsibly by setting limits on dangerous or antisocial behavior. Time-outs may help defuse anger. Be consistent with rules. Praise child when he plays well with others.

By Jennifer Lach

SOURCES; "THE EARLY CHILDHOOD YEARS: THE 2 TO 6 YEAR OLD," "THE SECOND TWELVE MONTHS OF LIFE," "THE FIRST TWELVE MONTHS OF LIFE" BY THERESA AND FRANK CAPLAN; "CARING FOR YOUR BABY AND YOUNG CHILD" BY STEVEN P. SHELOV, M.D.; "FIRST FEELINGS" BY STANLEY GREENSPAN; "YOUR BABY & CHILD" BY PENELOPE LEACH.

● For More Information

Many organizations offer advice on parenting and child development. Check with your public school for local groups. A few notable programs:

Home Instruction Program for Preschool Youngsters (HIPPY USA): 212-678-3500

MELD (Minnesota Early Learning Design): 612-332-7563

Parents as Teachers National Center: 314-432-4330

Birth To Three: 800-680-7888

Family Resources: 800-641-4546

Learning language, researchers are finding, is an astonishing act of brain computation—and it's performed by people too young to tie their shoes

BY SHANNON BROWNLEE

Inside a small, dark booth, 18-month-old Karly Horn sits on her mother Terry's lap. Karly's brown curls bounce each time she turns her head to listen to a woman's recorded voice coming from one side of the booth or the other. "At the bakery, workers will be baking bread," says the voice. Karly turns to her left and listens, her face intent. "On Tuesday morning, the people have going to work," says the voice. Karly turns her head away even before the statement is finished. The lights come on as graduate student Ruth Tincoff opens the door to the booth. She gives the child's curls a pat and says, "Nice work."

Karly and her mother are taking part in an experiment at Johns Hopkins University in Baltimore, run by psycholinguist Peter Jusczyk, who has spent 25 years probing the linguistic skills of children who have not yet begun to talk. Like most toddlers her age, Karly can utter a few dozen words at most and can string together the occasional two-word sentence, like "More juice" and "Up, Mommy." Yet as Jusczyk and his colleagues have found, she can already recognize that a sentence like "the people have going to work" is ungrammatical. By 18 months of age, most toddlers have somehow learned the rule requiring that any verb ending in *-ing* must be preceded by the verb *to be.* "If you had asked me 10 years ago if kids this young could do this," says Jusczyk, "I would have said that's crazy.

Linguists these days are reconsidering a lot of ideas they once considered crazy. Recent findings like Jusczyk's are reshaping the prevailing model of how children acquire language. The dominant theory, put forth by Noam Chomsky, has been that children cannot possibly learn the full rules and structure of languages strictly by imitating what they hear. Instead, nature gives children a head start, wiring them from birth with the ability to acquire their parents native tongue by fitting what they hear into a preexisting template for the basic structure shared by all languages. (Similarly, kittens are thought to be hard-wired to learn how to hunt.) Language, writes Massachusetts Institute of Technology linguist Steven Pinker, "is a distinct piece of the biological makeup of our brains." Chomsky, a prominent linguist at MIT, hypothesized in the 1950s that children are endowed from birth with "universal grammar," the fundamental rules that are common to all languages, and the ability to apply these rules to the raw material of the speech they hear—without awareness of their underlying logic.

The average preschooler can't tell time, but he has already accumulated a vocabulary of thousands of words—plus (as Pinker writes in his book, *The Language Instinct,*) "a tacit knowledge of grammar more sophisticated than the thickest style manual." Within a few months of birth, children have already begun memorizing words without knowing their meaning. The question that has absorbed—and sometimes divided—linguists is whether children need a special language faculty to do this or instead can infer the abstract rules of grammar from the sentences they hear, using the same mental skills that allow them to recognize faces or master arithmetic.

The debate over how much of language is already vested in a child at birth is far from settled, but new linguistic research already is transforming traditional views of how the human brain works and how language evolved. "This debate has completely changed the way we view the brain," says Elissa Newport, a psycholinguist at the University of Rochester in New York. Far from being an orderly, computer-like machine that methodically calculates step by step, the brain is now seen as working more like a beehive, its swarm of interconnected neurons sending signals back and forth at lightning speed. An infant's brain, it turns out, is capable of taking in enormous amounts of information and finding the regular patterns contained within it. Geneticists and linguists recently have begun to challenge the common-sense assumption that intelligence and language are inextricably linked, through research on a rare genetic disorder called Williams syndrome, which can seriously impair cognition while leaving language nearly intact (box, Rare Disorder Reveals Split between Language and Thought). Increasingly sophisticated technologies such as magnetic resonance imaging are allowing researchers to watch the brain in action, revealing that language literally sculpts and reorganizes the connections within it as a child grows.

The path leading to language begins even before birth, when a developing fetus is bathed in the muffled sound of its mother's voice in the womb. Newborn babies prefer their mothers' voices over those of their fathers or other women, and researchers recently have found that when very young babies hear a recording of their mothers' native language, they will suck more vigorously on a pacifier than when they hear a recording of another tongue.

At first, infants respond only to the prosody—the cadence, rhythm, and pitch—of their mothers' speech, not the words. But soon enough they home in on the actual sounds that are typical of their parents' language. Every language uses a different assortment of sounds, called phonemes, which combine to make syllables. (In English, for example, the consonant sound "b" and the vowel sound "a" are both phonemes, which combine for the syllable *ba,* as in *banana.*) To an adult, simply perceiving, much less pronouncing, the phonemes of a foreign language can seem impossible. In English, the p of *pat* is "aspirated," or produced with a puff of air; the p of *spot* or *tap* is unaspirated. In English, the two p's are considered the same; therefore it is hard for English speakers to recognize that in many other languages the two p's are two different phonemes. Japanese speakers have trouble distinguishing between the "l" and "r" sounds of English, since in Japanese they don't count as separate sounds.

Polyglot tots. Infants can perceive the entire range of phonemes, according to Janet Werker and Richard Tees, psychologists at the University of British Columbia in Canada. Werker and Tees found that the brains of 4-month-old babies respond to every phoneme uttered in languages as diverse as Hindi and Nthlakampx, a Northwest American Indian language containing numerous consonant combinations that can sound to a nonnative speaker like a drop of water hitting an empty bucket. By the time babies are 10 months to a year old, however, they have begun to focus on the distinctions among phonemes of their native language and to ignore the differences among foreign sounds. Children don't lose the ability to distinguish the sounds of a foreign language; they simply don't pay attention to them. This allows them to learn more quickly the syllables and words of their native tongue.

An infant's next step is learning to fish out individual words from the nonstop stream of sound that makes up ordinary speech. Finding the boundaries between words is a daunting task, because people don't pause ... between ... words ... when ... they speak. Yet children begin to note word boundaries by the time they are 8 months old, even though they have no concept of what most words mean. Last year, Jusczyk and his colleagues reported results of an experiment in which they let 8-month-old babies listen at home to recorded stories filled with unusual words, like *hornbill* and *python.* Two weeks later, the researchers tested the babies with two lists of words, one composed of words they had already heard in the stories, the other of new unusual words that weren't in the stories. The infants listened, on average, to the familiar list for a second longer than to the list of novel words.

The cadence of language is a baby's first clue to word boundaries. In most English words, the first syllable is accented. This is especially noticeable in words known in poetry as trochees—two-syllable words stressed on the first syllable—which parents repeat to young children (BA-by, DOG-gie, MOM-my). At 6 months, American babies pay equal amounts of attention to words with different stress patterns, like gi-RAFFE or TI-ger. By 9 months, however, they have heard enough of the typical first-syllable-stress pattern of English to prefer listening to trochees, a predilection that will show up later, when they start uttering their first words and mispronouncing giraffe as *raff* and banana as *nana*. At 30 months, children can easily repeat the phrase "TOM-my KISS-ed the MON-key," because it preserves the typical English pattern, but they will leave out the *the* when asked to repeat "Tommy patted the monkey." Researchers are now testing whether French babies prefer words with a second-syllable stress—words like *be-RET* or *ma-MAN*.

Decoding patterns. Most adults could not imagine making speedy progress toward memorizing words in a foreign language just by listening to somebody talk on the telephone. That is basically what 8-month-old babies can do, according to a provocative study published in 1996 by the University of Rochester's Newport and her colleagues, Jenny Saffran and Richard Aslin. They reported that babies can remember words by listening for patterns of syllables that occur together with statistical regularity.

The researchers created a miniature artificial language, which consisted of a handful of three-syllable nonsense words constructed from 11 different syllables. The babies heard a computer-generated voice repeating these words in random order in a monotone for two minutes. What they heard went something like "bidaku-padotigolabubidaku." *Bidaku*, in this case, is a word. With no cadence or pauses, the only way the babies could learn individual words was by remembering how often certain syllables were uttered together. When the researchers tested the babies a few minutes later, they found that the infants recognized pairs of syllables that had occurred together consistently on the recording, such as *bida*. They did not recognize a pair like *kupa*, which was a rarer combination that crossed the boundaries of two words. In the past, psychologists never imagined that young infants had the mental capacity to make these sorts of inferences. "We were pretty surprised we could get this result with babies, and with only brief exposure," says Newport. "Real language, of course, is much more complicated, but the exposure is vast."

Learning words is one thing; learning the abstract rules of grammar is another. When Noam Chomsky first voiced his idea that language is hardwired in the brain, he didn't have the benefit of the current revolution in cognitive science, which has begun to pry open the human mind with sophisticated psychological experiments and new computer models. Until recently, linguists could only parse languages and marvel at how quickly children master their abstract rules, which give every human being who can speak (or sign) the power to express an infinite number of ideas from a finite number of words.

There also are a finite number of ways that languages construct sentences. As Chomsky once put it, from a Martian's-eye view, everybody on Earth speaks a single tongue that has thousands of mutually unintelligible dialects. For instance, all people make sentences from noun phrases, like "The quick brown fox," and verb phrases, like "jumped over the fence." And virtually all of the world's 6,000 or so languages allow phrases to be moved around in a sentence to form questions, relative clauses, and passive constructions.

Statistical wizards. Chomsky posited that children were born knowing these and a handful of other basic laws of language and that they learn their parents' native tongue with the help of a "language acquisition device," preprogrammed circuits in the brain. Findings like Newport's are suggesting to some researchers that perhaps children can use statistical regularities to extract not only individual words from what they hear but also the rules for cobbling words together into sentences.

This idea is shared by computational linguists, who have designed computer models called artificial neural networks that are very simplified versions of the brain and that can "learn" some aspects of language. Artificial neural networks mimic the way that nerve cells, or neurons, inside a brain are hooked up. The result is a device that shares some basic properties with the brain and

that can accomplish some linguistic feats that real children perform. For example, a neural network can make general categories out of a jumble of words coming in, just as a child learns that certain kinds of words refer to objects while others refer to actions. Nobody has to teach kids that words like *dog* and *telephone* are nouns, while *go* and *jump* are verbs; the way they use such words in sentences demonstrates that they know the difference. Neural networks also can learn some aspects of the meaning of words, and they can infer some rules of syntax, or word order. Therefore, a computer that was fed English sentences would be able to produce a phrase like "Johnny ate fish," rather than "Johnny fish ate," which is correct in Japanese. These computer models even make some of the same mistakes that real children do, says Mark Seidenberg, a computational linguist at the University of Southern California. A neural network designed by a student of Seidenberg's to learn to conjugate verbs sometimes issued sentences like "He jumped me the ball," which any parent will recognize as the kind of error that could have come from the mouths of babes.

But neural networks have yet to come close to the computation power of a toddler. Ninety percent of the sentences uttered by the average 3-year-old are grammatically correct. The mistakes they do make are rarely random but rather the result of following the rules of grammar with excessive zeal. There is no logical reason for being able to say "I batted the ball" but not "I holded the rabbit," except that about 180 of the most commonly used English verbs are conjugated irregularly.

Yet for all of grammar's seeming illogic, toddlers' brains may be able to spot clues in the sentences they hear that help them learn grammatical rules, just as they use statistical regularities to find word boundaries. One such clue is the little bits of language called grammatical morphemes, which among other things tell a listener whether a word is being used as noun or as a verb. *The,* for instance, signals that a noun will soon follow, while the suffix *ion* also identifies a word as a noun, as in vibration. Psycholinguist LouAnn Gerken of the University of Arizona recently reported that toddlers know what grammatical morphemes signify before they actually use them. She tested this by asking 2-year-olds a series of questions in which the grammatical morphemes were replaced with other words. When asked to "Find the dog for me," for example, 85 percent of children in her study could point to the right animal in a picture. But when the question was "Find *was* dog for me," they pointed to the dog 55 percent of the time. "Find *gub* dog for me," and it dropped to 40 percent.

Fast mapping. Children may be noticing grammatical morphemes when they are as young as 10 months and have just begun making connections between words and their definitions. Gerken recently found that infants' brain waves change when they are listening to stories in which grammatical morphemes are replaced with other words, suggesting they begin picking up grammar even before they know what sentences mean.

Such linguistic leaps come as a baby's brain is humming with activity. Within the first few months of life, a baby's neurons will forge 1,000 trillion connections, an increase of 20-fold from birth. Neurobiologists once assumed that the wiring in a baby's brain was set at birth. After that, the brain, like legs and noses, just grew bigger. That view has been demolished, says Anne Fernald, a psycholinguist at Stanford University, "now that we can eavesdrop on the brain." Images made using the brain-scanning technique positron emission tomography have revealed, for instance, that when a baby is 8 or 9 months old, the part of the brain that stores and indexes many kinds of memory becomes fully functional. This is precisely when babies appear to be able to attach meaning to words.

Other leaps in a child's linguistic prowess also coincide with remarkable changes in the brain. For instance, an adult listener can recognize *eleph* as *elephant* within about 400 milliseconds, an ability called "fast mapping" that demands that the brain process speech sounds with phenomenal speed. "To understand strings of words, you have to identify individual words rapidly," says Fernald. She and her colleagues have found that around 15 months of age, a child needs more than a second to recognize even a familiar word, like *baby.* At 18 months, the child can get the picture slightly before the word is ending. At 24 months, she knows the word in a mere 600 milliseconds, as soon as the syllable *bay* has been uttered.

Fast mapping takes off at the same moment as a dramatic reorganization of the child's brain, in which language-related operations, particularly grammar, shift from both sides of the brain into the left hemisphere. Most adult brains are lopsided when it comes to language, processing grammar almost entirely in the left temporal lobe, just over the left ear. Infants and toddlers, however, treat language in both hemispheres, according to Debra Mills, at the University of California–San Diego, and Helen Neville, at the University of Oregon. Mills and Neville stuck electrodes to toddlers' heads to find that processing of words that serve special grammatical functions, such as prepositions, conjunctions, and articles, begins to shift into the left side around the end of the third year.

From then on, the two hemispheres assume different job descriptions. The right temporal lobe continues to perform spatial tasks, such as following the trajectory of a baseball and predicting where it will land. It also pays attention to the emotional information contained in the cadence and pitch of speech. Both hemispheres know the meanings of many words, but the left temporal lobe holds the key to grammar.

This division is maintained even when the language is signed, not spoken. Ursula Bellugi and Edward Klima, a wife and husband team at the Salk Institute for Biological Stud-

ies in La Jolla, Caiif., recently demonstrated this fact by studying deaf people who were lifelong signers of American Sign Language and who also had suffered a stroke in specific areas of the brain. The researchers found, predictably, that signers with damage to the right hemisphere had great difficulty with tasks involving spatial perception, such as copying a drawing of a geometric pattern. What was surprising was that right hemisphere damage did not hinder their fluency in ASL, which relies on movements of the hands and body in space. It was signers with damage to the left hemisphere who found they could no longer express themselves in ASL or understand it. Some had trouble producing the specific facial expressions that convey grammatical information in ASL. It is not just speech that's being processed in the left hemisphere, says MIT's Pinker, or movements of the mouth, but abstract language.

Nobody knows why the left hemisphere got the job of processing language, but linguists are beginning to surmise that languages are constructed the way they are in part because the human brain is not infinitely capable of all kinds of computation. "We are starting to see how the universals among languages could arise out of constraints on how the brain computes and how children learn," says Johns Hopkins linguist Paul Smolensky. For instance, the vast majority of the world's languages favor syllables that end in a vowel, though English is an exception. (Think of a native Italian speaking English and adding vowels where there are none.) That's because it is easier for the auditory centers of the brain to perceive differences between consonants when they come before a vowel than when they come after. Human brains can easily recognize *pad, bad,* and *dad* as three different words; it is much harder to distinguish *tab, tap,* and *tad.* As languages around the world were evolving, they were pulled along paths that minimize ambiguity among sounds.

Birth of a language. Linguists have never had the chance to study a spoken language as it is being constructed, but they have been given the opportunity to observe a new sign language in the making in Nicaragua. When the Sandinistas came to power in 1979, they established schools where deaf people came together for the first time. Many of the pupils had never met another deaf person, and their only means of communication at first was the expressive but largely unstructured pantomime each had invented at home with their hearing families. Soon the pupils began to pool their makeshift gestures into a system that is similar to spoken pidgin, the form of communication that springs up in places where people speaking mutually unintelligible tongues come together. The next generation of deaf Nicaraguan children, says Judy Kegl, a psycholinguist at Rutgers University, in Newark, N.J., has done it one better, transforming the pidgin sign into a full-blown language complete with regular grammar. The birth of Nicaraguan sign, many linguists believe, mirrors the evolution of all languages. Without conscious effort, deaf Nicaraguan children have created a sign that is now fluid and compact, and which contains standardized rules that allow them to express abstract ideas without circumlocutions. It can indicate past and future, denote whether an action was performed once or repeatedly, and show who did what to whom, allowing its users to joke, recite poetry, and tell their life stories.

Linguists have a long road ahead of them before they can say exactly how a child goes from babbling to banter, or what the very first languages might have been like, or how the brain transforms vague thoughts into concrete words that sometimes fly out of our mouths before we can stop them. But already, some practical conclusions are falling out of the new research. For example, two recent studies show that the size of toddlers' vocabularies depends in large measure on how much their mothers talk to them. At 20 months, according to a study by Janellen Huttenlocher of the University of Chicago, the children of talkative mothers had 131 more words in their vocabularies than children whose mothers were more taciturn. By age 2, the gap had widened to 295 words.

In other words, children need input and they need it early, says Newport. Parking a toddler in front of the television won't improve vocabulary, probably because kids need real human interaction to attach meaning to words. Hearing more than one language in infancy makes it easier for a child to hear the distinctions between phonemes of more than one language later on.

Newport and other linguists have discovered in recent years that the window of opportunity for acquiring language begins to close around age 6, and the gap narrows with each additional candle on the birthday cake. Children who do not learn a language by puberty will never be fluent in any tongue. That means that profoundly deaf children should be exposed to sign language as early as possible, says Newport. If their parents are hearing, they should learn to sign. And schools might rethink the practice of waiting to teach foreign languages until kids are nearly grown and the window on native command of a second language is almost shut.

Linguists don't yet know how much of grammar children are able to absorb simply by listening. And they have only begun to parse the genes or accidents of brain wiring that might give rise, as Pinker puts it, to the poet, the raconteur, or an Alexander Haig, a Mrs. Malaprop. What is certain is that language is one of the great wonders of the natural world, and linguists are still being astonished by its complexity and its power to shape the brain. Human beings, says Kegl, "show an incredible enthusiasm for discourse." Maybe what is most innate about language is the passion to communicate.

Boys will be Boys

Developmental research has been focused on girls; now it's their brothers' turn. Boys need help, too, but first they need to be understood.

BY BARBARA KANTROWITZ AND CLAUDIA KALB

IT WAS A CLASSIC MARS-VENUS ENCOUNTER. Only in this case, the woman was from Harvard and the man—well, boy—was a 4-year-old at a suburban Boston nursery school. Graduate student Judy Chu was in his classroom last fall to gather observations for her doctoral dissertation on human development. His greeting was startling: he held up his finger as if it were a gun and pretended to shoot her. "I felt bad," Chu recalls. "I felt as if he didn't like me." Months later and much more boy-savvy, Chu has a different interpretation: the gunplay wasn't hostile—it was just a way for him to say hello. "They don't mean it to have harsh consequences. It's a way for them to connect."

Researchers like Chu are discovering new meaning in lots of things boys have done for ages. In fact, they're dissecting just about every aspect of the developing male psyche and creating a hot new field of inquiry: the study of boys. They're also producing a slew of books with titles like "Real Boys: Rescuing Our Sons From the Myths of Boyhood" and "Raising Cain: Protecting the Emotional Life of Boys" that will hit the stores in the next few months.

What some researchers are finding is that boys and girls really are from two different planets. But since the two sexes have to live together here on Earth, they should be raised with special consideration for their distinct needs. Boys and girls have different "crisis points," experts say, stages in their emotional and social development where things can go very wrong. Until recently, girls got all the attention. But boys need help, too. They're much more likely than girls to have discipline problems at school and to be diagnosed with attention deficit disorder (ADD). Boys far outnumber girls in special-education classes. They're also more likely to commit violent crimes and end up in jail. Consider the headlines: Jonesboro, Ark.; Paducah, Ky.; Pearl, Miss. In all these school shootings, the perpetrators were young adolescent boys.

Even normal boy behavior has come to be considered pathological in the wake of the feminist movement. An abundance of physical energy and the urge to conquer—these are normal male characteristics, and in an earlier age they were good things, even essential to survival. "If Huck Finn or Tom Sawyer were alive today," says Michael Gurian, author of "The Wonder of Boys," "we'd say they had ADD or a conduct disorder." He says one of the new insights we're gaining about boys is a very old one: boys will be boys. "They are who they are," says Gurian, "and we need to love them for who they are. Let's not try to rewire them."

Indirectly, boys are benefiting from all the research done on girls, especially the landmark work by Harvard University's Carol Gilligan. Her 1982 book, "In a Different Voice: Psychological Theory and Women's Development," inspired Take Our Daughters to Work Day, along with best-selling spinoffs like Mary Pipher's "Reviving Ophelia." The traditional, unisex way of looking at child development was profoundly flawed, Gilligan says: "It was like having a one-dimensional perspective on a two-dimensional scene." At Harvard, where she chairs the gender-studies department, Gilligan is now supervising work on males, including Chu's project. Other researchers are studying mental illness and violence in boys.

While girls' horizons have been expanding, boys' have narrowed, confined to rigid ideas of acceptable male behavior no matter how hard their parents tried to avoid stereotypes. The macho ideal still rules. "We gave boys dolls and they used them as guns," says Gurian. "For 15 years, all we heard was that [gender differences] were all about socialization. Parents who raised their kids through that period said in the end, 'That's not true. Boys and girls can be awfully different.' I think we're awakening to the biological realities and the sociological realities."

But what exactly is the essential nature of boys? Even as infants, boys and girls behave differently. A recent study at Children's Hospital in Boston found that boy babies are more emotionally expressive; girls are more reflective. (That means boy babies tend to cry when they're unhappy; girl babies suck their thumbs.) This could indicate that girls are innately more able to control their emotions. Boys have higher levels of testosterone and lower levels of the neurotransmitter serotonin, which inhibits aggression and impulsivity. That may help explain why more males than females carry through with suicide, become alcoholics and are diagnosed with ADD.

The developmental research on the impact of these physiological differences is still in the embryonic stage, but psychologists are drawing some interesting comparisons between girls and boys (chart). For girls, the first crisis point often comes in early adolescence. Until then, Gilligan and others found, girls have an enormous capacity for establishing relationships and interpreting

Some Tips for Parents

• **Common sense helps.** So does a sense of humor. Most of all, boys need to know that the two most important people in their lives, their parents, are there for them.

• **Boys need hugs, too.** Don't try to turn him into Clint Eastwood at the age of 4. You're not coddling him by showing tenderness; you're developing emotional solidarity with your son and teaching him empathy.

• **Don't sweat the gun issue.** Even if you ban all guns, chances are your son will find a way to play at fighting: fingers or carrots work equally well. There's no evidence that this kind of play will turn your boy into a killer any more than playing with trucks will make him a truckdriver.

• **It's OK to get mad.** When he's at an appropriate age, you can help him understand the difference between legitimate feelings of anger and expressing it by hitting, kicking or screaming.

• **Stay in touch.** As they get older, boys still need their parents. Look for opportunities to communicate, like picking him up at school. He'll be strapped in a seat belt, so you know he can't get away.

emotions. But in their early teens, girls clamp down, squash their emotions, blunt their insight. Their self-esteem plummets. The first crisis point for boys comes much earlier, researchers now say. "There's an outbreak of symptoms at age 5, 6, 7, just like you see in girls at 11, 12, 13," says Gilligan. Problems at this age include bed-wetting and separation anxiety. "They don't have the language or experience" to articulate it fully, she says, "but the feelings are no less intense." That's why Gilligan's student Chu is studying preschoolers. For girls at this age, Chu says, hugging a parent goodbye "is almost a nonissue." But little boys, who display a great deal of tenderness, soon begin to bury it with "big boy" behavior to avoid being called sissies. "When their parents drop them off, they want to be close and want to be held, but not in front of other people," says Chu. "Even as early as 4, they're already aware of those masculine stereotypes and are negotiating their way around them."

It's a phenomenon that parents, especially mothers, know well. One morning last month, Lori Dube, a 37-year-old mother of three from Evanston, Ill., visited her oldest son, Abe, almost 5, at his nursery school, where he was having lunch with his friends. She kissed him, prompting another boy to comment scornfully: "Do you know what your mom just did? She kissed you!" Dube acknowledges, with some sadness, that she'll have to be more sensitive to Abe's new reactions to future public displays of affection. "Even if he loves it, he's getting these messages that it's not good."

There's a struggle—a desire and need for warmth on the one hand and a pull toward independence on the other. Boys like Abe are going through what psychologists long ago declared an integral part of growing up: individualization and disconnection from parents, especially mothers. But now some researchers think that process is too abrupt. When boys repress normal feelings like love because of social pressure, says William Pollack, head of the Center for Men at Boston's McLean Hospital and author of the forthcoming "Real Boys," "they've lost contact with the genuine nature of who they are and what they feel. Boys are in a silent crisis. The only time we notice it is when they pull the trigger."

No one is saying that acting like Rambo in nursery school leads directly to tragedies like Jonesboro. But researchers do think that boys who are forced to shut down positive emotions are left with only one socially acceptable outlet: anger. The cultural ideals boys are exposed to in movies and on TV still emphasize traditional masculine roles—warrior, rogue, adventurer—with heavy doses of violence. For every Mr. Mom, there are a dozen Terminators. "The feminist movement has done a great job of convincing people that a woman can be nurturing and a mother and a tough trial lawyer at the same time," says Dan Kindlon, an assistant professor of psychiatry at Harvard Medical School. "But we haven't done that as much with men. We're afraid that if they're too soft, that's all they can be."

And the demands placed on boys in the early years of elementary school can increase their overall stress levels. Scientists have known for years that boys and girls develop physically and intellectually at very different rates (time-line). Boys' fine motor skills—the ability to hold a pencil, for example—are usually considerably behind girls. They often learn to read later. At the same time, they're much more active—not the best combination for academic advancement. "Boys feel like school is a game rigged against them," says Michael Thompson, coauthor with Kindlon of "Raising Cain." "The things at which they excel—gross motor skills, visual and spatial skills, their exuberance—do not find as good a reception in school" as the things girls excel at. Boys (and girls) are also in academic programs at much younger ages than they used to be, increasing the chances that males will be forced to sit still before they are ready. The result, for many boys, is frustration, says Thompson: "By fourth grade, they're saying the teachers like girls better."

A second crisis point for boys occurs around the same time their sisters are stumbling, in early adolescence. By then, say Thompson and Kindlon, boys go one step further in their drive to be "real guys." They partake in a "culture of cruelty," enforcing male stereotypes on one another. "Anything tender, anything compassionate or too artis-

The Wonder (and Worry) Years

There may be no such thing as *child* development anymore. Instead, researchers are now studying each gender's development separately and discovering that boys and girls face very different sorts of challenges. Here is a rough guide to the major phases in their development.

Boys

0–3 years At birth, boys have brains that are 5% larger than girls' (size doesn't affect intelligence) and proportionately larger bodies—disparities that increase with age.

4–6 years The start of school is a tough time as boys must curb aggressive impulses. They lag behind girls in reading skills, and hyperactivity may be a problem.

Age 1	2	3	4	5	6	7

Girls

0–3 years Girls are born with a higher proportion of nerve cells to process information. More brain regions are involved in language production and recognition.

4–6 years Girls are well suited to school. They are calm, get along with others, pick up on social cues, and reading and writing come easily to them.

Trouble Spots: Where Boys Run Into Problems

Not all boys are the same, of course, but most rebel in predictable patterns and with predictable weapons: underachievement, aggression and drug and alcohol use. While taking chances is an important aspect of the growth process, it can lead to real trouble.

When Johnny Can't Read

Girls have reading disorders nearly as often as boys, but are able to overcome them. Disability rates, as identified by:

CLINICAL TESTS		SCHOOLS	
Boys	8.7%	Boys	13.6%
Girls	6.9%	Girls	3.2%

SOURCE: DR. SALLY SHAYWITZ, CONN. LONGITUDINAL STUDY

Suicidal Impulses

While girls are much more likely to try to kill themselves, boys are likelier to die from their attempts.

SUICIDE ATTEMPTS*		SUICIDE FATALITIES	
Boys	3,000	Boys	260
Girls	23,000	Girls	77

1995, AGES 5–14. *NEWSWEEK ESTIMATE. SOURCES: NCHS, CDC

Binge Drinking

Boys binge more on alcohol. Those who had five or more drinks in a row in the last two weeks:

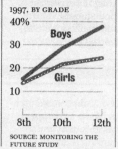

1997, BY GRADE

SOURCE: MONITORING THE FUTURE STUDY

Aggression That Turns to Violence

Boys get arrested three times as often as girls, but for some nonviolent crimes the numbers are surprisingly even.

Arrests of 10- to 17-year-olds: ■ Boys ▨ Girls

ESTIMATES, 1996. SOURCE: NAT'L CENTER FOR JUVENILE JUSTICE

Eating Disorders

Boys can also have eating disorders. Kids who used laxatives or vomited to lose weight:

1995, BY GRADE

SOURCES: CDC, YOUTH RISK BEHAVIOR SURVEY

---

tic is labeled gay," says Thompson. "The homophobia of boys in the 11, 12, 13 range is a stronger force than gravity."

Boys who refuse to fit the mold suffer. Glo Wellman of the California Parenting Institute in Santa Rosa has three sons, 22, 19 and 12. One of her boys, she says, is a "non-typical boy: he's very sensitive and caring and creative and artistic." Not surprisingly, he had the most difficulty growing up, she says. "We've got a long way to go to help boys . . . to have a sense that they can be anything they want to be."

In later adolescence, the once affectionate toddler has been replaced by a sulky stranger who often acts as though torture would be preferable to a brief exchange of words with Mom or Dad. Parents have to try even harder to keep in touch. Boys want and need the attention, but often just don't know how to ask for it. In a recent national poll, teenagers named their parents as their No. 1 heroes. Researchers say a strong parental bond is the most important protection against everything from smoking to suicide.

For San Francisco Chronicle columnist Adnir Lara, that message sank in when she was traveling to New York a few years ago with her son, then 15. She sat next to a woman who told her that until recently she would have had to change seats because she would not have been able to bear the pain of seeing a teenage son and mother together. The woman's son was 17 when his girlfriend dumped him; he went into the garage and killed himself. "This story made me aware that with a boy especially, you have to keep talking because they don't come and talk to you," she says. Lara's son is now 17; she also has a 19-year-old daughter. "My daughter stalked me. She followed me from room to room. She was yelling, but she was in touch. Boys don't do that. They leave the room and you don't know what they're feeling." Her son is now 6 feet 3. "He's a man. There are barriers. You have to reach through that and remember to ruffle his hair."

With the high rate of divorce, many boys are growing up without any adult men in their lives at all. Don Elium, coauthor of the best-selling 1992 book "Raising a Son," says that with troubled boys, there's often a common theme: distant, uninvolved fathers, and mothers who have taken on more responsibility to fill the gap. That was the case with Raymundo Infante Jr., a 16-year-old high-school junior, who lives with his mother, Mildred, 38, a hospital administrative assistant in Chicago, and his sister, Vanessa, 19. His parents divorced when he was a baby and he had little contact with his father until a year ago. The hurt built up—in sixth grade, Raymundo was so depressed that he told a classmate he wanted to kill himself. The classmate told the teacher, who told a counselor, and Raymundo saw a psychiatrist for a year. "I felt that I just wasn't good enough, or he just didn't want me," Raymundo says. Last year Raymundo finally confronted his dad, who works two jobs—in an office and on a construction crew—and accused him of caring more about work than about his son. Now the two spend time together on weekends and sometimes go shopping, but there is still a huge gap of lost years.

7–10 years While good at gross motor skills, boys trail girls in finer control. Many of the best students but also nearly all of the poorest ones are boys.

11–13 years A mixed bag. Dropout rates begin to climb, but good students start pulling ahead of girls in math skills and catching up some in verbal ones.

14–16 years Entering adolescence, boys hit another rough patch. Indulging in drugs, alcohol and aggressive behavior are common forms of rebellion.

8	9	10	11	12	13	14	15	16

7–10 years Very good years for girls. On average, they outperform boys at school, excelling in verbal skills while holding their own in math.

11–13 years The start of puberty and girls' most vulnerable time. Many experience depression; as many as 15% may try to kill themselves.

14–16 years Eating disorders are a major concern. Although anorexia can manifest itself as early as 8, it typically afflicts girls starting at 11 or 12; bulimia at 15.

SOURCES: DR. MICHAEL THOMPSON, BARNEY BRAWER. RESEARCH BY BILL VOURVOULIAS—NEWSWEEK

Black boys are especially vulnerable, since they are more likely than whites to grow up in homes without fathers. They're often on their own much sooner than whites. Black leaders are looking for alternatives. In Atlanta, the Rev. Tim McDonald's First Iconium Baptist Church just chartered a Boy Scout troop. "Gangs are so prevalent because guys want to belong to something," says McDonald. "We've got to give them something positive to belong to." Black educators like Chicagoan Jawanza Kunjufu think mentoring programs will overcome the bias against academic success as "too white." Some cities are also experimenting with all-boy classrooms in predominantly black schools.

Researchers hope that in the next few years, they'll come up with strategies that will help boys the way the work of Gilligan and others helped girls. In the meantime, experts say, there are some guidelines. Parents can channel their sons' energy into construc-tive activities, like team sports. They should also look for "teachable moments" to encourage qualities such as empathy. When Diane Fisher, a Cincinnati-area psychologist, hears her 8- and 10-year-old boys talking about "finishing somebody," she knows she has mistakenly rented a violent videogame. She pulls the plug and tells them: "In our house, killing people is not entertainment, even if it's just pretend."

Parents can also teach by example. New Yorkers Dana and Frank Minaya say they've never disciplined their 16-year-old son Walter in anger. They insist on resolving all disputes calmly and reasonably, without yelling. If there is a problem, they call an official family meeting "and we never leave without a big hug," says Frank. Walter tries to be open with his parents. "I don't want to miss out on any advice," he says.

Most of all, wise parents of boys should go with the flow. Cindy Lang, 36, a full-time mother in Woodside, Calif., is continually amazed by the relentless energy of her sons, Roger Lloyd, 12, and Chris, 9. "You accept the fact that they're going to involve themselves in risky behavior, like skateboarding down a flight of stairs. As a girl, I certainly wasn't skateboarding down a flight of stairs." Just last week, she got a phone call from school telling her that Roger Lloyd was in the emergency room because he had fallen backward while playing basketball and school officials thought he might have a concussion. He's fine now, but she's prepared for the next emergency: "I have a cell phone so I can be on alert." Boys will be boys. And we have to let them.

With KAREN SPRINGEN *in Chicago,*
PATRICIA KING *in San Francisco,*
PAT WINGERT *in Washington,* VERN E. SMITH
in Atlanta and ELIZABETH ANGELL *in New York*

Research in Review

The Education of Hispanics in Early Childhood: Of Roots and Wings

Eugene E. Garcia

As director of the Office of Bilingual Education and Minority Languages Affairs in the U.S. Department of Education, I sought to engage my *professional* experience and expertise as an educational researcher and my *personal* cultural and linguistic experience to address national education policy. The professional in me has been nurtured at some of the best educational institutions in the United States, while the nonprofessional has been nurtured in a large, rural, Mexican American family. Born in the United States and speaking Spanish as our first language for generations, our family included 10 children—four high school graduates and one college graduate.

Bringing these *personas* (Spanish for "persons") together was not as difficult as I had expected and the mixture was quite helpful to the wide variety of people I interacted with in my national role. Bringing together these personas, I communicated with individuals in ways not possible had I spoken only with one voice or separate voices.

This article presents my intersecting but distinct voices to help further our understanding of life in a diverse society—particularly of Hispanics growing up in the United States during their early childhood years. The historical pattern of the education of Hispanics in the United States is a continuous story of underachievement. It need not continue to be that way.

The three voices here address issues of the past, present, and future. They recognize the multiple selves that not only make up my own persona but those that are a

Eugene E. Garcia, Ph.D., is professor and dean of the Graduate School of Education at the University of California in Berkeley He continues to do research in areas related to language, culture, and schooling. He served as director of the Office of Bilingual Education and Minority Language Affairs in the U.S. Department of Education, 1993–95.

*This is one of a regular series of Research in Review columns. The column in this issue was invited by **Carol Seefeldt**, Ph.D., professor at the University of Maryland, College Park.*

reality for all of us. It is useful to recognize that we walk in varied and diverse cultures. There is great diversity within each individual, just as there is diversity among individuals and the many cultures they belong to or represent. We all live with diversity, some of us more than others. No one escapes this challenge or its advantages and disadvantages.

While English First, an organization committed to English as the official U.S. language, is passionately concerned that multilingualism will produce divisiveness and significant conflict, indigenous people whose roots in the Americas outdistance the "White man's" presence

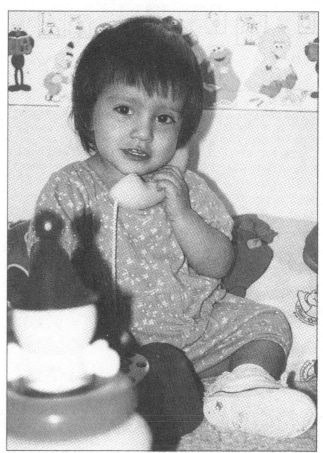

© Subjects and Predicates

The Voices

Eugene.

This voice often represents my intellectual upbringing and is recognized primarily by my academic credentials—degrees received and where and when, how successful I was in those environments, academic positions I have held and their status in the academic world, the empirical research I have done, my teaching, and, of course, the articles and books I have written. This set of experiences and accomplishments, at its core, attempts to expand in critical and strategic ways our broader understanding of language acquisition, teaching, learning, and schooling, and the specific relevance of these to language-minority populations—learners who come to the educational enterprise not knowing the language of that formal enterprise and particularly for students like me who are classified as Hispanic in the present jargon of educators and demographers. I did not begin my academic pursuits with this specific population in mind but have naturally gravitated toward using my professional skills to address issues of relevance to it, but not *only* to it.

Gene.

Other parts of me are more rooted in the nonacademic world, my social and cultural realities. I am a son, brother, husband, father, and so on. In such social and cultural roles, I have experienced a wonderful family environment, learning much from my father and mother—neither of whom ever had the opportunity to attend school. They taught me to respect them, my elders, my brothers and sisters, and others who were not members of my family—such as my teachers—or not like me, and, most of all, to respect myself. They never gave me a formal lesson about these things; they just lived them, in the harsh realities of poverty and the hard work any migrant or sharecropping family understands. This teaching and learning included experiences of outright racism and subtle institutional racism in which our language, color, and heritage were not always met with either individual or group respect. From these experiences and teachers emerged the voice of Gene (a name used most often by my family and friends).

This persona agreed to work as an undergraduate in the migrant camps, tutoring adults in English and related subjects so that they could earn the GED (general equivalency diploma). This persona realized early that he was different. I spoke primarily Spanish, my peers only English. I and my family worked in the fields; my peers and their families hired us to work in their fields. My peers enjoyed a much higher standard of living—I recall being embarrassed that my family did not take summer vacations or have running water and inside toilets. Quite honestly, most of the time, these differences did not weigh heavy on my mind or affect my behavior—I had lots of friends, some like me and others quite different from me.

It was likely more Gene than Eugene who accepted the invitation to join the Clinton administration and Secretary of Education Richard Riley in the Department of Education. In political/policy roles like this one, I realized that policymakers and practitioners of education do not always act based on the best theory, proven educational practices, or even promising educational innovations. They act mostly out of political interests. I realized the importance of the politics of education. Gene's voice is often dominated by these lessons, although Eugene is not totally unaffected by them.

mourn just as passionately the loss of their languages and cultures. As this country and the world shrinks communicatively, economically, socially, and intellectually, diversity is becoming harder to hide, but it has always been there. In the following pages, I address issues related to the education of Hispanics in early childhood with the varied voices within me.

The "Hispanic" debate

Eugene, Gene, and Gino realize that their voices are not alone nor are their views held by all Hispanics in the United States. Most critical of such views of the interactive relationship of "roots and wings" for Hispanics are two well-regarded and influential Hispanic authors, each in her or his own way refuting the importance of roots and the relationship of those roots to the educational development of Hispanics.

Linda Chavez, an adviser in the Reagan White House, journalist, commentator, and author of *Out of the Barrio: Toward a New Politics of Hispanic Assimilation*, suggests that

> Every previous group—Germans, Irish, Italians, Greeks, Jews, Poles—struggled to be accepted fully into the social, political and economic mainstream, sometimes against the opposition of a hostile majority. They learned the language, acquired education and skills, and adapted their own customs and traditions to fit an American context. (1991, 2)

The key for Hispanic success in America, Chavez argues, is minimizing the public/governmental recogni-

Gino.

Another voice within me is identified best by the endearing name that my mother used for me—Gino. In my large, quite Catholic family, to baptize a child is a distinct honor and, in recognition of that honor, *los padrinos*, the godparents, are given the authority to name the child. At my birth my parents selected my eldest sister and her husband to serve as my padrinos, and my sister was enchanted with the name Eugene. That is how I came to have a Greek name in a cohort of brothers and sisters named Antonio, Emelio, Cecelia, Caprianita, Abel, Federico, Tiburcio, and Christina, and born of parents named Lorenzo and Juanita. My mother could not pronounce *Eugene*, so to her and my immediate family I became Gino.

Gino carries a distinct sense of cultural "Hispanic-ness," "Chicanismo," "Latino-ness," or "Raza-ness." These concepts reflect a deep regard for the linguistic and cultural roots that foster identity—best exemplified by a lesson from my father:

> For farmworkers and sharecroppers, winter was a time to prepare for work—there was not much work during this period. One winter in the high plains of Colorado where I was born and raised, my father pointed to an *árbol*—a cottonwood tree. He asked, *Por qué puede vivir ese árbol en el frio del invierno y en el calor del varano?* (How can that tree survive the bitter cold winter and the harsh heat of summer?) My father was a man of few words—relatives often characterized him as quiet and shy—but when he spoke we all listened very carefully. I rambled on about how big and strong the tree was and how its limbs and trunk were like the strong arms and bodies of my elder brothers. Then he kindly provided a different perspective by referring to a common Spanish *dicho/consejo* (proverb): *El árbol fuerte tienen raíces maduros* (A strong tree has mature/strong roots).

In articulating this significant piece of the analysis that was absent from my youthful thoughts, my father made clear that without strong roots, strong trees are impossible—and we don't even see the roots! The roots of many Hispanics in this country have either been ignored or stripped away in the name of growing strong. Many have been directed to stop speaking Spanish, to perceive their culture as a "less-than" one, and to assimilate as quickly as possible so they can succeed in American society (Chavez 1991). Unfortunately, many have suffered the fate of the rootless tree—they have fallen socially, economically, academically, and culturally.

However, to Gino, my mother made it very clear: roots and their concomitant integrity and self-respect were not enough. She wanted the very best for all her children, certainly not the long and painful fieldwork that she had endured for a lifetime. She wanted us *bien educados*—to have a set of formal and marketable skills. She made very clear that children needed wings, like the wings she insisted we children grew every night upon falling asleep, so as to fly to heaven to be with God. "All children," she said, "are angels." In recent stories by Chicano author Victor Villaseñor, his mother elaborates further on this notion (Villaseñor 1991). She says that the children fly to God each night and station themselves as stars in His heaven. Both our mothers expressed a special regard for the sanctity of childhood and required children to have wings to perform their related roles. My mother emphasized that she could not provide the kind of wings that God and a good education could provide. She knew that the teachers and schools would have to take me further than she could personally. Education would need to provide the strong and elaborate wings for me to succeed where she often felt she had failed: "Go to school—strong wings like those of an eagle are also what you need in this world to raise your family and provide for them all that we have been unable to provide for you."

For Hispanics in this country, the emphasis on building wings in school has strategically focused on teaching English language skills: "Teach them English well and then they will succeed." Yet all educators realize that in today's information age, education must provide broad and strong intellectual wings related to fundamental linguistic, mathematical, scientific, and technological literacies. English literacy is important, but it is not enough. Gino feels that Hispanics, such as those he and his family represent, have been educationally shortchanged.

tion of Hispanic roots and the individual and governmental promotion of assimilation. She chides the federal government, particularly federal bilingual education programs, and Hispanic leaders for promoting permanent victim status and vying with Black Americans for the distinction of being the poorest, most segregated, and least educated minority, thereby entitling them to government handouts. These actions in turn, her conclusion advances, encourage Hispanics to maintain their language and culture and their specific identity in return for rewards handed out through affirmative action and federal, state, and local educational policies that thwart assimilation. This does not sound like my father's concern for the importance of roots or my mother's emphasis on wings.

Yet another Hispanic author, Richard Rodriguez, is very eloquent in his description of his upbringing in a Mexican home and a Catholic school where the English-speaking nuns literally beat the Spanish language and the "Hispanic-ness" out of him. His book *Hunger of Memory* (1982) describes this forced assimilation, painful as it was, that propelled him to new heights of educational achievement. Although he himself never articulates the conclusion, he leaves open the suggestion that such treatment of Hispanics is exactly what they need to get over their "problems." Eugene, Gene, and Gino reach a very different conclusion in this discussion. But you should know that the debate exists.

The following discussion indirectly addresses this debate but includes an expanded research-related discussion of vulnerability factors both within and outside the education arena along with data related to the "effective" treatment of this growing population of young children and families. The discussion addresses the following:

1. An overall demographic assessment of factors related to the schooling of culturally diverse populations, including issues of poverty, family stability, and immigrant status;

2. A particular analysis of the challenges associated with the growing number of language-minority students who are Hispanic—children who come to school with limited or no proficiency in English; and

3. A presentation of conceptual and empirical perspectives that sets the stage for a more informed approach to the education of Hispanics in early childhood.

The research

The demographic picture

The Census Bureau in its attempts to provide clarifying demographic information never fails in confusing us. In documenting the racial and ethnic heterogeneity of our country's population, it has arrived at a set of highly confusing terms that place individuals in separate exclusionary categories: White, White non-Hispanic, Black, Hispanic (with some five subcategories of Hispanics). Unfortunately, outside of the census meaning of these terms, they are for the most part highly ambiguous and nonrepresentative of the true heterogeneity which the Census Bureau diligently seeks to document. Therefore, it is important to note at the outset of this discussion that these categories are useful only as the most superficial reflection of our nation's true diversity. I do not know many census-identified "Whites," "Blacks," or "Hispanics" who believe they are "White," "Black," and so on, but given the forced-choice responses allowed them in census questionnaires, they are constrained by these choices.

Having consented to this significant restriction regarding efforts to document population diversity in this country, I still must conclude that an examination of the available data provides a fuzzy but useful portrait of our society and the specific circumstances of various groups within our nation's boundaries. That sketch is one of consummate vulnerability for non-White and Hispanic (usually referred to as "minority") families, children, and students. On almost every indicator, non-White and Hispanic families, children, and "at-risk" students are likely to fall into the lowest quartile on indicators of "well-being": family stability, family violence, family income, child health and development, and educational achievement. Yet this population has grown significantly in the last two decades and will grow substantially in the decades to come. The table ("Hispanic Demographics") summarizes these factors for census-derived information on Hispanics.

The demographic transformation that has become more evident in the last decade was easily foreseen at least that long ago. Our schools' future student profile is as predictable: in a mere 40 years, White students will be a minority in every category of public education as we know it today. Unfortunately, the emerging student majority of ethnic and racial background continues to be at risk in today's social institutions. The National Center for Children in Poverty (1995) provided a clear and alarming demographic window on these at-risk populations. Of the 21.9 million children under six years of age in 1990 who will move slowly through society's institutions—family, schools, the workplace—five million (25%) were living in poverty. Although less than 30% of all children under six years of age were non-White, more than 50% of the children in poverty were non-White. In addition, these children continued to live in racial/ethnic isolation. Some 56% lived in racially isolated neighborhoods in 1966; 72% resided in such neighborhoods in 1994; 61% of children in poverty live in concentrations of poverty where 20% of the population is poor.

High school or equivalent completion rates are alarming for these emerging majority student populations. In 1994 the high school completion rate for the U.S. population was 81.1% for 19-year-olds, 86.5% for 24-year-olds, and a very respectable 86% for 29-year-olds. For Blacks and Hispanics the rate of completion in all age groups was close to 60% (U.S. Department of Commerce 1990). With regard to academic achievement, in 1994, 30% of 13-year-old students were one grade level below the norm on standardized achievement measures. However, this differed significantly for emerging majority and White students: 27% for White students, 40% for Hispanic students, and 46% for Black students.

The qualitative description of education presented above is further affirmed for Hispanics by other quantitative descriptions. A recent study reported by de Leon Siantz (1996) uses descriptive data from the Hispanic Health and Nutrition Examination Survey, a national effort sampling stratified populations of Mexican American, Puerto Rican, and Cuban American families in three U.S. regions (southwest, northeast, and

While English First, an organization committed to English as the official U.S. language, is passionately concerned that multilingualism will produce divisiveness and significant conflict, indigenous people whose roots in the Americas outdistance the "White man's" presence mourn just as passionately the loss of their languages and cultures.

Hispanic Demographics

General demographic character

- Of the approximately 22.7 million Hispanics in the continental United States, the following information characterizes the population's ethnic diversity.

Country/area of origin	Number (in millions)	%
Mexico	14.6	64.3
Puerto Rico	2.4	10.6
Central/South America	3.0	13.4
Cuba	1.1	4.7
Other Hispanic countries	1.6	7.0

- 89.5% of the total Hispanic population in the United States is concentrated in three states: California (26%), Texas (25.5%), and New Mexico (38%). Other states with significant Hispanic populations are Arizona (19%), Colorado (13%), Florida (12%), and New York (12%).
- Average age of the Hispanic population in 1993 was 26.7 years.
- 200,000 Hispanics immigrate legally to the United States annually; Hispanics are 40% of all legal immigrants. (An estimated 200,000 Hispanics immigrate illegally.)
- The Hispanic population grew by 53% from 1980 to 1990, compared to the 9.8% growth in the general U.S. population.
- 17 million Hispanics report speaking Spanish in the home.
- 90% of Hispanics live in metropolitan areas; 52% in central cities.

Indices of "vulnerability"

- Median family income has fluctuated for Hispanics (1982—$23,814; 1991—$24,614; 1992—$23,912), remaining below that of non-Hispanics (1982—$35,075; 1991—$38,127; 1992—$38,015).
- In 1992, 26.2% of Hispanic families lived below the poverty line, compared to 27.2% in 1982. (In 1992, 10.4% of non-Hispanic White families lived below the poverty line.)
- In 1993, 1,239,094 Hispanic families (23.3%) were maintained by a female head-of-household (an increase of .5% from 1983 when it was 22.8% or 827,184); 48.8% of these households lived below the poverty line.
- 72.9% of Hispanics hold unskilled and semiskilled jobs, compared to 50.8% of non-Hispanics.

Education

- Approximately 50% of Hispanics leave school prior to graduation (70% by 10th grade).
- 38% of Hispanics are held back at least one grade.
- 50% of Hispanics are overage at grade 12.
- 90% of Hispanic students are in urban districts.
- 82% of Hispanic students attend segregated schools.
- Hispanics are significantly below national norms on academic achievement tests of reading, math, science, social science, and writing at grades 3, 7, and 11, generally averaging one to two grade levels below the norm. At grade 11, Hispanics average a grade 8 achievement level on these tests.
- Hispanics are placed in special education services six times more often than the general student population.

Sources: U.S. Bureau of the Census, *The Hispanic Population in the United States: March 1993* (Washington DC: U.S. Government Printing Office, 1993); U.S. Bureau of the Census, *Social and Economic Characteristics in the US: 1990 Census of the Population* (Washington DC: GPO, 1990); M.A. Reddy, *Statistical Record of Hispanic Americans* (Michigan: Gale Research, Inc., 1993); and U.S. Immigration and Naturalization Service, *Statistical Yearbook of the Immigration and Naturalization, 1993* (Washington DC: GPO, 1994).

---

southeast). This study reports very small differences in family well-being and child well-being indicators across these groups and regions. The Hispanic population was described as growing, youthful, poor, lacking parental care, and at high risk for AIDS.

Moreover, recent national Head Start data (Phillips & Cabrera 1996) indicate that only one-third of the programs had an enrollment characterized by a single language, with a range of 1 to 32 languages represented in programs, while 72% of programs had enrollments of between 2 and 3 languages. The predominant languages represented in these programs were Spanish and English.

Combined with the contemporary educational zeitgeist that embraces excellence and equity for all students, attention to the Hispanic children, families, and students has been significant. Following this theme are recent analyses and recommendations: the California State Department of Education efforts to better train infant and toddler caregivers in state-supported programs (California State Department of Education 1992), the U.S. Department of Education reforms for federally funded education programs (Garcia & Gonzales 1995), the National Academy of Education discussion of standards-based reform (McLaughlin & Shepard 1995), the National

Research Council's Roundtable on Head Start Research efforts to provide an issue analysis of research needed to produce a thriving future for Head Start for a highly diverse population of children and families (Phillips & Cabrera 1996), the National Council of Teachers of English and the International Reading Association's treatment of language arts standards (NCTE/ IRA 1996), and NAEYC's position statement on linguistic and cultural diversity (NAEYC 1996). All of these publications have attended to the vulnerabilities of Hispanics and have addressed issues of language and culture in light of this country's past treatment of this population and the present conceptual and empirical understanding of the need for institutions to be more responsive. Much of this thinking about policy and practice is based on the issues and research findings that follow.

Our past approach: Americanization

Historically, Americanization has been a prime institutional education objective for Hispanic young children and their families (Elam 1972; Gonzales 1990; Garcia 1994). Schooling practices were adapted whenever the Hispanic student population rose to significant numbers in a community. This adaptation resulted in special programs applied to both children and adults in urban and rural schools and communities. The desired effect of Americanizing was to socialize and acculturate the targeted diverse community. In essence, if public efforts could teach these children and families English and American values, then social, economic, and educational failure could be averted. Ironically, social economists have argued that this effort was coupled with systematic efforts to maintain disparate conditions between Anglos and minority populations. Indeed, more than anything else, past attempts at addressing the Black, Hispanic, Indian, Asian, etc., "educational problem" have actually preserved the political and economic subordination of these communities (Spencer 1988). Coming from a sociological theory of assimilation, Americanization has traditionally been recognized as a solution to the problem of immigrants and ethnicity in the modern industrialized United States. Linda Chavez (1991) continues to champion this solution for Hispanics.

The Americanization solution has not worked. Moreover, it depends on the flawed notion of group culture. The Americanization solution presumes that culturally different children are, as a group, culturally flawed. To fix them individually, we must act on the individual as a member of a cultural group. By changing the values, language, and so forth of the group, we will have the solution to the educational underachievement of students representing these groups. The challenge facing educators regarding Hispanic students is not to Ameri-

> **Part of the current push for excellence and equity for all students has been increased attention to Hispanic children.**

canize them but to understand them and act responsively to the specific diversity they bring and the educational goal of academic success for all students.

Early childhood practices that meet the challenge

The debate regarding early childhood education of Hispanic students in the United States has centered on the role of cultural and developmental appropriateness of curriculum and pedagogy, along with Spanish language use and the development of English in these early childhood settings. Discussion of this issue has included cross-disciplinary dialogues involving psychology, linguistics, sociology, politics, and education. (For a more thorough discussion of these issues, see Cummins 1979, Troike 1981, Baker and deKanter 1983, Garcia 1983, Willig 1985, Rossell and Ross 1986, Hakuta and Gould 1987, August and Garcia 1988, Crawford 1989, Baker 1990, Kagan and Garcia 1991, Garcia 1994, Cole 1995, Garcia and Gonzalez 1995, and Rossell and Baker 1996.) The central theme of these discussions relates to the specific role of the native language.

Supporters of culturally sensitive and native language instruction are at one end in this debate. Proponents of this specially designed instructional strategy recommend the utilization of the child's native language and mastery of that language prior to the introduction of an English, more mainstream curriculum. This approach (Cardenas 1986; Fishman 1989) suggests that the competencies in the native culture and language, particularly about academic learning, provide important cognitive and social foundations for second-language learning and academic learning in general—you really only learn to read once. At the other end in this debate, introduction to the English curriculum is recommended at the onset of the student's schooling experience, with minimal use of the native language. This specially designed approach calls for English language "leveling" by instructional staff (to facilitate the understanding on behalf of the student with limited English proficiency) combined with an English-as-a-second-language component. In essence, the earlier the student confronts English and the more times he or she is confronted, the greater the English linguistic advantage (Rossell 1992; Rossell & Baker 1996).

The native language debate has ignored the contributions of Friere (1970), Bernstein (1971), Cummins (1979, 1986), Heath (1986), Ogbu (1986), Trueba (1987), Levin (1988), Tharp (1989), Rose (1989), Moll (1991), Garcia

(1995), and Krashen (1996), who have suggested that the schooling vulnerability of such students must be understood within the broader contexts of this society's treatment of these students and their families in and out of educational institutions. That is, no quick fix is likely under social and early education conditions that mark the Hispanic-language minority student for special treatment of his or her language difference without consideration for the psychological and social-cultural circumstances in which that student resides. This is not to suggest that the linguistic character of this student is insignificant. Instead, it warns us against the isolation of this single attribute as the only variable of importance. This more comprehensive view of the education, particularly early childhood education, includes an understanding of the relationship between home and school, the sociocultural incongruities between the two, and the resulting effects on learning and achievement (Kagan & Garcia 1991; Garcia 1994).

Recent research findings have redefined the nature of the educational vulnerability of Hispanic children, destroyed common stereotypes and myths, and laid a foundation on which to reconceptualize present educational practices and launch new initiatives. This foundation recognizes the homogeneity and heterogeneity within and between diverse student populations. No one set of descriptions or prescriptions will suffice; however, a set of commonalties deserves particular attention.

Research focusing on early childhood classrooms, teachers, administrators, and parents revealed an interesting set of perspectives on the treatment of children

dents ("Everyone will learn to read in my classroom") and also served as advocates for their students. They rejected any conclusion that their students were intellectually or academically disadvantaged.

Parents expressed a high level of satisfaction and appreciation regarding their children's educational experience in these classrooms. All indicated or implied that academic success was tied to their children's future economic success. Anglo and Hispanic parents were both quite involved in the formal parent-supported activities of the schools. However, Anglo parents' attitudes were much more in line with a child advocacy view—somewhat distrustful of the school's specific interest in doing what was right for their child. Conversely, Hispanic parents expressed a high level of trust for the teaching and administrative staff.

This recent research addresses some significant practice questions regarding effective academic environments for Hispanic children:

1. *What role did native language instruction play?*

Teachers considered native language use in daily instruction as key. They implemented an articulated native language and literacy effort that recognized language as a tool for learning and not as a learning objective.

2. *Who were the key players in this effective schooling drama?*

Administrators and parents played important roles. However, teachers were the key players. They achieved

> **Be an advocate for our linguistically and culturally diverse children and families by nurturing, celebrating, and challenging them. They do not need our pity for what they do not have; they, like any individual and family, require our respect and the use of what they bring as a resource.**

(Hakuta & Gould 1987; Rose 1989; Garcia 1991; Moll 1991; Ramirez et al. 1991; Wong Fillmore 1991; Garcia 1994; Cole 1995). Classroom teachers were highly committed to the educational success of their students; perceived themselves as instructional innovators utilizing "new" learning theories and instructional philosophies to guide their practice; continued to be involved in professional development activities, including participation in small-group support networks; had a strong, demonstrated commitment to student-home communication (several teachers were utilizing a weekly parent interaction format); and felt they had the autonomy to create or change the instruction and curriculum in their classrooms even if it did not meet the district guidelines exactly. Significantly, these teachers "adopted" their students. They had high academic expectations for all their stu-

the educational confidence of their peers and supervisors. They worked to organize instruction, create new instructional environments, assess effectiveness, and advocate for their students. They were proud of their students, reassuring but consistently demanding. They rejected any notion of linguistic, cultural, or intellectual inferiority regarding their students. They were child advocates.

Imbedded in the activities of these educational enterprises for Hispanic students was the understanding that language, culture, and their accompanying values are acquired in the home and community environment; that children come to school with some knowledge about what language is, how it works, and what it is used for; that children learn higher-level metacognitive and metalinguistic skills as they engage in socially meaningful activities; and that children's development and learning are best understood in the interaction of linguistic, sociocultural, and cognitive knowledge and experiences. In particular for students who did not speak English, their native language was perceived as a resource instead of a problem. **In general terms, this research *suggests* moving away from a needs assessment and non-English-proficiency-as-a-problem approach to an asset inventory and native-language-as-a-resource approach.**

Conclusion

Effective early education curriculum, instructional strategies, and teaching staffs recognize that development and learning have their roots in sharing expertise and experiences through multiple avenues of communication. Further, effective early childhood education for linguistically and culturally diverse children encourages them to take risks, construct meaning, and seek reinterpretation of knowledge within the compatible social contexts. Within this nurturing environment, skills are tools for acquiring knowledge, not ends in themselves, and the language of the child is an incredible resource. The curriculum recognizes that any attempt to address the needs of these students in a deficit or subtractive mode is counterproductive. Instead, this knowledge base recognizes, conceptually, that educators must be additive in an approach to these students.

Recent statements about these challenges reinforce this charge. The National Council of Teachers of English and the International Reading Association (NCTE/IRA) in their enunciation of standards for English language arts recognize that

> Students develop an understanding of and respect for diversity in language use, patterns, and dialects across cultures, ethnic groups, geographic regions, and social roles.
> Students whose first language is not English make use of their first language to develop competency in the English language arts and to develop understanding of content across the curriculum.
> Celebrating our shared beliefs and traditions are not enough; we also need to honor that which is distinctive in the many groups that make up our nation. (1996, 3)

NAEYC echoes these same concerns in its position statement related to educational practices regarding linguistic and cultural diversity in early childhood:

> Early childhood educators can best help linguistically and culturally diverse children and their families by acknowledging and responding to the importance of the child's home language and culture. Administrative support for bilingualism as a goal is necessary within the educational setting. Educational practices should focus on educating children toward the "school culture" while preserving and respecting the diversity of the home language and culture that each child brings to the early learning setting. (1996, 12)

In the present era, this challenge must be met within the context of philosophical, ideological, and political debates surrounding our professional efforts to do things right and to do the right things for all children and families. Eugene, Gene, and Gino encourage you in these efforts, particularly for Hispanics, recognizing the significance of your role and regard for their roots and wings. Here are five practical applications that teachers can use to meet this challenge:

1. Know the linguistic and cultural diversity of your students. Like an ethnographer, be very observant and seek information regarding the languages and cultures represented by the children, families, and communities you serve. Learn to pronounce your student's name as the family pronounces it. For each student write down linguistic and cultural information so it becomes as important as the other things you write down.

2. Take on the new challenge of serving linguistic and culturally diverse children with resolve, commitment, and *ganas* (high motivation). Children and families will appreciate your willingness to learn their language—even small phrases of their language. They will also recognize paternalistic attitudes—attitudes that convey the notion that their children should negate their native language and culture.

3. Be up to date on the new knowledge base. We know so much more now about how better to deal with diversity. Most of us grew up or received our formal training in eras when diversity was not an issue. Incorporate personal and formal stories, games, songs, and poems from various cultures and languages into the curriculum.

4. Share the knowledge with the educational and noneducational community. There is so much strong feeling among educators and the general public that diversity is a problem and must be eliminated. Be clear about how you deal with diversity in ways that respect the need for common culture, shared culture, and individual integrity.

5. Above all else, care about and be an advocate for our linguistically and culturally diverse children and families by nurturing, celebrating, and challenging them. They do not need our pity or remorse for what they do not have; they, like any individual and family, require our respect and the use of what they bring as a resource.

References

August, D., & E. Garcia. 1988. *Language minority education in the United States: Research, policy and practice.* Chicago: Charles C. Thomas.

Baker, K.A. 1990. Bilingual education's 20-year failure to provide rights protection for language-minority students. In *Children at risk: Poverty, minority status and other issues in educational equity*, eds. A. Barona & E. Garcia, 29–52. Washington, DC: National Association of School Psychologists.

Baker, K.A., & A.A. deKanter. 1983. An answer from research on bilingual education. *American Education* 56: 157–69.

Bernstein, B. 1971. A sociolinguistic approach to socialization with some reference to educability. In *Class, codes and control: Theoretical studies towards a sociology of language*, ed. B. Bernstein, 146–71. London: Routledge & Kegan Paul.

California State Department of Education. 1992. *The program for infant/toddler caregivers: A guide to language development and communication.* Sacramento: Author.

Cardenas, J. 1986. The role of native-language instruction in bilingual education. *Phi Delta Kappan* 67: 359–63.

Chavez, L. 1991. *Out of the barrio: Toward a new politics of Hispanic assimilation.* New York: Basic.

Cole, R.W. 1995. *Educating everybody's children: What research and practice say about improving achievement.* Alexandria, VA: Association for Supervision and Curriculum Development.

Crawford, J. 1989. *Bilingual education: History, politics, theory, and practice.* Trenton, NJ: Crane.

Cummins, J. 1979. Linguistic independence and the educational development of bilingual children. *Review of Educational Research* 19: 222–51.

Cummins, J. 1986. Empowering minority students: A framework for intervention. *Harvard Educational Review* 56 (1): 18–35.

de Leon Siantz, M. 1996. Profile of the Hispanic child. In *Hispanic voices: Hispanic health educators speak out,* ed. S. Torres, 134–49. New York: NLN Press.

Elam, S. 1972. Acculturation and learning problems of Puerto Rican children. In *The Puerto Rican community and its children on the mainland,* eds. F. Corradasco & E. Bucchini, 116–38. Metuchen, NJ: Scarecrow.

Fishman, J. 1989. Bias and anti-intellectualism: The frenzied fiction of "English only." In *Language and ethnicity in minority sociolinguistic perspective,* ed. Multilingual Matters, 214–37. London: Multilingual Matters.

Friere, P. 1970. *Pedagogy of the oppressed.* New York: Seabury.

Garcia, E. 1983. *Bilingualism in early childhood.* Albuquerque: University of New Mexico Press.

Garcia, E. 1991. *Education of linguistically and culturally diverse students: Effective instructional practices. Education Report #1.* Washington, DC: Center of Applied Linguistics and the National Center for Research on Cultural Diversity and Second Language Learning.

Garcia, E. 1993. Language, culture and education. In *Review of research in education,* ed. L. Darling-Hammond, 51–97. Washington, DC: American Educational Research Association.

Garcia, E. 1994. *Understanding and meeting the challenge of student diversity.* Boston: Houghton Mifflin.

Garcia, E. 1995. Educating Mexican American students: Past treatments and recent developments in theory, research, policy, and practice. In *Handbook of research on multicultural education,* eds. J. Banks & C.A. McGee Banks, 372–426. New York: Macmillan.

Garcia, E., & R. Gonzalez. 1995. Issues in systemic reform for culturally and linguistically diverse students. *College Record* 96(3): 418-31.

Gonzalez, R. 1990. *Chicano education in the segregation era: 1915–1945.* Philadelphia: Balch Institute.

Hakuta, K., & L.J. Gould. 1987. Synthesis of research on bilingual education. *Educational Leadership* 44 (6): 39–45.

Heath, S.B. 1986. Sociocultural contexts of language development. In *Beyond language: Social and cultural factors in schooling language minority students,* ed. California Department of Education, 143–86. Los Angeles: Evaluation, Dissemination, and Assessment Center, California State University.

Kagan, S.L., & E. Garcia. 1991. Educating culturally and linguistically diverse preschoolers: moving the agenda. *Early Childhood Research Quarterly* 6: 427–43.

Krashen, S. 1996. *Under attack: The case against bilingual education.* Culver City, CA: Language Education Associates.

Levin, I. 1988. *Accelerated schools for at-risk students.* CPRE Research Report Series RR-010. New Brunswick, NJ: Rutgers University Center for Policy Research in Education.

McLaughlin, M.W., & L.A. Shepard. 1995. *Improving education through standard-based reform: A report by the national academy of education panel of standards-based education reform.* Stanford, CA: National Academy of Education.

Moll, L. 1991. *Funds of knowledge for change: Developing mediating connections between homes and classrooms.* Paper presented at the conference on "Literacy, Identity and Mind," University of Michigan, Ann Arbor.

NAEYC. 1996. NAEYC position statement: Responding to linguistic and cultural diversity—recommendations for effective early childhood education. *Young Children* 51 (2): 4-12.

National Center for Children in Poverty. 1995. *Welfare reform seen from a children's perspective.* New York: Columbia University School of Public Health.

NCTE/IRA (National Council of Teachers of English and International Reading Association). 1996. *Standards for the English language arts.* Urbana, IL: NCTE.

Ogbu, J. 1986. The consequences of the American caste system. In *The school achievement of minority children: New perspectives,* ed. U. Neisser, 73–114. Hillsdale, NJ: Erlbaum.

Phillips, D.A., & N.J. Cabrera. 1996. *Beyond the blueprint: Directions for research on Head Start's families.* Washington, DC: National Academy Press.

Ramirez, J.D., S.D. Yuen, D.R. Ramey, & D.J. Pasta. 1991. *Final Report: Longitudinal study of structured English immersion strategy, early-exit and late-exit transitional bilingual education programs for language-minority children.* San Mateo, CA: Aguirre International.

Rodriguez, R. 1982. *Hunger of memory.* New York: Bantam.

Rose, M. 1989. *Lives on the boundary.* New York: Free Press.

Rossell, C. 1992. Nothing matters? A critique of the Ramirez, et al. longitudinal study of instructional programs for language minority children. *Journal of the National Association for Bilingual Education* 16 (1–2): 159–86.

Rossell, C., & K. Baker. 1996. The education effectiveness of bilingual education. *Research in the Teaching of English* 30: 7–74.

Rossell, C., & J.M. Ross. 1986. *The social science evidence on bilingual education.* Boston: Boston University.

Spencer, D. 1988. Transitional bilingual education and the socialization of immigrants. *Harvard Educational Review* 58 (2): 133-53.

Tharp, R.G. 1989. *Challenging cultural minds.* London: Cambridge University Press.

Troike, R.C. 1981. Synthesis of research in bilingual education. *Educational Leadership* 38: 498-504.

Trueba, H.T. 1987. *Success or failure? Learning and the language minority student.* Scranton, PA: Harper & Row.

U.S. Department of Commerce. 1990. *The Hispanic population in the United States: March 1989.* Washington, DC: GPO.

Villaseñor, V. 1991. *Rain of gold.* New York: Delta.

Willig, A.C. 1985. A meta-analysis of selected studies on effectiveness of bilingual education. *Review of Educational Research* 55 (33): 269–317.

Wong Fillmore, L. 1991. When learning a second language means losing a first. *Early Childhood Research Quarterly* 6 (3): 323–46.

Unit 3

Key Points to Consider

❖ If you were designing the best space possible for the development of toddlers, what would it include?

❖ Comment on the idea that homework in the primary grades does not help children learn.

❖ What does inclusion mean? Brainstorm three activities in a preschool classroom for children with limited motor abilities.

 **Links**   # www.dushkin.com/online/

13. **American Academy of Pediatrics (AAP)**
    http://www.aap.org
14. **Canada's Schoolnet Staff Room**
    http://www.schoolnet.ca/home/e/
15. **Classroom Connect**
    http://www.classroom.net
16. **ERIC Clearinghouse on Disabilities and Gifted Education**
    http://www.cec.sped.org/gifted/gt-faqs.htm
17. **National Resource Center for Health and Safety in Child Care**
    http://nrc.uchsc.edu
18. **Online Innovation Institute**
    http://oii.org

These sites are annotated on pages 4 and 5.

Educational practices with young children seem to be always changing, yet always the same. The notion of what is good practice in early childhood education varies between two extremes. One approach is traditional, with an emphasis on skill and drill methods, segmented curriculum, and accuracy in work. The other approach, which includes curricular integration and an emphasis on play, is more constructivist. These two approaches coexist in early childhood but are based in very different philosophies of how teaching and learning occur. So the dilemma is to determine which educational practice is most appropriate for children.

"Simply Sensational Spaces: A Multi-"S" Approach to Toddler Environments" describes how good practice looks for very young children. The authors emphasize simplicity in room arrangement by creating two zones—one for large-motor skills and one for dramatic play. Softness is also important, both in equipment selections and in the environment. The curriculum focuses on discovery learning through the senses, with a variety of stimulating activities. Space for toddlers to learn is not a scaled-down version of preschool but is distinctly different, geared to the developmental needs of toddlers.

An intriguing finding from research is that one educational practice may not be as effective as we have traditionally thought. That practice is dreaded homework. The effect of homework on young learners may be particularly damaging to future learning, especially if the work is "busywork" and doesn't reinforce new concepts. The result of bad homework is a decrease in motivation to learn and an increase in poor study habits. Sharon Begley gives us something to ponder in "Homework Doesn't Help," a brief article from a popular news magazine.

Good practice means teaching children, not curriculum. "From Philosophy to Practice in Inclusive Early Childhood Programs" is a description of a conceptual framework for combining developmentally appropriate practices with early childhood special education in order to teach all children well. The authors are careful to define inclusion as "all children attending the same program, all of the time." No child is pulled out for special programs, instead, each child is given the appropriate support for success in the setting. Effective inclusion practices begin with functional goals that are designed with families. The services provided for the child are multidisciplinary. The article ends with a helpful example of how to merge developmentally appropriate practice with special education practices.

The research article for this unit is "Inclusion of Young Children with Special Needs in Early Childhood Education: The Research Base." It was chosen for its comprehensive review of recent literature on inclusion at the early childhood level. The authors use an "ecological systems" approach for examining the perspectives of family, social policy, community, and culture. Each of these systems affects the way inclusion occurs in actual practice. For instance, some factors in the community may act as barriers to inclusion of young children in programs. It is important to discover whether policies and community practices help facilitate or hinder the development of children with special needs.

Good practice, appropriate for children's development and based on active play, has no shortcuts and cannot be trivialized. It takes careful thought and planning, using the latest knowledge of early childhood education, to make curriculum and practice choices. By working out specifics of routines and procedures, curriculum, and assessment suitable for young children, the early childhood professional strengthens skills in decision making. These are crucial tasks for a teacher interested in developmentally appropriate practice.

It may cause anxiety, but day care can benefit kids

Day care has small but significant effects on both cognitive development and the mother-child relationship, new research shows.

By Beth Azar
Monitor staff

High-quality day care may be good for a child's cognitive development, according to several new studies. In fact, some new research implies that children who spend their early years in center-based care perform better on tests of language and mathematics than children who stay home with their mothers.

Such studies are beginning to answer questions that have plagued parents since women started working outside the home: Does the amount of time spent in child care or the quality of child care affect a child's development?

Psychologists have tried to design studies to measure the effect of day care above and beyond other factors known to affect development, including a child's innate predispositions, aspects of parental care and socioeconomic status.

Although mounting evidence suggests that day care has had far less of an impact on child development than these factors, there also seem to be small but significant effects of day care on both cognitive development and the mother-child relationship.

The biggest and best designed study to date, funded by the National Institute on Child Health and Human Development (NICHD), released findings in April showing that:

• Children in high-quality day care—care that provides a stimulating environment—do as well on cognitive and language tests as children who stay home with their mothers, regardless of how many hours a day they spend in such care.

• Mothers are slightly more affectionate and attentive to their children the less time their children spend in day care.

• Mothers are slightly more affectionate and attentive to their children the higher quality the day care setting.

The study was conducted by a team of 29 researchers—mostly psychologists—who are funded by a 7-year grant from NICHD. They have been following 1,300 families and their children from 10 sites since 1991, beginning when the children were one month old. The results on cognitive development and mother-child interaction are from data collected when the children were 15 months, 24 months and 36 months old.

Stimulating conversation

The quality of the interaction between day-care providers and the children in their care is the most important aspect of day care for fostering children's cognitive skills, reported the NICHD researchers at the annual meeting of the Society for Research on Child Development in April.

Children whose care-givers asked them questions, engaged them in conversation and responded to them when they spoke, scored highest on measures of cognitive and language ability. These child-care variables contributed between 1.3 percent and 3.6 percent of the variance in cognitive and language development—a rather small, but significant effect, said Sarah Friedman, PhD, NICHD coordinator of the study and one of its investigators.

Another recent study conducted in Sweden found that children in center-based child care scored significantly higher on tests of language skill and math proficiency than children cared for by their mothers or in family-based day care.

The study, conducted by Swedish researchers Anders Broberg, PhD, and

Philip Hwang, PhD, of Göteborgs University, and NICHD researchers Holger Wessels, PhD, and Michael Lamb, PhD, followed 146 children from age 16 months to age 8. The researchers regularly measured the quality of home and out-of-home care, child temperament and verbal abilities during the preschool years. And they measured cognitive ability when the children were in second grade.

As in the NICHD study, the researchers found that children who had more interaction with their caregivers scored better on tests of verbal ability. The best predictor of mathematical ability were aspects of care such as small day-care groups, a small ratio of children to caregivers and a narrow range of ages within the child-care group.

The bottom line is that "child care *per se* is not placing children at a disadvantage," said Friedman. "And those are wonderful results."

Relationships with mom

Based on results released last year, the NICHD study concluded that child care did not damage the security of children's attachment to their mothers at age 15 months, provided the children received relatively sensitive care from their mothers. In the most recent analysis, the study found a small link between the amount of time children spend in day care and how affectionate and attentive their mothers were when the children were age 3.

In particular, mothers were slightly less attentive, less responsive and less positively affectionate with their children, the more time their children spent in out-of-home care when they were very young, said University of Virginia psychologist Robert Pianta, PhD, one of the study investigators. But of all the possible predictors of the mother-child relationship, day care only accounted for about 1 percent, he added.

As for quality of day care, the more positive the relationship between children and their day-care providers, the more involved and sensitive mothers were to their children.

"Both quantity and quality of child care has a significant but small effect on maternal attachment," said Pianta.

One flaw in the NICHD study is the fact that the researchers did not systematically measure the quality of home-based care for children who received full-time care from their mothers, said Pianta. So there is no way to compare low-quality mother care with high-quality mother care or low-quality out-of-home care.

The researchers did, however, look to see if high-quality care could act as a buffer for children at high risk of poor development because of home factors such as poverty or mothers' depressive symptoms. For example, they looked to see if poor children in high-quality care had a better relationship with their mothers than poor children in low-quality care.

"We found slim to no buffer effects of high quality care for these children," said Pianta.

They also found that low-quality care did not put high-risk children at significantly more risk than high-risk children in high-quality care, he said.

The NICHD research group is conducting the same types of analyses for cognitive and language development, said Friedman.

In an analysis from the study now in press, the researchers found that at age 15 months, poor children in home-based day care received lower quality care than children from more affluent homes who were in home-based day care. However, of the children in child-care centers, those from the most affluent and the poorest homes received higher-quality care than children from homes just above the poverty level. This implies that government day-care subsidies provide a safety net for the poorest families while the near-poor must settle for less-expensive, lower quality care, said the researchers.

The next phase of the study will look at how training and experience of day-care providers affect child development, said Pianta. And they still have several years worth of data to analyze before they make any final conclusions about the long-term effect of child care on children.

More complex analyses will be welcome, said Harvard University psychologist Jerome Kag[a]n, PhD. This kind of research has therapeutic value for parents who are worried about how child care influences their children.

But it also highlights the need for more research on the complex interactions between social class, temperament and quality of care and the impact of those interactions on a child's behavior, anxiety level, and language and cognitive abilities, he added.

Infants and Toddlers

Meeting Basic Needs: Health and Safety Practices in Feeding and Diapering Infants

Janis Warrick[1,3] and **Mary Kay Helling**[2]

INTRODUCTION

The number of infants in group care settings continues to increase. According to the National Child Care Staffing Study (1989), 14% of the children in child care centers in 1977 were infants and toddlers, 2 years old or younger. By 1988, this increased dramatically to 30%. Along with the increase in center care, nearly 60% of the infants in out-of-home care are in family child care homes, while 40% are in centers (Committee for Economic Development, 1993).

Providing high quality care for infants is one of the priority areas in early childhood education. A key component of quality child care for children generally and infants in particular is attending to their basic needs for a healthy and safe environment. Based on findings from a four-state study, the quality of infant care was judged to be poor to mediocre. Almost half of the infants in the study were in rooms that were rated as having less than minimal quality (Helbrun *et al.*, 1995). What this means for infants is that they may not be in environments that meet their needs for health and safety. As reported in the study, infants in the poor quality centers are more susceptible to illness due to lack of sanitary conditions and are in danger due to lack of safe environments.

Child care providers and educators may at times wonder about the appropriateness of the routine procedures used in meeting the basic needs of infants within their programs. Information about health and safety changes rapidly in response to new research findings and suggestions for best practices.

Moreover, informal observations of students in pre-service programs as well as of providers in the field point out the need, in some cases, for opportunities to build on the knowledge base of infant basic care. Results from an exploratory survey of childcare providers and pre-service early childhood professionals also pointed out the need for better dissemination of information about infant basic care. For example, only 35.5% of the 170 students and caregivers who responded to the Infant Care Survey indicated they would wash a baby's hands after diapering (Warrick, 1994). At times, babies may touch their genitals or other areas within the diapering space; therefore it is important to wash their hands.

As this example illustrates, proper procedures for infant basic care may not be common knowledge among early childhood personnel. Also, the procedures used may work well from an efficiency standpoint, yet not be recommended from a health and safety perspective.

It is generally assumed that individuals learn these skills from their personal experiences in caring for children or from observing others caring for children. At times, a person may perform daily routines within the child care and education context without much

[1]Lake Area Technical Institute, Watertown, South Dakota.
[2]South Dakota State University, Brookings, South Dakota.
[3]Correspondence should be directed to Jan Warrick, Box 730, Lake Area Technical Institute. Watertown, South Dakota 57201.

From *Early Childhood Education Journal*, Vol. 24, No. 3, 1997, pp. 195-199. © 1997 by Human Sciences Press. Inc. Reprinted by permission.

thought. But the practices observed in the field are not always the ones necessary or recommended for maintaining a safe and healthy environment.

The purpose of this article is to encourage those who are responsible for the care and education of young children to periodically reassess the procedures used when involved in the daily routines of caring for infant basic needs. Basic needs include: diapering, sanitation, safety, feeding, handing infants, and caring for children not feeling well. This article provides an overview of two of the most basic care areas—diapering and feeding.

HEALTHY AND SAFE FEEDING PRACTICES

Feeding practices which are healthy and safe is a key element in providing quality care for infants. Recommendations for best practices in feeding infants are included in this section.

It is not necessary to heat formula but many caregivers prefer to do so. It is also likely that a microwave will be used to heat the formula. Because of this, it is important to follow the protocol developed by Sigman-Grant, Bush, and Anantheswaran (1992):

Prior to Heating:

1. Heat only bottles containing 4 oz. or more without the nipples.
2. Heat only refrigerated formula.
3. Always stand the bottle up.
4. Always leave bottle top uncovered to allow heat to escape.

Heating Instructions (with microwave set on full power).

1. 4 oz bottles: Heat for no more than 30 seconds.
2. 8 oz bottles: Heat for no more than 45 seconds.

Serving instructions

1. Always replace nipple assembly: then invert ten times (vigorous shaking is unnecessary).
2. Formula should be cool to the touch; formula warm to the touch may be too hot to serve.
3. Always test formula; place several drops on tongue or on top of the hand (not the inside wrist) (p. 414).

When heating formula in the microwave avoid using glass bottles because they absorb microwave energy, whereas plastic bottles do not (Sigman-Grant et al., 1992).

Discard any formula or breast milk left in the bottle and not consumed by the baby during each feeding (Deitch, 1987). Do not be tempted to save and reheat the milk again for a later feeding. This is because germs or salivary enzymes may mix in from the baby's sucking, according to Dr. Madeleine Rose, Assistant Professor, Nutrition and Food Science Department, South Dakota State University (personal communication, June 8, 1994).

Avoid feeding an infant directly out of the jar of commercially prepared baby food if the remaining contents will be fed to the baby at another time or to another child. Cover the remaining contents and label with the baby's name and date. Store the jar in the refrigerator and discard the contents if not used within 36 hours (Deitch, 1987).

To further assure safe handling of infant foods (Deitch, 1987; Martin & Lewis, 1994):

1. Require parents who bring their infant's food into your home or center to only bring unopened containers. Ready to serve formula should be in unopened containers as well.
2. Wash your hands with soap and water before preparing baby's formula and bottles to prevent infection.
3. Use bottles, caps, and nipples that have been washed in clean water and dishwashing detergent, or in the dishwasher. If you wash them by hand, use a bottle brush. Squeeze water through nipple holes to make sure they are open. Rinse well and let them stand in a rack to dry. Disinfect the rack frequently.
4. With canned formula, clean the top of the can with soap and water. Rinse. Use a clean punch-type can opener to open.
5. Use only fresh water from the tap or distilled water if you are mixing a concentrate or powder formula. If you use well water rather than water from a community water supply, have it tested before using it for an infant. High nitrate levels could harm the baby. Boiling the well water does not assure its safety.
6. Store prepared formula, tightly covered, in the refrigerator for no more than 48 hours after opening. Refrigerate formula you prepare from powder and use within 24 hours. Tightly cover the remaining powder. Store in a cool, dry place and use within 1 month. Label and date each bottle.

7. Discard any formula or milk left in an infant's bottle or cup after each feeding. Once the baby nurses from a bottle, microorganisms from the baby's mouth are introduced into the formula. Neither refrigeration nor reheating the milk will prevent microorganisms from growing.

8. You may safely keep breast milk in the refrigerator for 24–48 hours or keep frozen for several months. Do not defrost the milk until just before you intend to use it. At this time, remove the container from the freezer and run under cold water, then warmer water. Shake the contents gently. Set the container of milk in a pan of water until the milk reaches room temperature.

Because formula, milk, juices, and sweetened drinks (soda, Kool-Aid, Hi-C, Hawaiian Punch, Tang, etc.) contain sugar, infants should not be given these liquids when they are laid down to sleep. Existing or erupting teeth may decay creating a condition known as nursing bottle syndrome. This especially affects the front teeth, leading to an early loss of these teeth. Because of this, the child may not be able to chew food properly and the permanent teeth may be crowded as a result (Kendrick *et al.*, 1991). Dr. Robert A. Arnold, orthodontist (personal communication, May 19, 1994) explains that the primary teeth maintain space for the developing permanent teeth. An infant's permanent teeth begin developing on the average at age 6 months and take 4–6 years to develop. If the primary teeth are lost, so is the arch length needed for the permanent teeth.

Always try to have the child drink his/her bottle before lying down in bed. Children who drink their bottles lying down are prone to ear infections because the fluid may drain into the ear. If an infant wants to take a bottle to bed, fill it with plain water (Kendrick *et al.*, 1991). Explain this possible harm so the infant's parents will understand the importance for the baby to not drink while lying down.

Because an infant's digestive system and the skills for self-feeding and swallowing are not well-developed, experts recommend infants be 4-to 6-months-old before semisolid foods (for example, rice cereal) are introduced. Add vegetables and fruit between 6 and 8 months of age. At about 8 or 9 months, offer food that is lumpy or cut into one-quarter inch cubes. This would include table food that the infant can easily chew, mash, or swallow whole. By the time the child is 1 year old, most of their food should be table food (Kendrick *et al.*, 1991). Continue giving the infant breast milk or formula up to age one (Frankie & Owen, 1993). Neither whole milk nor skim milk is suitable for the first year (Robinson, Lawler, Chenoweth, & Garwick, 1990).

Some things to remember (Kendrick *et al.*, 1991):

1. Offer the baby water from a cup between meals, beginning at about 6 months of age when the baby is eating solid foods.

2. Avoid infant cereals that are premixed with formula, fruit, or honey. Dr. Madeleine Rose (personal communication, June 29, 1994) recommends starting with rice cereal because it does not cause as many allergies as wheat.

3. Use a baby-sized spoon to feed baby.

4. A baby's bottle is for water, formula, or diluted (one part juice to one part water) 100% juice only. Dr. Madeleine Rose (personal communication, June 29, 1994) says that very young infants (less than 6 months of age) do not need water. They get enough from the breast milk or formula. If they get too much water or juice, they may not get enough protein, calories, vitamins, and minerals that the milk provides.

5. Add one new food at a time. Wait 3–5 days before introducing another one. This will give the baby time to get used to the new food and to identify if the baby has an allergic reaction to it.

6. Sugar, salt, and butter should not be added to baby's food.

7. The best foods are: plain fruits, plain vegetables, plain meats, eggs (only 2–3 per week and after the child is 10 months of age), 100% fruit juice, unsalted crackers, rice, noodles, spaghetti, whole-wheat bread, hot or cold unsweetened cereals, plain yogurt, cottage cheese, and water.

8. Foods to avoid are: mixed dinners, bacon, luncheon meats, hot dogs, ham, creamed vegetables, corn, fruit desserts, puddings, cookies, candy, cakes, nuts, popcorn, whole grapes, and sweetened drinks. Food objects such as hot dogs, candies, nuts, and grapes pose a threat for death by choking (Ryan, Yacoub, Paton, & Avard, 1990). Other listed foods contain high amounts of sugar or fat.

9. Continue giving whole milk until the child is 2 years old. Infants need the nutrients and calories whole milk provides. Skim and low fat milk contain too few calories and too much protein.

10. Every baby is different. Encourage parents to consult their physicians for advice.

Parents may also choose to consult a dietitian, community health nurse, physician's assistant, or other professional for advice.

HEALTHY AND SAFE DIAPERING PROCEDURES

Anyone who cares for infants knows that the need to change diapers may seem like an endless yet necessary task. Caregivers are encouraged to give careful thought to the diapering routine to prevent the spread of illnesses and diseases.

For many, the floor seems like a likely place for safe diapering; but is not recommended due to the possibility of spreading infectious diseases. The preferred surface is at least 3 feet above the floor (Kendrick, Kaufmann, & Messenger, 1991).

Diapering needs to be done on a surface used only to change diapers. This surface should be as far away from any food-handling area as possible. Running water needs to be nearby, preferably within arm's reach (Kendrick et al., 1991). Other children should not be in the diaper-changing area (American Academy of Pediatrics and American Public Health Association, 1992). Never leave the child, even for a second. Always keep one hand on the baby even if using a strap on the changing table (Kendrick et al., 1991).

Cover fecal material by folding the soiled diaper inward (Yamauchi, 1991). Keep diapers in containers separate from other waste receptacles. Locate such containers near the diaper changing area. Line waste containers with plastic garbage bags and cover with a tight-fitting lid. Keep soiled clothing in a separate plastic bag. Frequently clean containers to prevent odors and the spread of disease (American Academy of Pediatrics and American Public Health Association, 1992). Empty diaper disposal containers at least daily, more often as needed (Kendrick et al., 1991).

When using cloth diapers, store clean diapers away from the area where soiled diapers are kept. Doing so prevents contamination (Yamauchi, 1991). Put the soiled diaper and/or soiled training pants into a labeled, sealed bag. Fecal contents of diapers can be emptied into the toilet. It is recommended to not rinse diapers in the toilet due to possible contamination of the toilet area for the next use (American Academy of Pediatrics and Ameri-

can Public Health Association, 1992). Store the bag out of children's reach. Send it home with the parent for proper laundering (Kendrick et al., 1991).

Caregivers may often give the baby something to play with to occupy the child during the diapering routine. Whatever the toy, disinfect it before using it again. Avoid giving a bottle of lotion or a container with talcum powder. These substances are dangerous to swallow or inhale, and an infant mouthing the container might eat some of the contents (Kendrick et al., 1991). Discourage routine use of talcum powder since the powder can cause severe respiratory problems (Pairaudeau, Wilson, Hall, & Milne, 1991).

Research indicates that when children wear clothing over diapers, there is a significant decrease in the likelihood of contamination (Van, Morrow, Reves, & Pickering, 1992). Therefore, make sure that you require parents to send extra changes of clothing for added protection. During summer months make sure that infants wear shorts over their diapers. Children also need to wear clothing over training pants as well.

In sum, the Centers for Disease Control (1984, pp. 10–11) recommends the following steps when changing diapers:

1. Check to make sure you have supplies ready.
2. Place roll paper or disposable towel on the part of the changing area where the infant's bottom will be.
3. Hold the infant away from your body as you carry them to the changing area. Lay the baby on the paper or towel.
4. Remove diaper. Put the diaper in a plastic bag or plastic-lined waste receptacle.
5. Clean the baby's bottom with a premoistened towelette or dampened paper towel. Dispose of the towelette in the same container as the soiled disposable diaper.
6. Remove the paper or towel from under the infant and dispose of it in the same way as the diaper.
7. Wipe your hands with a fresh premoistened towelette or a damp paper towel and dispose of it in the plastic bag or receptacle with the diaper. If you wear disposable gloves, discard now.
8. Diaper the infant.
9. Wash the baby's hands.
10. Return the child to play area.
11. Clean and disinfect the diapering area and any supplies that were touched.
12. Wash your hands.

13. Record the time of the diaper change and whether the baby was wet, dry, or had a bowel movement.

Recorded information provides valuable documentation for monitoring infant's activities. For example, the caregiver can easily scan the record sheet and note the frequency of loose stools. This, in turn, alerts the caregiver of the possibility the infant may be ill. Such a record is also important for the parents to have at the end of the child's day. The caregiver should feel comfortable recording such information so it is accurate for that infant and not confused or mixed up with another child's activity record.

To disinfect the diapering area, use a bleach solution of 1 tablespoon of bleach (5.25% sodium hypochlorite) to 1 quart of water (1/4 cup of bleach per 1 gallon of water) (Deitch, 1987). Look closely at the label found on the side of the bleach bottle to make sure the percentage of sodium hypochlorite is 5.25.

Mix a fresh solution of bleach each day because it deteriorates rapidly (Deitch, 1987). Put it in a labeled spray bottle to be used exclusively for cleaning and sanitizing the area. Keep out of children's reach (Kendrick *et al.*, 1991). Safely dispose the unused portions of the bleach solution at the end of the day. Do this by discarding the bleach solution in the sanitary sewer drain (Deitch, 1987).

SUMMARY

Diapering and feeding are two vitally important routines in meeting basic needs of infants. Such routine times provide opportunities for enhancing infants' development through interaction with others. Feeding and diapering times are ideal for one-to-one interaction with infants. Caregivers are encouraged to speak directly with children, asking questions and responding to infant vocalizations with verbal and nonverbal (e.g., smile, head nod) communications. Adults can also label infant body parts as well as the items used in the process of feeding and diapering. Singing simple songs and reciting rhymes can also be incorporated into routine times.

Early childhood professionals educating and caring for infants are encouraged to review the procedures used in diapering and feeding. Assessing whether procedures assure safe and healthy conditions for infants is an important component of quality care.

REFERENCES

American Academy of Pediatrics and American Public Health Association (1992). *Caring for our children—National health and safely performance standards: Guidelines for out-of-home child care programs.* Washington, DC: Author.

Centers for Disease Control (1984). *What you can do to stop disease in the child day care center* (Stock #017-023-00172-8). Washington, DC: U.S. Government Printing Office.

Committee for Economic Development (1993). *Why child care matters: Preparing young children for a more productive America.* New York: Author.

Deitch, S. (Ed.). (1987). *Health in day care: A manual for health professionals.* Elk Grove Village, IL: American Academy of Pediatrics.

Frankie, R. T., & Owen, A. L. (1993). *Nutrition in the community: The art of delivering services.* St. Louis, MO: Mosby.

Helbrun, S., Culkin, M., Howes, C., Bryant, D., Clifford, R., Cryer, D., Peisner-Fenberg, & Kagan, S. (1995). *Cost, quality, and child outcomes in child care centers* (executive summary). Denver, CO: University of Colorado, Economics Department.

Kendrick, A. B., Kaufman, R., & Messenger, K. P. (Eds.). (1991). *Healthy young children: A manual for programs.* Washington, DC: National Association of the Education of Young Children.

Martin, H. D., & Lewis, N. M. (1994). *Guidelines for bottlefeeding* (Report G94-1203-A). University of Nebraska, Lincoln: Cooperative Extension, Institute of Agriculture and Natural Resources.

Pairaudeau, P. W., Wilson, R. G., Hall, M. A., & Milne, M. (1991). Inhalation of baby powder: An unappreciated hazard. *British Medical Journal, 302,* 1200–1201.

Robinson, C. H., Lawler, M. R., Chenoweth, W. L., & Garwick, A. E. (1990). *Normal and therapeutic nutrition* (17th ed.). New York: Macmillan.

Ryan, A., Yacoub, W., Paton, B., & Avard, D. (1990). Childhood deaths from toy balloons. *American Journal of Diseases of Children, 144,* 1221–1224.

Sigman-Grant, M., Bush, G., & Anantheswaran, R. (1992). Microwave heating of infant formula: A dilemma resolved. *Pediatrics, 90,* 412–415.

Van, R., Morrow, A. L., Reves, R. R., & Pickering, L. K. (1991). Environmental contamination in child day-care centers. *American Journal of Epidemiology, 133,* 460–470.

Warrick, J. C. (1994). *Infant Care Survey.* Unpublished survey.

Whitebook, M., Howes, C., & Phillips, D. (1989). *Who Cares? Child Care Teachers and the Quality of Care in America.* Final Report of the National Child Care Staffing Study, Child Care Employee Project, Oakland, CA.

Yamauchi, T. (1991). Guidelines for attendees and personnel. In L. G. Donositz (Eds.), *Infection control in the child care center and preschool* (pp. 9–19). Baltimore, MD: Williams and Wilkins.

Simply Sensational Spaces: A Multi-"*S*" Approach to Toddler Environments

Linda H. Lowman and Linda H. Ruhmann

"**D**ifferent strokes for different folks" takes on new meaning when planning room arrangements for toddlers in group care settings. With a basic understanding of the special developmental needs of toddlers, caregivers can provide physical environments that help these children feel relaxed and successful throughout the day.

Our visits to a variety of toddler rooms over the last few years reveal a trend to treat toddlers as smaller preschoolers. Toddlers often are the victims of the "push-down" movement so common in many other educational settings. Most child

Linda H. Lowman, M.Ed., is an associate professor in the Child Development Department at San Antonio College in Texas. She is a former toddler teacher and infant/toddler CDA instructor.
Linda H. Ruhmann, M.Ed., is a professor in the Child Development Department at San Antonio College in Texas. Linda serves as the infant-toddler coordinator for the college's Child Development Center and has advised many infant/toddler CDA students.

care programs provide toddlers with environments, equipment, and activities that are similar to those found in classrooms for three- to five-year-olds. Several authors (for example, Greenman 1988; Dodge, Dombro, & Koralik 1991) have reported on this trend.

© Francis Wardle

Greenman notes,

Toddlers are child care's equivalent of junior high school students. They often appear to be more mature than they are, and the frequent result in toddler programs is the tendency to treat them as proto-preschoolers—smaller and less competent. (1988, 52)

Developmentally Appropriate Practice in Early Childhood Programs Serving Children from Birth through Age 8 clearly states, however, that "**Good programs for children from birth to age 3 are distinctly different from**

all other types of programs—they are *not* a scaled down version of a good program for preschool children" (Bredekamp 1987, 29).

One area in which this pushdown is particularly apparent is the arrangement of the physical environment. Many toddler rooms we have visited are simpler versions of preschool classrooms complete with seven or eight traditional learning centers and the same kinds of toys and materials. This type of physical environment frequently proves frustrating to both children and adults because it does not meet the unique developmental needs of this particular age group.

Between the ages of one and three, children move from babyhood into the larger world of early childhood. During these two years important development is occurring that will greatly in-

From *Young Children*, May 1998, pp. 11-17. © 1998 by the National Association for the Education of Young Children. Reprinted by permission.

fluence later growth and learning. Toddlers are in a different stage of cognitive development than their preschool counterparts. Many are still in what Piaget calls the sensorimotor period, where their learning style involves processing information primarily through sensory and motor input. That's why toddlers must have environments that allow them to move around easily and explore materials thoroughly.

Toddlers are also working on two important psychosocial tasks, the mastery of which is essential if they are to move confidently into the preschool years: development of a sense of trust and development of a sense of autonomy (Erikson 1956). Therefore, one- and two-year-olds need both interpersonal and physical environments that provide a sense of security (building trust) and allow opportunities to make choices and experience mastery (encouraging autonomy).

Accommodating toddlers' physical needs in a flexible way helps them feel secure. Younger toddlers in particular need schedules and spaces that allow them to eat and nap as their own body rhythms dictate. As toddlers begin to push for autonomy, the environment should encourage appropriate choices and opportunities for mastering self-help skills. Low shelves with a modest number of clearly displayed materials and step-ups to sinks, cubbies, and windows encourage independence. In addition, most of the day should be spent in free-choice activities either inside or out rather than in teacher-directed activities.

Based on toddlers' developmental needs, there are special environmental requirements for toddler rooms. These may be addressed in terms of a multi-S environment. These Ss—simplicity, seclusion, softness, senses, stimulation, stability, safety, and sanitation—are outlined in the accompanying boxes. They serve as guidelines for developing physical environments for toddlers that foster their unique growth and help facilitate the transition between babyhood and early childhood.

Simplicity

A **simplified** room arrangement provides toddlers a variety of appropriate experiences in a way that accommodates their unique movement patterns. We have found that four basic activity zones in a toddler room allow for ease of movement in and between areas and offer the kinds of materials that toddlers enjoy bringing together.

The four activity areas are a large-motor zone, a dramatic-play zone, a messy zone, and a quiet zone. These are normally placed in a modified peripheral arrangement and separated by low, sturdy dividers. A simplified arrangement also works well for mixed-age groups of which toddlers often are a part. In traditional preschool classrooms the zones are often subdivided into more elaborate learning centers.

1. A large-motor zone is essential in a toddler room. Considerable space allows children to work on rapidly developing gross-motor skills. Children at this age need many opportunities to challenge their growing ability to make their bodies work for them. If not provided with these challenges, they will find them by climbing on tables and shelves and pushing chairs around the room.

The large-motor zone can include various large-motor structures (climbers, slides, tunnels) as well as large lightweight blocks, push-and-

Courtesy of the authors

The large-motor zone should provide a variety of large-motor challenges.

pull toys, and riding toys. A CD or tape player and props encourage dancing and movement to music.

This is different from the preschool classroom in which there is often a separate area for blocks, music, and perhaps gross-motor activities.

2. The dramatic-play zone is particularly conducive to pretend play. One sign of toddlers' increasing cognitive maturity is the advent of pretend play (Piaget 1962). At this age children are most interested in imitating familiar adults in familiar settings, so a variety of realistic home props, including large dolls, are the most satisfying.

Home-center equipment (stoves, sinks, refrigerators) should be open rather than closed to avoid pinched fingers and to accommodate the toddlers' still somewhat vague concept of object permanence (things out of sight still exist).

Dress-up clothes should be safe and simple enough for the child to use without assistance. Hats, purses, vests, and the slip-on shoes of older children are favorite items.

Objects that can be moved, such as strollers, shopping carts, and vacuum cleaners, also get frequent use, as do doll beds big and strong enough to hold toddler bodies.

Placing the dramatic-play area close to the large-motor zone allows for easy movement between these two popular spaces.

While preschoolers enjoy a variety of changing themes in the dramatic-play area, toddlers prefer the stability of the "home" setting.

3. The messy zone is that area of the room where children are encouraged to "mess around" with a variety of fluid materials (sand, water, paint, paste, etc.) and make discoveries about both the natural and physical sciences. The messy area should be close to a water

The multi-S approach to toddler environments is designed to provide flexible guidelines within which teachers can work to meet the needs of their individual group of toddlers and the needs of individual children *within* the group. Careful observation and purposeful adjustments are

Courtesy of the authors

The dramatic-play zone should be toddler size and contain realistic items for pretend play.

Courtesy of the authors

The quiet zone includes books, manipulatives, and discovery materials.

Courtesy of the authors

The messy zone is easy to clean so children can explore many art and sensory materials.

source and have a washable floor covering. Tables for art experiences and eating can be in this area, as well as sensory tubs or tables, sturdy easels (at least two), and shelves for discovery items, art supplies (appropriate for the age), and perhaps an animal. Chairs can be put up during activity times since many toddlers prefer to stand when working with art and sensory materials and often see chairs as a large-motor challenge rather than a place to sit.

In a preschool room this area is often divided into three more complex centers—discovery, sensory, and art.

4. Every toddler room needs a haven where children can unwind, kick back, chill out, sink in, and just relax. The quiet zone provides such a spot. Here toddlers can enjoy cuddling with an adult, looking at books, working with manipulatives, or just doing nothing. As the softest and most inviting area of the classroom, the quiet zone includes books on a low shelf, stuffed animals and soft toys, manipulatives (which this age still prefers to play with on the floor), and additional discovery items. Terrariums and aquariums add interest. A comfortable chair or love seat that can accommodate an adult and one or two children should be included here.

Preschool children still need a quiet spot, which is often the library center. They prefer sitting at tables to use most manipulatives, so a separate table games center is often added.

Seclusion

Because toddlers frequently engage in onlooker and solitary play and can become easily overwhelmed in group settings, spaces that invite *seclusion* are very important in their environments (Cataldo 1983; Greenman 1988; Dodge 1992). An inviting alone space should be a part of each activity zone. Sturdy cardboard boxes or china barrels can serve this purpose.

Courtesy of the authors

Spaces to be alone in allow children retreats as well as spots from which to view others.

Softness

Many toddlers spend long hours away from home in a variety of child care settings. For such children it is essential that the environment be as homelike as possible. **Softness** in the environment helps a classroom seem more homey. Soft items, such as carpet fabric wall hangings, upholstered furniture, and stuffed toys, also help to absorb noise. Toddlers are attracted to soft spots for their sensory appeal as well as their comfort.

Remember, however, that the most inviting soft spots to toddlers are the arms and laps of favorite caregivers. Frequent touching gives toddlers confidence for further exploration. It is essential that each toddler receive appropriate cuddling throughout the day when *he* initiates or sends signals that he

essential to meet the changing needs of these unique learners. Our goal should always be to provide warm, stable relationships, especially one

primary caregiver for each toddler, and simply sensational spaces in which toddlers can feel both comfortable and competent.

Courtesy of the authors

Softness helps create a more homelike atmosphere and encourages children to relax.

needs it. Some caregivers only cuddle their favorites or impose cuddling on children. The best caregivers give *all* children good care and observe and respond to individuals.

The Senses

Because toddlers are sensorimotor learners, an environment rich in sensory appeal is important for encouraging optimal development. *Care must be taken, however, to avoid sensory overload.*

The toddler environment should appeal to all of the senses. There should be a variety of interesting things for children to look at, including the children's scribbles, pictures of real people and objects hung at the children's eye level, mirrors in standard and surprising places, and, if possible, opportunities to look outside. Bright-colored wind socks or streamers add visual interest as well. Because the figure-ground discrimination of this age is not yet well developed, it is important to surround both pictures and materials stored on shelves

Courtesy of the authors

The environment should include a variety of things to see, hear, and touch without being overwhelmed.

with space (Harris 1986). As we've said, keep it simple.

Toddlers enjoy listening to wind chimes, music boxes, an occasional

Stimulation

Environments for toddlers also need to be **stimulating,** providing a variety of appropriate challenges to meet growing skill levels. Skilled parents, family child care providers, and center-based caregivers observe individuals carefully and sense what would be a good "next step," a challenge, not a frustration (Berk & Winsler 1995).

Gonzalez-Mena and Eyer (1997) discuss the importance of the caregiver determining each child's level of optimum stress and providing activities accordingly. According to Cataldo (1983), materials that are open ended enough to be used by several age groups can provide realistic challenges for young children. Appropriate novelty and complexity of materials also maintain toddler interest (Dempsey & Frost 1993). Examples of such interesting, open-ended materials include a variety of common household objects, such as

plastic butter tubs, jars, and makeup containers; dump-and-fill containers that can be carried; and different sizes and shapes of soft blocks. As toddlers near age three, introduce wooden blocks.

Courtesy of the authors

The environment needs to include materials that not only allow children to feel successful but also provide challenges.

Open-ended art materials appropriate for toddlers include larger crayons and chalk, paper for tearing, flour-and-water paste, and paint (initially colored water and then nontoxic varieties for older toddlers).

The quantity of materials should be carefully monitored. Too many choices of materials all at once overwhelm toddlers and lead to random exploration rather than more focused play. And we all know that many small loose toys frequently lead to social difficulties (possession problems) in toddler rooms, whereas larger pieces of gross-motor equipment (such as multifunction climber) lead to more positive social interactions because they allow children to be in close proximity yet not invading upon each other's space.

tape or radio music, toys with built-in sounds, and tape recordings of their own voices or voices of loved adults.

Provide pleasant smells with scented water and playdough, fresh flowers, herb collages, smelling bottles, and an electric potpourri pot (placed out of the children's reach).

A variety of textures also should be included throughout the room. Toddlers love to feel things and learn about the properties of objects through their fingertips. Bubble wrap and contact paper (sticky side up) taped to the floor fascinate children as they explore with fingers and feet.

Safety

Toddlers are avid explorers with little sense of danger and little impulse control, so **safety** must be a primary consideration in their environments. Close supervision is essential.

Furniture and outdoor equipment should be sturdy enough to be climbed on and scaled to toddler size to lessen the danger of falls. All objects in the classroom should be too big to be swallowed since many toddlers still mouth objects. The room must be carefully inspected daily for any potential hazards, and a choke tube should be standard equipment in every toddler room.

Courtesy of the authors

Equipment needs to be carefully selected and arranged so children can explore freely and safely.

Stability

Toddler environments need to remain relatively **stable.** The world is so confusing if you've only been in it a year or two. Toddlers feel more secure and more in control when they know on a daily basis what to expect and where to find things. Schedules and room arrangements should stay consistent. Toddlers have a strong need for repetition and ritual and for opportunities to thoroughly practice emerging skills before moving on. They need to know that favorite books, dolls, toys, and their special

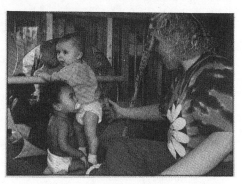

"loveys" (blankets, pacifiers) will remain in the environment as long as they are interested in them.

Materials in toddler rooms should be rotated slowly and with careful attention to current interests and skills. Do not change all materials at once. Add new manipulatives, books, dramatic-play props, and large-motor challenges as children lose interest in what is available rather than change many things on a weekly basis to go along with a new unit of study (as is often done in preschool classrooms). As the children become more mature, the environment should change and grow more complex with them, but it still needs to remain stable enough to meet their security needs.

Courtesy of the authors

A stable environment helps children feel more secure at an age where transitions are often difficult.

Sanitation

Last but by no means least—in fact, it should be a top priority in developing appropriate toddler environments—is good **sanitation.** Such essential toddler routines as diapering, toileting, feeding,

and napping require careful attention to keep children healthy.

Because toddlers still frequently prefer to play on the floor, floors must be well maintained. And since mouthing of toys does occur, all materials need to be washed daily in the dishwasher or by hand (first with detergent and water, then sprayed with a mix of one tablespoon of bleach to one quart of water). Convenient, adult-accessible storage of cleaning materials makes maintenance of sanitary environments much easier.

Courtesy of the authors

Easily accessible water, soap, and cleaning supplies help make keeping the room sanitary much easier.

References

Berk, L. E., & A. Winsler. 1995. *Scaffolding children's learning: Vygotsky and early childhood education.* Washington, DC: NAEYC.

Bredekamp, S., ed. 1987. *Developmentally appropriate practice in early childhood programs serving children from birth through age 8.* Exp. ed. Washington, DC: NAEYC.

Cataldo, C. Z. 1983. *Infant and toddler programs: A guide to very early childhood education.* Reading, MA: Addison-Wesley.

Dempsey, J. D., & J. L. Frost. 1993. Play environments in early childhood education. In *Handbook of research on the education of young children,* ed. B. Spodek, 306–21. New York: Macmillan.

Dodge, D. 1992. Making classrooms work for children and adults. *Child Care Information Exchange* (January): 21–23.

Dodge, D. T., A. L. Dombro, & D. G. Koralek. 1991. *Caring for infants and toddlers.* Vol. 1. Washington, DC: Teaching Strategies.

Erikson, E. 1956. *Childhood and society.* New York: Norton.

Gonzalez-Mena, J., & D. Eyer. 1997. *Infants, toddlers, and caregivers.* Mountain View, CA: Mayfield.

Greenman, J. 1988. *Caring spaces, learning places: Children's environments that work.* Redmond, WA: Exchange Press.

Harris, A. C. 1986. *Child development.* New York: West.

Piaget, J. 1962. *Play, dreams and imitation in childhood.* New York: Norton.

For further reading

Balaban, N. 1992. The role of the child care professional in caring for infants, toddlers, and their families. *Young Children* 47 (5): 66–71.

Bredekamp, S., & C. Copple, eds. 1997. Part 3, Developmentally appropriate practice for infants and toddlers. In *Developmentally appropriate practice for early childhood programs,* rev. ed., 55–94. Washington, DC: NAEYC.

Bronson, M. B. 1995. *The right stuff for children birth to 8: Selecting play materials to support development.* Washington, DC: NAEYC.

Carnegie Task Force on Meeting the Needs of Young Children. 1994. *Starting points: Meeting the needs of our youngest children.* New York: Carnegie Corporation. (Available through NAEYC.)

Caruso, D. A. 1988. Research in review. Play and learning in infancy: Research and implications. *Young Children* 43 (6): 63–70.

Daniel, J. E. 1993. Infants to toddlers: Qualities of effective transitions. *Young Children* 48 (6): 16–21.

Da Ros, D., & A. Wong. 1994. Naptime: A transition with ease. *Young Children* 50 (1): 69.

Dittmann, L. L., ed. 1984. *The infants we care for.* Washington, DC: NAEYC.

Dittmann, L. L. 1986. Finding the best care for your infant or toddler. *Young Children* 41 (3): 43–46.

French, L. 1996. "I told you all about it, so don't tell me you don't know": Two-year-olds and learning through language. *Young Children* 51 (2): 17–20.

Gonzalez-Mena, J. 1992. Taking a culturally sensitive approach in infant-toddler programs. *Young Children* 47 (2): 4–9.

Greenberg, P. 1987. Ideas that work with young children. What is curriculum for infants in family day care (or elsewhere)? *Young Children* 42 (5): 58–62.

Greenberg, P. 1991. *Character development: Encouraging self-esteem and self-discipline in infants, toddlers, and 2-year-olds.* Washington, DC: NAEYC.

Greenman, J., & A. Stonehouse. 1996. *Prime times: A handbook for excellence in infant and toddler programs.* St. Paul: Redleaf.

Gullo, D. F., C. B. Burton-Maxwell, & S. J. Bruk. 1995. Milwaukee Early Schooling Initiative: Making it happen for young children. *Young Children* 50 (6): 12–17.

Hignett, W. F. 1988. Food for thought. Infant/toddler day care, yes; but we'd better make it good. *Young Children* 44 (1): 32–33.

Honig, A. S. 1985. High quality infant/toddler care: Issues and dilemmas. *Young Children* 41 (1): 40–46.

Honig, A. S. 1989. Quality infant/toddler caregiving: Are there magic recipes? *Young Children* 44 (4): 4–10.

Honig, A. S. 1993. Mental health for babies: What do theory and research tell us? *Young Children* 48 (3): 69–76.

Honig, A. S. 1995. Singing with infants and toddlers. *Young Children* 50 (5): 72–78.

Howes, C. 1989. Research in review. Infant child care. *Young Children* 44 (6): 24–28.

Hrneir, E. J. 1985. Infant play: A window to motivational competence. In *When children play: Proceedings from the International Conference on Play and Play Environments,* eds. F. L. Frost & S. Sunderlin, 339–42. Washington, DC: Association for Childhood Education International.

Hughes, F. P., J. Elicker, & L. C. Veen. 1995. A program of play for infants and their caregivers. *Young Children* 50 (2): 52–58.

Kendrick, A. S., R. Kaufmann, & K. P. Messenger. 1995. *Healthy young children: A manual for programs.* Washington, DC: NAEYC.

Koralek, D. G., L. S. Colker, & D. T. Dodge. 1995. Toddlers. In *The what, why, and how of high-quality early childhood education: A guide for on-site supervision,* rev. ed., 41–65. Washington, DC: NAEYC.

Kupetz, B. N., & E. J. Green. 1997. Sharing books with infants and toddlers: Facing the challenges. *Young Children* 52 (2): 22–27.

Lowe, M. 1975. Trends in the development of representational play in infants from one to three years—An observational study. *Journal of Child Psychology, Child Psychiatry, & Allied Disciplines* 16: 33–47.

Meyerhoff, M. K. 1992. Viewpoint. Infant/toddler day care versus reality. *Young Children* 47 (6): 44–45.

Meyerhoff, M. K. 1994. Of baseball and babies: Are you unconsciously discouraging father involvement in infant care? *Young Children* 49 (4): 17–19.

Morris, S. L. 1995. Supporting the breastfeeding relationship during child care: Why is it important? *Young Children* 50 (2): 59–62.

Mueller, E., & J. Bergstrom. 1982. Fostering peer relations in normal and handicapped young children. In *The social life of children in a changing society,* ed. K. M. Borman. 191–215. Hillsdale, NJ: Erlbaum.

Raikes, H. 1996. A secure base for babies: Applying attachment concepts to the infant care setting. *Young Children* 51 (5): 59–67.

Reinsberg, J. 1995. Reflections on quality infant care. *Young Children* 50 (6): 23–25.

San Fernando Valley Child Care Consortium, A. Godwin & L. Schrag, cochairs. 1996. *Setting up for infant/toddler care: Guidelines for centers and family child care homes.* Rev. ed. Washington, DC: NAEYC.

Schreiber, M. E. 1996. Lighting alternatives: Considerations for child care centers. *Young Children* 51 (4): 11–13.

Shore, R. 1997. *Rethinking the brain: New insights into early development.* New York: Families and Work Institute.

Weissbourd, B., & J. S. Musick, eds. 1981. *Infants: Their social environments.* Washington, DC: NAEYC.

Zeavin, C. 1997. Toddlers at play: Environments at work. *Young Children* 52 (3): 72–77.

Homework Doesn't Help

Every night, millions of parents and kids shed blood,
sweat and tears over the kitchen table.
Now some researchers say these dreaded lessons are
generally pointless until middle school.

BY SHARON BEGLEY

THERE ARE AS MANY THEORIES ABOUT why so many of America's children need remedial tutoring as there are failing students. But more and more education researchers are drawing lessons from kids like Adam, whose long, sad battle with homework began in the first grade. His school, outside Chicago, assigned just a little in the beginning—maybe 15 minutes a night, plus reading. Now, in fourth grade, his load has rocketed to three hours a night, and Adam, identified as a gifted student, "is completely frustrated," says his mother. "Last night he was up until 10:15 finishing a project, and he is crying more and more. He asks me, 'I work hard six hours a day in school—how much do I have to do?' He is having trouble focusing in school, and I suspect it's because he is exhausted."

There was blood, sweat and a puddle of tears on kitchen tables across America this morning, the detritus of a long afternoon, stretching into evening, of yesterday's homework. Sure, some students probably whipped out their perfectly organized assignment pad, did each task cheerfully and finished with time to spare for reading, television or play. We just don't know any. Something that infuriates parents, sabotages family time and crowds out so much else in a child's life might be tolerable if it also helped kids learn

and if it imbued them with good study habits and a lifelong love of learning. Unfortunately, "for elementary-school students the effect of homework on achievement is trivial, if it exists at all," concludes psychologist Harris Cooper of the University of Missouri, whose analysis of more than 100 studies has stood up for 10 years.

The drive to discover why homework is not more useful in the early years, and to explain how to make it so, has generated more scientific interest in the subject "than ever before," says Cooper. Next month, at the annual meeting of the American Educational Research Association in San Diego, a symposium will examine the value of homework and ask what constitutes good assignments. For the new study he will present there, Cooper collected data on 709 students in grades two through four and six through 12. In lower grades, "there was a significant *negative* relationship between the amount of homework assigned and student attitudes," Cooper says, reflecting the not-surprising fact that kids resent the stuff. But in grades six and up, the more homework students completed, the higher their achievement. It is not clear, however, what is cause and what is effect: are already good students finishing more assignments because they are motivated and

good at academics, or is completing assignments causing students to do better? "You can't identify anything as causal," says Cooper. "But we do think that how much homework helps is a function of grade level. There is a tipping point where homework has negative consequences."

That suggests that the trend among schools to pile on more homework, starting in kindergarten, could backfire. In the lower grades, since homework does not improve student performance, it should fulfill different goals: fostering a love of learning, honing study skills. Instead, there is ample anecdotal evidence that it breeds poor attitudes, as Cooper finds, and resentment. Too many teachers are still assigning useless, even counterproductive, homework—work that duplicates without reinforcing material covered in class. Homework that frustrates or angers a child or otherwise makes learning unpleasant "is a quick route to academic dread," says Lyn Corno of Columbia University's Teachers College, convincing a child early on that school stinks and he's a rotten student. "Homework becomes a grind to get through, rather than a learning experience," Corno says. The prevalence of bad homework might explain the lack of a connection between homework and student achievement in elementary school.

What is good homework? Especially for younger children, short assignments quickly completed should be the goal; long assignments uncompleted or completed with tears and tantrums are deadly. Also, homework should be different from classwork. It "is most beneficial when it moves out of the drone mode and into the creative mode," says Gary Griffin of Teachers College. "Homework should be an opportunity to engage in creative, exploratory activity—doing an oral history of your family or determining the ecological effects of a neighborhood business." Rather than memorizing names, dates and battles of the Civil War, students might write fictional letters from a Northerner to a Southerner, expressing their feelings about the issues dividing the nation. The assignment should also be crucial to the next day's classwork to emphasize to students that homework matters and isn't just a plot to make them miserable. It should be focused: for example, don't ask the students to write about an open-ended theme from a novel the class is reading, ask them to pick one character and explain why he or she behaved in a particular way.

Even good assignments can be overdone, however. "If homework gets piled on, and if it's boring, kids will go through satiation and frustration, and parents will express negative attitudes that kids will pick up," warns Lyn Corno. David, a third grader in Oak Park, Ill, regularly spends from 7 to 9 p.m. on homework, "but sometimes we're up until 10:30 trying to finish," says his mother, a lawyer. "David is a very bright and inquisitive kid who has come to dislike school because of the homework."

More than 100 studies find that it is not until middle school that homework begins to pay off. Julian Betts of the University of California, San Diego, for instance, followed 3,000 seventh and 10th graders. "The amount of math homework assigned had a huge effect on math test scores," he finds. A seventh grader given 15 minutes of math homework every school night through 11th grade would wind up one full grade ahead in achievement compared with one who did no math homework for those years.

How can homework have little to no effect on learning in the elementary grades, but a noticeable effect beginning in sixth grade? It is easier in higher grades to assign imaginative, focused, substantive homework that requires students to integrate and apply knowledge—the kind of homework that promotes learning. "The theory," says Corno, "is that assignments given in high school relate more directly to the school curriculum and become more challenging. Also by high school, students usually have resigned themselves to the routine. Working hard after school, and having good study skills, is less of an issue." But teaching the high schooler to work independently and to value academics requires that a good foundation of attitudes and aptitude be laid in the early years. Because homework is too often turning kids off to school, says Corno, "homework is more a part of the problem than a part of the solution." If young students fail to acquire the basic foundation of learning, thanks to dumb homework or staggering amounts of it, tutors can look forward to more paying customers.

Working with Families

Don't Shut Fathers Out

Eugenia Hepworth Berger, Department Editor

INTRODUCTION

For those of you who were fortunate enough to have a nurturing father—model, encourager, guide, protector, care provider, breadwinner, teacher, story teller, play partner, and standard setter—you know how important a father can be. But did you know that as educators and child care providers you can make a difference in children's lives by encouraging fathers to get involved? If you provide a father friendly environment where fathers or father substitutes can participate, and if you model attitudes and activities that allow them to support their children, they will recognize their importance and the manner in which they can provide a human touch to children. Encourage participation and provide opportunities for men to become all that they can be to their children.

HISTORY

In past years, fathers in the United States have been viewed primarily as providers (breadwinners) even though there have always been other roles that fathers perform. At the turn of the twentieth century, fathers were viewed as the head of the family, the breadwinner, and standard setter. The philosophy for child care emphasized love and affection in the formation of character with the father participating as the standard setter and the mother providing the love. "The period of 1890 to 1910 stressed love and freedom, the period of 1910 to 1920 emphasized strict scheduling and discipline, and self-regulation appeared in the late 1920s and 1940s" (Berger, 1995, p. 60). "By the 1920s fathers were seeking information on everything . . . and in the ensuing years the new 'fatherhood' began to makes its cultural march as it became part of the experts' discourse on family life, personality development and psychological well-being" (Griswold, 1993, p. 6).

Children's Bureau. Interest in the welfare of families resulted in the establishment of the Children's Bureau in 1912 with the publication of *Infant Care* in 1914. The book's intention was to help mothers and fathers take care of their babies, but the focus was on the mother's role. In the 1942 issue of *Infant Care*, there was a shift in attitude and the father become a part of the parenting team. "Until this time, only women's identities were presumed to be tied to parenthood. Now it was possible for men's identities to be tied to parenthood too" (LaRossa, 1997, p. 55).

Responses in the 1940s. When young men were recruited for service in World War II, their examinations revealed that many young men had deficient mental health and physical development. Responses to these findings were illustrated by Dr. Benjamin Spock's book, *The Common Sense Book of Baby and Child Care* in which he urged parents to enjoy their children, thus influencing the rearing practices of many families, and Erik Erikson's book, *Childhood and Society*. Erikson looked at the child through bio-socio-psycho lenses, and recognized that the child's genetic being was also impacted by the child's world. A neo-Freudian, he described eight stages of growth, which continue to have relevance in human growth and development.

The 1950s. In the 1950s, the war was over, many women, who had worked or grown up during the war effort, married and began families; others welcomed their husband back from the war and returned to a two-parent family. The emphasis of parenting was on the mother with the father supporting her efforts and providing the breadwinner and standard-setting roles.

Diminishing Role of Fathers. Some who have studied fatherhood believe that fathers began to lose their dominant roles during the 1960s, continuing into the 1970s. It was suggested that children could be raised as well without fathers as with them. "The retreat from fatherhood began in the 1960s, gained momentum in the 1970s, and hit full stride in the 1980s. . . . It became relatively easy to argue fathers were not really necessary to the 'modern' family" (Horn, 1977, pp. 24–25).

During the second half of the twentieth century, changes in the father's role can be seen to be influenced by social changes and the varying beliefs in what was best for child development. One example of change was in the study of attachment. Initially, mother and infant attachment was studied and recognized as essential and the responsibility of the mother to care for the child. Later, it was recognized that attachment to fathers and significant others was valid as well.

Mothers in the Labor Force. The single greatest impact on change in family life came when women with young children joined the workforce. No longer is there a picture of a mother and children at home with the father going off to work each morning. In 1996, 78% of married women with children under the age of 18 were working; 38% of these women worked full time, year-round. Sixty-eight percent of women with children under the age of six worked with 31% working full time, year round. This compares with 44% working and 10% working full time, year round in 1970 (Bianchi & Spain, 1996, p. 21).

Single Parent Families. The second impact on families and fathers is the increase in single parent families. Unmarried women had nearly one in three births in 1995 compared to one in ten in 1970. The highest rate of births to unwed mothers was for the women in their early 20s (72 per 1000); second were women in their late 20s (59 per 1000). These were followed by teenagers with 46 per 1000 births (Bianchi & Spain, 1996, pp. 8, 9).

Single parents need support in providing their children with others that are significant to them including fathers, grandparents, relatives, and others who can help provide the love and caring children need. In order to paint a picture of the child's needs let us use Erikson's stages. The times suggested were not given by Erikson, are approximate, and each stage may carry back and over into another.

ERIKSON'S FIRST FIVE STAGES OF GROWTH

Trust vs. Mistrust (0–18 months)

During the first stage, the infant develops trust in his or her caregivers. Fathers, mothers, as well as other caregivers can begin the development of attachment with the infant. During the first 3 months, routine is important, infants are totally self-absorbed. But by the seventh or eighth month, the child identifies those that the child knows and shows separation anxiety toward others. "Consistency, continuity, and sameness of experience provide a rudimentary sense of ego identity" (Erikson, 1963, p. 147).

Traditionally, mothers have been recognized as the important person in attachment, with fathers supporting her, but fathers are also important attachment figures. "Researchers have gathered substantial evidence that infants form the attachment to both mothers and fathers at about the same period during the first year of life, although most infants develop a preference for the primary care providers" (Lamb, 1997, p. 15). Fathers can provide a loving, stable, predictable environment for the child. The child begins to recognize the world is a safe and stable place and they will be taken care of (LaCrosse, 1997). We know from recent studies that the brain is developing its connections and does this at a rapid rate during the first 3 years, so interaction with both parents increases the opportunity for the child to have the necessary brain development.

Autonomy vs. Shame and Doubt (18 months–3 years)

Toddlers are developing a sense of self. "If denied the gradual and well-guided experience of the autonomy of free choice, . . . the child turns against himself all his urge to discriminate and to manipulate. . . . From a sense of self control without loss of self-esteem comes a lasting sense of good will and pride" (Erikson, 1963, pp. 252, 254). Research shows that although fathers and mothers influence the children in similar rather than dissimilar ways, fathers are more apt to play with their young children with physically stimulating, unpredictable play and noncontaining interactions (Lamb, 1997, pp. 112, 113). Fathers can add to the children's development of selves during the period of autonomy as well as the next stage of initiative. "Young children need lots of verbal stimulation for developing the language centers of their brains, hence dads' style of parenting help children develop self regulation, while that of moms helps children acquire language skills" (Horn, 1997, p. 27).

Initiative vs. Guilt (3–5)

"Initiative adds to autonomy the quality of undertaking, planning and 'attacking' a task for the sake of being active and on the move" (Erikson, 1963, p. 255). Sex role identification, begun in the autonomy stage becomes stronger in the initiative vs. guilt stage. Father becomes important in role identity for both boys and girls.

The child's world widens and children begin to turn to other children through participation in preschool. Words become increasingly important for communication with other children. Mothers and teachers rely on words for guidance and self-control.

Industry vs. Inferiority (6–12)

The danger of this period of life, the elementary school days, is the feeling of inferiority. Children need to be supported and able to accomplish the challenges of education.

By the age of 12, the moral foundation is laid, and children are affected by the behavior of their parents. So the moral behavior of both parents is very important. Children develop their social skills and their beliefs in morality during this time. Most important to this development is the way the father and mother interact. Fathers teach their sons and daughters through modeling how women should be treated. If dads relate to their daughters in nonsexual ways, they make the daughters feel that they are important for who they are, not for their bodies. Girls with active and loving fathers do not need to use their bodies to relate to men (LaCrosse, 1997). Boys 6–12 are interested in many activities in which they and their fathers can participate together. During this period, it is important that both boys and girls have strong male models to help them in their development.

Identity vs. Role Confusion (12–18)

By this time, it is important that the moral rules of the family are internalized by the children so that they think about consequences before they act. It is again important for both father and mother to model the type of behavior that they want their children to have. Boundaries and expectations have been set and children now begin to set their own limits. Fathers can be extremely important if they will listen to and communicate with their children. Fathers continue to be important to both boys and girls. Fathers can help daughters know that love and sex are not synonymous (LaCrosse, 1997). If fathers continue to recognize their children's accomplishments, they will be able to handle the social issues of drugs and sex, and also able to function better as adults. Opportunities to work and play with their fathers allow fathers to have great influence on their sons's ability to handle the pressures of young adulthood.

WHY INVOLVE FATHERS?

Issues that make the need for encouraging fathers to be involved with their children include (1) the increase in single-parent families, (2) the need for children to have significant others who are men, and (3) the development of standards and morals.

Increase in Single Parent Families

In the two decades between 1970 and 1996, the number of children not living with their biological fathers almost tripled. In looking at family groups rather than total population, the numbers rose from 3 million, 480,000 single-parent mother family groups (11.5%) in 1970 to 9 million, 600,000 single-parent mothers (26.6%) in 1996. There were also more single-parent fathers in family groups going from 380,000 (1.3%) in 1970 to 1 million, 900,000 (5%) in 1996 (Bianchi & Spain, 1996, p. 14). The data makes it clear that resources to support both fathers and mothers in their roles as parents are necessary.

Outcomes Resulting from Fathers' Involvement

Research (Byrne, 1997, pp. 2, 3; Horn, 1997, p. 27; Levine, Murphy, & Wilson, 1997) indicates that children without fathers fail in school three times more often than those in two parent families. They are apt to have more emotional problems that need treatment. They have more behavioral problems and lower reading and mathematical ability. Suicide is three times higher for single-parent adolescents. The children are five times more likely to be in poverty. On the other hand, studies show that children of fathers who are involved in school activities complete more school and have greater incomes than those whose parents were not involved. And fathers who are positively involved with their children support their intellectual and emotional development (Byrne, 1997; Engle & Breaux, 1998; Lamb, 1997; Levine, Murphy, & Wilson, 1997).

Changes in Behavior

As boys get older, undesirable behavior increases. In a study by Harris and Associates (1995), conducted for the Boy Scouts of America, it was revealed that younger boys have higher moral standards than older boys. This study included boys in two-parent families as well as single-parent families, and they were asked "During the past year, I have . . ." Only 20% of the young group (7–10 years) cheated on tests or homework, while 76% of the 14–19 year old students had. In the 7–10-year-old group, only 7% had shoplifted; but in the older group, 33% had (p. 7). Eighty-three percent of young children thought spending time with their families was important, but only 41% of the older group thought so (p. 18). This suggests that caring and guidance needs to be established early in a child's life and that it needs to continue until adulthood.

INVOLVING FATHERS IN PROGRAMS

Fathers are an asset to a child's development, and communities can become an asset to a father's development. Here are a few strategies for an effective fatherhood program:

- Promote partnerships between fathers. Match up new dads with current participants and form peer support groups.
- Provide fathers with information on child development. Teach them techniques for raising sons and daughters of all ages.
- Make it easy for fathers to attend. Have flexible schedules, provide or pay for transportation, and offer child care.

- Offer life skills training. Teach classes on parenting, relationships, anger management, and leadership.
- Help identify the abilities and needs of fathers. Provide literacy, job training, and employment opportunities, information, and referrals.
- Have men in leadership roles of the program.
- Promote tolerance. Encourage cultural diversity and acknowledge the important roles of mothers.
- Teach standards and accountability for fatherhood. Let dads know there are rights, responsibilities, resources, and rewards ("4 Rs of Fatherhood") to being a good father.
- Listen and learn from fathers. Survey men for their ideas and interests, and let them know you value their opinions.
- Recognize all kinds of fathers. From teen dads, to men who serve as father-figures, to incarcerated fathers, remember that all dads need support (Governor Romer's Responsible Fatherhood Initiative, 1997, used with permission).

This list emphasizes the ways programs can get help from fathers and, at the same time, help them perfect their roles as fathers. They can also be helped in their development of skills needed for good employment opportunities, thus reducing unemployment and poverty and improving their self-esteem and ability to be the man they want to be.

MAKING INVOLVEMENT HAPPEN IN CENTERS AND SCHOOLS

When involving fathers, include any male who is serving as a friend or father substitute. "The stereotype that women alone should care for children—or that they alone are capable of caring for children—limits the opportunities and talents of both sexes" (Levine, Murphy, & Wilson 1997, p. 10). The term, father, includes father substitutes.

Father-Friendly Atmosphere

1. Create an atmosphere where men as well as women are expected to be involved.
2. Decorate bulletin boards so parents know they are welcome.
   a. Include displays of fathers, mothers and children.

b. Have children make posters that include men.

c. Include all ethnic groups with parents and children.

d. See if the children can bring photographs of their father or father substitute when he was young. Make a poster for the bulletin board.

3. Appoint a child to be a welcoming person (perhaps the V.I.P.—very important person of the day). Let them share a class notebook with the visitor. (Photographs will have to be taken. Include a father in one of the pictures).

4. Have nonthreatening activities with children that visitors can do when they first visit.

5. Make a special effort to help fathers with special needs children get involved with programs and other fathers (Davis & May, 1991).

6. Last, but not least, encourage all fathers to visit.

Communication

There are many opportunities to communicate and more can be planned.

1. During daily drop-off and pick-up, talk with fathers as well as mothers. If uncles, grandfathers, and others stand outside waiting for their children to come, find someone to watch the room and go out and talk with them. Always give them an opportunity to talk half of the time.

2. Encourage fathers to come early and participate with the children.

3. In newsletters include a picture and article about a father. As stated above, a father substitute, uncle, or friend will do. Send newsletters to both custodial and noncustodial parents unless the courts have found that the noncustodial parent should not be contacted. Parents who hear about their children continue to be involved.

4. Have parent teacher conferences at a time when both parents or single parents can attend. Have the noncustodial parent attend, too. You can have them at separate times if they prefer.

5. Make home visits. Try to visit when both parents can be present.

6. Advertise special days at convenient times for parents where fathers and mothers can share ideas and help prepare the center (complied from Berger, 1995, 1996; Levine, Murphy, & Wilson, 1993).

Activities

Special days can encourage parents to come. The following are just samples. Get the fathers together and let them think of more ideas.

1. Paint the pumpkin. Get pumpkins from a store or have fathers bring a pumpkin. Let the children classify the pumpkins according to size. Make graphs of the pumpkin sizes. Enlist the father to help with the action. Paint the pumpkin faces together.

2. Plan physical activities stations. The children rotate around the activity centers. Try centers such as a balance beam, jump rope, jump over the pretend stream, play catch, bean bags, and hop scotch. Let fathers supervise each center.

3. Go on field trips. Plan some exciting field trips that fathers would enjoy participating in. The zoo, farm, or history museum would be excellent choices (ideas compiled from Berger, 1995, Levine, 1997.)

Recruit

Getting Men Involved: Strategies for Early Childhood Programs. (Levine, Murphy, & Wilson, 1993): If you are having trouble recruiting, get a copy of this book; it is filled with suggestions. One that stands out is the use of bus drivers (pp. 74–75). Parents in Community Action from Indianapolis redefined the role of the bus driver and successfully used their 54 bus drivers to be part of the program and to also recruit other fathers. The drivers attend all educational staff meetings and also work 1 hour in the classroom. Some end up working longer periods of time in the centers. Drivers meet the parents because they pick up the children. They also need parent volunteer riders to ride with them in the bus. Through these contacts, they are able to recruit others to become involved in their Head Start centers.

CONCLUSIONS

If personnel in centers and schools recognize the importance of fathers in the lives of their children, they can respond by including men in their work. Each center and school will have to develop their own directions for involving fathers. They will examine where they are and how they can respond to fathers, where they want to be, and how they can get there. Action is next. Plans are only effective if they are put into action.

REFERENCES

Bianchi, S. M., & Spain, D. (December, 1996). Women, work and family in America. In *Population Bulletin, 51*(3). Washington, DC: Population Reference Bureau.

Berger, E. H. (1995). *Parents as partners in education: Families and schools working together.* Englewood Cliffs, NJ: Prentice Hall.

Berger, E. H. (1996). Don't leave them standing on the sidewalk. *Early Childhood Education, 24*(2), 131–133.

Byrne, G. (October 1997) Father may not know best, but what does he know? *Population Today, 25*(10), 1–3.

Davis, P. B., & May, J. F. (1991). Involving fathers in early intervention and family support programs: Issues and strategies. *Children's Health Center, 20*(2), 87–92.

Engle, P. L., & Breaux, C. (1998). Fathers' involvement with children: Perspectives from developing countries. In *Social policy report, 12*(1). Ann Arbor, MI: Society for Research in Child Development.

Erikson, E. H. (1963). *Childhood and Society* (2nd ed.). New York: W. W. Norton.

Governor Romer's Responsible Fatherhood Initiative (1997). *Colorado fathers' resource guide.* Denver, CO: Author.

Griswold, R. L. (1993). *Fatherhood in America.* New York: Basic Books.

Horn, W. F. (July, August 1997). You've come a long way, daddy. *Policy Review, 84,* 24–30.

Lamb, M. E. (Ed.) (1997). *The role of the father in child development* (3rd ed.). New York: Wiley.

LaCrosse, R. (October 1997) Stages of Development. Paper presented at Colorado Summit on Fatherhood, Denver, CO.

LaRossa, R. (1997). *The modernization of fatherhood: A social and political history.* Chicago: The University of Chicago Press.

Levine, J. A., Murphy, D. T., & Wilson, S. (1993). *Getting men involved: Strategies for early childhood programs.* New York: Scholastics.

From Philosophy to Practice in Inclusive Early Childhood Programs

Tom Udell
Joyce Peters
Torry Piazza Templeman

Two 4-year-olds are playing at the water table. Their teacher observes that Michelle splashes her hand on the surface repeatedly, chortling with delight. Carlos is busy pouring water from a large container into several smaller ones and then arranging them in a pattern to his liking.

These children of the same age are at different developmental points in their lives. How can a teacher or a child care provider allow Michelle to do all the splashing she needs to do, teach her social skills in water play, and also encourage Carlos to continue his absorption in measuring and artistic design—as well as learn the social skills of playing with Michelle? A simple water table activity is more complicated than it seems. Why is this play activity important? How can an inclusive program meet the needs of both children?

The Individuals with Disabilities Education Act has challenged all providers of service to young children with disabilities to provide services in natural community settings where young children without disabilities participate. Educators are looking for ways to merge developmentally appropriate practices with practices found effective in the field of early childhood special education. Although these two sets of practices converge at certain points, professionals agree that differences remain (Bredekamp & Rosegrant, 1992).

The Teaching Research Early Childhood Program has developed a conceptual framework to meet the challenge of blending developmentally appropriate practices with early childhood special education recommended practices. This blended approach has resulted in the delivery of quality services within an inclusive preschool/child care setting.

Elements of an Inclusive Program

In the context of early childhood education, what are the differences among practices known as *mainstreaming, reverse mainstreaming, integration,* and *inclusion*? All these terms denote the introduction of children with disabilities into a "typical" environment for some portion of the day, or in the case of reverse mainstreaming, the introduction of some typically developing peers into what is essentially a special education program.

Inclusion goes further in that no one is introduced into anyone else's program. All children attend the same program, all of the time. Each child is given the support he or she needs to be successful in the setting. For children age 3 to school age, these settings are most often public and private community preschool and child care programs.

The most comprehensive and widely disseminated guidelines defining quality services in these settings are *developmentally appropriate practices,* as defined by the National Association for the Education of Young Children (NAEYC).

Research in early childhood special education indicates that those using these developmental guidelines as the *sole* principles for providing services to young children with disabilities would fall short of provid-

ing the full range of services these children need. Carta, Schwartz, Atwater, and McConnell (1991) warned against the adoption of these guidelines to the potential exclusion of principles and practices that we know are effective for children with disabilities, but also suggest that educators not overlook developmentally appropriate practices in providing inclusive services for these children. Indeed, Bredekamp and Rosegrant stated in a 1992 NAEYC publication:

> Experiences with mainstreaming over the past two decades suggest a conclusion that probably will be made concerning the guidelines . . . and children with special needs 20 years from now: The guidelines are the context in which appropriate early education of children with spe-

From *Teaching Exceptional Children*, January/February 1998, pp. 44-49. © 1998 by The Council for Exceptional Children. Reprinted by permission.

PRINCIPLES OF EARLY CHILDHOOD SPECIAL EDUCATION

- **Intervention focused on functional goals**
- **Family-centered services**
- **Regular monitoring and adjustment of intervention**
- **Transition planning**
- **Multidisciplinary services**

cial needs should occur; however, a program based on the guidelines alone is not likely to be sufficient for many children with special needs. (p. 106)

Let's look at both recommended practices—developmentally appropriate practices and early childhood special education practices—and find points where educators, children, families, and communities can work together to make inclusive programs successful.

Developmentally Appropriate Practice

NAEYC published a widely used position statement about developmentally appropriate practices for serving young children from birth to age 8 in early childhood programs (Bredekamp, 1987). The association compiled and published this statement in reaction to the concern of early childhood educators with the increasing academic demands made of young children in early childhood programs and general misconceptions about how teachers should provide instruction to young children.

This position statement became the most widely recognized guideline in the field of early childhood education. In 1997 NAEYC published the revised *Developmentally Appropriate Practice in Early Childhood Programs* (Bredekamp & Copple, 1997), clarifying the misunderstandings and misinterpretations that arose from a decade of extensive dissemination of the original position statement.

Based on the developmental theories of Piaget and Vygotsky, the NAEYC guidelines convey the primary message that *learning occurs through exploratory play activities* and that formal instruction beyond the child's current developmental level will result in nonfunctional, rote learning at best. Developmentally appropriate practice suggests that teachers should not attempt to direct or tightly structure learning experi-

ences and that formal academic instruction at the preschool level should not occur.

These guidelines have three dimensions, as follows:

1. *Age appropriateness.* According to child development knowledge and research, all children grow and change in a universal, predictable sequence during the first 9 years of life. This knowledge about typical child development allows teachers to plan appropriate environments and experiences.
2. *Individual appropriateness.* Each child has his or her own unique pattern of growth, strengths, interests, experiences, and backgrounds. Both the curriculum and adults' interactions with children should be responsive to these individual differences.
3. *Cultural appropriateness.* To truly understand each child, teachers and child care providers must recognize and respect the social and cultural context in which the child lives. When teachers understand the cultural context in which children live, they can better plan meaningful experiences that are relevant for each child (Bredekamp & Copple, 1997).

Teachers should use knowledge of child development to identify the range of appropriate behaviors, activities, and materials for a specific age group. As well, they should use this knowledge in conjunction with an understanding of each child in the classroom and his or her unique personalities, backgrounds, and abilities to design the most appropriate learning environment.

NAEYC recommends that instructional practices emphasize child-initiated, child-directed play activities, based on the assumption that young children are intrinsically motivated to learn by their desire to understand their environment. Teaching strategies include hands-on exploratory activities with emphases on the use of concrete, real, and relevant activities.

Rationale of Early Childhood Special Education

Early childhood special education is based on the premise that early and comprehensive intervention maximizes the developmental potential of infants and children with disabilities. Such intervention produces child outcomes that would likely not occur in the absence of such intervention (McDonnell & Hardman, 1988).

Since the initiation of publicly supported services for preschool children with disabilities in the mid-1970s, professionals in early childhood special education have developed a body of practices. This body of practice has evolved from research, model demonstration, and evaluation ef-

forts and is currently referred to as *early childhood special education recommended practices.* Researchers have documented syntheses of desired characteristics, or recommended practices, of exemplary, early childhood special education models (DEC, 1993; McDonnell & Hardman, 1988; Wolery, Strain & Bailey, 1992; Wolery & Wilbers, 1994). We have selected components of these models and practices that researchers have shown to be essential, effective, and compatible with the NAEYC guidelines (see Carta et al., 1991, for evaluation criteria). These components include setting functional goals and monitoring children's progress toward these goals, planning for transitions, and working closely with families.

Intervention Focused on Functional Goals

Intervention for children with disabilities should focus on producing specific and measurable child goals. To make meaningful changes in children's behavior, these goals need to be functional for each child and for the environments in which the child participates. A *functional* skill is one that is essential to participation within a variety of integrated environments. In early childhood settings, functional skills are those that assist children to interact more independently and positively with their physical and social environments.

For example, it is probably more functional for a child to be able to carry out his or her own toileting functions independently than to be able to name 10 farm animals. Shouldn't we give preference to skills that will enable the child to participate more fully in an integrated setting, as

Effective early childhood instructional practices emphasize child-initiated, child-directed play activities, based on the assumption that young children are intrinsically motivated to learn by their desire to understand their environment.

opposed to those skills that would be indicated in the developmental hierarchy or sequence? If our answer is yes, these goals then become the focus for providing individualized intervention. Teachers or care providers design services and instruction to produce a specific outcome—like independent toileting—and this outcome becomes the standard against which the success of an intervention is measured.

Family-Centered Services

The family is the heart of all early childhood programs. Families participate in planning and decision making in all aspects of their children's program.

A good school-family partnership includes a system for a child's family to have regular communication with the classroom staff and have frequent opportunities to participate in their child's program. Quality programs also include procedures for helping families link into existing community resources.

Regular Monitoring and Adjustment of Intervention

Educators and care providers should systematically monitor the effects of specific interventions. Researchers have shown the effectiveness of using *formative* assessment data to monitor children's progress toward their individual goals and objectives. (McDonnell & Hardman, 1988).

We know that such data must be gathered frequently enough to monitor the subtleties of progress or failure. Data-collection systems must measure child progress toward the acquisition of predetermined goals, including the application of skills in a variety of settings.

Transition Planning

Educators and care providers of all children—and particularly children with disabilities—must plan for transition from one school or child care setting to the next one. Early childhood special educators are particularly concerned with transition from preschool to kindergarten because this move signals a major change for the child and the family from familiar and secure surroundings to a new, unknown setting.

This is a time of considerable stress, and teachers and child care providers must engage in careful, timely planning to smooth the process. Many people are involved in the transition planning process: the child's family, the sending teacher, the early intervention specialist, support personnel, and the future receiving teacher. An effective transition plan often begins 1–2 years before the actual move. This preliminary planning enables the sending teachers to identify skills needed in the future environment. These skills are included in the child's curriculum during the last preschool years.

Key Aspects of Developmentally Appropriate Practices
- **Developmental evaluation of children for program planning and implementation**
- **High staff qualifications**
- **High ratio of adults to children**
- **Strong relationship between home and program**

Multidisciplinary Services

Professionals from many disciplines need to participate in the planning of comprehensive services for children with disabilities and their families. Because many of these children and their families have complex needs, no single professional and no one discipline can provide a full range of services.

The specific needs of each child and family determine what disciplines should be involved in assessing, planning, implementing, and monitoring services. The following disciplines are commonly involved in early childhood special education:

- Speech and language therapy.
- Occupational and physical therapy.
- Health and medical services.
- Audiology.
- Disability-specific specialists, such as a vision specialist or autism specialist.

Professionals in these disciplines provide services in an integrated manner: They share knowledge and methods across disciplines, and the entire team develops and implements one comprehensive plan. Following this plan, team members provide consultation services within the early childhood environment.

Merging Programs Through Developmentally Appropriate Practices

The first step to merging these approaches is to recognize the advantages a program adhering to developmentally appropriate practices offers for the successful inclusion of children with disabilities. Such a program will have high-quality components, many of which facilitate the inclusion process.

Facilitating Inclusion

The nature of developmentally appropriate practices allows for the inclusion of children with great variation in development within the same setting. Even in a group

---

of young children without disabilities, of the same age, children can be as much as 2 years apart developmentally.

Thus, planning developmentally appropriate activities and providing equipment and materials for the preschool setting already accommodates children in a wide development range. This allowance in planning and material selection makes it possible to include children with mild and moderate disabilities without additional adaptation.

This developmental approach to planning creates an ideal environment for embedding instruction on individually targeted skills. The developmental emphasis on learning as a process rather than a product also facilitates targeting a variety of individualized objectives. To illustrate the process-versus-product approach, let's look at ways teachers might provide art experiences—and individualized instruction—for children.

The *process* approach to art allows children to explore available materials, experiment, and create individual designs with little regard for the end product. This approach also allows for intervention on a variety of instructional objectives for children with disabilities while all children are involved in the same activity. For example, all children are involved in a finger-painting activity; one child may be working on requesting objects, another on identifying colors, and yet another on staying with the group.

Providing Quality Indicators

Developmentally appropriate practices are not a curriculum, nor do they dictate a rigid set of standards. Developmental programs will not all look the same, but they will have a similar framework that pays careful attention to child development knowledge and will assist educators in providing quality services for children. The use of developmentally appropriate practices ensures quality in programs in many ways, such as developmental evaluation of children for program planning and implementation, high staff qualifications, a high ratio of adults to children, and strong relationship between home and program.

- *Developmental evaluation.* Decisions about enrollment and placement have a major effect on children. Educators and care providers base these decisions on multiple assessment data emphasizing observations by teachers and parents. Teachers use developmental assessment of child progress and achievement to adapt curriculum, communicate with families, and evaluate program effectiveness. Developmental evaluations of children use valid instruments developed for use with young children; these assessment tools are gender, culture, and socioeconomically appropriate (Bredekamp, 1987).

Children of the same age can be as much as 2 years apart developmentally.

- *Staff qualifications.* The NAEYC guidelines for developmentally appropriate practice emphasize the need for staff with preparation and supervised experiences specific to working with young children. Early childhood teachers should have college-level preparation in early childhood education and child development.
- *High adult/student ratios.* A key to implementing developmentally appropriate practices is to have a small number of children per classroom and a high ratio of adults to children. Ratios suggested in the NAEYC position statement are higher than those required for licensing in most states. NAEYC recommended standards describe a ratio of 2 adults to 20 children ages 4–5, with younger children requiring smaller groups with higher adult-to-child ratios.
- *Home-to-program relationship.* NAEYC guidelines recommend parent involvement in all decision making, regular communication between parents and teacher, and encouragement of parent involvement in the day-to-day happenings of the program. These practices help in building a strong relationship between home and the child's community program.

Developing a Conceptual Base

We have developed a conceptual base, recognizing the two sets of practice, that will allow both developmentally appropriate practices and special education principles to exist within the same setting. The Teaching Research Early Childhood Program has developed a philosophy that views developmentally appropriate practices as the foundation on which individualized programs are built, adding special education instruction when needed for individual children. We believe that the two approaches to early childhood are not mutually exclusive.

Figure 1 illustrates this dilemma. The builder has two sets of clearly different materials and cannot decide which to use. The key to moving beyond this dilemma is to recognize that these practices serve distinctively different purposes—and we can view them as different types of resources.

- *Developmentally appropriate practices* are used to design an age-appropriate, stimulating environment supportive of all children's needs. These practices, however, were not developed to reflect or address specific individual needs of children with disabilities and offer little information about specific intervention strategies needed to serve these children.
- *Early childhood special education* practices are used to complement the basic program for children with exceptional developmental needs and to emphasize individualized strategies to maximize children's learning opportunities. These practices, however, do not provide guidelines for designing a quality early childhood learning environment.

When educators recognize these practices as being different, but compatible, they can then plan a single comprehensive program, as shown in Figure 2. The completed school uses developmentally appropriate practices as the material from which the foundation is built and special education practices as the material that completes the structure.

Implementing Both Practices Within the Same Setting

Let's look more closely at how this merger might work. A well-designed early childhood education program, following developmentally appropriate practices, uses a planned, well-organized environment where children interact with materials, other children, and adults. Here the NAEYC guidelines are apparent: Young children are intrinsically motivated to learn by their desire to understand their environment; the program is set up to allow children to self-select activities from a variety of interest centers.

When children show they need further support, educators use special education strategies that are made available in the program. These strategies include the following:

- *Directly prompting practice* on individually targeted skills, based on functional behavioral outcomes.
- *Reinforcing* children's responses.
- *Collecting data* to monitor children's progress and make intervention changes.

Some educators view these strategies as conflicting with developmentally appropriate practices. Some people liken this direct prompting to the formal instruction that NAEYC deplored for use with young children. We believe that this view is a misinterpretation of NAEYC's position statement and the guidelines for developmentally appropriate practices.

As we mentioned earlier, however, NAEYC guidelines do not exclude intervention strategies for children with identified special needs (Bredekamp & Rosegrant 1993). We hope that by clarifying this misinterpretation, we might encourage teach-

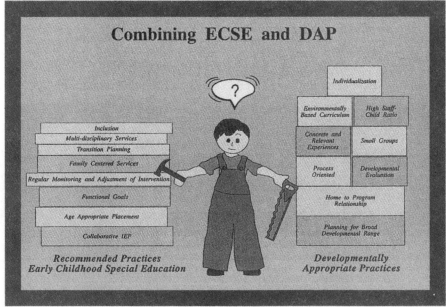

Figure 1

ers to view these intervention strategies as individually appropriate for some children.

As educators begin to merge these two approaches to early childhood education, we will find all children participating in the same well-organized, systematically planned environment—with direct instruction being provided to children who need this type of intervention. This direct instruction is blended into naturally occurring opportunities throughout the ongoing daily routine, such as play at the water table or learning independent toileting. An early childhood program adhering to developmentally appropriate practices provides a strong foundation for the provision of consultation services from professionals across different disciplines.

Consider transition services—an area of special education services that some educators believe conflicts with a child-centered developmental program. The transition planning process has an apparent conflict with developmentally appropriate practice because it presumes that the needs of some future environment should drive the child's curriculum at present. Guidelines for developmentally appropriate practices reject the idea of current curriculums being driven by the needs of a future environment.

To resolve this conflict we can look to the *foundation* concept. In developmentally appropriate practice, we find children participating in an environment planned to fit their current developmental demands and individual backgrounds and interests. Within this environment, children with special needs receive instruction on specific skills that will assist them to be successful in their next setting. Teachers have selected these specific skills or objectives with direct regard to the child's current needs and level of functioning, with some, but not predominant, focus on transition skills needs as dictated by future environments. Skills selected because of the demands of a future environment are ones that can be facilitated without disruption in the current environment. These skills are also within the boundaries of being developmentally appropriate in the future environment.

Mutually Beneficial, Not Mutually Exclusive

In inclusive early childhood education programs, we must caution against adopting developmentally appropriate practices to the exclusion of research-supported special education practices. Similarly, we must not fail to recognize the benefits offered by placing children with disabilities in developmentally appropriate programs. We need

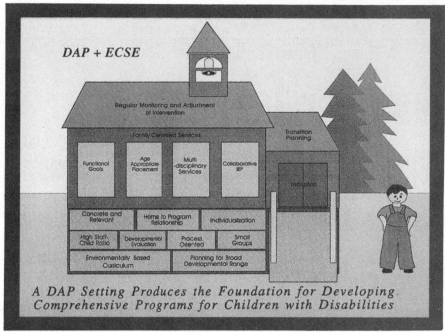

Figure 2

to develop an understanding of both sets of practices and to develop a program, from philosophy to practice, that merges practices.

References

Bredekamp, S. (Ed.). (1987). *Developmentally Appropriate Practices in Early Childhood Programs Serving Children from Birth Through Age 8* (Exp. ed.). Washington, DC: National Association for the Education of Young Children.

Bredekamp, S., & Copple, C. (Eds.). (1997). *Developmentally Appropriate Practices in Early Childhood Programs* (Rev. ed.) Washington, DC: National Association for the Education of Young Children.*

Bredekamp, S., & Rosegrant, T. (Eds.). (1992). *Reaching potentials: Appropriate curriculum and assessment for young children* (Vol. 1, pp. 92–112). Washington, DC: National Association for the Education of Young Children.

Carta, J. J., Schwartz, I. S., Atwater, J. B., & McConnell, S. R. (1991). Developmentally appropriate practice: Appraising its usefulness for young children with disabilities. *Topics In Early Childhood Special Education 11*(1), 1–20.

DEC Task Force on Recommended Practices. (1993). *DEC recommended practices: Indicators of quality in programs for infants and young children with special needs and their families*. Reston, VA: The Council for Exceptional Children, Division of Early Childhood Education. (ERIC Document Reproduction Service No. ED 370 253)

McDonnell, A., & Hardman, M. (1988). A synthesis of "best practice" guidelines for early childhood services. *Journal of the Division of Early Childhood, 12*, 328–337.

Wolery, M., Strain, P. S., & Bailey, D. B. (1992). Reaching potentials of children with special needs. In S. Bredekamp & T. Rosegrant (Eds.), *Reaching potentials: Appropriate curriculum and assessment for young children* (Vol. 1, pp. 92–112). Washington, DC: National Association for the Education of Young Children.*

Wolery, M., & Wilbers, J. S. (Eds.). (1994). *Including children with special needs in early childhood programs*. Washington, DC: National Association for the Education of Young Children.*

Books Now

To order books marked by an asterisk (*), please call 24 hrs/365 days: 1–800–BOOKS–NOW (266–5766) or (702) 258–3338 ask for ext. 1212 or visit them on the web at http://www.BooksNow.com/ TeachingExceptional.htm. Use Visa, M/C, or AMEX or send check or money order + $4.95 S&H ($2.50 each add'l item) to: Books Now, 660 W. Charleston Blvd., Las Vegas, NV 89102.

Tom Udell, *Assistant Research Professor;* **Joyce Peters,** *(CEC Oregon Federation), Associate Research Professor;* **Torry Piazza Templeman,** *(CEC Oregon Federation), Associate Director, Teaching Research Division, Western Oregon University, Monmouth.*

Address correspondence to Tom Udell, Teaching Research Division, Western Oregon University, 345 N. Monmouth Ave., Monmouth, OR 97361 (e-mail:udellt@wou.edu).

We would like to thank Kathy Haydon for her illustrations.

Together Is Better:

Specific Tips on How to Include Children with Various Types of Disabilities

Jane Russell-Fox

Develop a professional relationship with the child's parents. Keep communication lines open among all involved—parents, physicians, special education teachers, and other relevant people.

My experiences with both inclusive and noninclusive environments has led me to conclude that "together is better." I believe that early childhood professionals who are including children with special needs in their classrooms can set up the environment so that it accommodates these children as well as typically developing children. In doing this the professional takes the first steps toward successful inclusion.

While working in several different self-contained settings, I spent most of my time negotiating with

Jane Russell-Fox, M.Ed., is a preschool teacher for the inclusive "Wee Wildcat" program for the Eastmont School District in East Wenatchee, Washington.

Photographs © The Growth Program.

my peers and administrators to plan for inclusion of the special needs children in my group. Usually my plan was for inclusion that would operate 15 to 20 minutes of the school day to give my children a chance at least to hear others model language, involve themselves in cooperative play, and establish friendships.

Staff members who knew I was a strong supporter of inclusive classrooms tended continually to say to me, "That sounds like a good idea; we should try that next week." Next week always came, and we were no closer to the beginning of an inclusive environment than we were the week before.

After my experiences in inclusive environments, I know now that everyone has to be sold on inclusion before it can work successfully. After one is sold on inclusion, it's the job

of the team to set up the environment and offer choices to all children at a variety of levels so that all can learn together in the same room.

It is also the job of the team to continue updating skills and working to improve the effectiveness of the program. Children with special needs do need specialized services based on individual needs, including predictable routines, accurate record keeping of goals, effective teaching strategies, all performed in a developmentally appropriate environment. There is no blueprint to follow—each person is an individual.

The following ideas are only a way to get you started. A range of services needs to be provided to most children with special needs. You can't do it all by yourself. Expect your team members to be there for you. Team members can include

From *Young Children,* May 1997, pp. 81–83. © 1997 by the National Association for the Education of Young Children (NAEYC). Reprinted by permission.

everyone from a child care provider to an occupational therapist.

The following processes are adaptations that are easy and use many commonsense ideas and readily available materials. For example, Jennifer has a vision impairment and is not able to see some of the books you read during circle time. What can you do? Try storytelling, enlarging the books, using flannelboard characters, or giving Jennifer a designated spot toward the front during circle time.

Working with a child who has exceptional health needs

- Develop a professional relationship with the child's parents and physician, and in some cases with other care providers who may come in contact with the child.
- Keep communication lines open among all.
- Get informed about the child's health needs, including medicine and diet.
- Invite the school nurse to become a part of the team.
- Develop a program plan for the child who may be out of the classroom for long periods of time. Home visits, telephone calls, classmate phone lists, and care packages from classmates or activity packets from the teacher can assist the child and his or her family in continuing to be a part of the classroom.*

Working with a child who has exceptional hearing needs

- Develop a professional relationship with the child's parents, audiologist, hearing specialist, sign language interpreter, and speech and language therapist.
- Keep communication lines open with them.
- Learn to change a hearing aid battery and cord.

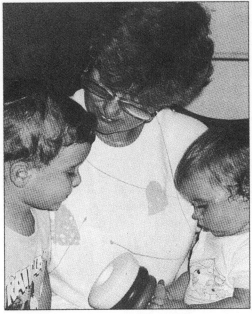

Facilitating social skills is an essential part of facilitating true inclusion. Teachers will want to keep groups relatively small so children can interact as children typically do.

- Use visual and tactile aids as much as you can.
- Use the child's name when seeking the child's attention.
- Make sure you have the child's attention before beginning the activity, giving directions, or introducing additional material.
- Speak at normal speed and volume without exaggerating lip movements.
- Make certain the child sits up close for good visibility of the teacher, activity, and other children.
- Encourage language in group activities by allowing time for the child to start and finish speaking.*

Working with a child who has exceptional learning needs

- Concentrate on the child's strengths, not weaknesses.
- Present content in short segments using a multisensory approach (audio, visual, manipulative).

Provide for as much overlearning or repeated practice as necessary.
- Praise the child's progress.
- Use task analysis.
- Be patient when it is necessary to show a child how to do something many times.
- Give directions one at a time until a child can handle more than one.
- Help parents to recognize their children's small successes.
- Plan for modeling and imitation.
- Provide clear transitions; try to avoid abrupt changes in activities.
- Present developmental-level challenges.
- Allow time and opportunity to practice new skills needed for activities.

Specific intervention strategies for working with a child with visual impairments

- Consult with the child's parents and vision specialists to determine what the child can see and what play materials would be most appropriate.
- Orient the child to the classroom layout and locations of materials. Give a new orientation whenever changes are made.
- Provide the child with a rich variety of tactile, manipulative, and auditory experiences.
- Encourage independent both by your actions and in the way the room is arranged.
- Be alert to the need for physical prompts.
- Before beginning a new activity explain what is going to happen.*

Working with a child who has exceptional communication needs

- Be a good listener.
- Use parallel talk. Broadcasting play-by-play action of the child's activity helps to stimulate the acquisi-

*Source: Adapted by permission, from R. E. Cook, A. Tessier, and M. D. Klein, *Adapting Early Childhood Curricula for Children with Special Needs,* 3d ed. New York: Merrill/Macmillan, 1992. 206–07, 209.

tion of language (e.g., "You're putting the ball in the basket").

• Use alternative communications as needed (e.g., sign language, augmentative communication).

• Have everyone in the classroom model good language by talking about and labeling what they are doing.

• Promote specific reasons for expressing language (i.e., giving information, requesting and getting attention, protesting, and commenting).

Working with a child who has exceptional physical needs

• Get input from the physical therapist on the proper handling and positioning of the child. Get specific directions on the length of time the child should be in a given position. Seek suggestions from the occupational therapist on adapting fine-motor materials so that the child participates in all of the classroom projects. (Of course parents must be included in all planning for the child.)

• Make sure materials and toys are accessible to the child.

• Remember that physical delays don't always have an accompanying mental disability.

• Become familiar with adaptive equipment and know how to use and care for it.

• Arrange the environment to accommodate adaptive equipment.

• Allow extra time for making transitions.

• Support and encourage that which the child can do physically.

• Foster independence by focusing on the child's nonphysical abilities.

⌘

Facilitating social skills is an essential part of facilitating true inclusion. Teachers will want to keep groups relatively small so children can interact as children typically do. Rewarding remarks reinforce specific desired behaviors. Materials appropriate to the skills of interaction desired need to be provided. For example, if your desired outcome is cooperation, set up situations in the classroom to encourage teamwork— "After we pick up the blocks, then we can get ready for snack." Making sufficient materials available helps promote cooperation and imitation.

With each new child with special needs, a few accommodations can be made to a classroom environment and the instruction to allow these children to be included. Placing children with special needs in a learning environment with their typical peers offers many challenges for families and staff, but the rewards reaped and the teamwork accomplished are well worth the effort.

Coming into a work environment that is already sold on inclusion and is *practicing* it has been one of the greatest rewards of my professional career. I strongly urge you to develop inclusive classrooms in *your* setting!

For further reading

Allen, K.E. 1980. *Mainstreaming in early childhood education*. Albany, NY: Delmar.

Barnes, E., C. Berrigan, & D. Biklen. 1978. *What's the difference: Teaching positive attitudes toward people with disabilities*. Syracuse, NY: Human Policy Press.

Buscaglia, L. 1983. *The disabled and their parents: A counseling challenge*. New York: Holt, Rinehart, & Winston.

Chandler, P.A. 1994. *A place for me: Including children with special needs in early care and education settings*. Washington, DC: NAEYC.

Cook, R.E., A. Tessier, & M.D. Klein. 1987. *Adapting early childhood curricula for children with special needs*. 3d ed. New York: Harcourt Brace Jovanovich.

Deiner, P.L. 1983. *Resources for teaching young children with special needs*. New York: Harcourt Brace Jovanovich.

Debelak, M., J. Herr, & M. Jacobson. 1981. *Creative innovative classroom materials for teaching young children*. New York: Harcourt Brace Jovanovich.

Froschl, M., L. Colon, E. Rubin, & B. Sprung. 1984. *Including all of us—An early childhood curriculum about disabilities*. New York: Project Educational Equity Concepts.

Fullwood, D. 1990. *Chances and choices: Making integration work*. Baltimore: Paul H. Brookes.

Trainer, M. 1991. *Differences in common. Straight talk on mental retardation, Down syndrome and life*. Bethesda, MD: Woodbine House.

Inclusion of Young Children with Special Needs In Early Childhood Education: The Research Base

Samuel L. Odom
University of North Carolina at Chapel Hill

Karen E. Diamond
Purdue University

Increasingly, early childhood programs include children with disabilities and typically developing children. The purpose of this paper is to review the recent empirical literature that underlies the practice of inclusion at the early childhood level in order to provide a context for the research articles appearing in this issue of ECRQ. We first describe the definitions of inclusion, rationales for inclusive classes, and demographics of inclusive programs and staff. Using Bronfenbrenner's ecological systems theory as a conceptual framework, we review research related to variables proximal to the program (i.e., microsystem and mesosystem levels) such as classroom practices, children's social interactions, teacher beliefs, and professional collaboration. Next, we examine research associated with variables occurring more distally from the classroom program (i.e., ecosystem and macrosystem levels): families' perspectives, social policy, community and culture. We conclude this review with an examination of research that illustrates the influence of variables a[t] one level of the ecological system on those occurring at a different levels and recommend directions for future research.

Direct all correspondence to: Samuel L. Odom, School Education, CB-3500. University of North Carolina at Chapel Hill, Chapel Hill, NC 27599-3500.

From *Early Childhood Research Quarterly*, Vol. 13, No. 1, 1998, pp. 3-25. © 1998 by Ablex Publishing Corporation. Reprinted by permission.

When a mother brings her child to the preschool program in her community, when a child steps off the bus to go into his Head Start classroom, and when the Montessori teacher looks around the class before beginning the day's activities, they all are likely to see children with different abilities and different family backgrounds. Developmental and cultural diversity characterizes early childhood education in the late 1990s, and these themes are likely to become more prominent in the next century. Including young children with disabilities in early childhood programs is one trend that exemplifies this diversity.

Although specific references to inclusive practices were missing from the original NAEYC publication of Developmentally Appropriate Practice (Bredekamp, 1987), the most recent revision contains some strategies for including children with special needs (Bredekamp & Copple, 1997). Leaders from the fields of early childhood education and early childhood special education have collaborated to identify ways in which programs might be modified to accommodate the individual needs of children with disabilities (Allen & Schwartz, 1996; Chandler, 1994; Wolery, Strain, & Bailey, 1992; Wolery & Wilbers, 1994). Researchers have noted the similarities between accepted practices in early childhood education and early childhood special education (Fox, Hanline, Vail, & Galant, 1994; McLean & Odom, 1993), and a call for collaboration among professionals providing services for both groups of children has been clear and persistent (Bredekamp, 1993; Burton, Hains, Hanline, McLean, & McCormick, 1992; Stayton & Miller, 1993; Wolery & Bredekamp, 1994).

Given the momentum generated by this movement toward inclusion, an examination of the research that underlies practice is timely and important. The current special issue of *ECRQ* provides a venue for the most recent research on inclusion. The purpose of this introductory article is to provide an "empirical" context for the articles in this issue through a review of the recent literature that has appeared in other journals and publications. Comprehensive reviews of the literature on inclusion, integration, and mainstreaming have appeared in the past (Karnes & Lee, 1979, Odom & McEvoy, 1988; Peck & Cooke, 1983), with Buysse and Bailey (1993) and Lamorey and Bricker (1993) having conducted the most recent reviews. Our review takes up where these earlier reviews left off—with research published in the early 1990s to the present. The review focused specifically on research with young children, primarily from the toddler years through kindergarten. Also, unless authors re-

ported conducting research with children having a single type of disability or diagnosis, the general descriptor, "children with disabilities" is used. A common practice in early childhood special education has been to identify children as having developmental delays, so often specific disability information is not available beyond a general identification of the magnitude of delay. In most cases, we report empirical research that has appeared or will appear in refereed journals, although in extending this discussion to issues of social policy, we expand our review to scholarly publications in which policy analyses appear.

CONCEPTUAL FRAMEWORK FOR REVIEW

An ecological systems framework, based on the work of Bronfenbrenner (1979), serves as the conceptual organizer for this review. Bronfenbrenner proposed that events occurring within specific settings affect children's behavior and development, and he identified these specific settings as *microsystems.* For our purposes, the microsystem is conceptualized as the inclusive classroom. Variables operating outside the immediate classroom setting influence the implementation of inclusion inside and outside the microsystem. A second level of the ecological system, identified as the *mesosystem,* consists of factors occurring in other settings in which the child or other key participants in the microsystem might participate. For example, mesosystem variables may include an event occurring in the home or family or interactions occurring among professionals outside of the immediate classroom setting (e.g., collaborative interactions among professionals).

The *exosystem,* the third ecological system level, consists of events or individual's actions occurring in settings in which microsystem participants do not participate, but which have an influence on events or actions in the microsystem. For example, social policies established by individuals not directly participating in the inclusive setting represent exosystem variables. *Macrosystem* variables are cultural or societal values and beliefs that affect participants or events in the microsystem. For example, cultural values related to disability or cultural roles related to authority represent macrosystem variables. Last, influences between variables at different levels could exist and Bronfenbrenner assumed that such influences could be reciprocal (e.g., influences could go from exosystem to microsystem or visa versa). For a more in-depth discussion of the ecological systems models and inclusion research, see Peck (1993) and Odom et al. (1996). In this paper, we will follow Bronfenbrenner's lead by first examining research on microsystem variables like classroom practices and teacher beliefs, and follow this initial section with reviews of research related to meso-, exo-, and macrosystem variables (e.g., family, social policy, and cultural influences on inclusive programs). We begin with a discussion of the definition of and rationales for inclusion.

DEFINITION OF INCLUSION

A commonly agreed upon definition of inclusion does not exist, and in fact the terminology associated with inclusion has changed over the years. Programs that first placed young children with and without disabilities in early childhood classroom settings were called *integrated* (Allen, Benning, & Drummond, 1972; Bricker & Bricker 1971; Guralnick, 1976). *Mainstreaming,* a term originating in public school settings for older children, was later applied to such programs. However, Bricker (1995) has noted that the mainstreaming term has never fit exactly, because often public school programs have not provided programs for typically developing preschool-aged children (although this trend is changing). The term *inclusion* began appearing in the early 1990s (Stainback & Stainback, 1990) in part as a reaction to the way in which mainstreaming was being poorly implemented in some public school settings for elementary school-aged children, and the term was rapidly applied to early childhood programs. The definition implied a more embedded (in regular education) and comprehensive (e.g., community as well as school settings) form of involvement of children with and without disabilities than occurred in mainstreamed programs. However, when authors currently write about inclusion at the early childhood level, they tend to define inclusion in different ways (compare Bricker, 1995; Filler, 1996; Odom et al., 1996; Salisbury, 1991; Siegel, 1996).

The single commonality across definitions of inclusion is that children with and without disabilities are placed in the same setting, which is most often a classroom. The specific contexts vary across organizations (e.g., private community-based child care programs, Head Start programs, pre-kindergarten programs in public schools) and service delivery models (e.g., itinerant-direct service, itinerant-collaborative, team teaching, etc.) (Odom et al., 1997; Wolery, Holcombe et al., 1993a). The ratio of children with disabilities to typically developing children also varies; however, researchers and practitioners appear to apply the term *inclusion* most frequently to programs in which the majority of the children are typically developing. Other descriptors such as *reverse mainstreaming, inclusive early childhood special education, or integrated special education* are often applied to programs in which the majority of children have disabilities and some typically developing children are also enrolled (Odom & Speltz, 1983). In this review, we will use the terminology that authors use in their respective papers (when describing their papers) or the generic term "inclusion" when multiple papers are cited.

RATIONALES FOR INCLUSION

Educational, legal, and philosophical rationales for inclusive programs are noted by Bricker (1978) and Bailey, McWilliam, Buysse, and Wesley (1998). In practice, these rationales appear to be implemented in ways that differentially affect the nature of inclusive programs. One philosophical rationale for placing children with disabilities in inclusive settings has been that all children have the right to a life that is as *normal* as possible. This philosophical/ethical rationale emphasizes that children with disabilities should experience the same quality preschool classroom program (presumably high quality) as typically developing children (Bailey et al., 1998); that they become members of the classroom community through participation in class activities (Schwartz, 1996); and that they develop positive social relationships with class members and teachers (Guralnick, in press; Storey, 1993).

Legal and legislative issues also provide a rationale for inclusive programs for preschool children. The Individuals with Disabilities Education Act (IDEA), passed in 1986 and recently re-authorized with similar language, extended its support for special education to preschool children and maintained the provision in the earlier law that children be placed in classes with typically developing peers to the extent appropriate. In addition, the Americans with Disabilities Act has stipulated that enrollment in regular child care settings cannot be denied to children with disabilities because of their disability. In combination, these laws provided impetus for the placement of children with disabilities in settings with typically developing children. However, as will be discussed in a later section on social policy, these laws are implemented through state and local policies, which sometime create barriers to inclusion.

An educational rationale is sometimes used to support inclusion. Following this rationale, children with disabilities are placed in inclusive settings because professionals and family members believe that the developmental benefits in inclusive settings are superior to nonintegrated settings. For some of these children, however, these settings may need to be adapted (Carta, Schwartz, Atwater, & McConnell, 1991; Wolery et al, 1993b) so that learning experiences become embedded in the ongoing developmentally appropriate curriculum (Cavallaro, Haney, & Cabello, 1993). In fact, Bailey et al. (1998, this issue) propose that the question of whether or not to place a child with a disability in an inclusive program would not be an issue if professionals and parents were confident that the program was [a] high quality program and staff planned individual learning experiences to meet the children's needs.

DEMOGRAPHICS OF INCLUSION

Inclusion appears to occur frequently in this country. In a series of studies, Wolery and his colleagues have examined the frequency of inclusion and personnel involved in such programs. Employing national random sampling strategies, they have found that children with disabilities have been included in Head Start (i.e., reported by 94% of the respondents), public school prekindergarten (73% of respondents), public school kindergarten (81.5% of respondents), and community-based programs (59.2% of respondents) (Wolery et al., 1993a). Across a four year period from 1986–1990, the percentage of programs enrolling at least one child with disabilities increased from 37% to 74.2% (Wolery et al., 1993b). In a recent study of AEYC accredited preschools, McDonnell, Brownell, and Wolery (1997) found a smaller percentage (56%) of programs, than in previous survey research, enrolling children with disabilities.

Other researchers have confirmed the finding by Wolery and colleagues that inclusion occurs in different organizational settings. Buscemi, Bennet, Thomas, and Deluca (1995) and Sinclair (1993) have noted that Head Start has become a frequent setting for inclusion, which corresponds to the mandate to enroll children with disabilities given to Head Start over a quarter century ago. In some states, inclusive preschool programs are beginning to be implemented in public schools. Barnett and Frede (1993) found that in Massachusetts, 67% of the 3 and 4 year old children with disabilities were in some form of inclusive placement within the public schools. In other states (TN and CT), Brown, Horn, Heiser and Odom (1996) and Bruder, Staff, and McMurrer-Kaminer (1997) have noted that community-based child care programs serve as inclusive placements. . . .

THE MICROSYSTEM: CLASSROOM AND TEACHER VARIABLES

Inclusive early childhood classes may be seen as a microsystem within a child's social ecology. Aspects of this microsystem, such as classroom characteristics, affect children's development. These characteristics include overall quality, the make-up of the class (e.g., same-age, mixed-age), the ways that teachers arrange the classroom environment, and their teaching strategies. In the next sections, we will discuss research that has examined the influence of classroom variables on children's experiences in inclusive preschool classes.

Curriculum

In inclusive early childhood programs, the curriculum followed will affect children's participation and outcomes. As noted earlier, NAEYC (Bredekamp & Copple, 1997) has proposed developmentally appropriate curriculum guidelines for all early childhood programs, including those that include children with disabilities. In their study of the quality of developmentally appropriate practice inclusive and segregated special education early childhood classrooms, Laparo, Sexton, and Synder (1998) found the quality of developmentally appropriate practice to be moderately high in both types of programs. They found no significant differences in quality across the two groups of programs.

Providing children the freedom to select their own play activities is an aspect of developmentally appropriate practices that may have an important influence on children's development. Hauser-Cram, Bronson and Upshur (1993) conducted naturalist study of 153 children with disabilities enrolled in community-based preschool programs. In classrooms where teachers offered more choice of activities, children with disabilities engaged in "more and higher levels of peer interaction . . . and appeared to be less distracted and more persistent when involved in mastering tasks" (p. 494). Similarly, Antia, Kreimeyer, and Eldredge (1994) found more positive interactions between children with and without hearing impairments when teachers provided consistent opportunities for children to work together in the same small groups.

Mixed-age Grouping

The age-grouping of children in inclusive programs also affects children's participation and development. Roberts, Burchinal, and Bailey (1994) found that children (2-, 3-, and 4-year-olds) in mixed-age groups took more turns in conversations with partners with disabilities and received more turns from partners with disabilities than did children in same-age groups. Other research in inclusive mixed-age group, has revealed that developmental trajectories for communication, motor, and cognitive development were enhanced for younger children (Bailey, Burchinal, & McWilliam, 1993) and interactions with peers were higher for younger children (Bailey, McWilliam, Ware, & Burchinal, 1993) when compared with children in same-age groups. Furthermore, children with disabilities in mixed-aged inclusive settings engaged in higher levels of play mastery (Blasco, Bailey, & Burchinal, 1993) when compared with peers with disabilities in same-age classes. McWilliam and Bailey (1995) reported, however, that attentional engagement (i.e., attending to another child or adult or playing nearby with similar materials) was affected only modestly by age grouping, and there was no effect of age grouping on other measures of engagement.

Social Competence in Classroom Settings

In the 1970s and 1980s, most research focused on the effectiveness of different interventions in promoting cognitive, communicative, and motor outcomes for children with disabilities. When these variables were used to define outcomes for children, research demonstrated that children with disabilities benefited from early intervention, and that having a well-defined curriculum was associated with more positive outcomes for children regardless of the curriculum that was chosen (Shonkoff & Hauser-Cram, 1987). With the emergence, in the early 1980's, of social competence as an important developmental construct (Hartup, 1983), research that focused on social competence as an important outcome for children with disabilities soon followed.

Guralnick and Neville (1997) describe social competence as the way "individuals define and solve the most fundamental problems in human relationships" (p. 579). To develop social competence requires that children integrate cognitive, communication, affective and motor skills to meet their own interpersonal goals. A young child's social competence has important implications for later development, since young children's difficulties in peer interaction are predictive of social adjustment problems during later childhood and adolescence (Parker & Asher, 1987). While social competence includes cognitive (information-processing) and emotional components (Dodge, Pettit, McClaskey, & Brown, 1986), interactions with peers provide an avenue for children to put into practice their social skills.

Recent research examining social interaction among peers with and without disabilities supports earlier findings that peer interaction for children with disabilities occurs more frequently in inclusive settings than in noninclusive setting containing only children with disabilities. Using play groups of boys with mild developmental delays and boys without disabilities, Guralnick, Connor, Hammond, Gottman, and Kinnish (1996) found that all children were more interactive when in an inclusive setting than when they were in segregated settings including only children with disabilities (similar to special education preschools) or only typically developing children (similar to regular preschools). The difference was evident in the first week and was most consistently apparent for children with developmental disabilities. . . .

As noted earlier, social competence includes cognitive and emotional components, as well as peer-related behaviors. In a recent study, Diamond, Hestenes, Carpenter, & Innes (in press) examined the influence of children's participation in an inclusive preschool program on acceptance of classmates with disabilities. They found that typically developing children in inclusive classes gave higher social acceptance ratings in response to scenarios about imaginary classmates with physical and sensory disabilities than did children in noninclusive early childhood programs. Children without disabilities in both types of classes gave the highest social acceptance ratings to imaginary classmates without disabilities. To examine the relationship of acceptance ratings and children's behavior in the classroom, Okagaki, Diamond, Kontos, & Hestenes (1988, this issue) observed children in university-based and community-based classrooms. Typically developing children with more positive attitudes toward children with disabilities (i.e., as measured through a hypothetical assessment) also played more often with children with disabilities in their class than did children with less positive attitudes. These authors also found a positive relationship between parental attitudes toward their children's play with children with disabilities and their children's interaction with children with disabilities. The studies just reported, along with recent work by Stoneman and her colleagues (Stoneman, Rugg, & Rivers, 1996) suggest that teachers and parents may play important roles in promoting children's acceptance of peers with disabilities.

Understanding the ways in which adults influence children's ideas about, and interactions with, other children is an area for future research. Bailey (1997) suggests that a primary factor that differentiates approaches to adult-child interaction, including teaching, is whether the adult (teacher or parent) assumes a directive or responsive role in relationship to the child. A question that has been of particular interest in recent years has been the ways in which such directive or responsive classroom teaching practices may promote interactions among children in inclusive classrooms . . .

Collaboration and Consultation. Cooperation, collaboration and mutual respect between "regular" and "special" early childhood teachers and therapists are important components of successful inclusive programs (Kontos & File, 1993). When receiving services and supports by consultants, early childhood teachers report preferring a consultative model rather than a medical or expert model approach (Buysse, Schulte, Pierce, & Terry, 1994). This finding is consistent with the work of Peck et al. (1993) who found that collaborative relationships among early childhood teachers and specialists were a hallmark of successful inclusive programs.

Barriers to successful collaboration also exist. In this issue, research by Stoiber, Gettinger, and Goetz (1998, this issue) suggests that limited time and opportunities for collaboration among teachers and therapists are viewed by practitioners as major barriers to inclusion. Similarly, Buysse, Wesley and Keyes (1998, this issue) found that the complexities of coordinating services for children with disabilities and their families often serves as a barrier to inclusion, at least from the perspective of practitioners and administrators. In their examination of the relationships among professionals working in inclusive programs, Lieber et al. (1997) identified a range of factors that functioned as barriers to or—alternatively—as facilitators of collaboration. These included having a shared philosophy, perceived "ownership" of the child with disabilities, staff communication, role release, and administrative support.

MESOSYSTEM VARIABLES: FAMILY PERSPECTIVES

For inclusive programs, most research related to families may be viewed as mesosystem level variables in that families represent a second microsystem context in which the child participates and which may affect the inclusive program. A rich history of research on family members' perspectives on early childhood inclusion exists (Bailey & Winton, 1987; Turnbull & Winton, 1983; Winton & Turnbull, 1981) and has been summarized well in an earlier review (Winton, 1993). The general findings across studies have been that family members: (a) have positive feelings about inclusive settings; (b) have identified some benefits for their children, and (c) share some fears or concerns about inclusive placements. . . .

EXOSYSTEM VARIABLES: SOCIAL POLICY

Social policies that affect inclusive programs often are formulated outside of the microsystem and, as such, can be considered exosystem variables. Gallagher, Harbin, Eckland, & Clifford (1994) have defined policy as: "the rules and standards that are established in order to allocate scarce public resources to meet a particular social need (p. 235)." Policies that affect preschool inclusion occur at the national (Federal regulations of Education or Head Start), state (State Departments of Education or Human Resources), and local levels (individual programs, see Smith & Rose, 1993). Kochanek and Buka (1997) noted that, along with families' desires for their child's placement, the increasing incidence of inclusion at the preschool level has been given impetus by the congressional action and statutes related to the Individual with Disabilities Education Act (PL 99-457) and Civil Rights legislation (i.e., Americans with Disabilities Act). However, the translation of national policy at the state level may also affect early childhood inclusion. Smith and Rose (1993) surveyed administrators, state policy makers, family members, and other constituents from 10 states. These respondents felt that state policies influenced most the provision of inclusive services at the local level. In their study of implementation of policy in Colorado, North Carolina, and Pennsylvania, Harbin, McWilliam, and Gallagher (in press) identified three policy factors that affected the number of children served in inclusive settings: (a) policymakers' interpretations of the federal law; (b) the emphasis (on inclusion) they choose to follow in policy development; and (c) the specificity of the policy created. . . .

Across this range of studies, key issues consistently appear as barriers. The first set of issues relates to *program standards or policies* regulating programs; such policies often require that children with disabilities be served in categorical (i.e., Special Education) classes in public school buildings. These policies have been identified as barriers that prevent placement of children in community-based or Head Start settings (Janko & Porter, 1997; Smith & Rose, 1993). *Financial or fiscal policies* represent a second set of issues; these refer to policies that prevent the use of special education funds for services involving typically developing children, the blending of funds across agencies, and the availability of funds

(ACF, 1997; Bailey et al., 1998 this volume; Harvey et al., 1997; Janko & Porter, 1997; Smith & Rose, 1993). *Personnel issues and staffing* represent another policy issue that can be a barrier. For example, regulations sometimes specify that young children with disabilities be placed only in classes with a licensed special education teacher, which precludes services in many community-based or Head Start programs (ACF 1997; Harvey et al., 1997; Smith & Rose, 1993). Another personnel issue relates to *preservice and inservice training*. In several states a barrier was identified because personnel were not trained to work in inclusive early childhood programs (Harvey et al., 1997; Janko & Porter, 1997; Smith & Rose, 1993). Although not a formal policy issue, the *attitudes of policy makers and implementers* (e.g., special education administrators, program directors) toward preschool inclusion exert a major influence on the provision of services (Rose & Smith, 1993). Likewise, Kochanek and Buka (1997) found attitudes and beliefs of adults in decision making roles to be a more powerful influence on placement decisions than either the availability of community placements or the families' attitudes toward inclusion.

MACROSYSTEM VARIABLES: CULTURE AND COMMUNITY

Issues related to community and culture fall within Bronfenbrenner's conceptualization of macrosystem variables. Attention to cultural values is a key and distinctive feature of accepted practice in early childhood education (Bredekamp & Copple, 1997) and early childhood special education (McLean & Odom, 1996). However, research on the relationship between cultural values and inclusive practices is just beginning to appear. In their examination of cultural variables, Hanson et al. (1996, this issue) found that cultural beliefs influenced family members' explanations for and understanding of their child's disability; the concerns and desires by families from different cultures for their children were sometime in conflict with classroom goals; cultural differences sometimes affected the social relationships children with disabilities and families formed with others; and programs varied in how they responded to cultural diversity and difference. . . .

Separating culture, community, and family is somewhat artificial. Characteristics of the community certainly affect the availability and nature of inclusive classroom programs for young children with disabilities (Beckman et al., this issue; Hanson et al., this issue: Kochanek & Buka, 1997). However, "inclusion" as a concept extends beyond classroom settings to the broader participation of individuals with disabilities in communities (Allen & Schwartz, 1996). Research describing community participation of young children with disabilities and their families is just emerging. Ehrman, Aeschleman, and Svanum (1995) surveyed parents of children with and without disabilities about the community activities in which their children participated. Although noting similarities for the two groups, the authors found that children with disabilities participated in fewer community activities than typically developing children, with the primary difference occurring for activities related to family enrichment (e.g., eating in a restaurant, going to a movie, activity with a sibling). To examine factors in the community that may serve as barriers to or facilitators of community inclusion for young children, Beckman et al. (1998, this issue) drew upon a cross-site qualitative data base. Facilitators included the family's sense of community, school-community connections, families' social contacts, deliberate strategies to foster participation, and environmental adaptations. Factors that limited community participation included neighborhood safety and stability, limited resources, family schedules, and unavailability of peers.

CONCLUSION

The research base on early childhood inclusion in the mid- to late-1990s is extensive. While much research continues to address questions related to classroom practices and families' perspectives, the topics have expanded greatly. Studies have generated information on practical issues such as the frequency of inclusive placements, the characteristics of personnel in inclusive settings, and the barriers to and facilitators of inclusion. Important new directions in research on cultural values, community, and social policy are emerging and may well influence practice in the future.

Using Bronfenbrenner's ecological systems theory as our conceptual organizer, it seems appropriate to note that research is rich and active within system levels, and researchers are beginning to examine linkages of variables across systems. For example, Janko, Schwartz, Sandall, Anderson, and Cottam (1997) examined the organizational features (i.e., policies, rules and regulations) of inclusive programs (an exosystem variable) and their linkages to the way inclusion occurred at the classroom level (microsystem). Kochanek, Harbin, and their colleagues have examined how social policy characteristics (exosystem) affect program provision (microsystem) (Harbin, McWilliams & Gallagher in press; Kochanek & Buka, 1997). In a study that illustrates the reciprocal influences across system variables, Harvey et al. (1997) described a process by which factors operating at the local program level (microsystem) influenced the development of policy at the state level (exosystem level), which in turn influenced local program practice. Hanson and colleagues (1998, this issue) have begun to examine cultural values (macrosystem) and issues within classrooms (microsystem). This systems analysis of factors related to inclusion may well contribute to our understanding of how inclusive programs work well for children and families and the range of factors related to such operation.

The emerging themes for future research come from each level of the ecological system model Bronfenbrenner proposed. At the microsystem level, specific practices for promoting developmental outcomes for children and for influencing the quality of inclusive settings are fertile areas for future research. At the mesosystem level, research on strategies for collaboration among professionals and between professionals and families will contribute strongly to the implementation of inclusive programs. At the exosystem level, research on the development and implementation of social policy, the reciprocal influences between policy and practice, the analysis of costs and flexible models for funding may well serve as the foundation for future inclusive programs. At the macrosystem level, our understanding of how cultural and linguistic diversity affect inclusive preschool programs is just beginning to become apparent. The significant and far reaching challenge for investigators in the future will be to step beyond the research *within* levels to examine how linkages *across* levels affect the everyday experiences of children in inclusive early childhood programs and their families.

Acknowledgment: Support for preparation of this paper was provided by Grant No. HO24K60001-97 from the U.S. Department of Education. The authors wish to thank Ruth Wolery and Sylvia Mewborn for assistance in final preparation of this manuscript.

REFERENCES

Administration for Children and Families. (1995). *Passages to inclusion.* Washington, DC: Administration for Children and Families Child Care Bureau (Available on WWW through http://ericps.crc.uiuc.edu/ncci/nccicome.html).

Allen, K. E., Benning, P. M., & Drummond, W. T. (1972). Integration of normal and handicapped children in a behavior modification preschool: A case study. In G. Semb (Ed.), *Behavior analysis and education* (pp. 127–141). Lawrence, KS: University of Kansas.

Allen, K. E., & Schwartz, I. S. (1996). *The exceptional child: Inclusion in early childhood education,* 3rd Ed. Boston: Del Mar Publishers.

Antia, S. D., Kreimeyer, K. H.,& Eldredge, N. (1994). Promoting social interaction between young children with hearing impairments and their peers. *Exceptional Children, 60,* 262–275.

Arnold, D., & Tremblay, A. (1979). Interaction of deaf and hearing preschool children. *Journal of Communication Disorders, 12,* 245–251.

Bailey, D. B., & Winton, P. (1987). Stability and change in parents' expectations about mainstreaming. *Topics in Early Childhood Special Education, 7,* 73–88.

Bailey, D. B. (1996). An overview of interdisciplinary training. In D. Bricker & A. Widerstrom (Eds.), *Preparing personnel to work with infants and young children and their families: A team approach,* (pp. 3–22). Baltimore, MD: Paul Brookes.

Bailey, D. B. (1997). Evaluating the effectiveness of curriculum alternatives for infants and preschoolers at risk. In M. J. Guralnick (Ed.), *The effectiveness of early intervention* (pp. 227–248). Baltimore, MD: Paul H. Brookes.

Bailey, D. B., Burchinal, M. R., & McWilliam, R. A. (1993). Age of peers and early childhood development. *Child Development, 64,* 848–862.

Bailey, D. B., McWilliam, R. A., Buysse, V., & Wesley, P. W. (1988). Inclusion in the context of competing values in early childhood education. *Early Childhood Research Quarterly, 15*(1).

Bailey, D. B., McWilliam, R. A., Ware, W. B., & Burchinal, M. A. (1993). The social interactions of toddlers and preschoolers in same-age and mixed-age play groups. *Journal of Applied Developmental Psychology, 14,* 261–276.

Barnett, W. S., & Frede, E. C. (1993). Early childhood programs in the public schools: Insights from a state survey. *Journal of Early Intervention, 17,* 396–413.

Beckman, P., Barnwell, D., Horn, E., Hanson, M., Gutierrez, S., & Lieber, J. (1998). Communities, families, and inclusion. *Early Childhood Research Quarterly, 15*(1).

Bennett, T., Delucca, D., & Bruns, D. (1997). Putting inclusion into practice: Perspectives of teachers and parents. *Exceptional Children, 64,* 115–131.

Bennett, T., Lee, H. & Lueke, B. (in press). Expectations and concerns: What mothers and fathers say. *Education and Training in Mental Retardation and Other Developmental Disabilities.*

Blasco, P. M., Bailey, D. B., & Burchinal, M. R. (1993). Dimensions of mastery in same-age and mixed-age integrated classrooms. *Early Childhood Research Quarterly, 8,* 193–206.

Bredekamp, S. (1987). *Developmentally appropriate practice in early childhood programs serving children from birth through age 8.* Washington, D.C. NAEYC.

Bredekamp, S. (1993). The relationship between early childhood education and early childhood special education: Healthy marriage or family feud? *Topics in Early Childhood Special Education, 13*(3), 258–273.

Bredekamp, S., & Copple, C. (1997). *Developmentally appropriate practice in early childhood programs,* Revised ed. Washington, D.C.: National Association for the Education of Young Children.

Bricker, D. D. (1978). A rationale for the integration of handicapped and nonhandicapped preschool children, in M. Guralnick (Ed.), *Early intervention and the integration of handicapped and nonhandicapped children* (pp. 3–26). Baltimore, MD: University Park Press.

Bricker, D. (1995). The challenge of inclusion. *Journal of Early Intervention, 19,* 179–194.

Bricker, D., & Bricker, W. (1971). Toddler Research and Intervention Project Report—Year 1. *IMRID Behavioral Science Monograph No. 20*, Nashville, TN: Institute on Mental Retardation and Intellectual Development, 1971.

Bronfenbrenner, U. (1979). *The ecology of human development: Experiments by nature and design.* Cambridge, MA: Harvard University Press.

Brown, W. H., Horn, E. M., Heiser, J. G., & Odom, S. L. (1996). Project BLEND: An inclusive model of early intervention services. *Journal of Early Intervention, 20,* 364–375.

Bruder, M. B., Staff, I., & McMurrer-Kammer, E. (1997). Toddlers receiving early intervention in child care centers: A description of a service delivery system. *Topics in Early Childhood Special Education, 17,* 185–208.

Burton, C. B., Hains, A. H., Hanline, M. F., McLean, M., & McCormick, K. (1992). Early childhood intervention and education: The urgency of professional unification. *Topics in Early Childhood Special Education, 11*(4), 53–69.

Buscemi, L.,Bennett, T., Thomas, D., & Deluca, D. A. (1995). Head Start: Challenges and training needs. *Journal of Early Intervention, 20,* 1–13.

Buysee, V., & Bailey, D. B. (1993). Behavioral and developmental outcomes in young children with disabilities in integrated and segregated settings: A review of comparative studies. *Journal of Special Education, 26,* 434–461.

Buysse, V. (1993). Friendships of preschoolers with disabilities in community-based child care settings. *Journal of Early Intervention, 17,* 380–395.

Buysse, V., Bailey, D. B., Smith, T. M., & Simeonsson, R. J. (1994). The relationship between child characteristics and placement in specialized versus inclusive early childhood programs. *Topics in Early Childhood Special Education, 14,* 419–435.

Buysse,V., Schulte, A. C., Pierce, P. P., & Terry, D. (1994). Models and styles of consultation: Preferences of professionals in early intervention. *Journal of Early Intervention, 18,* 302–310.

Buysse, V., Wesley, P., Keyes, L., & Bailey, D. B. (1996). Assessing the comfort zone of child care teachers in serving young children with disabilities. *Journal of Early Intervention, 20,* 189–203.

Buysse, V., Wesley, P. W., & Keyes, L. (1998). Implementing early childhood inclusion: Barrier and support factors. *Early Childhood Research Quarterly, 13*(1), 169–184.

Carta, J. J., Schwartz, I. S., Atwater, J. B., & McConnell, S. R. (1991). Developmentally appropriate practice: Appraising its usefulness for young children with disabilities. *Topics in Early Childhood Special Education, 11*(1), 1–20.

Cavallaro, C. C., Haney, M., & Cabello, B. (1993). Developmentally appropriate strategies for promoting full participation in early childhood settings. *Topics in Early Childhood Special Education, 13,*293–307.

Chandler, P.A. (1994). *A place for me: Including children with special needs in early care and education settings.* Washington, D.C.: National Association for the Education of Young Children.

Cole, K. N., Mills, P. E., Dale, P. S., & Jenkins, J. R. (1991). Effects of preschool integration for children with disabilities. *Exceptional Children, 58,* 36–45.

Derman-Sparks, L. And the A.B.C. Task Force (1989). *Anti-Bias Curriculum: Tools for empowering young children.* Washington, D.C.: NAEYC.

Diamond, K., Hestenes, L., Carpenter, E., & Innes, F. (in press). Relationships between enrollment in an inclusive class and preschool children's ideas about people with disabilities. *Topics in Early Childhood Special Education.*

Dodge, K. A., Petit, G. S., McClaskey, C. L., & Brown, M. M. (1986). Social competence in children. *Monographs of the Society for Research in Child Development, 51,* (2, Serial No. 213).

Ehrmann, L., Aeschleman, S., & Svanum, S. (1995). Parental reports of community activity patterns: A comparison between young children with disabilities and their nondisabled peers. *Research in Developmental Disabilities, 16,* 331–343.

English, K., Goldstein, H., Schafer, K., & Kaczmarek, L. (1997). Promoting interactions among preschoolers with and without disabilities: Effects of a buddy skills-training program. *Exceptional Children, 63,* 229–243.

Erwin, E. J. (1993). Social participation of young children with visual impairment in specialized and integrated environments. *Journal of Visual Impairments and Blindness, 87,* 138–142.

Favazza, P. C., & Odom, S. L. (1997). Promoting positive attitudes of kindergarten-age children toward people with disabilities. *Exceptional Children, 63,* 405–418.

Filler, J. (1996). A comment on inclusion: Research and social policy. *Social Policy Report: Society for Research in Child Development, 10*(2 & 3), 31–33.

File, N. (1994). Children's play, teacher-child interactions, and teacher beliefs in integrated early childhood programs. *Early Childhood Research Quarterly, 9,* 223–240.

File, N., & Kontos, S. (1993). The relationship of program quality to children's play in integrated early intervention settings. *Topics in Early Childhood Special Education, 13,* 1–18.

Fishbein, H. D., & Imai, S. (1993). Preschoolers select playmates on the basis of gender and race. *Journal of Applied Developmental Psychology, 14,* 303–316.

Fox, L., Hanline, M. F., Vail, C. O., & Galant, K. R. (1994). Developmentally appropriate practice: Applications for young children with disabilities. *Journal of Early Intervention, 18,* 243–257.

Gallagher, J. J., Harbin, G., Eckland, J., & Clifford, R. (1994). State diversity and policy implementation: Infants and toddlers. In L. Johnson, et al. (Eds.), *Meeting early intervention challenges: Issues from birth to three,* (pp. 235–250). Baltimore: Paul H. Brookes.

Gemmel-Crosby, S., & Handik, J. R. (1994). Preschool teachers' perceptions of including children with disabilities. *Education and Training in Mental Retardation, 19,* 279–290.

Goldstein, H., Kaczmarek, L. A., & Hepting, N. H. (1996). Indicators of quality in communication interventions. In S. Odom & M. McLean (Eds.), *Early intervention and early childhood special education: Recommended practices* (pp. 197–221). Austin, TX: PRO-ED.

Graham, M. A., & Bryant, D. M. (1993). Characteristics of quality, effective service delivery systems for children with special needs. In D. M. Bryant & M. A. Graham (Eds.), *Implementing early intervention: From research to effective practice* (pp. 233–252). NY: Guilford Press.

Guralnick, M. J. (in press). The nature and meaning of social integration for young children with mild developmental delays in inclusive settings. *Journal of Early Intervention.*

Guralnick, M. J. (1976). The value of integrating handicapped and nonhandicapped preschool children. *American Journal of Orthopsychiatry, 46,* 236–245.

Guralnick, M. J. (1994). Mothers' perceptions of the benefits and drawbacks of early childhood mainstreaming. *Journal of Early Intervention, 18,* 168–183.

Guralnick, M. J. (1997). Second generation research in the field of early intervention. In M. Guralnick (Id.), *The effectiveness of early intervention* (pp. 3–23), Baltimore: Paul H. Brookes.

Guralnick, M. J., Connor, R., & Hammond, M. (1995). Parents' perspectives of peer relations and friendships in integrated and specialized programs. *American Journal on Mental Retardation, 99,* 457–476.

Guralnick, M. J., Connor, R. T., Hammond, M. A., Gottman, J. M., & Kinnish, K. (1996a). Immediate effects of mainstreamed settings on the social interactions and social integration of preschool children. *American Journal on Mental Retardation, 100,* 359–377.

Guralnick, M. J., Gottman, J. M., & Hammond, M. A. (1996b). Effects of social setting on the friendship formation of young children differing in developmental status. *Journal of Applied Developmental Psychology, 17,* 625–651.

Guralnick, M. J. & Neville, B. (1997). Designing early intervention programs to support children's social competence. In M. Guralnick (Ed.), *The effectiveness of early intervention* (pp. 579–610). Baltimore, MD: Paul H. Brookes.

Hanline, M. F. (1993). Inclusion of preschoolers with profound disabilities. An analysis of children's interactions. *Journal of the Association for Persons with Severe Handicaps, 18,* 28–35.

Hanson, M. J., Guitierrez, S., Morgan, M., Brennan, E. L., & Zercher, C. (1997). Language, culture, and disability: Interacting influences on preschool inclusion. *Topics in Early Childhood Special Education, 17,* 307–336.

Hanson, M. J., Wolfberg, P., Zercher, C., Morgan, M., Gutierrez, S., Barnwell, D., & Beckman, P. (1998). The culture of inclusion: Recognizing diversity at multiple levels. *Early Childhood Research Quarterly, 13* (1), 185–210.

Hartup, W. (1983). Peer relations. In E. M. Hetherington (Ed.), P. H. Mussen (Series Ed.), *Handbook of child psychology, Vol 4: Socialization, personality, and social development* (pp. 103–196). New York: John Wiley.

Harbin, G. L., McWilliam, R. A., & Gallagher, J. (in press). Services to young children with disabilities: A descriptive analysis. In S. Meisels & J. Shonkoff (Eds.), *Handbook of early childhood intervention,* 2nd ed. New York: Cambridge University Press.

Harvey, J., Voorhees, M. D., & Landon, T. (1997). The role of the State Department of Education in promoting integrated placement options for preschoolers: Views from the field. *Topics in Early Childhood Special Education, 17,* 387–409.

Hauser-Cram, P., Bronson, M. B., & Upshur, C. C. (1993). The effects of the classroom environment on the social and mastery behavior of preschool children with disabilities. *Early Childhood Research Quarterly, 8,* 479–498.

Hundert, J., Mahoney, B., Mundy, F., & Vernon, M. L. (1998). A descriptive analysis of developmentally appropriate and social gains of children with severe disabilities in segregated and inclusive preschools in southern Ontario. *Early Childhood Research Quarterly, 13* (1).

Hundert, J., Mahoney, W. J., & Hopkins, B. (1993). The relationship between the peer interaction of children with disabilities in integrated preschools and research and classroom teacher behaviors. *Topics in Early Childhood Special Education, 13,* 328–343.

Janko, S., & Porter, A. (Eds.). (1997). *Portraits of inclusion through the eyes of children, families, and educators.* Seattle, WA: Early Childhood Research Institute on Inclusion.

Janko, S., Schwartz, I., Sandall, S., Anderson, K., & Cottam, C. (1997). Beyond microsystems: Unanticipated lessons about the meaning of inclusion. *Topics in Early Childhood Special Education, 17,* 286–306.

Johnson, R., & Johnson, D. W. (1986). Building friendships between handicapped and nonhandicapped students: Effects of cooperative and individualistic instruction. *American Educational Research Journal, 18,* 415–424.

Karnes, M. D., & Lee, R. C. (1979). Mainstreaming in the preschool. In L. Katz (Ed.), *Current topics in early childhood education, Vol. 2* (pp. 13–42). Norwood, NJ: Ablex.

Kochanek, T. T., & Buka, S. L. (1997). *Influential factors in inclusive versus noninclusive placements for preschool children with disabilities.* Manuscript submitted for publication.

Kontos, S., & File, N. (1993). Staff development in support of integration. In C. Peck, S. Odom, & D. Bricker (Eds.), *Integration of young children with disabilities into community programs* (pp. 169–186). Baltimore: Paul H. Brookes.

Lamorey, S., & Bricker, D. D. (1993). Integrated programs: Effects on young children and their parents. In C. Peck, S. Odom, & D. Bricker, (Eds.), *Integrating young children with disabilities into community-based programs: From research to implementation* (pp. 249–269). Baltimore: Paul H. Brookes.

LaParo, K. M., Sexton, D., & Snyder, P. (1998). Program quality characteristics in segregated and inclusive early childhood settings. *Early Childhood Research Quarterly, 13* (1), 151–168.

Lieber, J., Beckman, P. J., Hanson, M. J., Janko, S., Marquart, J. M., Horn, E., & Odom, S. L. (1997) The impact of changing roles on relationship between professionals in inclusive programs for young children. *Early Education and Development, 8,* 67–82.

Lieber, J., Capell, K., Sandall, S. R., Wolfberg, P., Horn, E., & Beckman, P. (1998). Inclusive preschool programs: Teachers' beliefs and practices. *Early Childhood Research Quarterly.*

Maccoby, E. E. (1988). Gender as a social category. *Developmental Psychology, 55,* 755–765.

McConnell, S. R., Sisson, L. A., Cort, C. A., & Strain, P. S. (1991). Effects of social skills training and contingency management on reciprocal interaction of preschool children with handicaps. *Journal of Special Education, 24,* 473–495.

McDonnell, A. P., Brownell, K., & Wolery, M. (1997). Teaching experience and specialist support: A survey of preschool teachers employed in programs accredited by NAEYC. *Topics in Early Childhood Special Education, 17,* 263–285.

McLean, M. E., & Odom, S. L. (1996). Establishing recommended practices in early intervention/early childhood special education. In S. Odom & M. McLean (Eds.), *Early intervention and early childhood special education: Recommended practices* (pp. 1–22). Austin, TX: PRO-ED.

McLean, M. E., & Odom, S. L. (1993). Practices for young children with and without disabilities; A comparison of DEC and NAEYC identified practices. *Topics in Early Childhood Special Education, 13,* 274–293.

McWilliam, R. A., & Bailey, D. B. (1995). Effects of classroom structure and disability on engagement. *Topics in Early Childhood Special Education, 15,* 123–147.

McWilliam, R. A., Lang, L., Vandeviere, P., Angell, R., Collins, L., & Underdown, G. (1995). Satisfaction and struggles: Family perceptions of early intervention services. *Journal of Early Intervention, 19,* 43–60.

Miller, L. J., Strain, P. S., Boyd, K., Hunsicker, S., McKinley, J., & Wu, A. (1992). Parental attitudes toward integration. *Topics in Early Childhood Special Education, 12,* 230–246.

Odom, S. L., & McEvoy, M. A. (1988). Integration of young children with handicaps and normally developing children. In S. Odom & M. Karnes (Eds.), *Early intervention for infants and children with handicaps: An empirical base* (pp. 241–268). Baltimore: Paul H. Brookes.

Odom, S. L., & Speltz, M. L. (1983). program variations in preschools for handicapped and nonhandicapped children: Mainstreaming vs. integrated special education. *Analysis and Intervention in Developmental Disabilities, 3,* 89–104.

Odom, S. L., Horn, E. M., Marquart, J., Hanson, M. J., Wolfberg, P., Beckman, P., Lieber, J., Li, S., Schwartz, I., Janko, S., & Sandall, S. (1997). *On the definition(s) of inclusion: Organizational context and service delivery models.* Manuscript submitted for publication.

Odom, S. L., Peck, C. A., Hanson, M., Beckman, P. J., Kaiser, A. P., Lieber, J., Brown, W. H., Horn, E. M., & Schwartz, I. S. (1996). Inclusion at the preschool level: An ecological systems analysis. *Social Policy: Society for Research on Child Development, 10* (2 & 3), 18–30.

Okagaki, L, Diamond, K. E., Kontos, S. J., & Hestenes, L. L. (1988). Correlates of young children's interactions with classmates with disabilities. *Early Childhood Research Quarterly, 13* (1), 67–86.

Parker, J. G., & Asher, S. R. (1987). Peer relations and later personal adjustment: Are low-accepted children at risk? *Psychological Bulletin, 102,* 357–389.

Peck, C. A. (1993). Ecological perspectives on the implementation of integrated early childhood programs. In C. Peck, S. Odom, & D. Bricker, (Eds.), *Integrating young children with disabilities into community-based programs: From research to implementation* (pp. 3–15). Baltimore: Paul H. Brookes.

Peck, C. A., & Cooke, T. P. (1983). Benefits of mainstreaming at the early childhood level: How much can we expect? *Analysis and Intervention in Development Disabilities, 3,* 1–22.

Peck, C. A., Carlson, P., & Helmstetter, E. (1992). Parent and teacher perceptions of outcomes for typically developing children enrolled in early childhood programs: A statewide survey. *Journal of Early Intervention, 16,* 53–63.

Peck, C. A., Furman, G. C., & Helmstetter, E. (1993). Integrated early childhood programs: Research on the implementation of change in organizational contexts. In C. Peck, S. Odom, & D. Bricker (Eds.), *Integration of young children with disabilities into community programs* (pp. 187–206). Baltimore: Paul H. Brookes.

Ramsey, P. G., & Myers, L. C. (1990). Salience of race in young children's cognitive, affective, and behavioral responses to social environments. *Journal of Applied Developmental Psychology, 11,* 49–67.

Roberts, J. E., Burchinal, M. R., Bailey, D. B. (1994). Communication among preschoolers with and without disabilities in same-age and mixed-aged classes. *American Journal on Mental Retardation, 99,* 231–249.

Rose, D. F., & Smith, B. J. (1993). Preschool mainstreaming: Attitude barriers and strategies for addressing them. *Young Children, 48* (4), 59–62.

Salisbury, C. L. (1991). Mainstreaming during the early childhood years. *Exceptional Children, 58,* 146–155.

Schwartz, I. S. (1996). Expanding the zone: Thoughts about social validity and training. *Journal of Early Intervention, 20,* 204–205.

Siegel, B. (1996). Is the emperor wearing clothes? Social policy and the empirical support of full inclusion of children with disabilities in the preschool and early elementary grades. *Social Policy Report: Society for Research in Child Development, 10* (1 & 2), 2–17.

Shonkoff, J. P., & Hauser-Cram, P. (1987). Early intervention for disabled infants and their families: A quantitative analysis. *Pediatrics, 80,* 650–658.

Sinclair, E. (1993). Early identification of preschoolers with special needs in Head Start. *Topics in Early Childhood Special Education, 13,* 184–201.

Smith, B. J., & Rose, D. F. (1993). *Administrator's policy handbook for preschool mainstreaming.* Cambridge, MA: Brookline Books.

Stainback, W., & Stainback, S. (Eds), (1990). *Support networks for inclusive schooling: Interdependent integrated education.* Baltimore, MD: Paul H. Brookes.

Stayton, V. D., & Miller, P. S. (1993). Combining general and special early childhood education standards in personnel preparation programs: Experience of two states. *Topics in Early Childhood Special Education, 13,* 372–387.

Stoiber, K. C., Gettinger, M., & Goetz, D. (1998). Exploring factors influencing parents' and early childhood practitioners' beliefs about inclusion. *Early Childhood Research Quarterly.*

Stoneman, Z., Rugg, M. E., & Rivers, J. (1996, December). *How do young children learn about peers with disabilities? Examining the role of parents as teachers of values, attitudes and prosocial behavior.* Paper presented at the International Early Childhood Conference on Children with Special Needs.

Storey, K. (993). A proposal for assessing integration. *Education and Training in Mental Retardation, 28,* 279–287.

Task Force on Recommended Practices (1993). *DEC Recommended Practices: Indicators of quality in programs for infants and young children with special needs and their families.* Reston, VA: Council for Exceptional Children.

Turnbull, A. P., & Winston, P. (1983). A comparison of specialized and mainstreamed preschools from perspectives of parents of handicapped children. *Journal of Pediatric Psychology, 8,* 57–71.

Winton, P. J. (1993). Providing family support in integrated settings: Research and recommendations. In C. A. Peck, S. L. Odom, & D. D. Bricker, (Eds.), *Integrating young children with disabilities into community programs: Ecological perspectives on research and implementation* (pp. 65–80). Baltimore: Brookes.

Winton, P. J., & Turnball, A. (1981). Parent involvement as viewed by parents of handicapped children. *Topics in Early Childhood Special Education, 1* (2), 11–20.

Wolery, M., & Bredekamp, S. (1994). Developmentally appropriate practice and young children with disabilities: Contextual issues in the discussion. *Journal of Early Intervention, 18,* 331–341.

Wolery, M., Holcombe, A., Brookfield, S., Huffman, K., Schroeder, C., Martin, C. G., Venn, M. L., Weits, M. G., & Fleming, L. A. (1993). The extent and nature of preschool mainstreaming: A survey of general early educators. *Journal of Special Education, 27,* 222–234.

Wolery, M. R., Martin, C. G., Schroeder, C., Huffman, K., Venn, M. L., Holcombe, A., Brookfield, J., & Fleming, L. A. (1994a). Employment of educators in preschool mainstreaming: A survey of general early educators. *Journal of Early Intervention, 18,* 64–77.

Wolery, M., Holcombe, A., Venn, M. L., Brookfield, J., Huffman, K., Schroeder, C., Martin, C. G., & Fleming, L. A. (1993). Mainstreaming in early childhood programs. Current status and relevant issues. *Young Children, 49,* 78–84.

Wolery, M., Strain, P. S., & Bailey, D. B. (1992). Reaching potentials of children with special needs. In S. Bredekamp & T. Rosegrant (Eds.), *Reaching potentials: Appropriate curriculum and assessment for young children,* Vol. 1 (pp. 92–113). Washington, D.C.: National Association for the Education of Young Children.

Wolery, M., Venn, M. L., Schroeder, C., Holcombe, A., Huffman, K., Martin, C. G., Brookfield, J., & Fleming, L. A. (1994b). A survey of the extent to which speech-language pathologists are employed in preschool programs. *Language, Speech, and Hearing Services in Schools, 25,* 2–8.

Wolery, M., & Wilbers, J. S. (1994). *Including children with special needs in early childhood programs.* Washington, D.C.: National Association for the Education of Young Children.

Unit 4

Unit Selections

Key Points to Consider

❖ What does family involvement mean in a child care program? A preschool? A primary grades school?

❖ What is the difference between guidance and punishment? How is that difference reflected in a teacher's approach to classroom management?

❖ What are the reasons for young children's motivation to diminish as they reach school age?

❖ In what ways are young children jeopardized when they are homeless?

 **Links** www.dushkin.com/online/

These sites are annotated on pages 4 and 5.

No subject in early childhood education seems to attract more attention from teachers and parents than how to guide behavior. New teachers are concerned that they will not be able to keep the children "under control." Mature teachers wrestle with the finer points of how to guide behavior positively and effectively. Parents have strong feelings on the subject of behavior, often based on their own childhood experiences. Teachers spend many hours thinking and talking about the best ways to guide young children's behavior: What should I do about the child who is out of bounds? What do I say to parents who want their child punished? Is punishment the same as discipline? How do I guide a child who has experienced violence and now acts out violently?

Schools that include families in significant ways find problems decrease and academic performance increases. With the diversity of family-school environments across the nation, family involvement means many different things. The most successful family involvement programs are based on doing careful planning and having an underlying philosophy. This is the premise of Mick Coleman and Susan Churchill's report, "Challenges to Family Involvement." Teachers and families both benefit from open communication of themes to guide family-school interactions. To improve collaboration, they outline excellent strategies for family life educators to use with teachers, communities, and parents.

Dan Gartrell in "Beyond Discipline to Guidance" clearly defines and applies the approach to working with children called guidance. He gives us a thorough history of the guidance approach, including international leaders such as Froebel, Montessori, and Dewey. These all believed that the goal of guidance was self-control and self-discipline. Gartrell sorts out five misunderstandings about guidance and provides six key guidance practices. He believes that "the objective is to teach children to solve problems rather than punish them for having problems they cannot solve."

Conflict resolution and social responsibility are important skills for all of us, whether adult or child. Teaching children to live at peace starts in the preschool classroom by helping children to be generous to each other and teaching through community projects. Teachers can learn techniques for conflict resolution to incorporate in the routines of everyday classroom life. They can also integrate peace into the curriculum in a variety of ways. These are the ways to teach peace concepts to children, according to author Anarella Cellitti.

The rise of homelessness in America is causing teachers to be concerned for children who move between shelters or migrate across the nation. Teachers who deal with homeless children are considering the climate and obstacles of schooling. Experiences of homelessness can hinder children's progress and affect their behavior.

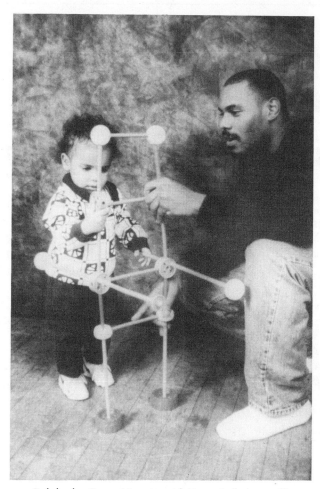

Ralph da Costa Nunez and Kate Collignon offer insight into the specialized education such children need in "Creating a Community of Learning for Homeless Children." They advise that the basis for working with these children is by lowering barriers to school attendance and participation. Model programs offer intensive services, ranging from tutoring children and parent literacy to health and nutrition care. Da Costa Nunez and Collignon emphasize the necessity of community and school partnerships. They illustrate this with examples of programs around the nation, whose goal is to ensure children's continuous access to schooling. While in child care or primary grades, homeless children should feel school is a safe, stable place. They need affectionate, supportive teachers who refrain from labeling or excluding them.

The theory article for this unit is "Fostering Intrinsic Motivation in Early Childhood Classrooms." It is an in-depth review of the patterns of motivation established during the early childhood years. Martha Carlton and Adam Winsler's premise is that young children are born with an innate need to interact with the environment, yet this need diminishes as children reach school age. The authors include a comprehensive definition of mastery motivation at four age ranges and conclude with principles for fostering the development of intrinsic motivation in early childhood programs.

Challenges to Family Involvement

Mick Coleman and Susan Churchill

Mick Coleman is Associate Professor and Susan Churchill is a doctoral student in the Department of Child and Family Development, University of Georgia, Athens.

The percentage of 3- and 4-year-olds enrolled in early childhood education programs has risen more than threefold since the mid-1960s (U.S. General Accounting Office, 1990). Public schools increasingly provide child care, preschool education and before- and after-school care for young children. Such school-based early childhood programs reflect a growing interest in early educational enrichment experiences for children in general, as well as an expansion of compensatory education programs for children who are judged to be at risk for school failure because of poverty, lack of proper health care, inadequate home-learning environments and a lack of adult protection (Swick & Graves, 1993, pp. 26, 93).

Recognizing the mutuality of families' and schools' concerns about children's growth and development, educators are seeking new ways to involve families in their children's education (Boyer, 1991; Silvern, 1988; U.S. Department of Education, 1991). While family involvement is a concept that has wide appeal, only limited institutional support exists (Epstein & Dauber, 1991; Greenberg, 1989; Swick & McKnight, 1989).

Challenges to Family Involvement

No conclusive evidence exists that family involvement programs are uniformly effective (White, Taylor & Moss, 1992), despite the many positive ways families can affect their children's academic efforts (see, for review, Henderson, 1988; Hess & Holloway, 1984; Peters, 1988; Rutter, 1985; White et al., 1992), and the many positive ways quality early childhood programs can affect families (see Pence, 1988; Powell, 1989; Schorr & Schorr, 1988). Family involvement efforts face two challenges aside from the difficulties associated with the diverse methodologies used in family involvement studies (White et al., 1992).

■ *Ambiguous definitions of family involvement.* It is hard to find consensus on the meaning of family involvement (Haseloff, 1990; White et al., 1992). Family involvement may include the following elements, among others: providing parents with facts about their child's development, teaching parents to become effective change agents for their child, providing parents with emotional support, training parents to guide and teach their child, exchanging information about a child between parents and teachers, hosting joint parent/teacher activities like childhood assessments or program planning, and helping parents get access to community services (McConachie, 1986; Peterson & Cooper, 1989).

Ambiguous definitions of family involvement can result in programs that are merely a series of disconnected activities with little relevance to family or classroom environments. To be effective, family involvement planners must address the ambiguous boundaries that exist between home and school (Johnston, 1990), and the resulting sense of intrusion and power imbalance that can occur when parents and teachers attempt to coordinate their interactions with children (Haseloff, 1990).

In practice, family involvement planning must include the formulation of a family involvement philosophy and supportive goals. In the course of conducting inservice workshops on family involvement, the authors have discovered that sufficient attention is not always paid to this conceptual process. Subsequent discussions about the meaning and purpose of family involvement, however, often uncover a common set of philosophical themes (see Table 1). Teachers can use the themes in Table 1 as an aid to beginning the reflective process. Teachers should delete from, or add to, the list so that it meets their schools' particular concerns and interests.

The list of themes is used as a planning device so that teachers can prioritize their family involvement goals while thinking about past family involvement experiences. In most cases, teachers can select one theme that best reflects their family involvement goal for the upcoming year. They can then develop specific family involvement objectives that reflect their school's diverse family-school environments.

■ *Diversity of family-school environments.* The call for greater collaboration between families and schools is admirable in that it recognizes the different contexts in which children learn. Nevertheless, the discontinuities between a young child's home and school lives can pose numerous challenges (Hess & Holloway, 1984; Peters, 1988; Silvern, 1988). A school's customs, schedules, spaces, resources, expectations, experiences, languages and values, for example, may not be reflected in the same way or to the same degree at home. This may be especially true for children from racial and cultural minority families, as well as those from lower socioeconomic families.

In particular, school environments may fit better with the family environments of children from middle-class families because public schools are often staffed with middle-class administrators and teachers. Middle-class families subsequently may be more responsive to school policies and family involvement programs than lower socioeconomic families.

Parent education and family socioeconomic status are two factors that may create discontinuity between schools and families. Although it is true that parents with higher levels of education and from higher socioeconomic backgrounds show greater family involvement, this trend does not necessarily indicate differential *interest* in family involvement (Epstein & Dauber, 1991;

Stevenson & Baker, 1987). In fact, parents from low-income families are as supportive of the family involvement concept as parents with higher incomes (Chavkin & Williams, 1989).

One way parents from lower and higher income families may differ is where they are willing or able to be involved in their children's education. Researchers have found a positive relationship between socioeconomic status and school-based family involvement activities such as parent conferences and volunteering, as well as teacher perceptions of parent support; socioeconomic status, however, has not been associated with home-based activities like tutoring (Hoover-Dempsey, Bassler & Brissie, 1987). This finding may reflect the difficulty or hesitancy parents from lower socioeconomic backgrounds may experience when directly interacting with schools. Some parents may have conflicting work and family demands. Others may limit their involvement with schools because of their own negative school experiences and feelings of academic inadequacy.

Parents with higher levels of education tend to be more involved in school activities, and their children are more likely to be doing well in school (Stevenson & Baker, 1987). These findings may reflect parental attitudes, work schedules and lifestyle priorities that are congruent with those found in schools. Parents with more education may have more positive attitudes toward school, resulting in more frequent and positive interactions with teachers and more reinforcement of classroom activities in the home. Parents with higher levels of education also may have more flexible work schedules, allowing them to assist with homework projects and attend school functions. Also, these families' adult-child interactions and childhood behavioral expectations may resemble more closely those found in the school.

To develop strategies that link the early learning experiences in home and school settings, planners must address the discontinuities between those environments. The authors have summarized in Table 2 some of the themes that they have found useful in helping family-school coordinators and teachers link family and school environments.

Teachers can use Table 2's themes to further expand their family involvement philosophies. Using the guides, for example, can facilitate the planning and implementation of enrollment interviews, home visits, parent-teacher meetings and classroom activities. Some teachers use the themes to formulate questions and possible explanations about family-school disagreements (e.g., home-school differences in behavior

Table 1

THEMES FOR GUIDING FAMILY INVOLVEMENT PHILOSOPHIES*

Theme	Goal
Empowerment	To provide families with the information and support they need to actively participate in school-related discussions regarding their children's education
Parenting	To support parents in nurturing and guiding their children
Family Strengths	To assist families in identifying and developing strengths and coping mechanisms as a means of managing family life stressors
Child-Siblings	To prepare school-age children and their younger siblings for schooling
Community Resources	To provide parents with the information, support and skills necessary to identify and manage community services
Educational Modeling	To involve parents in identifying education objectives and providing supportive in-home learning opportunities for their children
Family-Teacher Relations	To improve the quality of interpersonal relations between teachers and children's families

*The purpose of the themes is to help structure ideas about family involvement and their implications for planning practical family involvement strategies. Some overlap is expected.

management and self-help expectations). Or, the themes can be used to structure classroom activities that build upon children's home experiences (e.g., childhood interests, home routines, family relationships). The themes in Table 2, like those in Table 1, are only a beginning point. Teachers can add themes that reflect their school's individual concerns.

Working with Family Professionals

Stamp and Groves (1994) suggested that family involvement be viewed as a "third institution" whose primary purpose is to strengthen family-school linkages. As we already have noted, the diversity of family structures and lifestyles can present barriers to creating such a "third institution."

On the other hand, a conclusion that families and schools cannot be linked would be based on too narrow an interpretation of family and school goals regarding early childhood education. The traditionally stated goals of child care (protection, nurturing and socialization) and school (education and socialization) always have been interdependent (Caldwell, 1990). Today, more than ever, academic education (learning to read and write) and life-skills education (learning self-help and social responsibilities) are mutually supportive endeavors that occur across family and school settings. Likewise, parents and teachers, although sometimes depicted as adversarial, have similar educational goals (Epstein, 1991) and philosophies (Stipek, Milburn, Clements & Daniels, 1992).

Thus, creating a "third institution" of family involvement is not impossible, although greater attention must be given to devising practical strategies for linking families and schools (Sexton, Aldridge & Snyder, 1994). The authors will now examine some ways in which three types of family professionals can work with schools to develop practical strategies for strengthening family involvement.

■ *Teacher training: Family life educators.* Teachers whose training in family relations is limited have only their own family experiences to guide them when developing a family involvement program. Family life educators can help address teachers' questions about potential barriers to family involvement. During inservice training, teachers should brainstorm questions. Some common questions regarding family involvement follow:

- What are the challenges that confront families from different socioeconomic backgrounds, and how do they influence families' involvement with schools and other social institutions?
- What concerns do families from different ethnic, religious, racial and sexual orientation backgrounds have regarding how their families are depicted in school?
- What are the potential stressors associated with divorce, death and remarriage in relation to child-teacher and parent-teacher relations?
- What strategies can be used to acknowledge the roles of foster parents, grandparents and other extended family guardians?

Barriers to family involvement go beyond school-based issues. Family life educators can help coordinate and facilitate the following professional learning experiences:

- Selected teachers might receive release time for social service internships in order to better understand the diversity of family life within a community context.
- Teachers might be asked to develop a family involvement program that is tied to a youth program, or that is based at a work site, community center or church.
- Inservice training can be provided to highlight the different roles that parents can play in supporting their children's development and education within and outside school and home settings.

One of the most popular topics in education today is diversity (Jacob & Jordan, 1993; McCracken, 1993; Neugebauer, 1992). Teachers need opportunities to explore their own respective cultures, as well as

---

Table 2

THEMES FOR GUIDING FAMILY-SCHOOL INTERACTIONS

Theme	Example
Home Routines	Child's typical daily schedule and activities
Child's Interests	Child's favorite toys, television programs, foods, games, books, etc.
Behavior Management	Types of encouragement, reinforcements, limits and consequences used by parents to guide child's behavior
Communication	Verbal and nonverbal strategies used by parents to instruct
Child's Fears	Objects, events and situations feared by a child
Community Involvement	Community events, activities and institutions that families attend (e.g., church, library, recreational, cultural)
Relationships	Child's most important interpersonal relationships within and outside the home setting
Self-Help Expectations	Self-help skills relating to personal hygiene and home chores that parents expect child to perform
Instructional Strategies	Strategies used by parents to teach a child (e.g., instruction, demonstrations, play)

those of others, in relation to curriculum issues. They should be careful, however, not to overgeneralize or stereotype, since all families are unique regarding their rates of cultural assimilation or their racial, ethnic, religious, socioeconomic and sexual orientation backgrounds. Family life educators can facilitate the following activities:

- Keep personal journals related to positive and negative family-school interactions to encourage reflective thought on teaching practices involving children from different family backgrounds.
- Discuss the meaning of "family diversity" and its implications for classroom practices to facilitate group creativity and problem-solving. The authors have found it useful to ask teachers to reflect upon their own meaning of "family" as a beginning reference point.
- Ask teachers to develop parent workshops on topics of their choosing that take into account the different family backgrounds represented in their respective classrooms.

■ *Community education: Family life advocates.* Early childhood advocates warn that educators must not promise more than early childhood programs can deliver, since legislators tend to view early childhood programs as a means by which to achieve sweeping education and social reforms (Morado, 1986). Family life advocates can work with teachers to ensure that family involvement expectations are kept realistic.

- Form task forces to identify barriers and recommend strategies for strengthening family-school-community linkages. School-community linkages may be needed, for example, to ensure the efficient delivery of social services to families who are recent immigrants and/or who have limited means of transportation or income.
- Encourage school administrators to make family life education an integral part of the curriculum. The concept of "families" rather than "family" should be stressed in order to reflect the diversity of family structures and lifestyles in contemporary society.
- Provide training to expand parents' child advocacy efforts. Such training might include establishing parent advisory boards, arranging co-teaching experiences and informing parents of child advocacy efforts in the community.

■ *Family involvement research: Family researchers.* Although the effectiveness of family involvement programs has not been adequately documented, parents and teachers continue to search for meaningful ways to support each other. Teachers can work with family and education researchers to clarify the importance of family involvement through examination of the following questions:

- Are parents better able to understand and implement information regarding child guidance and education when it is presented in parent-led support groups as opposed to teacher-led educational groups? A study about strategies for coordinating family-school expectations and practices regarding children's guidance and education would be useful.
- Do children from certain family backgrounds (e.g., well-established versus recently immigrated; different socioeconomic levels) perform better in the classroom when classroom activities include materials found in their homes, rather than standard classroom materials? Teachers could benefit from learning how to use home materials to support and expand the classroom curriculum.
- Are community-based programs that link families with human services agencies more effective than similar school-based programs? This question could be answered by comparing the joint efforts of teachers and family service workers with those of schools and human service agencies.
- In what ways does family involvement serve as a mediating variable in children's short- and long-term academic and social adjustment? Educators could benefit from studies about family involvement programs' timing, structure and content.
- What are the secondary effects of family involvement programs? Research is needed, for example, on how family involvement programs may benefit younger siblings still at home and the ability of parents to advocate for their children across community settings.

Conclusion

Understanding family lives is central to building a meaningful family involvement program. Family professionals can work with school administrators and teachers to meet the challenges associated with family involvement by helping to develop a family involvement plan that is both practical and relevant to community needs.

References

Boyer, E. L. (1991). *Ready to learn: A mandate for the nation.* Lawrenceville, NJ: Princeton University Press.

Caldwell, B. M. (1990). Educare: A new professional identity. *Dimensions, 18,* 3–6.

Chavkin, N. F., & Williams, D. L. (1989). Low-income parents' attitudes toward parent involvement in education. *Journal of Sociology and Social Welfare, 16,* 17–28.

Epstein, J. L. (1991). Paths to partnership: What we can learn from federal, state, district, and school initiatives. *Phi Delta Kappan, 72,* 344–349.

Epstein, J. L., & Dauber, S. L. (1991). School programs and teacher practices of parent involvement in inner-city elementary and middle schools. *The Elementary School Journal, 91,* 289–305.

Greenberg, P. (1989). Parents as partners in young children's development and education: A new American fad? Why does it matter? *Young Children, 44,* 61–75.

Haseloff, W. (1990). The efficacy of the parent-teacher partnership of the 1990s. *Early Child Development and Care, 58,* 51–55.

Henderson, A. T. (1988). Parents are a school's best friends. *Phi Delta Kappan, 70,* 148–153.

Hess, R. D., & Holloway, S. D. (1984). Family and school as educational institutions. In R. D. Parke, R. N. Emde, H. P. McAdoo, & G. P. Sackett (Eds.), *Review of child development research: The family* (Vol. 7) (pp. 179–222). Chicago: University of Chicago Press.

Hoover-Dempsey, K. V., Bassler, O. C., & Brissie, J. S. (1987). Parent involvement: Contributions of teacher efficacy, school socioeconomic status, and other school characteristics. *American Educational Research Journal, 24,* 417–435.

Jacob, E., & Jordan, C. (1993). *Minority education: Anthropological perspectives.* Norwood, NJ: Ablex.

Johnston, J. H. (1990). *The new American family and the school.* Columbus, OH: National Middle School Association.

McConachie, H. (1986). *Parents and young mentally handicapped children: A review of research issues.* Cambridge, MA: Brookline Books.

McCracken, J. B. (1993). *Valuing diversity: The primary years.* Washington, DC: National Association for the Education of Young Children.

Morado, C. (1986). Prekindergarten programs for 4-year-olds: Some key issues. *Young Children, 41,* 61–63.

Neugebauer, B. (1992). *Alike and different: Exploring our humanity with young children.* Washington, DC: National Association for the Education of Young Children.

Pence, A. (1988). *Ecological research with children and families.* New York: Teachers College Press.

Peters, D. L. (1988). Head Start's influence on parental and child competence. In S. K. Steinmetz (Ed.), *Family and support systems across the life span* (pp. 73–97). New York: Plenum.

Peterson, N. L., & Cooper, C. S. (1989). Parent education and involvement in early intervention programs for handicapped children. In M. J. Fine (Ed.), *The second handbook on parent education: Contemporary perspectives* (pp. 197–233). New York: Academic.

Powell, D. (1989). *Families and early childhood programs.* Washington, DC: National Association for the Education of Young Children.

Rutter, M. (1985). Family and school influences on cognitive development. *Journal of Child Psychology and Psychiatry, 26,* 683–704.

Schorr, D., & Schorr, L. (1988). *Within our reach: Breaking the cycle of disadvantage.* New York: Doubleday.

Sexton, D., Aldridge, J., & Snyder, P. (1994). Family-driven early intervention. *Dimensions, 22,* 14–18.

Silvern, S. (1988). Continuity/discontinuity between home and early childhood education environments. *The Elementary School Journal, 89,* 147–159.

Stamp, L. N., & Groves, M. M. (1994). Strengthening the ethic of care: Planning and supporting family involvement. *Dimensions of Early Childhood, 22,* 5–9.

Stevenson, D. L., & Baker, D. P. (1987). The family-school relation and the child's school performance. *Child Development, 58,* 1348–1357.

Stipek, D., Milburn, S., Clements, D., & Daniels, D. H. (1992). Parents' beliefs about appropriate education for young children. *Journal of Applied Developmental Psychology, 13,* 293–310.

Swick, K., & Graves, S. B. (1993). *Empowering at-risk families during the early childhood years.* Washington, DC: National Education Association.

Swick, K., & McKnight, S. (1989). Characteristics of kindergarten teachers who promote parent involvement. *Early Childhood Research Quarterly, 4,* 19–29.

U.S. Department of Education. (1991). *Preparing young children for success: Guideposts for achieving our first national educational goal.* Washington, DC: Author.

U.S. General Accounting Office. (1990). *Early childhood education: What are the costs of high-quality programs?* (GAO/HRD-90-43BR). Washington, DC: Author.

White, K. R., Taylor, M. J., & Moss, V. D. (1992). Does research support claims about the benefits of involving parents in early intervention programs? *Review of Educational Research, 62,* 91–125.

PUNISHMENT, DISCIPLINE, AND GUIDANCE

Beyond Discipline to Guidance

Dan Gartrell

A student teacher in a Head Start classroom recorded in her journal an anecdotal observation of two children involved in a confrontation (printed with permission); the children here are named Charissa and Carlos.

Observation: Charissa and Carlos were building with blocks. Charissa reached for a block, and Carlos decided he wanted the same one. They both tugged on the block, and then Carlos hit Charissa on the back. Charissa fought back tears and said, "Carlos, you're not s'posed to hit—you're s'posed to use the 'talking stick.'"

Carlos said yeah and got the stick. I couldn't hear what they said, but they took turns holding the stick and talking while the other one listened. After only a minute, the two were playing again, and Charissa was using the talking stick. Later I asked her what the talking stick helped them decide. She said, "That I use the block first this time. Carlos uses it next time."

Reflection: I really got concerned when Carlos hit Charissa, and I was just about to get involved. I couldn't believe it when Charissa didn't hit back but told Carlos to

Dan Gartrell, Ed.D., is professor of early childhood education at Bemidji State University in Minnesota. This article is based on his forthcoming text, titled A Guidance Approach for the Encouraging Classroom, *and the writings of many other early childhood educators and developmental psychologists over the years.*

get the talking stick—and he did! Then they solved the problem so quickly. DeeAnn [the teacher] told me she has been teaching the kids since September [it was now April] to solve their problems by using the talking stick. Usually she has to mediate, but this time two children solved a problem on their own. It really worked!

> **Firm guidance and calm coaching help children solve social problems.**

Preschoolers do not typically solve a problem like this, on their own, by using a prop like a talking stick! But DeeAnn had been working with the children all year to teach them this conflict management skill. To ensure consistency, she had persuaded the other adults in the room to also use the talking stick (even once themselves!). Utilizing the ideas of Wichert (1989), the adults started by using a lot of coaching (high-level mediation) but over time encouraged the children to take the initiative to solve their problems themselves.

Conflict management—in this case through the technique of a decorated, venerable talking stick—is an important strategy in the overall approach to working with children called *guidance* (Janke & Penshorn Peterson 1995). By now guidance is a familiar term in early childhood education, as is its companion term, *developmentally appropriate practice* (DAP). However,

like the misinterpretations of DAP that have surfaced in recent years, some interpretations of guidance show a misunderstanding of what the approach is about. Erroneous interpretations have led to the misapplication of guidance ideas: some teachers may think they are using guidance when they are not.

This article is an effort to amplify the concept of guidance. It defines guidance, traces the guidance tradition in early childhood education, examines the present trend toward guidance, explains what guidance is not, and illustrates key practices in classrooms where teachers use guidance.

Guidance defined

Teachers who practice guidance believe in the positive potential of children, manifest through a dynamic process of development (Greenberg 1988). For this reason, teachers who use guidance think beyond conventional classroom discipline—the intent of which is to keep children (literally and figuratively) in line. Rather than simply being a reaction to crises, guidance involves developmentally appropriate, culturally responsive education to reduce the occurrence of classroom problems. Guidance means creating a positive learning environment for each child in the group.

Guidance teaches children the life skills they need as citizens of a democracy (Wittmer & Honig 1994): respecting others and one's self, working together in groups, solving problems using words, expressing strong emotions in acceptable ways, making decisions ethically and intelligently. Teachers who use guidance realize that it takes well into adulthood to master these skills and that, in learning them, children—like all of us—make mistakes. Therefore, because children are just beginning this personal development, teachers regard behaviors traditionally considered *mis*behaviors as *mistaken* behaviors (Gartrell 1987b, 1995). The interventions teachers make to address mistaken behaviors are firm but friendly, instructive and solution oriented but not punitive. The teacher helps children learn from their mistakes rather than punishing them for the mistakes they make; empowers children to solve problems rather than punishing them for having problems they cannot solve; helps children accept consequences but consequences that leave self-esteem intact.

Guidance teaching is character education in its truest, least political sense—guiding children to develop the empathy, self-esteem, and self-control needed for autonomy, Piaget's term for the capacity to make intelligent, ethical decisions (Kamii 1984). In contrast to the notion that the teacher handles all problem situations alone, guidance involves teamwork with professionals and partnerships with parents on behalf of the child.

The guidance tradition

The only task harder than learning democratic living skills is teaching them to others. Guidance has always been practiced by the kind of teacher whom, if we were fortunate, we had ourselves; whom we would want our children to have; whom we would like to emulate. From time immemorial there probably have been "guidance teachers." A rich guidance tradition spanning more than 150 years has been documented in the early childhood field.

The pioneers

Educators interested in social reform long have viewed children as being in a state of dynamic development and adults as patterning effective education and guidance practices responsive to the developmental pattern of the child. During the nineteenth century the European educators Herbart, Pestalozzi, and Froebel began fundamental educational reform, in no small part as a result of their views on the child's dynamic nature (Osborn 1980). Herbart and Pestalozzi recognized that children learn best through activities they can tie to their own experiences rather than through a strictly enforced recitation of facts.

German born Friedrich Froebel was the originator of the kindergarten, at the time intended for children aged three to six. Froebel incorporated such practices as manipulatives-based instruction, circle time, home visits, "mothers' meetings," and the use of women teachers (Lilley 1967). (In the 1870s, his kindergartens were barred in Germany for being "too democratic.") For Froebel

the whole purpose of education was guidance so that the "innate impulses of the child" could be developed harmoniously through creative activity. As part of his early developmental orientation, Froebel believed that the nature of the child was essentially good and that "faults" were the product of negative experiences, sometimes at the hand of the educator (Lilley 1967).

Similarly, Maria Montessori took a developmental viewpoint, maintaining that "the child is in a continual state of growth and metamorphosis, whereas the adult has reached the norm of the species" (cited in Standing 1962, 106). Montessori's remarkable vision included not only the innovations of the "prepared environment" and a child-oriented teaching process but also the idea that intelligence is greatly influenced by early experience. It interesting to note that Montessori's early theory of "sensitive periods" of learning is supported in graphic fashion by the brain research of today.

Montessori—as well as her American contemporary, John Dewey—abhorred the traditional schooling of the day, which failed to consider children's development. She criticized didactic teaching practices with children planted behind desks, expected to recite lessons of little meaning in their lives, and kept in line by systematic rewards

© Blakely Fetridge Bundy

© Bob Loveland

Often, friendly adult intervention and assistance can help children work through a seemingly insoluble social problem themselves. Most of the time, children want to solve what they perceive as the problem.

and punishments (Montessori 1964). Her approach made the child an active agent in the education process; through this responsibility children would learn *self*-discipline.

Like Montessori, Dewey viewed discipline as differing in method depending on the curriculum followed. The "pre-primary" level in Dewey's University of Chicago Laboratory School featured project-based learning activities that built from the everyday experience of the young learners. Dewey saw the connection between school and society, postulating that our democratic ideals need to be sustained through the microcosm of the classroom. In his 1900 monograph *The School and Society,* Dewey states,

> If you have the end in view of forty or fifty children learning certain set lessons, to be recited to the teacher, your discipline must be devoted to securing that result. But if the end in view is the development of a spirit of social co-operation and community life, discipline must grow out of and be relative to such an aim. There is a certain disorder in any busy workshop; there is not silence; persons are not engaged in maintaining certain fixed physical postures; their arms are not folded; they are not holding their books thus and so. They are doing a variety of things, and there is the confusion, the bustle that results from activity. Out of the occupation, out of doing things that are to produce results, and out of doing these in a social and co-operative way, there is born a discipline of its own kind and type. Our whole conception of discipline changes when we get this point of view. (1969, 16–17).

Dewey, of course, was not just speaking of early childhood education but of schooling at all levels. Almost 100 years later, his words still challenge America's educators and eloquently capture the "guidance difference."

Midcentury influences

In the first half of the twentieth century, progressive educators and psychologists increasingly viewed children not in traditional moralistic terms (good and bad) but in terms responsive to a positive developmental potential. The nursery school movement in Britain and the United States was imbued with these progressive ideas and influ-

© BmPorter/Don Franklin

Comfort the hurt child first, then have a conversation with others involved. The objective is to increase empathy and interpersonal problem-solving skills.

enced the writings of two midcentury early childhood educators, James L. Hymes Jr. (1949, 1955) and Katherine Read (1950).

Katherine Read Baker was a nursery education leader. Her classic *The Nursery School: A Human Relations Laboratory* is currently reprinted under a new title in a ninth edition. For Read, the classroom is a supportive environment for both children and adults to gain understanding in the challenging area of human relationships. Read speaks clearly of the child's need for understandable, consistent limits and of the use of authority to encourage self-control:

> Our goal is self-control, the only sound control. But self-control can be sound only when there is a stable mature self. Our responsibility is to help the child develop maturity through giving him the security of limits maintained by responsible adults while he is growing. (Read [1950] 1993, 233)

Hymes distinguished himself as director of the noted Kaiser Day Care Centers during World War II and later as one of the people who strongly influenced the educational approach basic to Head Start. Hymes wrote frequently about early childhood edu-

cation matters, including the landmark Effective Home-School Relations (1953). His Discipline (1949) and Behavior and Misbehavior (1955) stressed the importance of understanding the reasons for children's behavior. He argued that the causes of problems often are not in the child alone but a result of the program placing inappropriate developmental expectations on the child.

Hymes and Read both stressed the need for teachers to have high expectations of children—but expectations in line with each child's development. They articulated a key guidance premise, that the teacher must be willing to modify the daily program for the benefit of children, not just hold the program as a fixed commodity, against which the behavior of the child is to be judged.

The basic educational and child guidance philosophy of Head Start, which was created as a nationwide program by War on Poverty leaders in 1965, was the nursery school/kindergarten philosophy developed long before and taught to several generations of teachers by Read, Hymes, and others of like persuasion.

Jean Piaget, often considered the preeminent developmental psychologist of the twentieth century, discussed implications of his work for the classroom in The Moral Judgment of the Child ([1932] 1960). The Swiss psychologist shared with Montessori the precept that children learn through constructing knowledge by interacting with the environment. Further, he shared with Dewey and leaders of nursery school and kindergarten education a high regard for the social context of learning—insisting that peer interaction is essential for healthy development. He maintained that education must be an interactive endeavor and that discipline must respect and respond to this fact. Speaking directly about the uses of conventional classroom discipline. Piaget points out,

> If one thinks of the systematic resistance offered by pupils to the authoritarian method, and the admirable ingenuity employed by children the world over to evade disciplinary constraint, one cannot help regarding as defective a system which allows so much effort to be wasted instead of using it in cooperation ([1932] 1960, 366–67)

Like Dewey, Read, and Hymes, Piaget saw the classroom as a "laboratory" in which the practice of democracy was to be modeled, taught, and learned. For these writers, the means to social, personal, and intellectual development was guidance practiced in the classroom by a responsible adult.

As Piaget's work demonstrates, midcentury psychologists as well as educators have enhanced guidance ideas. Important names that readers may have encountered in college educational psychology classes are Erikson, Adler, Maslow, Rogers, Combs, Purkey, and Jersild, among others (Hamacheck 1971).

Two such psychologists who have greatly influenced guidance views are Dreikurs (1968) and Ginott (1972). In line with Adler's theory about personality development, Dreikurs's construct of Mistaken Goals of Behavior has contributed to the present concept of mistaken behavior. Ginott, a particular influence on my writing, has contributed much to the language of guidance, illustrated by one of his more famous quotes: "To reach a child's mind, a teacher must capture his heart. Only if a child feels right can he think right" (1972, 69). Across the middle of the century, a broad array of educators and psychologists nurtured and sustained the guidance tradition.

The 1980s

Through the 1970s the guidance tradition was sustained by writers such as Jeannette Galambos Stone (1978) and Rita Warren (1977), who authored widely read monographs for the National Association for the Education of Young Children (NAEYC), along with many other well-known early childhood educators. While guidance was becoming important in preschool programs, a new trend in the public schools threatened to stop the percolating up of guidance ideas, a long-sought goal of early childhood educators. "Back to the basics" became the call of public school educators, and curriculum and teaching methods grew more proscribed. During this time academic and disciplinary constraints were even put on kindergarten and preschool children. With disregard for young children's development, teachers were pressured to "get students ready" for the academics of the next level—a pressure still felt by some early childhood teachers today.

During these years, the interactive nature of the guidance approach did not fit the regimen of the academic classroom. New "obedience-driven" discipline systems, such as assertive discipline, came into widespread use at all levels of public education—and even in some preschool programs (Gartrell 1987a; Hitz 1988). In Discipline with Dignity, Curwin and Mendler lamented the widespread adoption of obedience models of discipline by public schools:

It is ironic that the current mood of education is in some ways behind the past. The 1980s might someday be remembered as the decade when admiration was reserved for principals, cast as folk heroes walking around schools with baseball bats, and for teachers and whole schools that systematically embarrassed students by writing their names on the chalkboard. But we do have hope that the pendulum will once again swing to the rational position of treating children as people with needs and feelings that are not that different from adults. Once we begin to understand how obedience is contrary to the goals of our culture and education, the momentum will begin to shift. Our view is that the highest virtue of education is to teach students to be self-responsible and fully functional. In all but extreme cases, obedience contradicts these goals. (1988, 24)

The guidance trend

Throughout the 1980s and up to the present, educators and writers at the early childhood level maintained their independence from the obedience emphasis in conventional discipline. In 1987 NAEYC published its expanded *Developmentally Appropriate Practice in Early Childhood Programs Serving Children from Birth through Age 8* (Bredekamp).

Now in its revised edition (Bredekamp & Copple 1997), the position statement and document advocate the interactive teaching practices responsive to the development of each child that our profession always has. In relation to behavior management, the document reflects the guidance approach and draws a sharp distinction with conventional elementary school classroom discipline. In *appropriate* teaching practice,

Teachers facilitate the development of social skills, self-control, and self-regulation in children by using positive guidance techniques, such as modeling and encouraging expected behavior, redirecting children to more acceptable activities, setting clear limits, and intervening to enforce consequences for unacceptable, harmful behavior. Teachers' expectations respect children's developing capabilities. Teachers are patient, realizing that not every minor infraction warrants a response. (Bredekamp & Copple 1997, 129)

Inappropriate practices are those in which

Teachers spend a great deal of time punishing unacceptable behavior, demeaning children who misbehave, repeatedly putting the same children who misbehave in time-out or some other punishment unrelated to the action.... Teachers do not set clear limits and do not hold children accountable to standards of acceptable behavior. The environment is chaotic, and teachers do not help children set and learn important rules of group behavior and responsibility. (Bredekamp & Copple 1997, 129)

At both the preprimary and primary-grade levels, these NAEYC documents illustrate the ambiguous distinction between conventional discipline techniques and the use of punishment (Bredekamp & Copple 1997). In fact, a growing number of early childhood professionals have become dissatisfied in recent years with the very term "discipline" (MnNAEYC 1991; Reynolds 1996). The reason is that teachers have a hard time telling where discipline ends and punishment begins. Other educators argue that discipline is a "neutral" term and does not have to mean punishment (Marion 1995). However, when most teachers

One of the major areas in which kindergarten and nursery education historically have distinguished themselves from elementary and secondary education is in the area of "behavior education." The former advocates guidance rather than punishment.

> ## The ideas in this article are not new, but many teachers are not yet putting them into practice.

use discipline, they tend to include acts of punishment; they mix up discipline and punishment out of anger or because they feel the child "deserves it." The very idea of "disciplining" a child suggests punishment, illustrating the easy semantic slide of the one into the other.

Teachers who go beyond discipline do so because of the baggage of punishment that discipline carries. These teachers reject punishment for what it is by definition: the infliction of "pain, loss, or suffering for a crime or wrongdoing."

For many years educators and psychologists have recognized the harmful effects of punishment on children (Dewey [1900] 1969; Piaget [1932] 1960; Montessori 1964; Slaby et al. 1995). Some of the effects of punishment are

- low self-esteem (feeling like a "failure"),
- negative self-concept (not liking one's self),
- angry feelings (sometimes under the surface) toward others, and
- a feeling of disengagement from school and the learning process.

A teacher who uses guidance knows that children learn little when the words they frequently hear are "Don't do that" or "You're naughty" or "You know better than that." When discipline includes punishment, young children have difficulty understanding how to improve their behavior (Greenberg 1988). Instead of being shamed into "being good," they are likely to internalize the negative personal message that punishment carries (Gartrell 1995).

Experts now recognize that through punishment children lose their trust in adults (Clewett 1988; Slaby et al. 1995). Over time young people come to accept doing negative things and being punished for them as a natural part of life. By contrast, the increasing use of conflict management (teaching children to solve their problems with words) fosters children's faith in social processes. Conflict management and other guidance methods are being used more now because they work better than punishment (Carlsson-Paige & Levin 1992). These methods teach children how to solve problems without violence and help children to feel good

about themselves, the class, and the teacher (Levin 1994). Young children need to learn how to know better and do better. The guidance approach is positive teaching, with the teacher having faith in the young child's ability to learn (Marion 1995).

Guidance: What it isn't

The term "discipline" remains in wide use at the elementary, middle-school, and secondary levels. Whether educators embrace the term "guidance" or attach a positive qualifier to "discipline," new notions about classroom management can be expected that claim the use of guidance principles. With the never-ending parade of new information, it is important for us to recognize what guidance is not—so as to better understand what it is.

Five misunderstandings about guidance

1. Guidance is *not* just reacting to problems.

Many problems are caused when a teacher uses practices that are not appropriate for the age, stage, and needs of the individual child. Long group times, for instance, cause young children to become bored and restless. (They will sit in large groups more easily when they are older.) The teacher changes practices—such as reducing the number and length of group activities—to reduce the need for misbehaviors. Changes to other parts of the education program—including room layout, daily schedule, and adult-to-child ratios—also help reduce the need for misbehavior. Guidance prevents problems; it does not just react to them.

2. Guidance does *not* mean that the program won't be educational.

When activities are developmentally appropriate, *all* children succeed at them, and *all* children are learning to be successful students. The Three *R*s are a part of the education program, but they are integrated into the rest

of the day and made meaningful so that children want to learn. This "basic" of Progressive Education, the parent of what we now call developmentally appropriate practice, is well explained in the original and revised editions of *Developmentally Appropriate Practice in Early Childhood Programs* and both volumes of *Reaching Potentials* (Bredekamp 1987; Bredekamp and Rosegrant 1992, 1995; Bredekamp & Copple 1997). When teachers use guidance, however, the Three *R*s are not all there is.

The importance of guidance, according to Lilian Katz, means that the teacher makes *relationships* the first *R* (cited in Kantrowitz & Wingert 1989). The social skills that are learned through positive relationships come first in the education program. Children need to know how to relate with others in all parts of their lives. Beginning to learn social skills in early childhood will help children in their years of school and in adult life (Wittmer & Honig 1994). (Social skills, after all, are really social studies skills and language arts skills.)

3. Guidance is *not* a "sometimes thing."

Some teachers think that it is natural to use "guidance" in one set of circumstances and "discipline" in another. Yet nonpunitive guidance techniques exist for all situations and, once learned, are effective (Carlsson-Paige & Levin 1992; Reynolds 1996). For example, a common discipline technique is the time-out chair, but the time-out chair usually embarrasses the child, seldom teaches a positive lesson, and is almost always punishment (Clewett 1988). The teacher can cut down on the use of this punishment by reducing the need for mistaken behavior and helping children to use words to solve their problems.

If a child does lose control and needs to be removed, the teacher can stay with the child for a cooling-down time. The teacher then talks with the child about how the other child felt, helps the child find a way to help the other child feel better (make restitution), and teaches a positive alternative for next time. Guidance encompasses a full spectrum of methods, from prevention to conflict resolution to crisis intervention to long-term management strategies. Teamwork with parents and other adults is frequently part of the overall approach.

The objective is to teach children to solve problems rather than to punish children for having problems they cannot solve. The outcomes of guidance—the ability to get along with others, solve problems using words, express strong feelings in acceptable ways—are the goals for citizens of a democratic society.

4. Guidance is *not* permissive discipline.

Teachers who use guidance are active leaders who do not let situations get out of hand. They do not make children struggle with boundaries that may not be there (Gartrell 1995). Guidance teachers tend to rely on guidelines—positive statements that remind children of classroom conduct—rather than rules which are usually stated in the negative, as though the adult expects the child to break them. When they intervene, teachers direct their responses to the behavior and respect the personality of the child (Ginott 1972). They avoid embarrassment, which tends to leave lasting emotional scars. They make sure that their responses are friendly as well as firm.

The objective is to teach children to solve problems rather than to punish children for having problems they cannot solve. The outcomes of guidance—the ability to get along with others, solve problems using words, express strong feelings in acceptable ways—are the goals for citizens of a democratic society. For this reason, guidance has a meaning that goes beyond traditional discipline. Guidance is not just keeping children in line; it is actively teaching them skills they will need for their entire lives (Wittmer & Honig 1994).

5. Guidance is *not* reducible to a commercial program.

The guidance tradition is part of the child-sensitive educational practice of the last two decades. Guidance is part of the movement toward developmentally appropriate and culturally responsive education. Teachers who use guidance rely on a teaching team (adults in the classroom working together) and positive parent-teacher relations. Guidance involves more than a workshop or a program on paper; it requires reflective commitment by the teacher, teamwork by the staff, and cooperation with families and the community.

Six key guidance practices

Teachers who use guidance have classrooms that are encouraging places to be in. In the words of one teacher, when guidance is present, children want to come to school even when they are sick. Both children and adults feel welcome in guidance classrooms. An informed observer who visits such a classroom quickly sees that "guidance is practiced here." Six key guidance practices follow. When they are evident in a classroom, the teacher is using guidance.

1. The teacher realizes that social skills are complicated and take into adulthood to fully learn.

In the process of learning social skills, children—like all of us—make mistakes. That's why behaviors traditionally considered to be "misbehaviors" are regarded as "mistaken behaviors" (Gartrell 1987a, b; 1995). The teacher believes in the positive potential of each child. He recognizes that mistaken behaviors are caused by inexperience in social situations, the influence of others on the child, or by deep, unmet physical or emotional needs. Understanding why children show mistaken behavior permits the teacher to teach social skills with a minimum of moral judgment about the child. He takes the attitude that "we all make mistakes; we just need to learn from them."

The teacher shows this understanding even when the children demonstrate "strong-needs" (serious) mistaken behavior (Gartrell 1987b, 1995). Such children are sometimes regarded as "bad" children, but the teacher using guidance knows that they are children with bad problems that they cannot solve on their own. In working with strong-needs mistaken behavior, the teacher takes a comprehensive approach. He seeks to understand the problem, modifies the child's program to reduce crises, intervenes consistently but nonpunitively, builds the relationship with the child, involves the parents, teams with staff and other professionals, and develops, implements, and monitors a long-term plan.

2. The teacher reduces the need for mistaken behavior.

One major cause of mistaken behavior is a poor match between the child and the educational program (the program expects either too much or too little from the child). The teacher improves the match by using teaching practices that are developmentally appropriate and culturally sensitive (Bredekamp 1987; Bredekamp & Copple 1997). She reduces wait times by offering many activities in learning centers and small groups. She gives children choices so they can work at their own levels in activities. To avoid problems, she anticipates when particular children will need support and encouragement. She changes activities, adjusts the schedule, and modifies the room arrangement as circumstances warrant. She uses adults in the classroom to increase individual attention and expand opportunities for positive adult-child attachments. When children's development, learning styles, and family backgrounds become the main priorities of a program, children become positively involved and feel less need to show mistaken behavior.

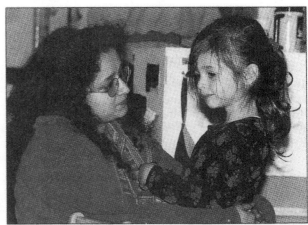

© Blakely Fetridge Bundy

One-on-one guidance works better than scolding.

3. The teacher practices positive teacher-child relations.

The teacher works to accept each child as a welcome member of the class (Warren 1977). To prevent embarrassment and unnecessary competition, the teacher avoids singling out children either for criticism or praise. Instead, she uses private feedback with the individual and group-focused encouragement with the class (Hitz & Driscoll 1988).

Even if children are preschoolers, the teacher holds class meetings both for regular business and for problems that arise (Brewer 1992). The teacher relies more on guidelines—positive statements of expected behaviors—than on rules with negative wording and implied threats. She models and teaches cooperation and empathy-building skills. She models and teaches acceptance of children who might be singled out negatively for physical, cultural, or behavioral reasons. She teaches that differing human qualities and circumstances are natural, to be appreciated and learned from. She understands that children who feel accepted in the classroom have less need to show mistaken behavior.

4. The teacher uses intervention methods that are solution oriented.

The teacher creates an environment in which problems can be solved peaceably (Levin 1994). He intervenes by modeling and teaching conflict management—initially using high-level mediation and continually encouraging the children to negotiate for themselves. He avoids public embarrassment and rarely uses removal (redirection and cooling-down times) or physical restraint, and then only as methods of last resort. After intervention, the teacher assists the child with regaining composure, understanding the other's feelings, learning more acceptable behaviors, and making amends and reconciling with the other child or group.

The teacher recognizes that, at times, he too shows human frailties. The teacher works at monitoring and managing his own feelings. The teacher learns even as he teaches. As a developing professional, the teacher models the effort to learn from mistakes.

5. The teacher builds partnerships with parents.

The teacher recognizes that mistaken behavior occurs less often when parents and teachers work together. The teacher also recognizes that being a parent is a difficult job and that many parents, for personal and cultural reasons, feel uncomfortable meeting with educators (Gestwicki 1992). The teacher starts building partnerships at the beginning of the year. Through positive notes home, phone calls, visits, meetings, and conferences, she builds relationships. It is her job to build partnerships even with hard-to-reach parents. When the invitations are sincere, many parents gradually do become involved.

6. The teacher uses teamwork with adults.

The teacher recognizes that it is a myth that she can handle all situations alone. She creates a teaching team of fellow staff and volunteers (especially parents), who work together in the classroom. She understands that children gain trust in their world when they see adults of differing backgrounds working together. When there is serious mistaken behavior, the teacher meets with parents and other adults to develop and use a coordinated plan. Through coordinated assistance, children can be helped to overcome serious problems and build self-esteem and social skills. The teacher knows that effective communication among adults builds a bridge between school and community. Through working together, teachers accomplish what they cannot do alone.

In summary, guidance goes beyond the traditional goal of classroom discipline: enforcing children's compliance to the teacher's will. On a day-to-day basis in the classroom, guidance teaches children the life skills they need as citizens of a democracy. Teachers encourage children to take pride in their developing personalities and cultural identities. Guidance teaches children to view differing human qualities as sources of affirmation and learning.

Guidance involves creating a successful learning environment for each child. The teacher plans and implements an educational program that is developmentally appropriate and culturally responsive. She serves as leader of a classroom community and helps all children to find a place and to learn. The teacher uses nonpunitive intervention techniques, in firm but friendly ways, to establish guidelines and guide children's behavior. She uses conflict resolution as a regular and important tool.

The guidance approach involves teamwork on the part of adults, especially in the face of serious mistaken behavior. Guidance links together teacher, parent, and child on a single team. Success in the use of guidance is measured not in test scores or "obedient" classes but in positive attitudes in the classroom community toward living and learning.

References

Bredekamp, S., ed. 1987. *Developmentally appropriate practice in early childhood programs serving children from birth through age 8.* Exp. ed. Washington, DC: NAEYC.

Bredekamp, S., & C. Copple, eds. 1997. *Developmentally appropriate practice in early childhood programs.* Rev. ed. Washington, DC: NAEYC.

Bredekamp, S., & T. Rosegrant, eds. 1992. *Reaching potentials: Appropriate curriculum and assessment for young children— volume 1.* Washington, DC: NAEYC.

Bredekamp, S., & T. Rosegrant, eds. 1995. *Reaching potentials: Transforming early childhood curriculum and assessment—volume 2.* Washington, DC: NAEYC.

Brewer, J.A. 1992. Where does it all begin? Teaching the principles of democracy in the early years. *Young Children* 47 (3): 51–53.

Carlsson-Paige, N., & D.E. Levin. 1992. Making peace in violent times: A constructivist approach to conflict resolution. *Young Children* 48 (1): 4–13.*

Clewett, A.S. 1988. Guidance and discipline: Teaching young children appropriate behavior. *Young Children* 43 (4): 22–36.*

Curwin, R.L., & A.N. Mendler. 1988. *Discipline with dignity.* Alexandria, VA: Association for Supervision and Curriculum Development.

Dewey, J. [1900] 1969. *The school and society.* Chicago: University of Chicago Press.

Dreikurs, R. 1968. *Psychology in the classroom.* New York: Harper & Row.

Gartrell, D.J. 1987a. Assertive discipline: Unhealthy for children and other living things. *Young Children* 42 (2): 10–11.

Gartrell, D.J. 1987b. Punishment or guidance. *Young Children* 42 (3): 55–61.

Gartrell, D.J. 1995. Misbehavior or mistaken behavior? *Young Children* 50 (5): 27–34.

Gestwicki, C. 1992. *Home, school and community relations.* Albany, NY: Delmar.

Ginott, H. 1972. *Teacher and child.* New York: Avon.

Greenberg, P. 1988. Avoiding 'me against you' discipline. *Young Children* 43 (1): 24–25.*

Hamacheck, D.E. 1971. *Encounters with the self.* New York: Holt, Rinehart, & Winston.

Hitz, R. 1988. Viewpoint. Assertive discipline: A response to Lee Canter. *Young Children* 43 (2): 25–26.

Hitz, R., & A. Driscoll. 1988. Praise or encouragement? New insights into praise: Implications for early childhood teachers. *Young Children* 43 (4): 6–13.

Hymes, J.L. 1949. *Discipline.* New York: Bureau of Publications, Columbia University.

Hymes, J.L. 1953. *Effective home-school relations.* Englewood Cliffs, NJ: Prentice Hall.

Hymes, J.L. 1955. *Behavior and misbehavior.* Englewood Cliffs, NJ: Prentice Hall.

Janke, A.J., & J. Penshorn Peterson. 1995. *Peacemaker's A, B, Cs for young children.* S. Marine on St. Croix, MN: Growing Communities for Peace.*

Kamii, C. 1984. Autonomy: The aim of education envisioned by Piaget. *Phi Delta Kappan* 65 (6): 410–15.

Kantrowitz, B., & P. Wingert. 1989. How kids learn, *Newsweek,* 17 July, 50–56.

Levin, D.E. 1994. *Teaching young children in violent times.* Cambridge, MA: Educators for Social Responsibility.

Lilley, I.M., ed. 1967. *Friedrich Froebel: A selection from his writings.* London: Cambridge University Press.

Marion, M. 1995. *Guidance of young children.* 5th ed. Columbus, OH: Merrill.

Minnesota Association for the Education of Young Children (MnAEYC). 1991. *Developmentally appropriate guidance of children birth to eight.* Rev. ed. St. Paul: Author.

Montessori, M. 1964. *The Montessori method.* New York: Schocken.

Osborn, D.K. 1980. *Early childhood education in historical perspective.* Athens, GA: Education Associates.

Piaget, J. [1932] 1960. *The moral judgment of the child.* Glencoe, IL: Free Press.

Read, K.H. [1950] 1993. *Early childhood programs: Human relations and learning.* 9th ed. Fort Worth, TX: Harcourt Brace.

Reynolds, E. 1996. *Guiding young children: A child-centered approach.* 2d ed. Mountain View, CA: Mayfield.

Slaby, R.G., W.C. Roedell, D. Arezzo, & K. Hendrix. 1995. *Early violence prevention: Tools for teachers of young children.* Washington, DC: NAEYC.

Standing, E.M. 1962. *Maria Montessori: Her life and work.* New York: New American Library.

Stone, J.G. 1978. *A guide to discipline.* Rev. ed. Washington, DC: NAEYC.

Warren, R.M. 1977. *Caring: Supporting children's growth.* Washington, DC: NAEYC.

Wichert, S. 1989. *Keeping the peace: Practicing cooperation and conflict resolution with preschoolers.* Philadelphia: New Society.*

Wittmer, D.S., & A.S. Honig. 1994. Encouraging positive social development in young children. *Young Children* 49 (5): 61–75.*

* Recommended reading

For further reading

Gartrell, D.J. 1994. *A guidance approach to discipline.* Albany, NY: Delmar.

Greenberg, P. 1990. Ideas that work with young children. Why not academic preschool? (Part 1). *Young Children* 45 (2): 70–80.

Greenberg, P. 1992. Why not academic preschool? (Part 2) Autocracy or democracy in the classroom? *Young Children* 47 (3): 54–64.

Greenberg, P. 1992. Ideas that work with young children. How to institute some simple democratic practices pertaining to respect, rights, roots, and responsibilities in any classroom (Without losing your leadership position). Young Children 47 (5): 10–17.

Hendrick, J. 1992. Where does it all begin? Teaching the principles of democracy in the early years. *Young Children* 47 (3): 51–64.

Teaching Peace Concepts to Children

ANARELLA CELLITTI

Children's everyday group experiences contain important opportunities for adults to model and teach skills and understandings that can lead to a more peaceful world.

Subjects & Predicates

Look for active, contemporary, positive pictures of people of various ages, from many cultures, with a range of capacities.

Components of teaching peace
- create a peaceful classroom
- teach conflict resolution and social responsibility

Many children today are exposed to acts of violence on television, in their communities, and sometimes within their families. Although the violence is frightening and puts children in danger, some children become accustomed to high levels of violence in their surroundings. As a result of their observations and experiences, many children are learning that violence is an apparently viable way to resolve conflicts between people (Eisenberg & Mussen, 1989).

In other homes, early childhood programs, and schools, young children learn that violence is not the only option, nor is it even an effective one, to resolve problems. Children in these peaceful environments routinely experience and use nonviolent ways to relate to peers and adults.

As early educators, it is our responsibility to expand children's thinking, to help them learn positive social skills if they are not familiar with them, and to assure that children know how to engage in peaceful interactions with others.

Teaching peace to young children involves two major components: creating a peaceful classroom environment, and teaching children conflict resolution and social re-

From *Dimensions of Early Childhood,* Spring 1998, pp. 38-42. © 1998 by the Southern Early Childhood Association (SECA), Little Rock, AR. Reprinted by permission.

sponsibility for themselves, others, and the world. The environment and curriculum can be shaped in ways that enable children to learn positive concepts about how people can live in harmony.

Create a Peaceful Atmosphere

In order to create a peaceful learning environment, teachers first establish an atmosphere in which adults model and facilitate peaceful interactions. Teachers maintain a climate of caring tolerance and mutual respect at all times, among children, staff, families, and visitors. Adults and children model communication skills, conflict resolution, tolerance, and honesty. Children in the group are expected to be generous to each other, to exhibit empathy, and to be increasingly aware of how their behaviors affect others.

Learning materials and activities are free from gender, racial, age, and other stereotypes. Caring adults build on typical everyday incidents (disagreements about turns on equipment, for example) to promote appropriate peacemaking skills such as communication, accepting no for an answer, standing up for what is fair, and taking turns. Children develop a sense of understanding about and empathy for others when they engage in meaningful community projects. Collect items for a toy or food drive, make cards or sing for nursing home residents or children in the hospital.

Families are an important ally in the peace-learning process. Talk with parents or guardians about how their children use their positive social skills and are learning to respect people. Encourage families to observe children at play, or videotape representative classroom interactions to show during conferences or meetings. Include information about conflict resolution, anti-bias activities, and other topics when you exchange information about children's progress.

Consider a peace center

In addition to incorporating peace into the daily routine, some teachers may want to set up a Peace Center in which children can read, listen to music, and practice their conflict resolution strategies. These are a few suggestions about how to set up such an area.

1. Designate a comfortable space. Decorate it with children's words and artwork depicting their ideas about peace. Post pictures of children engaged in activities at the Peace Center. Choose soothing music from a variety of cultures. "Peace Is the World Smiling" (Music for Little People, 1989) is one such recording. Select children's books in which the characters model peaceful behaviors.

2. Display pictures and posters that depict human diversity. Hang them at children's eye level. Look for active, contemporary, positive pictures of people of various ages, from many cultures, with a range of capacities. Catalogs, travel brochures, and magazines are excellent sources. Local newspapers often publish pictures of community members who are volunteers.

3. Set a few positive rules about expectations for children's behavior in the group, such as "We use our words to solve problems."

4. Teach children how to resolve conflicts with others. Explain all four steps (Table 1) as children resolve their disagreements. At first, and nearly always with toddlers, an adult is there to assure that children follow each step. Preschoolers soon learn to use these strategies independently. This democratic conflict resolution process also can be used by adults.

5. Post the program's rules and conflict resolution steps, so that adults are aware of what is expected. Explain their purpose. Encourage families to implement similar positive childrearing strategies.

Table 1

Steps to teach children conflict resolution

Step	Action
1. "Tell us what happened."	Allow each child to explain the problem.
2. Summarize.	Summarize what they say. Include each child's point of view.
3. "What could you do about this problem?"	Ask children for possible solutions. Consider all possibilities. You may say, "I wonder if there is another way to handle this problem," but don't suggest any solution.
4. Help the children choose a solution.	Do not give any hint of what you think they should do—it is their decision.

Note. From *Helping Children Love Themselves and Others: A Professional Handbook for Family Day Care* (p. 26), by J. McCracken (ed.), 1990, Washington, DC: The Children's Foundation. Copyright © 1990 by The Children's Foundation.

Subjects & Predicates

Teaching peace to children is a daily process.

6. Have a log that children fill in each time they use the center. Activities to be logged could include being at the center to resolve problems, read, write, or chat. For children who are still learning to read, use symbols to denote each activity.

7. Create a "Getting Along" word bank for your readers.

Suggest words that children can use to express their feelings and or describe actions so they can communicate more effectively. Offer substitute words for hurtful language (hate, stupid), such as angry or confused.

Integrate Peace in The Curriculum

Peace concepts are effectively taught only when they make sense to children and are embedded within the curriculum and classroom routines. Teaching peace to children is a daily process, rather than a special week or a project. These ideas describe how peace concepts can be incorporated into traditional academic areas, all of which are integrated in a developmental early childhood curriculum.

1. Social studies. Broaden children's true understanding about the uniqueness and similarities among individuals, families, communities, states, and countries around the world. Make sure information is accurate and about real people. Ask community volunteers to share

aspects of their heritage, such as artifacts or family photos. Ensure that children realize all people, including themselves, are unique individuals within a particular culture. Regularly incorporate authentic ethnic foods and real clothing into the pretend play area. Engage children in appropriate ways to solve current social problems in the community, such as writing letters about trash on their playground. Children learn about the democratic process when they vote on meaningful issues (Gunnels, 1997), build consensus in small groups, and use negotiation skills.

2. History/news. Read children's stories that recognize and celebrate people who work to establish human rights and a better life for others. Select such books often, rather than reading about Martin Luther King, Jr. only on his birthday holiday, for example. Talk with children about people they know who are working for peace and justice—neighbors, educators, decision makers in their community. Invite these people to describe their work to children. The president of the library board, for example, might explain how he talks with people and writes letters to ask for donations to buy new books.

3. Music and oral traditions. Music from any time periods and cultures can be integrated into discussions about geography and social studies. Find out what children know about a topic, and then build on that information. In what states or countries do children's friends and relatives live? What areas have they heard about in the news? To what kinds of music do they listen? Choose authentic music—familiar and new—from many different styles. Select songs, games, and finger plays that promote the values of understanding and helping others. Learn the words to songs in several languages, including signing.

4. Authentic literature. Books can greatly enhance children's knowledge of others. Look for accurate, balanced portrayals of diverse peoples. Limit the number of books that deal only with holidays or offer a "tourist" approach—make sure children gain a more realistic perspective of daily life. Choose children's books that portray children and adults engaging in friendly, peaceful behaviors. Extend children's literature experiences by providing hands-on activities that enable them to gain a fuller understanding of the situation portrayed.

5. Visual arts. Art experiences that relate to taking care of the earth or that come from different cultures can promote children's social responsibility and their understanding of other perspectives. Show children paintings or weavings, for example and talk with them about these pieces. Provide children with the necessary materials and tools, and demonstrate new techniques. Then encourage them to represent their own ideas and concepts.

6. Natural sciences. Science activities concerning recycling, reforestation, and taking care of sea animals and the ocean could be included as children discover the process of erosion, decomposition of waste, and animal life. Or follow up on children's understanding about human similarities and differences in skin color, hair texture, and teeth.

7. Number concepts. Math could incorporate studies of the classroom population such as helping children create graphs of classmates' eye color, food preferences, or other characteristics. Prepare ethnic foods using favorite recipes provided by families in the program. Children make a shopping list for, measure, and mix ingredients, and when it is done, divide the food in portions. Nutrition, money, and many other concepts could be explored.

Teachers have daily opportunities to increase children's abilities to communicate, respect each other, resolve conflicts, and accept social responsibility—skills they will carry into adulthood. Inclusion of peace-making skills in the curriculum is as important as learning to read and write.

References

Damon, W. (1988). *The moral child: Nurturing children's natural moral growth.* New York, NY: Free Press.

Eisenberg, N., & Mussen, P. (1989). *The roots of prosocial behaviors in children.* Cambridge, MA; Cambridge University Press.

Gunnels, J. A. (1997, Fall). A class pet campaign: Experiencing the democratic process. *Dimensions of Early Childhood, 25* (4), 31–34.

Kostelnik, M., Stein, L., Whiren, A., & Soderman, A. (1993). *Guiding children's social development.* Albany, NY: Delmar.

Kreidler, W. (1984). *Creative conflict resolution.* Glenview, IL: Scott Foresman.

McCracken, J. (Ed). (1990). *Helping children love themselves and others: A professional handbook for family day care.* Washington, DC: The Children's Foundation.

Peace is the world smiling. (1989). A peace anthology for families (Cassette Recording No. MLP D-2104). Redway, CA: Music for Little People.

Wolfgang, C., & Glickman, C. D. (1986). *Solving discipline problems: Strategies for classroom teachers.* Boston, MA: Allyn & Bacon.

Anarella Cellitti, Ph.D., is Assistant Professor at Texas A&M University-Kingsville in Kingsville.

Creating a Community of Learning for Homeless Children

**The shocking truth is that the average age
of a homeless person in the United States is 9 years.
More than 750,000 homeless children are of school age.
How are we educating these children?**

Ralph da Costa Nunez and Kate Collignon

By 1997, more than 1 million American children were homeless, moving between shelters and overcrowded or inadequate housing. Of these, more than 750,000 were school-aged, and the overwhelming majority performed well below grade level (Education for Homeless Children 1994; Nunez 1996).

These children are at risk of far more than academic failure. Plagued by domestic violence, family substance abuse, parental uninvolvement, and the psychological devastation of homelessness, they need more than help with their homework: They need a safe haven where they will receive the educational and emotional support to keep them from falling farther into the cracks of society.

Many U.S. public schools provide academic assistance for homeless children, but only a handful of innovative model programs—whether functioning as shelters within schools or schools within shelters—provide comprehensive approaches to education. They have established "communities of learning" by incorporating referrals to adult education and family support services into *specialized*—rather than special—education for children. By

broadening our vision beyond traditional children's education, we can learn from these models and effectively break the cycles of poverty and homelessness to ensure that the next generation will succeed.

Educational Pitfalls Facing Homeless Children

Homeless children face monumental obstacles in their pursuit of education. They lag far behind other children, both educationally and developmentally (Molnar et al., 1991; Rafferty 1991, 1995; Bassuk and Rubin 1987). Although all children in poverty fare similarly, homeless children face seemingly insurmountable logistical problems and emotional and psychological pressures.

The most visible hindrances to homeless children's education are the obstacles to enrollment and participation created by movement to and residence in a shelter. While allowed by law to continue at the school they attended before becoming homeless, many children end up in shelters so far from their previous home that they must choose between transferring schools or spending hours commuting. At new schools, the traumatized fami-

lies face an obstacle course of residency, guardianship, and immunization requirements; inadequate record-keeping systems; and a lack of continuity of programs like special education and gifted education. For most homeless families, this happens two or three times during the school year (Rafferty 1991; Anderson et al. 1995).

Even after enrollment, homeless children struggle to reorient themselves to new schools, teachers, classmates, and curriculums; and teachers are forced to reassess their new students' skill levels and needs. Often teachers do not even know that their students are homeless. Even if they do, few teachers are trained in the special needs of homeless children. Homeless students are frequently left out of extended class projects and are three times more likely to be recommended for special education programs than their peers—and many never escape (Nunez 1996).

These impediments only hint at the devastation to a child's education caused by the psychological impact of homelessness. The loss of a home robs a child of the familiarity and sense of place that most people take for granted. At school, classmates are quick to ridicule homeless children, adding stigma to the displacement homeless children suffer.

What about the parents? The average homeless parent—a young single mother with one or two children—reads at or below the 6th grade level and left school by the 10th grade. Many parents feel alienated from school, and most are unable to reinforce school lessons. A constant crisis mode leaves parents no room for long-term goals such as education and stability. As a result, most homeless children fail to attend school regularly. One study found that homeless children in New York City had missed an average of three weeks of school even before entering the shelter system (Nunez 1996).

To help homeless children and their families move beyond the crises of homelessness, we must provide not just specialized tutoring but also a safe place, stability, and direct services. The Education of Homeless Children and Youth Program of the 1987 Stewart B. McKinney Homeless Assistance Act has taken significant steps toward ensuring equal access to public education for homeless children. But much remains to be done.

Communities of Learning

Schools must work to ameliorate the barriers to school attendance and participation, as well as the environmental conditions that fail to support—or at worst, sabotage—a child's education. Model programs have combined the educational expertise of schools with the experience and services of shelters into school-or shelter-based communities of learning.

Communities of learning immerse children in an environment of education, while enabling them to see their parents embracing learning as well, and to receive the basic care that schools usually assume children receive at home. A community of learning includes the following:

■ Specialized education for homeless children.

■ Contextualized education for parents.

■ Linkages to needed services.

The educational curriculums for children at these centers incorporate traditional techniques used for special education, but do not replace regular school attendance. The centers work to accommodate the frequent and unpredictable disruptions in participation common among homeless children, not to isolate homeless children from the educational mainstream.

Again, what about the parents? Many homeless parents are embar-

> The Brownstone after-school program provides one-on-one tutoring, homework help, and creative educational activities that are organized around themes to provide continuity from one day to the next.

rassed by their lack of literacy skills and feel humiliated by memories of academic failure. By addressing the educational needs of parents, we can encourage parental involvement and pave the way to much-needed stability. Here are some guidelines for an adult education curriculum:

■ Be basic enough to help those with even the lowest literacy skills.

■ Be flexible to accommodate the same unpredictable participation rates that plague homeless children.

■ Be relevant to a parent's day-to-day life.

■ Be provided in a one-on-one or workshop format—anything to avoid negative associations with previous classroom-based experiences.

Model Programs

The Brownstone School, operated by Homes for the Homeless at the Prospect Family Inn in the Bronx, is a shelter-based after-school program that takes an accelerated—rather than remedial—approach to helping homeless children address specific academic difficulties while keeping up with their peers. The Brownstone provides one-on-one tutoring, homework help, and creative educational activities that are organized around themes to provide continuity from one day to the next. The tutors modify these activities for multiple skill levels and offer them in brief cycles to accommodate new students who arrive at the shelter (Nunez 1994).

At the Prospect Family Inn, adult education begins with basic literacy workshops. In these, parents read, write, and talk about parenting, health and nutrition, stress management, budgeting, housing, and apartment maintenance. Many parents attend an alternative high school on site at the shelter that prepares them to receive their General Equivalency Diploma (GED). Parents then attend employment workshops and qualify for internships and placement. Parents' participation in these programs and children's participation in Brownstone and on-site day care supplement parenting and literacy training with the opportunity for parents and children to read and spend time together in a structured and safe place (Nunez 1994).

Yet homeless parents and children cannot be expected to make education their priority so long as they must continue to worry about where they will be sleeping the next night or when an abuser will resurface. Communities of learning must attend to these other issues.

Such attention begins by providing for basic needs. The Recovering the Gifted Child Academy, a public alternative middle school in Chicago founded by Corla "Momma Hawk" Hawkins to serve children who come from poverty (and many from homelessness), maintains a "survival kit" including clean underwear, socks, deodorant, toothpaste, and toothbrushes for any student who needs them. The Academy also offers three meals a day for its students—operating on the assumption that no assumptions can be made about what children are provided with outside of school (Pool and Hawk 1997). Once these basic needs are attended to, communities of learning still must attend to less visible needs, such as the effects of domestic violence and substance abuse. Teachers can listen when children want to talk, be prepared to discuss personal issues, and provide resources and referrals for specialized counseling and direct services.

Housing referrals and placement are critical needs. The Benjamin Franklin Day Elementary School— "B.F. Day"—a public school in Seattle with a high percentage of homeless students and a specialized program to meet their needs, acts as a liaison between landlords and families to ensure that buildings in undesirable neighborhoods do not fall into disrepair, but remain occupied and maintained by families (Quint 1994).

Community and School Partnerships

Communities of learning must establish lines of communication between schools and community-based organizations. This common thread of communication and collaboration unites the efforts of model programs to make them successful. Yet this critical step in providing a safe haven for homeless children is the piece most often missing from many programs.

Although schools are legally responsible for making sure that homeless children receive the special educational attention they need, lack of understanding of the needs of homeless children among school administrators and staff has left the few existing programs woefully inadequate. On the other hand, the few shelters and community-based organizations offering children's education programs have difficulty in implementing educational curriculums. Even when children's education, adult education, and family support are well provided within one environment or the other, the lack of communication between schools and shelters impedes the education of homeless children. Schools often lose track of students

making frequent moves, and shelter programs fail to reach children who are *almost* homeless—who are being shuttled between the apartments of family and friends.

Both schools *and* shelters hold a treasury of institutional expertise and resources necessary to provide effective programs for homeless children. To make the best use of all these resources, schools must work with community-based organizations and shelters to develop their own communities of learning. Here are three important steps to follow:

1. Identify community resources and their locations.

2. Develop an information-sharing relationship between schools and these organizations. At a minimum, this relationship should facilitate the education of school administrators and staff about the presence and specific needs of homeless children.

3. Update administrators of both schools and shelters on progress and developments within their programs to ensure that the programs are complementary, not conflicting.

Even such basic communication can make a significant difference in the life of a homeless child. In South Bend, Indiana, children residing at the Center for the Homeless shelter would get on the school bus at the stop in front of the shelter to taunts and jeers by their nonhomeless classmates. Open lines of communication between the shelter and the school district made it possible to alter the route of the bus to make the shelter the first stop in the morning and last in the afternoon so that no students would be identified as "shelter kids."

From this information-sharing relationship, collaboration develops. The B.F. Day School developed a relationship with the Mercer Island United Methodist Church, which provided volunteers to assist in moving families into permanent housing and to collect and distribute household items. Volunteers also assisted parents with household maintenance, budgeting, and cooking. Then, other partnerships emerged. For example, a clinic sent a physician's assistant to the school

every Monday to examine children and provide immunizations and prescriptions (Quint 1994).

In other school/community collaborations, schools have provided services on site at shelters. The Alternative High Schools, a New York City public preparatory and vocational training program for teen parents and high school dropouts, agreed to establish a branch at the Prospect Family Inn so that homeless parents attend class among familiar faces, rather than traveling across town and getting involved in yet another bureaucracy (Nunez 1994).

The ultimate goal of this collaboration is seamless integration of children's education, adult education, and support services, making full use of school and shelter resources to establish effective communities of learning either in schools or in shelters. Thus homeless children already living in shelters can receive the educational assistance they need to avoid returning to the shelters as adults, and children on the verge of homelessness can be linked to the services their families need to keep from having to enter a shelter.

Perhaps the greatest example is set by the Homeless Children and Families Program in the Salem Keizer Public School system in Oregon. In addition to identifying homeless students and ensuring that these children have continuous access to schooling, the program has become involved in the activities of five local family shelters to engage the parents of homeless children in education and case management services. Program staff members serve as a bridge between the schools and shelters. They work with homeless children while they are in school and then go to local shelters to provide after-school and preschool enrichment programs for the children and case management, referrals, and life-skills classes for their parents.

An Opportunity for Action
The challenge that faces our schools is less a mandate to stretch under-

funded services still further and more an opportunity to fulfill their potential as the spine of society. Schools have the greatest ongoing contact with all members of the community—children, parents, aunts, uncles, grandparents, neighbors—and the ability to steer the direction of lives through supportive measures. By addressing children's needs through collaboration with local service providers, schools have the power to make a difference not only for homeless children in shelters but also for families on the verge of homelessness. Indeed, it is ironic that out of the problems of homeless children, solutions have developed that meet the needs of many children at risk of educational neglect.

Though the goal of communities of learning is to educate children, the process must first focus on educating the educators. Every school administrator and teacher must understand that childhood homelessness is not something that flares up only during periods of media attention. We must recognize that the boy or girl who acted up in math class may be missing far more than the principles of long division. Only then will all children—homeless and otherwise—receive both the educational and developmental support they need from schools.

> Schools must work with community-based organizations and shelters to develop their own communities of learning.

Individual schools can make a difference in their district, and individual teachers can make a difference in their schools. By learning about the needs of homeless children and accepting the opportunity to take responsibility for more than a child's grades, individual educators can begin the collaborative approaches needed to develop a community of learning.

References

Anderson, L.M., M.I. Janger, and K.L.M. Panton. (1995). *An Evaluation of State and Local Efforts to Serve the Educational Needs of Homeless Children and Youth.* Washington, D.C.: U.S. Department of Education, Office of the Undersecretary.

Bassuk, E.L, and L. Rubin. (1987). "Homeless Children: A Neglected Population." *American Journal of Orthopsychiatry* 57, 2: 279–286.

Education for Homeless Children and Youth Program. (1994). *Report to Congress: Fiscal Year 1994.* Washington, D.C.: U.S. Department of Education.

Molnar, J., W.R. Rath, T.P. Klein, C. Lowe, and A.H. Hartmann. (1991). *Ill Fares the Land: The Consequences of Homelessness and Chronic Poverty for Children and Families in New York City.* New York: Bank Street College of Education.

Nunez, R. (1994). *Hopes, Dreams and Promise: The Future of Homeless Children in America.* New York: Homes for the Homeless.

Nunez, R. (1996). *The New Poverty: Homeless Families in America.* New York: Insight Books/Plenum Publishing.

Pool, C.R., and M. Hawk. (April 1997). "Hope in Chicago." *Educational Leadership* 54, 7: 33–36.

Quint, S. (1994). *Schooling Homeless Children.* New York: Teachers College, Columbia University.

Rafferty, Y. (1991). *And Miles to Go . . . Barriers to Academic Achievement and Innovative Strategies for the Delivery of Educational Services to Homeless Children.* New York: Advocates for Children of New York.

Rafferty, Y. (Spring 1995). "The Legal Rights and Educational Problems of Homeless Children." *Perspectives: Journals of the Children's Institute of the Dyson College of Arts and Sciences* (Vol. 2). New York: Pace University.

Ralph da Costa Nunez is President and CEO of the Institute for Children and Poverty and a Professor at Columbia University's School of International and Public Affairs. **Kate Collignon** is Research and Training Associate with the Institute for Children and Poverty. Contact the authors at the Institute for Children and Poverty, 36 Cooper Square, 6th Floor, New York, NY 10003 (e-mail: hn4061@handsnet.org). World Wide Web: http://www.opendoor.com/hfh/

Fostering Intrinsic Motivation in Early Childhood Classrooms

Martha P. Carlton[1,3] and Adam Winsler[2]

Young children are born with an innate curiosity to learn about their world. This intrinsically instigated learning is often called mastery motivation. Patterns of motivation are established at an early age. The early childhood years are crucial for establishing robust intrinsic motivational orientations which will last a lifetime. By the time many children reach school, much of their motivation has been lost or replaced with extrinsically motivated learning strategies. Preschools and elementary schools have been criticized for contributing to such negative motivational patterns in children. This can be changed. Early child care situations and preschools can instead be instrumental in the strengthening of children's motivation. The goal of this paper is to show that through an understanding of the beginnings of motivation, we can begin to find ways to build strong motivational patterns in children that can carry on to later years of learning.

KEY WORDS: Motivation; classroom, preschool; infant.

INTRODUCTION

When a child is born, there is within that child an innate need to interact with the environment. These interactions lead to learning and the acquisition of knowledge. The motivation that drives this learning is based solely within the child and requires no outside rewards for its continuation. This motivation has been seen as humans' inherent intrinsic motivation to learn (Deci, 1975). As children reach school age, however, many do not seem to possess this interest in learning (Stipek, 1988). What happens to this motivation? What can we do to foster its development? By looking at the origins and development of intrinsic motivation, it is possible to identify some of the factors that can result in the strengthening or weakening of motivational patterns in young children. The purpose of this article is to explore the development differences in children from birth to 5 years with respect to motivation, and to provide several ideas, activities, and principles that early childhood educators can use to foster intrinsic motivation in all young children. Children's development will be divided into four age ranges: birth to 9 months, 9–24 months, 24–36

[1] College of Education, University of Alabama, Tuscaloosa, Alabama.
[2] Department of Psychology, George Mason University, Fairfax, Virginia.
[3] Correspondence should be directed to Martha Carlton, Educational Psychology, College of Education, University of Alabama, Box 870231, Tuscaloosa, Alabama 35487; email: mcarlton@bamaed.ua.edu.

From *Early Childhood Education Journal*, Vol. 25, No. 3, Spring 1998, pp. 159-166. © 1998 by Plenum Publishing Corporation. Reprinted by permission.

months, and 3–5 years. During each of these age ranges, specific activities will be discussed that can foster the development of intrinsic motivation in early childhood settings and at the close, a table will be given summarizing ten major motivational principles for early childhood professionals.

A DEFINITION OF MOTIVATION

Motivation can be defined as the process by which children's goal-directed activity is instigated and sustained (Pintrich & Schunk, 1996). Goal-directed behavior may be intrinsically motivated, extrinsically motivated, or motivated by a combination of the two. Intrinsic motivation refers to the desire to participate in an activity merely for the pleasure derived from that activity (Pintrich & Schunk, 1996). Conversely, an extrinsically motivated activity would be one that is engaged in for the sake of a desirable outcome, such as praise or reward. Intrinsic motivation is associated with greater learning and achievement in children (Gottfried, 1985; Pintrich & Schunk, 1996). This enhancement of learning occurs presumably because intrinsically motivated students are more involved in their learning, and they use strategies to promote deeper understanding and future application of that learning. Intrinsically motivated children experience more enjoyment from their learning, gain greater knowledge and insight, feel better about themselves, and are more likely to persist in goal-directed activities (Barrett & Morgan, 1995; Deci, Vallerand, Pelletier, & Ryan, 1991; Ford & Thompson, 1985; Harter, 1978; Pintrich & Schunk, 1996). If intrinsically motivated learning is better than extrinsically motivated learning, then it would appear to be to the benefit of all educators to understand the functioning and development of this type of motivation.

INTRINSIC MOTIVATION IN THE EARLY CHILDHOOD YEARS

Intrinsic motivation is made up of three basic psychological needs that are thought to be innate in human beings: the needs for competence, relatedness, and autonomy or self-determination (Deci et al., 1991). Competence is understanding how to achieve various outcomes and having the belief that you are capable of obtaining those outcomes. Relatedness involves the ability to develop se-cure and stable relationships with others in a social context. Autonomy is the self-regulating and self-initiating quality of one's own actions. The development of these three areas can be seen in the context of the young child.

The newborn is filled with the desire to respond to the many stimuli presented by her environment. As the child interacts with the environment, certain events occur. If the child can relate her action with the reaction of the environment, a sense of control over the environment is gained. This sense of control strengthens feelings of competence within the child and leads to further exploration and experimentation. With each successful interaction, the sense of competence grows (Ford & Thompson, 1985).

This growing sense of competence is closely linked with the child's attachment to significant caregivers. As children develop secure relationships with caregivers, they become freer to exhibit more exploration within the environment. They are also able to use the caregiver as a secure base for explorations as they attempt to master the environment (Ford & Thompson, 1985). The security of initial warm attachment relationships facilitates the ability to develop other meaningful relationships in later childhood. Feelings of relatedness to early childhood teachers motivate and free children to explore the learning environment (Ryan & Powelson, 1991).

As the child becomes older, autonomy becomes more important. Autonomy is the need to regulate one's own behavior and to govern the initiation and direction of one's actions (Ryan & Powelson, 1991). Children from homes where autonomy is supported tend to transfer their feelings of autonomy to school situations. Learning environments can also be seen as either autonomy-supportive or controlling. Autonomy denotes an inner sense that one's actions are coming from within one's self and that the individual has control of those actions. Controlling situations cause the individual to feel a lack of personal control over actions and little personal responsibility for those actions. Learning gained through autonomy-supportive events facilitates a feeling of self-determination and often results in greater understanding of the material being learned (Deci & Ryan, 1987).

As children become older, motivational patterns become differentiated by various subject and task areas. For example, each individual will have different motivational patterns for mathematics, reading, music, etc., depending on their history of experiences in those domains. All motivational levels do not have to be equal across demands for each individual (White, 1959). Infants and young children, conversely, are seen to have an undifferentiated need for competence; they have only a general need to master their environment. This is often referred to as "mastery motivation" (Barrett & Morgan, 1995). All mastery motivation is intrinsic in nature since children find the behavior rewarding in itself with no need for external rewards. Some aspects of mastery motivation include: (a) persistence at tasks that are somewhat difficult, (b) a preference for one's own control over environmental events (as opposed to passive observation), and (c) preference for some degree of challenge (Barrett & Morgan, 1995). All children start out with an optimal degree of motivation at birth, with the exception of some children whose special needs may compromise their motivation. The differences in older children's motivation is determined by what happens to them in their early years.

How does motivation manifest itself within the early childhood classroom? Here are two different children in the same preschool classroom. Sarah is 3 years old. She enjoys coming to school and is seldom ready to go home at the end of the day. She chooses activities that present a challenge to her and she persists until completing the activity to her own satisfaction. She decides what she would like to do during the day, and is pleased with her own abilities. Although she occasionally seeks the teacher's help with more difficult activities, she is content to work on her own, and she persists on activities for extended periods of time. Sally, on the other hand, needs constant help from the teacher. She seldom is able to select her own activity or plan what she would like to do during the day. When she does make a decision, she selects only those activities that are easy enough to complete rapidly, and demands the teacher's approval when she is finished. Sally quits an activity at the slightest obstacle, and rarely completes anything. One essential difference between these two children is their motivational orientation. While Sarah is very intrinsically motivated, Sally's activities are mostly extrinsically motivated.

As can be seen from this illustration, motivation is an important topic for early childhood educators. It determines a child's total functioning in learning environments. There is little published material dealing with these issues that caretakers can turn to for information. While much is known about different motivational patterns seen in children and their relation to academic performance and achievement in the later school years (Pintrich & Schunk, 1996), less information is available about the development of early motivation in the preschool years.

A DEVELOPMENTAL SEQUENCE FOR MOTIVATION

Infants (Birth to 9 Months)

Description of Infant Motivation. At birth, infants are capable of limited voluntary motor movements. They can turn their heads, kick their legs, and fling their arms about. They are also capable of controlling their sucking responses. From this state, infants rapidly gain control of more motor functions as muscle coordination develops. Within 9 months, the average infant has progressed from a state of random movements to a child who can crawl across the room and pull himself to a standing position, possibly even move a few steps. During these great changes, what can help maintain the child's motivation?

Research on Infant Motivation. Infants are predisposed to try to control their environments from birth. When infants can see the actual consequences of their actions, they are motivated to continue the actions. Young infants, of course, have a very limited behavioral repertoire for controlling their environment. Cries, vocalizations, facial expressions, and small limb actions are what most people can observe in the infant as attempts at control. Psychologists, however, in the laboratory have been able to capitalize on another important and natural infant behavior—sucking. By using pressure-sensitive pacifiers wired to computers which control the presentation of different stimuli, researchers have learned that infants within the first few weeks of life will control the rate of their sucking (i.e., increase or decrease sucking speed) in order to view or repeatedly view pleasant visual stimuli. That is, infants will systematically suck on the pacifier at the rate that presents desired (i.e., face-like) stimuli rather than the rate that presents either other, less attractive stimuli or no stimuli, and infants early on prefer to use the pacifier which controls the presentation of stimuli rather than one that does not (Rovee-Collier, 1987). Also, infants remember (in terms of repeating/increasing their sucking rates later) which stimuli were previously under their control and which stimuli were not (DeCasper & Carstens, 1981). Such research suggests that infants are much more sophisticated than had been previously thought and that infants' motivation and goals can be assessed if one carefully interprets infant behavior from the perspective of their own behavioral repertoire.

Slightly older infants begin to gain additional control over muscle movements and use more involved means to interact with their environment. Several studies have illustrated this point. Infants who are given a mobile that is activated by their own movements, become more active and escalate the frequency of their movements when viewing the mobile again later (Shields & Rovee-Collier, 1992). Continued exposure will also result in social reactions to the movements, such as smiling and cooing (Watson & Ramey, 1972). Children react similarly to a string tied around their wrists which activates pictures and pleasant music. If the pulled string no longer results in music and pleasant pictures, the child will become angry and unhappy (Lewis, Alessandri, & Sullivan, 1990). Although infant care centers are not likely to have computerized pacifiers which present stimuli, nor might they wish to attach strings between infants' arms and their mobiles, infant caregivers can learn to recognize infants' cues and attempts at mastering the environment and arrange the environment such that infants have multiple opportunities to do so.

Recommendations for Caregivers. Caregiver actions are also critical in the development of the infant's motivation. The beginnings of mastery feelings develop as a child sees that his actions upon the environment have an effect. If the child's actions are consistently responded to and reinforced by caregivers, the infant develops an expectancy that his/her actions have an effect on the environment (Lewis & Goldberg, 1969). By providing toys that would reinforce this feeling of environmental control (i.e., toys that actually manifest a change when manipulated), the caregiver can insure that the child will continue to experience feelings of control over the environment.

Both the inanimate environment (including the physical surroundings and the toys presented to the child) and the social environment (including the individuals that the child comes in contact with) function independently to foster mastery motivation within the child (Yarrow, Rubenstein, Pedersen, & Jankowski, 1972). Social stimulation extends the development of so-

cial responsiveness and language, and occurs when caregivers respond to the child's social actions. This might include responding to the child's verbalizations, playing peek-a-boo, or responding to smiles by smiling back. Social stimulation also leads to stronger attachment to caregivers and feelings of relatedness to others. Stimulation from the inanimate environment furthers exploratory behaviors. This can be facilitated by providing toys that are interesting and responsive to the child. The infant's orientation to both objects and people become part of a feedback system with the environment which influences the infant's functioning over a long time period. A wider variety of inanimate objects leads to a greater amount of exploratory behavior exhibited by the child. The responsiveness of both the social and the inanimate environments facilitates motivational and skill development (Yarrow *et al.*, 1972).

Specific activities that are appropriate for this age group and that would enhance exploratory behavior are: mobiles that are activated by the child's movements; brightly colored objects that can easily be grasped, and that make sounds when moved; objects with interesting taste, texture, and smell; small, soft dolls or animals with emphasis on the face, especially the eyes.

Infants/Toddlers (9–24 Months)

Description of Infant/Toddler Motivation. During the period from 9 to 24 months, infants continue to try to control events and are better able to decide what to do to accomplish particular ends (Barrett & Morgan, 1995). Success is still not based on externally imposed standards because caregivers tend to reward all attempts, but is based on the infant's ability to accomplish desired ends. Infants begin to evaluate themselves and are motivated to do things for themselves. (Barrett & Morgan, 1995)

Research on Infant/Toddler Motivation. Although most research has been done with mothers and their children, it is likely the same for all caregivers. It has been found that the mother's responsive behavior to the child is the most important factor of determining future competence across all types of exploratory behavior (Hendrickson & Hansen, 1977). Mothers who were responsive, but who did not instantly answer every request from the children were more likely to rear motivated and competent children. These children are able to independently explore with little mother–child interaction, knowing that mother is there when needed. This enhanced freedom of exploration leads to greater development of competence. On the other hand, infants whose mothers are constantly choosing and directing the child's activities tend to initiate fewer of their own explorations, resulting in infants who show less competence and mastery motivation. Mothers who interact less often but facilitate discovery and exploration in their infants when they do play with them, tend to have children who persist longer on difficult tasks (Jennings, Harmon, Morgan, Gaiter, & Yarrow, 1979).

There appears to be a negative relation between the level of a child's mastery with objects and the amount of parental interference in the child's interactions with those objects (Wachs, 1987). The more a parent interferes with the child's independent exploration of objects, the less the child will progress toward mastery of that object. It is the independent exploration that leads to mastery. Providing responsive toys in one setting also helps the child learn strategies to deal with new toys in other settings. The child has learned the necessary strategies to deal with responsive toys at home, and these strategies can be applied to unfamiliar situations away from home. If a child has not learned how to deal with these toys at home, he faces difficult circumstances when in an unfamiliar situation. He not only has to deal with the new situation, but also with new toys, which may cause unmanageable stress (Wachs, 1987).

Infants of mothers who support their child's autonomy by allowing them to freely explore the environment tend to exhibit more overall persistence plus more competence and positive affect at 20 months of age (Frodi, Bridges, & Grolnick, 1985). Maternal sensitivity, defined as effectively reading infant cues and being responsive to the child's communications, relates highly with persistence and competence. Finally, these authors found that mothers who control their children's behaviors through the use of supportive rather than punitive corrections tend to have children who score higher on ratings of persistence, competence, and positive affect.

Adult attention-focusing skills become an important factor in caregiver interactions with the older infants (Yarrow et al., 1984). Maternal stimulation teaches a child how to focus his or her own attention, enhancing the child's exploratory competence (Belsky, Goode, & Most, 1980). Infants who display the greatest amount of competence while exploring have mothers who frequently focus their attention on objects and events within the environment, in a responsive, respectful, and nonintrusive manner.

Recommendations for Caregivers. Caregivers can be effective in many ways when focusing the child's attention. The caregiver can arouse a child's interest when it is waning, redirect attention to a new area, or inhibit actions in an overstimulated child. While demonstrations can increase a child's interest in a particular toy, extended demonstrations can decrease that same interest. A single demonstration of a new object may be enough to interest the child, with the adult then allowing the child to explore on its own (Ruff & Rothbart, 1996). An important principle for adults to follow when trying to foster joint attentional states with infants while simultaneously trying to avoid being intrusive, is for adults to present various toys and stimuli but for them to follow the gazes, cues, and interests of the infant.

Language development is also influenced by joint attention with the caregiver. When the adult focuses verbally on an object that the child is interested in, the child can more easily establish the joint attentional focus with the adult. This facilitates greater opportunities for verbal development and other nonlinguistic scaffolding of the child's language development (Tomasello & Farrar, 1986).

A mother's emotional response to particular aspects of the environment can also have consequences for the child's responses in ambiguous situations (Gunnar & Stone, 1984). If mother is happy and positive, the infant is reassured and can respond positively to an uncertain situation. Infants look to adults for ways of reacting and positive caregiver responses can elicit the same responses in children.

Appropriate activities for children in this age range that would support autonomy and help focus attention are: play songs that are repetitive and simple enough for the child to repeat; flutter/action balls; bristle-type blocks; grasping toys that require complex manipulations (dials, switches, doors that open); push toys with sturdy handles for walking; puzzles with large knobbed pieces; round nesting materials.

Toddlers/Preschoolers 24–36 Months)

Description of Toddler/Preschooler Motivation. By the age of 24–36 months, children are developing an appreciation for standards, self-awareness, and self-evaluation. They are also developing the ability to execute a sequence of behavior to achieve a goal. By 3 years of age, children become interested in doing well rather than just accomplishing socially valued tasks (Barrett & Morgan, 1995).

Research on Toddler/Preschooler Motivation. Children in this age group are able to evaluate their own behavior and to respond appropriately to successes and failures. Children are able to sense which activities are harder for them, and experience greater pride when accomplishing these difficult tasks, with less shame when failing to accomplish them. When tasks are determined to be easy, shame is apparent if the task is failed, but only minimal pride is exhibited for successes (Lewis, Alessandri, & Sullivan, 1992).

Adult teaching styles remain of importance during the toddler years. Parents and teachers can help their children work through tasks by giving less support after success and more support after failures (Pratt, Kerig, Cowan, & Cowan, 1988). Successful parents respond to improvements of their children by systematically reducing their own involvement and allowing children to participate and accomplish as much of the task on their own as possible, using a strategy that is known as "scaffolding."

The basis of scaffolding is the establishment of a joint problem solving situation where two individuals interact while trying to reach a common goal. The adult is warm and responsive to the child's needs, but provides only enough support to keep the child engaged in the task and interacting. The adult carefully structures the task to maintain the child's interest by providing an obtainable challenge at all times. The amount of adult involvement lessens as the child gains competency in the task and is more able to function on his own. By allowing the child more freedom and by providing questions that allow the child to discover his own solutions to the problem, self-regulation skills, motivation, and learning are increased (Berk & Winsler, 1995).

Children early in the toddler years are becoming increasingly aware of the multistep nature of tasks (Barrett & Morgan, 1995). While simple cause-and-effect toys such as a pop-up toaster, were appropriate at earlier ages, more complex combination toys are now needed. A ring stacking toy that requires a sequence of actions for solution would be a more appropriate example for the toddler. Early in their second year, children become able to select appropriate tasks on their own due to a rapidly developing self-awareness (Busch-Rossnagel, Knauf-Jenson, & DesRosiers, 1995). Since the provision of appropriately challenging toys is positively related to persistence, the caregiver still has a very necessary role in selecting the range of activities that will be at the child's disposal and in providing the guidance and scaffolding necessary for children's effective learning of these more complex, sequential skills.

Recommendations for Caregivers. Appropriate activities for this age range that allow for self-evaluation, encourage multistep solutions, and provide situations for scaffolding would include: all sizes of balls to throw and catch; simple pop-up books; dress-me dolls; simple matching games; rhythm instruments to play with accompanying music; tunnels to crawl through; boards with magnetic shapes; 5–10 piece wooden puzzles; rocking horses; housecleaning sets; matching and sorting materials.

Preschoolers (3–5 Years)

Description of Preschooler Motivation. By three years of age, children are becoming more involved with the use of verbal problem solving skills, and the internalization of speech. Children are beginning to direct their own learning, with private speech, or children's self-talk, being a critical component in this development. Private speech begins as social conversation, but develops into a means of self-regulation of activity (Berk & Winsler, 1995). The child uses overt verbal communication to direct her own behavior in problem solving situations. When the young child is challenged by an activity, she will talk herself through the solution to the problem. Just as the adult scaffolded the child's behavior in joint problem solving situations earlier, the child can now scaffold her own behavior through the use of private speech (Winsler, Diaz, & Montero, in press). The child is now able to accept the role of self-regulator which was once fulfilled by the adults in his environment.

Research on Preschooler Motivation. When children have reached a level of self-regulation, they are able to feel that they have gained some level of control over their own environment which leads to feelings of self-competence. This ties back to two of the three innate needs that are required for the development of intrinsic motivation: competence and autonomy. The ability to be self-regulated is the basis for autonomy, while the establishment of that autonomy leads to feelings of competence, all of which lead to strengthened intrinsic motivation. Private speech is an indicator that the child is involved in motivated, engaged activity. Rather than urging children to work quietly, caregivers should encourage children to verbalize about their activities, carefully scaffolding their interactions to provide the child with the appropriate level of help (Berk & Winsler, 1995).

The appropriate use of rewards is also of extreme importance at this age. As caregivers of young children, our intuition may tell us that if we reward children for completing a task, we will strengthen their motivation for engaging in that task. This notion is linked to the idea that children are devoid of their own motivation and that it is the job of caregivers to motivate children from the outside. However, we now know from a large body of research that this is simply not true. Giving rewards to children for an activity that is already interesting to them actually reduces their motivation for the activity and makes them less likely to repeat the activity later (Cameron & Pierce, 1994). Lepper, Greene, and Nisbett (1973), for example, compared two groups of preschool children who initially liked to draw. One group was given rewards (an award) for drawing and another group did not receive rewards for drawing. The two groups were then measured as to how much time children voluntarily spent drawing a week or so later. Children who received the rewards spontaneously chose to draw significantly less often than those who were not rewarded for drawing earlier. The reason is that young children are filled with their own internal, intrinsic motivation for various activities. When children are rewarded for doing a task for which they were already intrinsically interested, they tend to reinterpret that the reason for doing the activity is to get rewards rather than to do the activity for fun. The child can become focused on the extrinsic reward and lose sight of the intrinsic nature of learning. Another problem is that children often feel like they are under external rather than internal control when they receive excessive rewards, praise, and punishments. What results is that children are less likely in the future to want to repeat the task simply for fun (Lepper, 1983).

When rewards are used, they should be infrequent and given only as feedback that focuses on the effort of the child rather than the quality of the final accomplishment (Ames, 1992). By focusing on the accomplishment, rewards can lead to feelings of inadequacy and

focus the child on his work in relation to others rather than on his own abilities and efforts (Solomon, 1996). Praise of the child's effort, on the other hand, will help instill feelings of self-worth that strengthen motivation (Deci et al., 1991).

Recommendations for Caregivers. The role of the teacher is significant at this age level. The teacher provides the framework of goals and multiple activities for obtaining those goals. If the goals are appropriate for the children and the activities are well organized, then the teacher should be able to step back and allow the children to pursue their own learning with guidance from the teacher as needed. However, it is important that early childhood teachers not conclude from the above that the role of the teacher is to stand back and not intervene or get involved with the children's activities. Teachers need to provide structure and assistance, without completely controlling every learning activity. Neither extreme of the totally teacher-directed or the completely child-centered classroom seen in many early childhood programs is optimal for promoting motivation and self-regulation (Berk & Winsler, 1995). Rather, preschool programs which fall in the middle of the continuum, in which children are given independence within intermediate amounts of structure and adults sensitively direct children's activities, are perhaps the best models for developing children's intrinsic motivation and competence (Berk & Winsler, 1995). Children's persistence, motivation, and participation in learning-directed activities is greatest during early childhood curricular activities which are pursued in a semistructured environment (Winsler & Diaz, 1995).

When applied to older children who are moving on to preschool classes and pre-kindergarten situations, the same suggestions for activities should apply. Children need structure that allows for free exploration. They should be challenged and allowed to set their own goals and to evaluate their own successes. Setting the environment up for this type of learning is of utmost importance. Activities need to be carefully selected to provide the correct amount of challenge and to engage curiosity. Guidance and scaffolding techniques properly utilized will help children develop to their highest potential.

Appropriate activities for this age range which will provide the atmosphere for learning may include: large and small trucks, cars, animals of all types; simple machines; measuring materials; beginning computer software; props for dress-up and pretend play; more complex puzzles including jigsaw as well as fit-in pieces; realistic ride-on toys; puppets and elaborate puppet theater; mosaic blocks; climbing structures; picture bingo, and matching games.

SUMMARY

From birth, children are instilled with an innate desire to learn about their world. What happens during the early years may determine the strength and type of motivation the child will have in later years. Caregivers play an extremely important role in the motivational life of the developing child. Table 1 provides a summary of what we feel are the ten most important principles for fostering intrinsic motivational patterns in early childhood classrooms. If the caregiver can remain flexible and respond to the changing needs of the child, then mastery motivation can be enhanced throughout the child's early development. Scaffolding techniques can be employed to further enhance the development of motivation, self-regulation, and learning skills. The careful and selective use of appropriate rewards focusing on the process of learning rather than the product will also enhance motivational skills. Allowing children to develop to their fullest potential can help them maintain their motivation and excitement in learning throughout the school years.

REFERENCES

Ames, C. (1992). Classrooms: Goals, structures, and student motivation. *Journal of Educational Psychology, 84*, 261–271.

Barrett, K. C., & Morgan, G. A. (1995). Continuities and discontinuities in mastery motivation during infancy and toddlerhood. A conceptualization and review. In R. H. MacTurk & G. A. Morgan (Eds.) *Mastery moti-*

Table 1. Ten Key Principles For Strengthening Children's Intrinsic Motivation in Early Childhood Classrooms

1. *Provide a Responsive Environment.* Present toys and activities that allow the child to actually see the effect that s/he has on the environment.

2. *Give Consistent and Responsive Caregiving.* Respond to the child in consistent ways. This allows the child to develop a sense of expectancy for reactions to his/her behavior. Responding to the child's cries and vocalizations builds the child's sense of agency in the world.

3. *Support Children's Autonomy.* Allow for children's free exploration and choice within the parameters you have set up in your classroom.

4. *Establish Close Relationships.* Young children are more comfortable exploring and challenging themselves when they are in the presence of caregivers with whom they have close, warm, and caring relationships.

5. *Establish Joint Attention.* Provide many opportunities for joint attention and joint collaboration with children on specific objects and/or tasks and talk about the object/task. Such episodes increase feelings of relatedness and agency and advance language, a tool children will use later to regulate their own motivation.

6. *Provide a Good Motivational Role Model.* By showing confidence in your abilities as a teacher, keeping a positive emotional tone and attitude, modeling persistence and a preference for challenge, and showing enthusiasm in learning for learning's sake, early childhood professionals can maximize the chances that young children will exhibit these same motivational qualities.

7. *Provide Challenge.* Children's self-efficacy is increased as they succeed at more and more challenging tasks. Provide developmentally-appropriate, yet challenging, activities for the children and gradually increase the difficulty level as children become more competent.

8. *Scaffold Children's Problem Solving.* In order to insure that children remain engaged in goal-directed pursuits and succeed on challenging tasks, teacher guidance may be needed in the form of sensitive scaffolding. Scaffolding refers to an adult–child interaction style during joint collaboration in which the adult carefully and dynamically modifies task difficulty and adult verbal assistance (i.e., asking leading questions) to allow the child to become increasingly more responsible for completing the task on his or her own.

9. *Foster Self-Evaluation.* Give children opportunities to evaluate their own activities and performances. Explicit questions to children may be needed to get the children to do this (i.e., "How do you feel about your (product)?" "Are you happy with that or do you want to do more?"), or to get the children to realize that they are already self-evaluating (i.e., "I like the way you looked at your (product), decided it wasn't the way you wanted it, and changed it.")

10. *Use Rewards Sparingly and Cautiously.* External rewards can reduce children's intrinsic motivation. Rewards should be used sparingly in the classroom. When rewards are used, they should emphasize the child's effort, persistence, and process, rather than performance, and they should be given in an informational, rather than controlling, manner.

vation: Origins, conceptualizations and applications (pp. 57–94). Norwood, NJ: Ablex.

Belsky, J., Goode, M. K., & Most, R. K. (1980). Material stimulation and infant exploratory competence: Cross-sectional, correlational, and experimental analysis. *Child Development, 51*, 1163–1178.

Berk, L. E., & Winsler, A. (1995). *Scaffolding children's learning: Vygotsky and early childhood education.* Washington, DC: National Association for the Education of Young Children.

Busch-Rossnagel, N. A., Knauf-Jensen, D. E., & Des-Rosiers, F. S. (1995). Mothers and others: The role of the socializing environment in the development of mastery motivation. In R. H. MacTurk & G. A. Morgan (Eds.), *Mastery motivation: Origins, conceptualizations and applications* (pp. 117–145), Norwood, NJ: Ablex.

Cameron, J., & Pierce, W. D. (1994). Reinforcement, reward, and intrinsic motivation: A meta-analysis. *Review of Educational Research, 39*, 363–423.

DeCasper, A. J., & Carstens, A. A. (1981). Contingencies of stimulation: Effects on learning and emotion in neonates. *Infant Behavior and Development, 4*, 19–35.

Deci, E. L. (1975). *Intrinsic motivation.* New York: Plenum Press.

Deci, E. L., & Ryan, R. M. (1987). The support of autonomy and the control of behavior. *Journal of Personality and Social Psychology, 53*, 1024–1037.

Deci, E. L., Vallerand, R. J., Pelletier, L. G., & Ryan, R. M. (1991). Motivation and education: The self-determination perspective. *Educational Psychologist, 26*, 325–346.

Ford, M. E., & Thompson, R. A. (1985). Perceptions of personal agency and infant attachment: Toward a life-span perspective on competence development. *International Journal of Behavioral Development, 8*, 377–406.

Frodi, A., Bridges, L., & Grolnick, W. (1985). Correlates of mastery-related behavior: A short-term longitudinal study of infants in their second year. *Child Development, 56*, 1291–1298.

Gottfried, A. E. (1985). Academic intrinsic motivation in elementary and junior high school students. *Journal of Educational Psychology, 77*, 631–645.

Gunnar, M. R., & Stone, C. (1984). The effects of positive maternal affect on infant responses to pleasant, ambiguous, and fear-provoking toys. *Child Development, 55*, 1231–1236.

Harter, S. (1978). Effectance motivation reconsidered: Toward a developmental model. *Human Development, 21*, 34–64.

Hendrickson, N. J., & Hansen, S. L. (1977). Toddlers: Competence and behavior patterns. *Child Study Journal, 7*, 79–97.

Jennings, K. D., Harmon, R. J., Morgan, G. A., Gaiter, J. L., & Yarrow, L. J. (1979). Exploratory play as an index of mastery motivation: Relationships to persistence, cognitive functioning, and environmental measures. *Developmental Psychology, 15*, 386–394.

Lepper, M. R. (1983). Extrinsic reward and intrinsic motivation: Implications for the classroom. In J. M. Levine & M. C. Wang (Eds.) *Teacher and student perceptions: Implications for learning* (pp. 281–317). Hillsdale, NJ: Erlbaum.

Lepper, M. R., Greene, D., & Nisbett, R. E. (1973). Undermining children's intrinsic interest with extrinsic rewards: A test of the overjustification hypothesis. *Journal of Personality and Social Psychology, 28*, 129–137.

Lewis, M., Alessandri, S. M., & Sullivan, M. W. (1990). Violation of expectancy, loss of control, and anger expressions in young infants. *Developmental Psychology, 26*, 745–751.

Lewis, M., Alesssandri, S. M., & Sullivan, M. W. (1992). Differences in shame and pride as a function of children's gender and task difficulty. *Child Development, 63*, 630–638.

Lewis, M., & Goldberg, S. (1969). Perceptual-cognitive development in infancy: A generalized expectancy model as a function of the mother-infant interaction. *Merrill-Palmer Quarterly, 15*, 81–100.

Pintrich, P. R., & Schunk, D. H., (1996). *Motivation in education: Theory, research, and applications.* Englewood Cliffs, New Jersey: Prentice-Hall.

Pratt, M. W., Kerig, P., Cowan, P. A., & Cowan, C. P. (1988). Mothers and fathers teaching 3-year-olds: Authoritative parenting and adult scaffolding of young children's learning. *Developmental Psychology, 24*, 832–839.

Rovee-Collier, C. K. (1987). Learning and memory. In J. D. Osofsky (Ed.), *Handbook of infant development* (2nd ed., pp. 98–148). New York: Wiley.

Ruff, H. A., & Rothbart, M. K. (1996). *Attention in early development: Themes and variations.* New York: Oxford University Press.

Ryan, R. M., & Powelson, C. L. (1991). Autonomy and relatedness as fundamental to motivation and education. *Journal of Experimental Education, 60*, 49–66.

Shields, P. J., & Rovee-Collier, C. K. (1992). Long-term memory for context-specific category information at six months. *Child Development, 63*, 245–259.

Solomon, M. A. (1996). Impact of motivational climate on students' behaviors and perceptions in a physical education setting. *Journal of Educational Psychology, 88*, 731–738.

Stipek, D. J. (1988). *Motivation to learn: From theory to practice.* Englewood Cliffs, New Jersey: Prentice-Hall.

Tomasello, M., & Farrar, M. J. (1986). Joint attention and early language. *Child Development, 57*, 1454–1463.

Wachs, T. D. (1987). Specificity of environmental action as manifest in environmental correlates of infants' mastery motivation. *Development Psychology, 23*, 782–790.

Watson, J. S., & Ramey, C. T. (1972). Reactions to response-contingent stimulation in early infancy. *Merrill-Palmer Quarterly, 18*, 219–227.

White, R. W. (1959). Motivation reconsidered: The concept of competence. *Psychological Review, 66*, 297–333.

Winsler, A., & Diaz, R. M. (1995). Private speech in the classroom: The effects of activity type, presence of others, classroom context, and mixed-age grouping. *International Journal of Behavioral Development, 18*, 463–487.

Winsler, A., Diaz, R. M., & Montero, I. (in press). The role of private speech in the transition from collaboration to independent task performance in young children. *Early Childhood Research Quarterly.*

Yarrow, L. J., MacTurk, R. H., Vietze, P. M., McCarthy, M. E., Klein, R. P., & McQuiston, S. (1984). Developmental course of parental stimulation and its relationship to mastery motivation during infancy. *Developmental Psychology, 20*, 492–503.

Yarrow, L. J., Rubenstein, J. L., Pedersen, F. A., & Jankowski, J. J. (1972). Dimensions of early stimulation and their differential effects on infant behavior. *Merrill-Palmer Quarterly, 18*, 205–218.

Unit Selections

26. **Why Curriculum Matters in Early Childhood Education,** Lawrence J. Schweinhart and David P. Weikart
27. **Fostering Creativity in the Early Childhood Classroom,** Mary K. Smith
28. **Challenging Movement Experiences for Young Children,** Stephen W. Sanders and Bill Yongue
29. **Learning to Read and Write: Developmentally Appropriate Practices for Young Children,** *The Reading Teacher*
30. **NAEYC Position Statement: Responding to Linguistic and Cultural Diversity—Recommendations for Effective Early Childhood Education,** *Young Children*
31. **Beginning to Implement the Reggio Philosophy,** Lynn Staley
32. **Supporting Math Thinking,** Alice P. Wakefield
33. **Documenting Children's Learning,** Judy Harris Helm, Sallee Beneke, and Kathy Steinheimer

Key Points to Consider

❖ What type of curriculum model provides for optimal learning for preschoolers? What role do the diverse lifestyles of the children in a classroom play in the development of the curriculum?

❖ What are some appropriate movement experiences all preschool children should have?

❖ Indicate literacy experiences that should be a part of early childhood classrooms. How can the teacher provide for these types of early literacy experiences to develop and flourish?

❖ How can active thinking play a key role in mathematics?

❖ What are the benefits of designing curriculum based on the interests of the children?

 **Links**   **www.dushkin.com/online/**

22. **California Reading Initiative**
    http://www.sdcoe.k12.ca.us/score/promising/prreading/prreadin.html
23. **Education Week on the Web**
    http://www.edweek.org
24. **Kathy Schrock's Guide for Educators**
    http://www.discoveryschool.com/schrockguide/
25. **Phi Delta Kappa**
    http://www.pdkintl.org
26. **Reggio Emilia**
    http://ericps.ed.uiuc.edu/eece/reggio.html
27. **Teachers Helping Teachers**
    http://www.pacificnet.net/~mandel/
28. **Verio Pittsburgh**
    http://pittsburgh.verio.net

These sites are annotated on pages 4 and 5.

We begin this unit with an article that sheds light on the ongoing debate about early childhood curriculum. Larry Schweinhart and David Weikart have conducted a major portion of the research that exists on the benefits of early childhood education. They now provide information on curriculum and the role of the teacher in early childhood settings. With many still teaching in a teacher-directed format we now have clear evidence of the importance of children participating in child-initiated, active, hands-on learning experiences. Just as we now know not to put butter on a burn because medical research has proved that to be harmful, we must use educational research to change those ingrained educational practices that do not provide for optimal learning.

Education will be very different as we move into the twenty-first century. The amount of information children are required to learn has increased over the past generation, and more is available every day. Children cannot possibly be responsible for knowing all this new information, but they will be required to know how information can be accessed. Where would be the best place to look? What Web site should they check? What information have they gathered, and what conclusions can they draw? These are the types of questions our young children will be asked in the not-too-distant future.

At the end of a busy day, most teachers would relish the thought of walking into a restaurant where they would not have to make any choices about what to eat or to do any of the shopping and cooking. All the food would be prepared by others and set before the hungry teachers to consume. Sounds wonderful! Maybe for two or even three nights the idea would be appealing, but come the fourth night, some teachers really would not like what was being served, or would cook it differently. In this restaurant, there are no opportunities for customer suggestions.

Does this sound like some classrooms? The adults choose the topic of study and spend weeks preparing the materials and activities. The teachers then lay everything out in front of the children and wait for them to eagerly lap up the information and activities prepared by the teacher. Unfortunately, this is how many classrooms operate.

Teachers in these classrooms do all the work, with no input from the children, their families, or their environment. Topics of study are often decided months in advance. A strict schedule is adhered to so that all the teacher-chosen topics can be covered in a particular time frame. Each year, themes are covered at the same time, and little, if any, deviation from the master calendar occurs. Unknowingly, teachers are making more work for themselves by ignoring the ideas and expertise that children and their families could contribute. The skills children acquire, such as investigating, predicting, and hypothesizing, can be more useful in future learning than knowing specific facts about a particular topic. Every teacher cannot teach the same information about every possible topic of study. What every

teacher can do, however, is to ensure that all children have equal opportunities to develop the learning skills they will need as they move through their formal education and into their chosen professions. It is not important if a particular preschool teacher does an in-depth investigation of boats and her friend who teaches in another part of the country does not. What is important is that the children in both classrooms have opportunities to develop and use skills, such as exploring, expression, and investigating, that extend their learning. Nor should any child be denied the opportunity to investigate, solve problems, and come to conclusions. These are the skills they will need in the future, more so than specific information on boats or any other topic of study. In "Beginning to Implement the Reggio Philosophy" Lynn Staley provides a glimpse of how staff in one early childhood program moved to a child-centered project approach to learning.

Why do the quality learning experiences so readily available in early childhood programs have to end as children get older? A fourth grader remarked one day, "My brain works better when my hands are working too." The saying "Hands On = Minds On" is so true.

After extensive reviews and input by professionals in both the fields of early childhood education and reading, a joint position statement was released in 1998 by the International Reading Association (IRA) and the National Association for the Education of Young Children (NAEYC). This statement provides clear and direct strategies for educators, as well as answers to key questions raised by both parents and teachers. The reader is encouraged to review carefully the continuum of children's development in early reading and writing contained in the article. This information could be posted for parents or used in determining which material to collect for portfolios.

Articles addressing creativity and motor development are also included in this unit. Many educators focus attention mainly on cognitive development and often have little time for opportunities for creative exploration or for teaching motor skills. Teaching correct motor skills requires more than allowing the children time to run around outside or in the gym, just as learning to read requires more than offering a room full of books.

Documenting children's learning has emerged as a key responsibility for teachers. Teachers who collect, analyze, make appropriate comments, and display the work of the children are adding greatly to their overall program quality. Parents, administrators, children, and community members all benefit from having opportunities to view evidence of the learning that has taken place.

A truly child-centered curriculum in a developmentally appropriate program is constantly changing, just like the children who attend that program. It is the job of the teachers and caregivers to keep pace with the children's needs and interests as they grow and learn.

Why Curriculum Matters in Early Childhood Education

A long-running study of the effects of preschool programs for children in poverty shows the benefits of a child-initiated, teacher-facilitated curriculum.

Lawrence J. Schweinhart
and David P. Weikart

A widespread consensus has developed in favor of public support for preschool programs for young children living in poverty. Head Start and state prekindergarten programs today serve about two-thirds of U.S. 4-year-olds living in poverty. Federal Head Start spending has tripled in the past decade, and nearly two-thirds of the states provide similar programs for 4-year-olds (see box, "Children in Poverty").

Influential groups of citizens, such as the Committee for Economic Development, have lent their political clout to this development—partly because of the findings of the High/Scope Perry Preschool Study that a high-quality preschool program cuts participants' lifetime arrest rate in half, significantly improves their educational and subsequent economic success, and provides taxpayers a return equal to 716 percent of their original investment in the program, a return that outperformed the U.S. stock market during the same period of time (Schweinhart et al. 1993; Barnett 1996).

We have less consensus on the goals of preschool programs. The National Association for the Education of Young Children (Bredekamp and Copple 1997) strongly favors *developmentally appropriate practice,* but this position has found detractors. Academic critics, such as Mallory and New (1994), argue that developmentally appropriate practice is socially constructed, context-bound, and insensitive to cultural and individual differences in development. Conservative critics, such as Hirsch (1997), see it as progressive ideology without adequate research support.

Should early childhood curriculum be adult-directed or child-initiated? Or should there be a balance of these two approaches? Is there a well-defined, research-proven model we can follow? The High/Scope Preschool Curriculum Comparison Study (the study that followed the

Because all three groups had biweekly home visits, home visits alone cannot explain the differences that were found.

High/Scope Perry Preschool Study), which was begun in 1969 and now includes data through age 23, sheds new light on these questions (Schweinhart and Weikart 1997 a and b).

This study assesses which of three theoretically distinct preschool curriculum models works best. The study has followed the lives of 68 young people born in poverty who were randomly assigned at ages 3 and 4 to one of three groups, each experiencing a different curriculum model.

Three Curriculum Models

The Curriculum Comparison Study included the following curriculum models:

• *Direct Instruction* was a scripted approach in which the teacher presented activities and the children responded to them. Classroom activities were sequences of academic lessons, emphasizing positive reinforcements of correct responses. Teachers clearly defined academic goals in reading, arithmetic, and language. The psychological tradition was behaviorist (Bereiter and Engelmann 1966).

• *The High/Scope Curriculum* was an open-framework approach in which teacher and child planned and initiated activities and worked together. Classroom activities were partly the result of the *plan-do-review* sequence, planned by the children themselves and supported by the teachers. These activities reflected experiences intended to promote intellectual, social, and physical development. The psychological tradition was constructivist and cognitive-developmental (Hohmann and Weikart 1995).

• *The traditional Nursery School* was a child-centered approach in which children initiated activities and the teachers responded to them. The teachers created classroom themes from everyday events and encouraged children to actively engage in free play. The goal was to create an environment in which children could develop naturally, and the psychological tradition was psychoanalytic (Sears and Dowley 1963).

Children in Poverty

Here are resources on the number of preschool children in poverty and the programs that serve them:

• The number of Head Start 4-year-olds living in poverty (http://www.acf.dhhs.gov/programs/hsb/statfact.htm).

• The number of children served by state prekindergarten programs (Adams and Sandfort 1994).

• The number of 4-year-olds living in poverty (one-sixth of the number of children under 6 living in poverty) (http://www.census.gov/hhes/poverty/poverty96/pv96est1.html).

Program staff implemented the curriculum models independently and to high standards, in two-and-a-half-hour classes five days a week and home visits every two weeks. Because all three groups had biweekly home visits, these visits alone cannot explain the differences that were found, although they may have intensified the curriculum models' effects. All other

aspects of the program were virtually identical. So, having taken into account slight differences in the groups' gender makeup, we are confident that outcome differences represent the effects of the three curriculum models.

Advantages at Age 23

Based on reports by the young people, either the High/Scope group or the Nursery School group had a total of 10 significant advantages over the Direct Instruction group, but the Direct Instruction group had no significant advantages over these groups. The High/Scope and Nursery School groups did not differ significantly from one another on any outcome variable.

By age 23, the High/Scope and Nursery School groups had two significant advantages over the Direct Instruction group:

• *Only 6 percent of either the High/Scope or the Nursery School group needed treatment for emotional impairment or disturbance during their schooling, as compared to 47 percent of the Direct Instruction group.* Because 47 percent is well above the typical rate for this population (17 percent of the comparable no-program group in the High/Scope Perry Preschool Study required such treatment), the Direct Instruction program experience appears to have left some of its participants with serious negative emotional residue.

• *Forty-three percent of the High/Scope group and 44 percent of the Nursery School group at some time up to age 23 engaged in volunteer work, as compared to 11 percent of the Direct Instruction group.* The programs that encouraged children to initiate their own activities had more

Child-initiated learning acitivities help children develop social responsibility and interpersonal skills.

graduates engaging in volunteer work in the community as young adults, suggesting greater awareness of the needs of others and their responsibility to take action to help.

The High/Scope group had six additional significant advantages over the Direct Instruction group:

• *Only 10 percent of the High/Scope group had ever been arrested for a felony, as compared to 39 percent of the Direct Instruction group.* Given the intractability of crime, this fourfold reduction in felony arrests is of great importance. It parallels the finding of the High/Scope Perry Preschool Study through age 27 that only 7 percent of the program group (which used child-initiated activities) but 35 percent of the no-program group had been arrested five or more times (Schweinhart et al. 1993). These data indicate the clearly different levels of personal and social responsibility that the High/Scope and Direct Instruction groups developed.

• *None of the High/Scope group had ever been arrested for a property crime, as compared to 38 percent of the Direct Instruction group.* Property crime may be distinguished from violent and drug-related crimes by its emphasis on assaulting authority. The High/Scope model places authority (teachers) in the role of resource and support. Direct Instruction gives teachers power and control and requires children to submit. As young adults, more of the former Direct Instruction preschoolers strike out at authority.

• *Twenty-three percent of the High/Scope group reported at age 15 that they had engaged in 10 or more acts of misconduct, as compared to 56 percent of the Direct Instruction group.* Although this finding did not

reappear in self-reports at age 23, it presaged the age-23 arrest findings.

• *Thirty-six percent of the High/Scope group said that various kinds of people gave them a hard time, as compared to 69 percent of the Direct Instruction group.* Apparently, the High/Scope group more willingly accepted responsibility for their own actions than did the Direct Instruction group and had developed ways to relate positively to authorities and others, rather than to blame or attack them for their actions.

• *Thirty-one percent of the High/Scope group had married and were living with their spouses, as compared to none of the Direct Instruction group.* Marriage may be seen as a step that takes personal responsibility and a willingness to adapt to others.

• *Seventy percent of the High/Scope group planned to graduate from college, as compared to 36 percent of the Direct Instruction group.* While no differences were found in actual high school graduation rates or in the highest year of schooling, such planning by the High/Scope group reflects greater optimism, self-confidence, and aspirations for the future.

The Nursery School group had two additional significant advantages over the Direct Instruction group, both of which resemble the felony arrest difference between the High/Scope group and the Direct Instruction group.

• *Only 9 percent of the Nursery School group had been arrested for a felony at ages 22–23, as compared to 34 percent of the Direct Instruction group.*

• *None of the Nursery School group had ever been suspended from work, as compared to 27 percent of the Direct Instruction group.*

Goals of Early Childhood Education

This study through age 23 found that young people born in poverty experienced fewer emotional problems and felony arrests if they had attended a preschool program based on child-initiated learning activities focused broadly on children's development, rather than scripted direct instruction focused specifically on academics.

These findings suggest that the goals of early childhood education should not be limited to academic preparation for school, but should also include helping children learn to make decisions, solve problems, and get along with others. Scripted teacher-directed instruction, touted by some as the surest path to school readiness, may purchase a temporary improvement in academic performance at the cost of a missed opportunity for long-term improvement in personal and social behavior. On the other hand, child-initiated learning activities seem to help children develop their social responsibility and interpersonal skills so that they become more personally and socially competent, fewer of them need treatment for emotional impairment or disturbance. Fewer are arrested for felonies as young adults.

Although the High/Scope and Nursery School groups did not differ significantly on any outcome variable at age 23, the High/Scope curriculum model is easier to replicate than the Nursery School approach because of High/Scope's extensive documentation, training program, and assessment system. Well-documented, research-proven curriculum models based on child-initiated learning appear to have the best potential for supporting successful child development.

References

Adams, G., and J. Sandfort. (1994). *First Steps, Promising Futures: State Prekindergarten Initiatives in the Early 1990s.* Washington, D.C.: Children's Defense Fund.

Barnett, W.S. (1996). *Lives in the Balance: Age 27 Benefit-Cost Analysis of the High/Scope Perry Preschool Program* (Monographs of the High/Scope Educational Research Foundation, 11). Ypsilanti, Mich.: High/Scope Press.

Bereiter, C., and S. Engelmann. (1966). *Teaching the Disadvantaged Child in the Preschool.* Englewood Cliffs, N.J.: Prentice-Hall.

Bredekamp, S., and C. Copple, eds. (1997). *Developmentally Appropriate Practice in Early Childhood Programs,* rev. ed. Washington, D.C.: National Association for the Education of Young Children.

Hirsch, E.D. (June 18, 1997). "On Faddism, Guruism and Junk Research." *Los Angeles Times.* (Available online for $1.50; use search terms E.D. Hirsch and 1997 at http://www.latimes.com/home/archives).

Hohmann, M., and D.P. Weikart. (1995). *Educating Young Children: Active Learning Practices for Preschool and Child Care Programs.* Ypsilanti, Mich.: High/Scope Press.

Mallory, B.L, and R.S. New. (1994). *Diversity and Developmentally Appropriate Practices: Challenges for Early Childhood Education.* New York: Teachers College Press.

Schweinhart, L.J., H.V. Barnes, and D.P. Weikart. (1993). *Significant Benefits: The High/Scope Perry Preschool Study Through Age 27* (Monographs of the High/Scope Educational Research Foundation, 10). Ypsilanti, Mich.: High/Scope Press.

Schweinhart, L.J., and D.P. Weikart. (1997a). "The High/Scope Preschool Curriculum Comparison Study Through Age 23." *Early Childhood Research Quarterly* 12: 117–143.

Schweinhart, L.J., and D.P. Weikart. (1997b). *Lasting Differences: The High/Scope Preschool Curriculum Comparison Study Through Age 23.* (Monographs of the High/Scope Educational Research Foundation, 12). Ypsilanti, Mich.: High/Scope Press.

Sears, P.S., and E.M. Dowley. (1963). "Research on Teaching in the Nursery School." In *Handbook of Research on Teaching,* edited by N. L. Gage. Chicago: Rand McNally.

Lawrence J. Schweinhart is Research Division Chair and **David P. Weikart** is President of High/Scope Educational Research Foundation, 600 North River St., Ypsilanti, MI 48198-2898 (e-mail: LarryS@highscope.org).

Fostering Creativity in the Early Childhood Classroom

Mary K. Smith, Ed.D.[1,2]

Most early childhood teachers would tell you that creativity is important; and that creativity should be considered an integral part of every early childhood classroom. Yet, too often, it is slighted in some areas or limited to being a part of art education. How can creativity can be nurtured and developed in all cognitive and social aspects of an early childhood classroom? The key to this fostering of creativity is for each teacher to examine his or her own filters that can help to. foster, or hinder, as the case may be, creativity in that classroom setting. By examining adult attitudes, classroom atmosphere, and children's activities and materials, and adjusting where necessary, to incorporate certain positive elements for creativity, early childhood educators are more likely to establish a trusting, flexible, and safe environment that allows and stimulates the creative process in an atmosphere of respect.

KEY WORDS: creativity; child autonomy; teacher attitudes; resourcefulness; classroom climate.

INTRODUCTION

Scott and Andy were playing in the housekeeping area. Suddenly Andy threw the fake fur piece on the floor and told Scott that there was a skunk and they should get out. The two boys proceeded to evacuate the area while pretending to call the fire department to come and help them. The teacher was working with another child close to this scene. She told the children that they had probably better move due to the skunk. More children got involved in the adventure. The original boys asked the teacher if the fire department was the right place to call. The teacher replied that she had never encountered the situation before, but if the fire department didn't respond, they might want to try the Humane Society.

This story is an entertaining example of the value of play in the early childhood classroom. But it is more than that. The story is also an example of children being creative; and it is an example of children being encouraged to be creative. Why is this important?

Most early childhood teachers realize the importance of educating the whole child. These teachers are supported by the developmental guidelines published by the National Association for the Education of Young Children. These guidelines state that a curriculum of exploration and integration addresses the physical, emotional, social, and cognitive aspects of a child's education (Bredekamp, 1987; Haiman, 1991). Yet, the whole child in that early childhood classroom can never really be served unless the issue of developing creativity is also considered. Without considering creativity, a unique part of the individuality of each child is slighted. Thus, a key question for early childhood teachers to ask is "What is creativity for young children, and how can teachers in early childhood classrooms foster it?"

[1]Teacher, Westgate Elementary, Westside Community Schools, Omaha, Nebraska, and Doctoral Student, Department of Educational Administration, University of Nebraska at Lincoln, Lincoln, Nebraska.

[2]Correspondence should be directed to Dr. Mary K. Smith, Westgate Elementary, 7802 Hascall, Omaha, Nebraska 68124.

From *Early Childhood Education Journal*, Vol. 24, No. 2, Winter 1996, pp. 77-82. © 1996 by Human Sciences Press, Inc. Reprinted by permission.

8-02-1980

Fig. 1. The painter.

Creativity is the process of being original, spontaneous, and/or unique. The child, using previous knowledge, sees or acts upon selected appropriate new relationships (Edwards & Nabors, 1993; Meador, 1993; Isenberg & Jalongo, 1993; Whitson, 1994). The child uses all information available to arrive at this new way of thinking or acting. In fact, the child's awareness is heightened in general (Fowler, 1990). To illustrate, the child who turns the fur piece in the housekeeping area into a skunk and evacuates everyone is being creative. He has taken his knowledge of skunks and extended that to the new setting of school where skunks would not likely be found. Likewise, a child, who draws a picture of the painting contractor as a message for his mother to return the painter's call, is being creative (Figure 1). Combining knowledge of what the painter looks like and the knowledge of how to take a message, the child uses his crayons to make the picture of the painter as a unique way of communicating—without written words—the news of the painter's call to his mother.

From the example of the boys and the skunk, as well as from the example of the child noting the painter's call, cognition and skills are necessary because these serve as the base for creativity. However, the child does not actually cross over into creativity without taking some distinctive steps (Whitson, 1994; Tegano, Moran, & Sawyers, 1991). To take those extra steps, children must find themselves in an environment that not only supports this effort but, more importantly, encourages it in specific ways. Some teachers might be looking for a formula to make creativity happen. A formula like that cannot be given. What can be given are some ways of

thinking, or facilitating strategies. Central to these ways of thinking or strategies will be the early childhood teacher who realizes and believes that creativity is not narrowly defined as a part of art education, but is, more broadly, able to be found and nurtured in every area of learning. Teachers cannot make children be creative. However, the teacher can provide a classroom that displays the appropriate attitude, the appropriate atmosphere, and the appropriate activities and materials for those children who wish to explore or demonstrate creative expression. These three ingredients—appropriate teacher attitude, appropriate classroom atmosphere, and appropriate activities and materials—which will be the focus of the rest of this article, can foster creativity. The absence of them can hinder creativity. The choice is really up to the teacher.

CREATIVITY CAN BE FOSTERED BY THE TEACHER'S ATTITUDE

An attitude of trust is paramount to developing creativity. Adults must trust that children will choose activities that will interest and engage them; and that children will self-regulate those choices without a lot of adult imposed regulations (Whitson, 1994). Most early childhood educators have been in a classroom where the teacher uses a planning board for the children to decide what area they will each work in for the next worktime period. This practice has the potential of limiting a child's thinking to just one area or aspect of the learning environment, particularly if every child is required to do the same task at that center. Further, many times children are asked to stay for a specified amount of time in order to "finish" that center before moving on to another choice. Surely, some of that practice is needed by teachers for accountability; but too much of it could hamper a child's potentially creative side. Now, think of a classroom without a daily planning board or without requirements for a certain number of centers to be visited or "completed" during worktime. This setting would allow each child to stay with a task for as long as he or she wished—or even continue the task when others have stopped working. The teacher is, in effect, telling the children that each of them is invited to go beyond the minimum amount of work or investment. "Getting done" is not the focus. The focus is on these children becoming competent decision makers, as well as on these young decision makers exploring fully and engaging in what interests them (Kamii & Devries, 1978). Engagement in a chosen activity fosters creative expression. Why? If a child knows that he was trusted to choose the activity in which he now finds himself engaged, he will also know that he will be trusted, if he wishes, to take a common or everyday activity and carry it to a new level (Whitson, 1994). An extension of this trust is demonstrated when the teacher elects to "teach to the moment" about something children find intriguing (Haiman, 1991). Trust, engagement, and extension are evident in this scene:

> Worktime was taking place after a group lesson on fire safety. Quite suddenly, half of the class met over in one corner of the room. The children had the scrap box with them. They were using the scrap paper to make fire badges for themselves; and they were splitting up into teams to check for fire hazards in the room. They were also making drawings of the play area and dividing that area up so that they could check the playground for safety when they went outside later.

These children absolutely went beyond the minimum expected, and their engagement led them into a creative way of expressing their combined knowledge. Consider the result if the teacher insisted that each child go back to the center area in which each had been working. Children, experiencing a situation similar to the one above, learn quickly that their interests are important; and that they are trusted to make decisions about what they choose in which to invest their time and inquiry.

Now, someone might suggest that in the real world, children must do certain work during certain times as well as stop work at certain times. Of course, sometimes that is true, but many times the subject matter or the stopping point is an arbitrary one chosen by the adult who has decided it is time to work on a particular idea or to move on simply because that was the original plan. When schedules cannot be changed to accommodate productive engagement, work can be saved and, therefore, respected until the child can resume the work.

There is, however, another important consideration regarding that sense of trust described in the scene of the children working on fire safety. That trust is not just immediately known by the children because trust is in the mind of the teacher. Communication of this sense of trust by the teacher to the stu-

dents is critical. First, a teacher must be able to clearly state permission to try something new. Second, that teacher must state what it is that the children accomplished by the unique process or by the achievement of some form of novel work. Young children do not necessarily have the terms readily available to them to describe what is going on when they are thinking or working creatively; but children can be gradually helped and encouraged to learn to put these ideas into their own words. Third, that teacher must verbally give value to what is taking place (Segal & Segal, 1994). This does not mean a gushy display of enthusiasm, but rather a simple positive statement that can establish a climate of value. This climate is then made more meaningful when the communication interaction moves from teacher-to-student to student-to-student. This interaction is critical. Children should have access to each other and have permission to collaborate or discuss projects with which they are involved. Learning with and from peers should be seen as highly valuable. Children should be able to mingle freely, to display work that they wish to share, and to invite others to see and discuss the work. These concepts of interaction and collaboration among students can be seen in the following example:

> The children had just had a group lesson from the art teacher. Many of them were working on the activity which involved making flowers with small pieces of tissue paper wrapped around a pencil so that the pieces would stand up when glued onto the paper. Other children were working in the housekeeping area, the block area, or on other independent choice activities. The teacher noticed that Alex had crushed his tissue paper so that it had a flat appearance. When she asked him how he had discovered that technique, Alex launched into telling her about his "accident"—he lost his balance and crushed his work. He, quite dramatically, knocked his head with his palm and said that he was sure then that his work was ruined until he looked at it again. That second look made him decide that he liked it that way! When the teacher asked Alex if he would like to share the discovery of his technique with the other children, he used some of the teacher's descriptive words along with his own to describe his discovery and his feeling about it. Children stopped working and listened to him. Two other children joined in with comments about something that they had learned by experimenting with the tissue. Several children walked around to look at the various works in progress to get ideas.

Much of the above example would have been lost if the children had not had access to each other. Obviously, a ground work of trust had been developed and communicated to the students by the teacher long before this day. Such rich scenes do not just happen in a vacuum.

Someone might say that teachers do not have time for all this communication. That is true if they do not make time for it in their day. This does not mean adding it in like one more thing to do, but simply not crowding each day by "making sure that those kids are busy" every minute. A little flexibility with the day can go a long way.

CREATIVITY CAN BE FOSTERED BY THE ATMOSPHERE OF THE CLASSROOM

Children benefit creatively from an atmosphere that is relaxed and based on common sense and respect. That atmosphere tells children that they can test an idea as long as it falls within the confines of safety and appropriateness (Segal & Segal, 1994). The classroom climate communicates to students that it is all right to take a risk and make a mistake. No one can be permitted to "put down" another person for an unusual answer or approach. Everyone should have time to explain what it is that they are trying to say or do. Students should be able to brainstorm about the positive parts of any attempt. Lists can be made of what was learned from the attempt. Children learn from doing—and children learn to be creative from trying creative things.

According to Scott (1991), children need to develop their internal sense of worth before they will take risks. Therefore, the atmosphere needs, also, to be one of self-governance in regard to discipline. Earlier, trust was addressed in regard to work—now apply the same issue of trust to discipline or prosocial behavior. Children can be taught or given models of the ways of being prosocial. Then these tools of prosocial behavior can be used to allow children to "take care of themselves" without an adult watching their every move. Yes, children will make mistakes but they can correct these mistakes and modify the results of these mistakes without an atmosphere of consequences and retribution as you can see from this scene that took place after recess:

The children had been outside with the paraprofessional. When they came in, the paraprofessional told the teacher that Andy had thrown a rock at Tommy. Luckily, it had missed. When the teacher sat down with the class to discuss the situation, Alex said that she didn't need to do that. He said that they just did what they would have done with her—the boys had talked about the problem. Their talking showed them that the running game they were playing was too hard for Andy; and he threw the rock when he got frustrated. The boys had then come up with a way to play that would keep the game fun for everyone, yet would make it easier for Andy; and, Andy, in return, had agreed not to throw rocks at his friends. The boys, with the paraprofessional's backing, told the teacher that they had all agreed and had successfully tried the new plan for the rest of recess. The teacher declared the matter closed and outlined for the class what the boys had achieved

These boys had learned that they could take care of themselves and solve their own problems in an equitable and agreeable manner. The internal motivation for self-regulation that each student will have in such a setting will help develop self-confidence and, therefore, the comfort to take a risk regarding creativity not only in problem solving but in all aspects of the classroom.

After reading the story of the boys and the rock above, someone might strongly suggest that a rule was broken; and that a consequence for breaking that rule should be given. Of course, you need classroom rules but some classrooms have too many, and place all the control completely outside of the child. Further, sometimes consequences are imposed so often that they become meaningless. The focus becomes one of remembering and adhering to all the rules rather than on learning how to get along, and on how to solve problems. Common sense has to be the focus. Creativity will not be fostered in a classroom that is a free-for-all place that is loud and out of control. Who could think well enough to have a creative thought in a setting like that? But neither will creativity be fostered in a room where all the control lies with the adult, and where conformity is the norm.

Because creative children may exhibit behaviors that will be different from other children, the classroom climate needs to reflect an atmosphere of respect for each person and each person's individuality. All children may be curious or sensitive, but a creative child may be those and more. A creative child may be unusually quiet or talkative, may have a strongly developed sense of humor, may do things considered odd by others, may be outspoken, or may be every bit a nonconformist (Meador, 1993; Tegano et al., 1991). Even though a creative child might be considered unusual, a pervasive atmosphere of respect should help everyone (teacher included) to think of that child as unique in some positive sense. An atmosphere of acceptance must be in place so that children displaying unusual tendencies along with their creativity do not become ostracized or the recipient of negative behavior and/or words. Consider this situation:

> Adam was a first grader in a multi-age classroom of first and second graders. He was a highly gifted child who was reading on the high school level as well as being a creative computer programmer in the class. Adam was also so highly disorganized that his messes often spilled over into areas belonging to classmates. One day, a small group of second graders approached Adam and said that they would be willing to help him organize his materials in order to help him, and the class in general. Adam gratefully accepted the offer; and worked right along with the organizing group.

The teacher had looked ahead to what might happen and used a proactive approach by talking about and role playing similar situations, thereby preparing all students for both sides of such a situation; and by teaching and modeling for them the tools of coping with such reactions (Segal & Segal, 1994). The teacher might have given Adam a consequence for his disorganization or chided the students for anger they might have directed at Adam for the mess in their areas; but rather than using rewards or punishments to handle such situations, the teacher worked toward setting a tone that says everyone respects each other, helps each other get through the difficult moments as quickly as possible, learns from those moments, regroups, and goes on with life.

CREATIVITY CAN BE FOSTERED BY THE CLASSROOM ACTIVITIES AND MATERIALS

Activities based on the interests of the children are conducive to fostering creativity. Young children are capable of telling what they know about a topic of interest, what they want to know, and how they want to explore the topic (Haiman, 1991; Scott, 1991). A toy or nature sample brought to school by one of the

children may cause the other children to display a spontaneous interest or curiosity. This is the time to explore that interest or curiosity; and let the interests drive the curriculum rather than let the curriculum drive what children can do.

Certainly, teachers often have curricular guidelines to follow, however, almost any topic can be tied to some element of the standard curriculum, and can offer the promise of a new slant on the old. Both students and teachers may experience creativity in such a setting. Teachers who value and act upon these ideas give children a sense of ownership in the work. Ownership leads to investment and engagement. Engagement leads to creative behavior. Examine this story about Jenny and her dinosaur:

> The children were asked to draw a favorite dinosaur and tell why it was their favorite. Jenny spent a great deal of time and used a great deal of detail in drawing a "princessasorus" complete with crown as well as scaly skin. She had a story to tell about this creature. When she was at home, she extended this by drawing a "Dimend Bartasorus" (Diamond Brontasaurus) for her teacher (Figure 2).

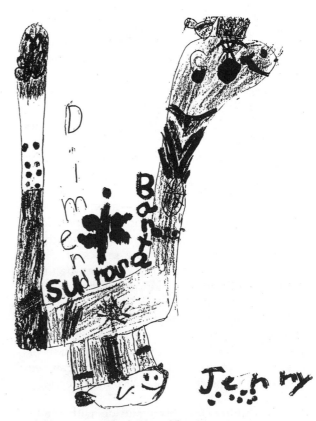

Fig. 2. Dimend Bartasorus.

Jenny spent more time on this project because she had an investment with her imagination. She did follow the instructions, and she is still within the confines of the curriculum for "dinosaurs"—she just went further, combined some ideas, and ventured into something new.

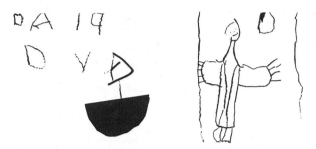

Fig. 3. Columbus and his boat—the other two sank.

Activities should also be open-ended. Rather than giving a strict model of what the product should be, discuss the product that you and/or the students want and then let them have reasonable control over deciding what materials they want to use or how they want to approach the product. If the materials are available to the children, they can get the ones they want at any time. Further, for young children, the product is not as important as the process by which the product was achieved. Some children may even want to abandon the product before it is finished. Teachers often view the product as a reflection on their teaching, rather than what it really is—a concrete reflection of the child's work and work process. Therefore, in such a process-oriented classroom, supplemental materials are important, but maybe not as important as the child's thought process while working on the product. Consider David's thought processes:

> The children were making cut paper and crayon pictures of the voyage of the three boats of Columbus. David finished his work with one boat and a picture of an unidentified person. When the teacher asked him about his work, he told her that the person in the picture was Columbus; but there was only one boat because the other two had sunk (Figure 3). The teacher accepted his work readily.

No, David did not complete the project exactly, but the assignment was done to his satisfaction and his version of reality. He had done the basic task with, obviously, some extra thought processes if he could explain his work in the manner he did. His "supplemental" materials were not concrete. David's "extra" materials were in his mind, and consisted of the mental manipulation of ideas.

As for those optional concrete materials, teachers may feel stressed to "find" or provide them. However, one has to ask, how can children try the unusual if they never see or have the opportunity to work with anything unusual? Families can be a convenient and willing resource for donating or locating unusual materials. Parental involvement has another plus—this involvement gives parents more opportunity to notice and value creativity—especially if the child can convince them as to why certain "junk" would be considered outstanding material at school.

Classroom activities should be planned in such a way that an ample amount of uninterrupted worktime is given for investigation and discussion. Creativity will not develop in a vacuum. The main idea is to have children who have the time to see new concepts or extensions—in the materials they have, rather than have children who need new materials to be stimulated. At first, the teacher can be the model by showing or telling about some extensions. Later, the children can take over this role, as Laura and Katie did:

> During worktime, Laura and Katie spent the better part of an hour sitting with the newly hatched chicks. They had an appropriate running conversation with each other during this time. They then approached the teacher with a song about chicks that they had created. The song was based on a familiar one that the children had learned about dinosaurs but it had been changed by the girls to incorporate what they knew or had learned about the chicks. The song was printed on the computer for the girls to use as they wished—for sharing, for a play, or for adding pictures for a story.

The girls were allowed to stay as long as they wished at the chicks, rather than being asked to leave after a certain amount of time or to leave in order to get another center done. This gave them the time and the permission to think of the chicks in a new way, and in combination with previous knowledge.

Finally, activities, processes, and products should be the intrinsic reward for learning. External rewards cause the shift of importance to go from the learning to "What do I get?"

and cause creativity to drop off (Kohn, 1993). Why would a child want to invest time and interest in something after a reward was given for a minimal accomplishment? The focus should be on the description of what is taking place or has taken place—and what was learned. Again, the teacher takes the lead in establishing this, but the children will follow.

CONCLUSION

None of these classroom scenes are spectacular in any way. They are simply examples of what can happen to begin or continue to creative process. These samples are not ends in themselves but stepping stones to more creative ideas. If teachers can identify in themselves, and alter or eliminate, the filters that prevent or hinder children from trying something new, then creativity will have a greater chance to be fostered. Teachers may be more encouraged to modify or remove those filters if they keep in mind that "the creation of new ideas does not come from minds trained to follow doggedly what is already known. Creation comes from tinkering and playing around, from which new forms emerge" (Wassermann, 1991, p. 135).

References

Bredekamp, S. (Ed.). (1987). *Developmentally appropriate practice in early childhood programs serving children from birth through age 8.* Washington, D.C.: NAEYC.

Edwards, L., & Nabors, M. (1993). The creative arts process. *Young Children, 48*(3), 77–81.

Fowler, C. (1990). Recognizing the role of artistic intelligences. *Music Educator's Journal, 77*(1), 24–27.

Haiman, P. (1991). Developing a sense of wonder in young children. There is more to early childhood education than cognitive development. *Young Children, 46*(6), 52–53.

Isenberg, J. P., & Jalongo, M. R. (1996). *Creative expression and play in early childhood* (2nd ed.). Englewood Cliffs, NJ: Merrill/Prentice Hall.

Kamii, C., & DeVries, R. (1978). *Physical knowledge in preschool education: Implications of Piaget's theory.* New York: Prentice Hall.

Kohn, A. (1993). *Punished by rewards.* Boston: Houghton Mifflin company.

Meador, K. (1993). Surviving a creative child's early years. *Gifted Child Today, 16*(2), 57–59.

Scott, M. (1991). Parental encouragement of gifted-talented-creative (GTC) development in young children by providing freedom to become independent. *The Creative Child and Adult Quarterly, 16*(1), 26–29.

Segal, J., & Segal, Z. (1994). Nurturing creativity in all your students. *LEARNING94, 23*(2), 26–27.

Tegano, D., Moran, J., & Sawyers, J. (1991). *Creativity in early childhood classrooms.* Washington, D.C.: National Education Association.

Wassermann, S. (1991). Serious play in the classroom: How messing around can win you the Nobel Prize. *Childhood Education, 68*(3), 133–139.

Whitson, S. (1994). The creative minority in our schools. *Childhood Education, 71*(1), 2–3.

Challenging Movement Experiences for Young Children

STEPHEN W. SANDERS
BILL YONGUE

Ten four-year-old children enter a large, carpeted room. A colorful parachute is on the floor in the middle. Against the wall are containers filled with a variety of balls and beanbags. The children move quickly in anticipation of what is about to happen. It is time for movement.

Every day, thousands of young children develop their physical skills by participating in a variety of movement experiences. Today we know more than ever about how to remain healthy. Regular participation in physical activity is one of the most important ways to live a longer, fuller life. Daily movement experiences are an integral part of high-quality early childhood programs. In the mid-1980s, the National Association for the Education of Young Children (NAEYC) published a position statement that described developmentally appropriate practice for children from birth through age eight (see Bredekamp & Copple, 1997).

The Council on Physical Education for Children (COPEC), a division of the National Association for Sport and Physical Education (NASPE), used NAEYC's model to develop *Developmentally Appropriate Practice in Movement Programs for Young Children Ages 3–5* (NASPE, 1992). The document consists of 25 integrated components, each suggesting guidelines for appropriate and inappropriate practice in movement programs for young children.

In a developmentally appropriate program for young children what kinds of movement experiences should children have? Four major areas from the NASPE guidelines are emphasized here: child development, teaching strategies, content, and assessment.

Developmental Physical Education

Developmental physical education as defined by Gallahue (1995) is physical activity that emphasizes the acquisition

> **Developmentally Appropriate Practice in Movement Programs for Young Children Ages 3–5 (NASPE, 1992) can assist educators of young children to:**
>
> - make informed decisions about the curriculum and content of movement programs
> - determine how to present content appropriately
> - evaluate curriculum and teaching methods
> - advocate for program improvement
> - more fully integrate movement activities within the curriculum

of sequential movement skills and increased physical competency based on the unique developmental level of the individual. It recognizes and incorporates the many contributions that systemic, sensitive teaching can make to a child's cognitive and affective development. Developmental physical education encourages the uniqueness of individuals and is based on the fundamental proposition that although motor development is age related, it is not age dependent.

Three components that are critical in developmentally appropriate physical education are: age appropriateness, developmental appropriateness, and instruction (NASPE, 1992).

From *Dimensions of Early Childhood*, Winter 1998, pp. 9-17. © 1998 by the Southern Early Childhood Association (SECA), Little Rock, AR. Reprinted by permission.

Table 1.

Characteristics of 3- to 5-year-old children

Physical
1. Perceptual-motor abilities rapidly develop, but confusion often exists in body, directional, temporal, and spatial awareness.
2. Rapidly developing fundamental movement abilities in a variety of motor skills. Unilateral movements are easier than bilateral movements such as skipping.
3. Often active and energetic and would rather run than walk, but still need rest periods.
4. Body functions and processes become well regulated.
5. Body builds of boys and girls are very similar.
6. Fine-motor control is yet to be fully established, and gross-motor control is still developing.

Cognitive
1. Increasing ability to express thoughts and ideas verbally.
2. Learn through play.

3. Very imaginative and continue to investigate and discover.
4. This preoperational thought phase of development results in a period of transition from self-satisfying behavior to fundamental socialized behavior.
5. Attention span depends on whether activity keeps child's interest.

Affective
1. Some children may be somewhat egocentric and assume that everyone thinks the way they do. This may result in reluctance to share and cooperate with others.
2. May be fearful of new situations, shy, self-conscious.
3. Beginning to distinguish right from wrong.
4. Self-concept is rapidly developing. Success-oriented experiences and positive reinforcement are especially important.

Age appropriateness. High-quality programs are not based on chronological age or grade level but are influenced by both. The process of development proceeds from simple to complex and from general to specific as young children strive to increase their competence in all domains. As a result, patterns of behavior emerge that help guide the selection of movement experiences that are typically appropriate for specific age groups (Gallahue, 1995).

For example, most 5-year-old children do not yet have the skills to compete in a regulation soccer game, but they can participate in activities that involve kicking a ball. It would be developmentally inappropriate, then, to force all 5-year-old children to participate in a regulation soccer game.

Individual appropriateness. Each child has a unique timing and pattern of growth and development. Therefore, movement activities are based on children's individual stages of motor development and levels of movement skill learning. The inclusion of specific movement experiences is considerably influenced by children's fitness levels, as well as their cognitive and affective development (Gallahue, 1995).

Some children, for example, may not develop the necessary skills to play soccer until late elementary school; others may never achieve the skills or have interest necessary to participate in the game.

Instruction. In a developmentally appropriate program, it is also important to incorporate instructional strategies that maximize opportunities for learning and success for all children. Teacher decisions concerning what, when, and how to teach are based primarily on the appropriateness of the activity for the individual and

secondarily on its suitability for a certain age group (NASPE, 1992, 1995).

It would be considered developmentally inappropriate to require children to participate in activities such as Duck-Duck-Goose or a relay race where activity time is limited because children spend most of their time waiting in lines for a turn.

Child Development

Movement activities are designed with the physical, cognitive, and affective development of children in mind. (NASPE, 1992, p. 6)

Each child is a whole, integrated person (Gallahue, 1995). In order to plan an appropriate learning environment and develop suitable experiences for young children, adults first need to understand children's development, including the cognitive, affective, and psychomotor characteristics and needs of the age group.

The characteristics briefly reviewed in *Table 1* are among those that determine not only how teachers work with children but also the types of movement experiences provided (Gallahue & Ozmun, 1995). Based on these characteristics, the Council on Physical Education for Children (NASPE, 1992) developed five premises of a developmentally appropriate movement program for young children.

1. Three-, four-, and five-year-old children are different from elementary-age children. When teachers understand the continuum of development, their focus can be on teaching children rather than teaching activities.

Young children need a variety of experiences that will lead them to more mature movement patterns.

2. **Young children learn through interaction with their environment.** This well-established concept has been stated in many ways—children learn by doing; children learn through active involvement with people and objects. Developmentally appropriate movement programs for young children are designed so that all children are active participants, not passive listeners or observers except for brief demonstrations and explanations of the activity.

3. **Teachers of young children act as guides or facilitators.** Teachers construct the environment with specific objectives in mind, then guide children toward these goals. By carefully observing children's responses and interests, teachers can adapt learning experiences to best meet individual needs. In high-quality programs, children make choices and seek creative solutions. Teachers actively engage children in experiences to broaden and deepen their learning, a strategy which is called "child-centered" rather than "subject-centered" approach to curriculum.

4. **Young children learn and develop in an integrated fashion.** Children's physical, emotional, social, and cognitive development are interrelated, so learning through movement encompasses all areas of development. Regularly-scheduled movement experiences focus upon the development of physical skills which are incorporated in the child's total development and integrated into the entire curriculum.

5. **Planned movement experiences enhance play.** A combination of play and planned movement experiences, specifically designed to help children develop physical skills, are the most beneficial in assisting young children in their development. When frequent, regular, appropriate movement experiences are combined with daily indoor and outdoor play, children freely practice and develop their skills.

Teaching Strategies

Movement exploration, guided discovery, and creative problem solving are the predominant teaching strategies employed. Children are provided the opportunity to make choices and actively explore their environment; while teachers serve as facilitators, preparing a stimulating environment and challenging activities. (NASPE, 1992, p. 6)

One of the most important tasks a teacher does is establish a safe, challenging environment in which all children can learn (Sanders, 1992). Make sure children know what is expected of them during movement activities. Children must be aware of any space restrictions, the movement patterns of other children, and their own potential for moving. A developmentally appropriate movement class for 4-year-old children might look something like the one described in *Figure 1*.

Table 2.

Skill themes in physical education for young children

Locomotor	Nonmanipulative	Manipulative
Walk	Push/pull	Throw
Run	Swing/sway	Catch
Leap	Bend/stretch	Strike
Hop	Twist/turn	Kick
Jump	Balance	Dribble
Gallop	Transfer weight	Bounce
Slide		Roll
Skip		

Curriculum Content

The movement curriculum has an obvious scope and sequence based on goals and objectives that are appropriate for all children. It includes a balance of skills and concepts designed to enhance the cognitive, motor, affective, and physical development of every child. (NASPE, 1992, p. 6)

There are two parts to curriculum development in physical education for young children. First, the content of a movement program for young children is made up of movement skills and concepts. Skills themes, the actual physical movements or skills that children will learn and perform, can be divided into three categories: locomotor, nonmanipulative, and manipulative *(Table 2)*.

Movement concepts modify skill themes and describe how skills are performed. For example, running is a skill. Fast, zigzag, and forward are concepts that describe running. During a lesson for older preschoolers, where the emphasis is on developing skill in running, the challenge might be, "Can you run very fast in a zigzag path while moving forward?" Movement concepts are expressed in categories of body awareness, (what the body can do), space awareness, (where the body moves), effort, (how the body moves), and relationships, (relationships of the body to its parts, objects, individuals, and groups).

The movement vocabulary in *Table 3* identifies appropriate concepts for young children to learn through movement (Graham, Holt/Hale, & Parker, 1993; Kruger & Kruger, 1989). This skill theme approach is developmentally appropriate with young children because it helps them become more capable movers. There is plenty of time to learn to play games such as soccer or basketball in later years after they have developed their skills.

The second part of a movement curriculum for young children includes providing children with information, or cues, on how to correctly perform the movement skills. *Cues* are key points children should learn about each skill (Graham et al., 1993). Some cues that are ap-

Figure 1.

Visit an appropriate movement class for four-year-olds

Ten four-year-old children walk quietly down a school hallway and enter a large, carpeted room. One of the first sights they see is the smiling face of Mrs. Phillips, their classroom teacher. "We are really going to have run learning today!" Mrs. Phillips tells the students.

Mrs. Phillips asks each child to pick a small carpet square from a pile and carry it to the center of the room. "Let's place our carpet squares in a circle and then sit on the carpets," she says. As the children sit, Mrs. Phillips observes that the shape is more a figure eight than a circle and that many children are sitting very close to each other. "Does this look like a circle?" she asks. Some children say no, others are not sure what a circle is supposed to look like. Mrs. Phillips helps arrange the carpets in a circle and then leads the children in a discussion about what a circle is, general and self-space, and not getting too close to friends while moving around the room. About two minutes have passed.

Mrs. Phillips explains the two rhythm sticks she holds. "These two sticks are my 'stop' signal. When I strike them together I would like you to stop, freeze your body, and not move." She demonstrates by striking the sticks together and freezing. "Can you stand up and start walking around the room and stay as far away from your friends as you can? If you see anyone getting close to you, it is your job to stay away from them." The children jump up and start moving. "This is fun!" David shouts.

Every 15 to 20 seconds, Mrs. Phillips strikes the sticks together and all children stop moving. Mrs. Phillips asks if they can move backward, and the children are off again. Each time Mrs. Phillips strikes the sticks, the children stop for about five seconds and she gives them the next challenge. "Show me you can hop on one foot." "Show me you can gallop around the room, but be careful not to get close to your friends." When the children have trouble with a challenge, Mrs. Phillips strikes the sticks together to stop the children so she can demonstrate how to do the challenge. The children move again, walking, hopping, galloping and running. Mrs. Phillips also guides the students in the directions, pathways, and speeds in which the movements can be performed.

After about four minutes, Mrs. Phillips can see the children are getting tired. She strikes the sticks together and points to three piles of beanbags. "Would you walk over, without touching any of your friends, pick up a beanbag, and then place it on your head? Can you balance the bean-

bag on your shoulder? Can you balance the beanbag on your elbow?" For the next four minutes the children practice balancing beanbags as suggested by the teacher. They also have ideas of their own, and Mrs. Phillips praises their creative efforts.

When the activity ends, the children place the beanbags in a box, and then Mrs. Phillips asks them to pick up large balloons [see note]. The balloons seem to spark an interest in the children, and they begin to bounce and strike them. After a short time, she gains their attention, talks about the balloons, and challenges the children to practice throwing, catching, and kicking. After about six minutes, Mrs. Phillips tells the children to put away their balloons and pick up hoops.

The hoops, spaced along a wall, are easy for children to pick up without collision. Children play with the hoops for a while without direction. Mrs. Phillips then asks them to line the hoops straight on the floor and challenges them to jump on two feet from hoop to hoop.

After practicing jumping for about five minutes or so, Mrs. Phillips wonders out loud, "How am I going to pick up all the equipment?" The children then eagerly volunteer to help.

The equipment stowed, Mrs. Phillips asks the children again to sit on their carpets. The children sing a song in which they touch parts of their bodies corresponding with the music. The children talk briefly about what they did during class and what they just learned, and Mrs. Phillips tells them they did an excellent job. The children then put their carpet squares away. The class period filled with movement activities, lasted about 30 minutes.

Note: **Balloons are an aspiration hazard and should only be offered to four- and five-year-old children if the balloons are properly inflated (American Public Health Association & American Academy of Pediatrics, 1992). Carefully supervise children whenever balloons are available, and remove all pieces of any popped balloons immediately. Infants and toddlers, who often explore items by chewing, should never be given balloons.**

Note: From Designing Preschool Movement Programs **pp. 11–12), by S.W. Sanders, 1992, Champaign, IL: Human Kinetics. Copyright © 1992 by Human Kinetics. Adapted with permission.**

---

propriate for assisting preschool children to develop movement skills are listed in *Table 4*.

Teachers who stress one cue at a time are less likely to confuse children (Graham et al., 1993). For example, the cues for teaching preschool children to throw are to step with the opposite foot, throw hard, and to turn the opposite side of the body toward the target. These three cues are introduced one at a time.

The more often a cue is stressed, the more likely the children are to improve their skills (Sanders, 1992), and the movement will soon become automatic. Preschool

children who learn cues for each skill will be more capable movers in elementary school.

Assessment

Systematic assessment is based on knowledge of developmental characteristics and ongoing observations in children as they participate in activities. This information is used to individualize instruction, plan objective-oriented lessons, identify children with special needs, communicate with parents, and evaluate the program's effectiveness. (NASPE, 1992, p. 10)

Photo courtesy of the authors

As children's skills and interests change, adults adjust the program to further accommodate each growing child

Table 3.

Movement concepts in physical education for young children

Space Awareness	Body Awareness
Personal Space	**Whole Body**
Self space	Front/back
Place in space	Sides
General Space	**Body Parts**
Middle of	Hands/head
Sides of	Feet/knees/toes
Boundaries of	Fingers/elbows
Directions	Shoulders/hips
Up/down	Stomach/eyes
Forward/backward	Mouth/neck
Right/left	Face/chin/ears
Sideways	Nose/ankles/wrist
Level	**Actions**
High/medium/low	Moving/still
Size	Weight on feet
Big/small	Weight on other parts
Pathways	Balancing
Straight/curved	**Body Shapes**
Angular/twisted	Wide/narrow
Figure eight	Round/twisted
Zigzag	
Shapes	
Round/square	
Triangular	
Rectangular	

Effort/Quality	Relationships
Time	**Space Words**
Fast/slow	Under/over
Faster/slower	On/off
Sudden/sustained	Around/through
Force	Between/among
Heavy/light	Near/far
Strong/weak	**Contact**
Hard/soft	Touching/not touching
Harsh/gentle	Together/apart
Flow	**People**
Bound/free	By yourself/with people
Stopping/going	Leading/following
Jerky/smooth	Mirroring/matching
	Unison/contrast

Teachers in developmentally appropriate programs continually and thoroughly assess children's progress. As children's skills and interests change, adults adjust the program to further accommodate each growing child (Grace & Shores, 1992). NASPE developed physical education benchmarks for students from kindergarten through the 12th grade. These benchmarks (see Table 5) are reasonable skill and knowledge outcomes that students would expect to achieve as a result of participating in a quality physical education program (NASPE, 1990).

How do teachers use these benchmarks to see if the children are progressing? The criteria for assessing physical skills are not unlike the criteria used to assess the social, emotional, and mental development of young children. The Southern Early Childhood Association (Grace & Shores, 1992) established these criteria that can be used as a foundation for assessing the physical skills of children.

1. Assessment must be valid. It must provide information related to the goals and objectives of a program.

2. Assessment must encompass the whole child. Programs must have goals and assessment procedures which relate to children's physical, social, emotional, and mental development.

3. Assessment must involve repeated observations. Repeated observations help teachers to find patterns of behaviors and avoid quick decisions.

4. Assessment must be continuous. Each child should be compared to his or her own individual course of development over time, rather than to average behavior for a group.

5. Assessment must use a variety of methods. Gathering a wide variety of information from different sources permits informed and professional decisions.

An assessment portfolio is a collection of a child's work which demonstrates the child's efforts, progress,

Table 4.

Example cues for selected skill themes

Catch
Use large colorful balls to help in tracking
Emphasize catching with the hands
Use a ball on a string for a more consistent toss
Use soft textured balls
If ball is above the waist, keep thumbs together
If ball is below the waist, hold pinkies together
Keep eyes on the ball [as it comes] into hands

Throw
Use visual aids (footprints or tape on floor) to help
  in the stepping position
Use large targets
Emphasize using opposition
Step, turn toward the target, throw hard

Kick
Use large targets
Use soft textured balls
Keep eye on the ball
Step beside the ball
Kick hard

Balance
Encourage alternate foot stepping
Begin walking by holding onto a rope or hoop

Gradually move to balance beam
Increase height of balance beam as children improve
Look straight ahead, move slowly, balance before taking
  next step

Spatial Awareness (Personal and general space)
Learn how to move, dodge, and stop
Keep head up when moving
Look left and right
Watch where you are going

Jump (Vertical and distance)
Two feet take off and two feet land
Maintain balance
As arms go up, feet come off the floor
Jump as high or as far as possible
Use arms for balance

Strike
Have ball on tee or suspended on string
Place ball at child's waist level
Bat should have large hitting surface and small handle
  (one-liter plastic bottles make good bats)
Step toward target, keep eye on ball, swing level and
  hard

---

and achievements over time (Grace & Shores, 1992). The portfolio can be made up of a variety of different assessment tools such as work samples, screening tests, rating scales, checklists, and systematic observations of the child's performance or behavior. When this collection of information is put together for each child, families and teachers can get an accurate picture of children's learning.

Table 5.

Benchmarks for kindergarten physical education

- Demonstrates competency in many movement forms and proficiency in a few movement forms
- Applies movement concepts and principles to the learning and development of motor skills
- Exhibits a physically active lifestyle
- Achieves and maintains a health-enhancing level of physical fitness
- Demonstrates responsible personal and social behavior in physical activity setting
- Demonstrates understanding and respect for differences among people in physical activity setting
- Understands that physical activity provides the opportunity for enjoyment, challenge, self expression and social interaction

Table 6 illustrates a checklist that might be used by teachers to see if kindergarten children are achieving the NASPE benchmarks.

Another tool to record children's progress is the video camera (see Reynolds & Milner in this issue). Videotape children individually as they perform a number of skills such as running, jumping, throwing, catching, and striking. Bring families into the assessment and learning process by viewing and discussing the video with them.

Teachers who continue to improve their professional practices help ensure that children will continue to have positive attitudes about physical education, and all learning, in the future.

References

American Public Health Association, & American Academy of Pediatrics. (1992). *Caring for our children: National health and safety performance standards: Guidelines for out-of-home child care programs.* Washington, DC, and Elk Grove Village, IL: Authors.

Bredekamp, S., & Copple, C. (Eds.). (1997). *Developmentally appropriate practice in early childhood programs* (Rev. ed.). Washington, DC: National Association for the Education of Young Children.

Gallahue, D.L. (1995). Transforming physical education curriculum. In Bredekamp, S. & Rosegrant, T. (Eds.), *Reaching potentials: Transforming early childhood curriculum and assessment* (pp. 125–137). Washington DC: National Association for the Education of Young Children.

Gallahue, D.L., & Ozmun, J.C. (1995). *Understanding motor development: Infant, children, adolescents, adults.* Dubuque, IA: W.C. Brown & Benchmark.

Grace, C., & Shores, E. (1992). *The portfolio and its use: Developmentally appropriate assessment of young children.* Little Rock: Southern Early Childhood Association.

Photo courtesy of the authors

Incorporate instructional strategies that maximize opportunities for learning and success for all children.

Graham, G., Holt/Hale, S., & Parker, M. (1993). *Children moving: A reflective approach to teaching physical education.* Palo Alto, CA: Mayfield.

Kruger, H., & Kruger, J. (1989). *The preschool teacher's guide to movement education.* Baltimore: Gerstung.

National Association for Sport and Physical Education (NASPE). (1990). *Definition of the physically educated person. Report of the NASPE Outcomes Committee.* Reston, VA: American Association for Health, Physical Education, Recreation, and Dance (AAHPERD).

NASPE. (1992). *Developmentally appropriate physical education practices for children. A position statement of the Council on Physical Education for Children of NASPE.* Reston, VA: AAHPERD.

Sanders, S.W. (1992). *Designing preschool movement programs.* Champaign, IL: Human Kinetics.

Stephen W. Sanders, Ed.D., is Assistant Professor of Health and Human Performance at Auburn University in Auburn, Alabama.

Bill Yongue, Ed.D., is Assistant Professor, Department of Health, Physical Education, and Recreation at Florida International University, Miami.

Table 6.

Sample checklist for physical education benchmarks

Child's name_____

Date _____

Check the appropriate column
   Demonstrated = D   Not Demonstrated = ND

Skill	D	ND
Kicks a stationary ball using a smooth, continuous running approach prior to the kick	____	____
Rolls sideways without hesitating or stopping	____	____
Makes both large and small body shapes while traveling	____	____
Walks and runs using a mature motor pattern	____	____
Tosses a ball and catches it before it bounces twice	____	____

A joint position statement of the International Reading Association (IRA) and the National Association for the Education of Young Children (NAEYC), adopted 1998

LEARNING TO READ AND WRITE: DEVELOPMENTALLY APPROPRIATE PRACTICES FOR YOUNG CHILDREN

Learning to read and write is critical to a child's success in school and later in life. One of the best predictors of whether a child will function competently in school and go on to contribute actively in our increasingly literate society is the level to which the child progresses in reading and writing. Although reading and writing abilities continue to develop throughout the life span, the early childhood years—from birth through age 8—are the most important period for literacy development. It is for this reason that the International Reading Association (IRA) and the National Association for the Education of Young Children (NAEYC) joined together to formulate a position statement regarding early literacy development. The statement consists of a set of principles and recommendations for teaching practices and public policy.

The primary purpose of this position statement is to provide guidance to teachers of young children in schools and early childhood programs (including child care centers, preschools, and family child care homes) serving children from birth through age 8. By and large, the principles and practices suggested here also will be of interest to any adults who are in a position to influence a young child's learning and development—parents, grandparents, older siblings, tutors, and other community members.

Teachers work in schools or programs regulated by administrative policies as well as available resources. Therefore secondary audiences for this position statement are school principals and program administrators whose roles are critical in establishing a supportive climate for sound, developmentally appropriate teaching practices; and policy makers whose decisions determine whether adequate resources are available for high-quality early childhood education.

A great deal is known about how young children learn to read and write and how they can be helped toward literacy during the first 5 years of life. A great deal is known also about how to help children once compulsory schooling begins, whether in kindergarten or the primary grades. Based on a thorough review of the research, this document reflects the commitment of two major professional organizations to the goal of helping children learn to read well enough by the end of third grade so that they can read to learn in all curriculum areas. IRA and NAEYC are commit-

Excerpted from *The Reading Teacher,* October 1998, pp. 196-214. © 1998 by the International Reading Association. Reprinted by permission.

ted not only to helping young children learn to read and write but also to fostering and sustaining their interest and disposition to read and write for their own enjoyment, information, and communication.

First, the statement summarizes the current issues that are the impetus for this position; then it reviews what is known from research on young children's literacy development. This review of research as well as the collective wisdom and experience of IRA and NAEYC members provides the basis for a position statement about what constitutes developmentally appropriate practice in early literacy over the period of birth through age 8. The position concludes with recommendations for teaching practices and policies.

Statement of the issues

Why take a position on something as obviously important as children's learning to read and write? The IRA and NAEYC believe that this position statement will contribute significantly to an improvement in practice and the development of supportive educational policies. The two associations saw that a clear, concise position statement was needed at this time for several reasons.

• It is essential and urgent to teach children to read and write competently, enabling them to achieve today's high standards of literacy.

Although the U.S. enjoys the highest literacy rate in its history, society now expects virtually everyone in the population to function beyond the minimum standards of literacy. Today the definition of *basic proficiency* in literacy calls for a fairly high standard of reading comprehension and analysis. The main reason is that literacy requirements of most jobs have increased significantly and are expected to increase further in the future. Communications that in the past were verbal (by phone or in person) now demand reading and writing—messages sent by electronic mail, Internet, or facsimile as well as print documents.

• With the increasing variation among young children in our programs and schools, teaching today has become more challenging.

Experienced teachers throughout the U.S. report that the children they teach today are more diverse in their backgrounds, experiences, and abilities than were those they taught in the past. Kindergarten classes now include children who have been in group settings for 3 or 4 years as well as children who are participating for the first time in an organized early childhood program. Classes include both children with identified disabilities and children with exceptional abilities, children who are already independent readers and children who are just beginning to acquire some basic literacy knowledge and skills. Children in the group may speak different languages at varying levels of proficiency. Because of these individual and experiential variations, it is common to find within a kindergarten classroom a 5-year range in children's literacy-related skills and functioning (Riley, 1996). What this means is that some kindergarteners may have skills characteristic of the typical 3-year-old, while others might be functioning at the level of the typical 8-year-old. Diversity is to be expected and embraced, but it can be overwhelming when teachers are expected to produce uniform outcomes for all, with no account taken of the initial range in abilities, experiences, interests, and personalities of individual children.

• Among many early childhood teachers, a maturationist view of young children's development persists despite much evidence to the contrary.

A readiness view of reading development assumes that there is a specific time in the early childhood years when the teaching of reading should begin. It also assumes that physical and neurological maturation alone prepared the child to take advantage of instruction in reading and writing. The readiness perspective implies that until children reach a certain stage of maturity all exposure to reading and writing, except perhaps being read stories, is a waste of time or even potentially harmful. Experiences throughout the early childhood years, birth through age 8, affect the development of literacy. These experiences constantly interact with characteristics of individual children to determine the level of literacy skills a child ultimately achieves. Failing to give children literacy experiences until they are school-age can severely limit the reading and writing levels they ultimately attain.

• Recognizing the early beginnings of literacy acquisition too often has resulted in use of inappropriate teaching practices suited to older children or adults perhaps but ineffective with children in preschool, kindergarten, and the early grades.

Teaching practices associated with outdated views of literacy development and/or learning theories are still prevalent in many classrooms. Such practices include extensive whole-group instruction and intensive drill and practice on isolated skills for groups or individuals. These practices, not particularly effective for primary-grade children, are even less suitable and effective with preschool and kindergarten children. Young children especially need to be engaged in experiences that make academic content meaningful and build on prior learning. It is vital for all children to have literacy experiences in schools and early childhood programs. Such access is even more critical for children with limited home experiences in literacy. However, these school experiences must teach the broad range of language and literacy knowledge and skills to provide the solid foundation on which high levels of reading and writing ultimately depend.

• Current policies and resources are inadequate in ensuring that preschool and primary teachers are qualified to support the literacy development of all children, a task requiring strong preservice preparation and ongoing professional development.

For teachers of children younger than kindergarten age in the United States, no uniform preparation requirements or licensure standards exist. In fact, a high-school diploma is the highest level of education required to be a child care teacher in most states. Moreover, salaries in child care and preschool programs are too low to attract or retain better qualified staff. Even in the primary grades, for which certified teachers are required, many states do not offer specialized early childhood certification, which means many teachers are not adequately prepared to teach reading and writing to young children. All teachers of young children need good, foundational knowledge in language acquisition, including second-language learning, the processes of reading and writing, early literacy development, and experiences and teaching practices contributing to optimal development. Resources also are insufficient to ensure teachers continuing access to professional education so they can remain current in the field or can prepare to teach a different age group if they are reassigned.

What research reveals: Rationale for the position statement

Children take their first critical steps toward learning to read and write very early in life. Long before they can exhibit reading and writing production skills, they begin to acquire some basic understandings of the concepts about literacy and its functions. Children learn to use symbols, combining their oral language, pictures, print, and play into a coherent mixed medium and creating and communicating meanings in a variety of ways. From their initial experiences and interactions with adults, children begin to read words, processing letter-sound relations and acquiring substantial knowledge of the alphabetic system. As they continue to learn, children increasingly consolidate this information into patterns that allow for automaticity and fluency in reading and writing. Consequently reading and writing acquisition is conceptualized better as a developmental continuum than as an all-or-nothing phenomenon (see "continuum of children's development in early reading and writing" for an illustration . . .).

But the ability to read and write does not develop naturally, without careful planning and instruction. Children need regular and active interactions with print. Specific abilities required for reading and writing come from immediate experiences with oral *and* written language. Experiences in these early years begin to define the assumptions and expectations about becoming literate and give children the motivation to work toward learning to read and write. From these experiences children learn that reading and writing are valuable tools that will help them do many things in life.

The beginning years (birth through preschool)

Even in the first few months of life, children begin to experiment with language. Young babies make sounds that imitate the tones and rhythms of adult talk; they "read" gestures and facial expressions, and they begin to associate sound sequences frequently heard—words—with their referents (Berk, 1996). They delight in listening to familiar jingles and rhymes, play along in games such as peek-a-boo and pat-a-cake, and manipulate objects such as board books and alphabet blocks in their play. From these remarkable beginnings children learn to use a variety of symbols.

In the midst of gaining facility with these symbols systems, children acquire through interactions with others the insights that specific kinds of marks—print—also can represent meanings. At first children will use the physical and visual cues surrounding print to determine what something says. But as they develop an understanding of the alphabetic principle, children begin to process letters, translate them into sounds, and connect this information with a known meaning. Although it may seem as though some children acquire these understandings magically or on their own, studies suggest that they are the beneficiaries of considerable, though playful and informal, adult guidance and instruction (Anbar, 1986; Durkin, 1966).

Considerable diversity in children's oral and written language experiences occurs in these years (Hart & Risley, 1995). In home and child care situations, children encounter many different resources and types and degrees of support for early reading and writing (McGill-Franzen & Lanford, 1994). Some children may have ready access to a range of writing and reading materials, while others may not; some children will observe their parents writing and reading frequently, others only occasionally; some children receive direct instruction, while others receive much more casual, informal assistance.

What this means is that no one teaching method or approach is likely to be the most effective for all children (Strickland, 1994). Rather, good teachers bring into play a variety of teaching strategies that can encompass the great diversity of children in schools. Excellent instruction builds on what children already know and can do, and provides knowledge, skills, and dispositions for lifelong learning. Children need to learn not only the technical skills or reading and writing but also how to use these tools to better their thinking and reasoning (Neuman, in press).

The single most important activity for building these understandings and skills essential for reading success appears to be *reading aloud to children* (Bus, Van IJzendoorn, & Pellegrini, 1995; Wells, 1985). High-quality book reading occurs when children feel emotionally secure (Bus & Van IJzendoorn, 1995; Bus et al., 1997) and are active participants in reading (Whitehurst et al., 1994). Asking predictive and analytic questions in small-group settings appears to affect children's vocabulary and comprehension of stories (Karweit & Wasik, 1996). Children may talk about the pictures, retell the story, discuss their favorite actions, and request multiple rereadings. It is the talk that surrounds the storybook reading that gives it power, helping children to bridge what is in the story and their own lives (Dickinson & Smith, 1994; Snow, Tabors, Nicholson, & Kurland, 1995). Snow (1991) has described these types of conversations as "decontextualized language" in which teachers may in-

duce higher level thinking by moving experiences in stories from what the children may see in front of them to what they can imagine.

A central goal during these preschool years is to enhance children's *exposure to and concepts about print* (Clay, 1979, 1991; Holdaway, 1979; Stanovich & West, 1989; Teale, 1984). Some teachers use Big Books to help children distinguish many print features, including the fact that print (rather than pictures) carries the meaning of the story that the strings of letters between spaces are words and in print correspond to an oral version, and that reading progresses from left to right and top to bottom. In the course of reading stories, teachers may demonstrate these features by pointing to individual words, directing children's attention to where to begin reading, and helping children to recognize letter shape and sounds. Some researchers (Adams, 1990; Roberts, in press) have suggested that the key to these critical concepts, such as developing word awareness, may lie in these demonstrations of how print works.

Children also need opportunity to practice what they've learned about print with their peers and on their own. Studies suggest that the physical arrangement of the classroom can promote time with books (Morrow & Weinstein, 1986; Neuman & Roskos, 1997). A key area is the classroom library—a collection of attractive stories and informational books—that provides children with immediate access to books. Regular visits to the school or public library and library card registration ensure that children's collections remain continually updated and may help children develop the habit of reading as lifelong learning. In comfortable library settings children often will pretend to read, using visual cues to remember the words of their favorite stories. Although studies have shown that these pretend readings are just that (Ehri & Sweet, 1991), such visual readings may demonstrate substantial knowledge about the global features of reading and its purposes.

Storybooks are not the only means of providing children with exposure to written language. Children learn a lot about reading from the labels, signs, and other kinds of print they see around them (McGee, Lomax, & Head, 1988; Neuman & Roskos, 1993). Highly visible print labels on objects, signs, and bulletin boards in classrooms demonstrate the practical uses of written language. In environments rich with print, children incorporate literacy into their dramatic play (Morrow, 1990;

Neuman & Roskos, 1997; Vukelich, 1994), using these communication tools to enhance the drama and realism of the pretend situation. These everyday, playful experiences by themselves do not make most children readers. Rather, they expose children to a variety of print experiences and the processes of reading for real purposes.

For children whose primary language is other than English, studies have shown that a strong basis in a first language promotes school achievement in a second language (Cummins, 1979). Children who are *learning English as a second language* are more likely to become readers and writers of English when they are already familiar with the vocabulary and concepts in their primary language. In this respect, oral and written language experiences should be regarded as an additive process, ensuring that children are able to maintain their home language while also learning to speak and read English (Wong Fillmore, 1991). Including non-English materials and resources to the extent possible can help to support children's first language while children acquire oral proficiency in English.

A fundamental insight developed in children's early years through instruction is the *alphabetic principle*, the understanding that there is a systematic relationship between letters and sounds (Adams, 1990). The research of Gibson and Levin (1975) indicates that the shapes of letters are learned by distinguishing one character from another by its type of spatial features. Teachers will often involve children in comparing letter shapes, helping them to differentiate a number of letters visually. Alphabet books and alphabet puzzles in which children can see and compare letters may be a key to efficient and easy learning.

At the same time children learn about the sounds of language through exposure to *linguistic awareness* games, nursery rhymes, and rhythmic activities. Some research suggests that the roots of phonemic awareness, a powerful predictor of later reading success, are found in traditional rhyming, skipping, and word games (Bryant, MacLean, Bradley, & Crossland, 1990). In one study, for example (MacLean, Bryant, & Bradley, 1987), researchers found that 3-year-old children's knowledge of nursery rhymes specifically related to their more abstract phonological knowledge later on. Engaging children in choral readings of rhymes and rhythms allows them to associate the symbols with the sounds they hear in these words.

Although children's facility in *phonemic awareness* has been shown to be strongly related to later reading achievement, the precise role it plays in these early years is not fully understood. Phonemic awareness refers to a child's understanding and conscious awareness that speech is composed of identifiable units, such as spoken words, syllables, and sounds. Training studies have demonstrated that phonemic awareness can be taught to children as young as age 5 (Bradley & Bryant, 1983; Bryne & Fielding-Barnsley, 1991; Cunningham, 1990; Lundberg, Frost, & Petersen, 1988). These studies used tiles (boxes) (Elkonin, 1973) and linguistic games to engage children in explicitly manipulating speech segments at the phoneme level. Yet, whether such training is appropriate for younger children is highly suspect. Other scholars find that children benefit most from such training only after they have learned some letter names, shapes, and sounds and can apply what they learn to real reading in meaningful contexts (Cunningham, 1990; Foorman, Novy, Francis, & Liberman, 1991). Even at this later age, however, many children acquire phonemic awareness skills without specific training but as a consequence of learning to read (Ehri, 1994; Wagner & Torgesen, 1987). In the preschool years sensitizing children to sound similarities does not seem to be strongly dependent on formal training but rather from listening to patterned, predictable texts while enjoying the feel of reading and language.

Children acquire a working knowledge of the alphabetic system not only through reading but also through writing. A classic study by Read (1971) found that even without formal spelling instruction, preschoolers use their tacit knowledge or phonological relations to spell words. *Invented spelling* (or phonic spelling) refers to beginners' use of the symbols they associate with the sounds they hear in the words they wish to write. For example, a child may initially write *b* or *bk* for the word *bike*, to be followed by more conventionalized forms later on.

Some educators may wonder whether invented spelling promotes poor spelling habits. To the contrary, studies suggest that *temporary* invented spelling may contribute to beginning reading (Chomsky, 1979; Clarke, 1988). One study, for example, found that children benefited from using invented spelling compared to having the teacher provide correct spellings in writing (Clarke, 1988). Although children's invented spellings did not comply with cor-

Continuum of children's development in early reading and writing

Note: *This list is intended to be illustrative, not exhaustive. Children at any grade level will function at a variety of phases along the reading/writing continuum.*

Phase 1: Awareness and exploration (goals for preschool)

Children explore their environment and build the foundations for learning to read and write.

Children can

- enjoy listening to and discussing storybooks
- understand that print carries a message
- engage in reading and writing attempts
- identify labels and signs in their environment
- participate in rhyming games
- identify some letters and make some letter-sound matches
- use known letters or approximations of letters to represent written language (especially meaningful words like their name and phrases such as "I love you")

What teachers do

- share books with children, including Big Books, and model reading behaviors
- talk about letters by name and sounds
- establish a literacy-rich environment
- reread favorite stories
- engage children in language games
- promote literacy-related play activities
- encourage children to experiment with writing

What parents and family members can do

- talk with children, engage them in conversation, give names of things, show interest in what a child says
- read and reread stories with predictable texts to children
- encourage children to recount experiences and describe ideas and events that are important to them
- visit the library regularly
- provide opportunities for children to draw and print, using markers, crayons, and pencils.

Phase 2: Experimental reading and writing (goals for kindergarten)

Children develop basic concepts of print and begin to engage in and experiment with reading and writing.

Kindergartners can

- enjoy being read to and themselves retell simple narrative stories or informational texts
- use descriptive language to explain and explore
- recognize letters and letter-sound matches
- show familiarity with rhyming and beginning sounds
- understand left-to-right and top-to-bottom orientation and familiar concepts of print
- match spoken words with written ones
- begin to write letters of the alphabet and some high-frequency words

What teachers do

- encourage children to talk about reading and writing experiences
- provide many opportunities for children to explore and identify sound-symbol relationships in meaningful contexts
- help children to segment spoken words into individual sounds and blend the sounds into whole words (for example, by slowly writing a word and saying its sound)
- frequently read interesting and conceptually rich stories to children
- provide daily opportunities for children to write
- help children build a sight vocabulary
- create a literacy-rich environment for children to engage independently in reading and writing

What parents and family members can do

- daily read and reread narrative and informational stories to children
- encourage children's attempts at reading and writing
- allow children to participate in activities that involve writing and reading (for example, cooking, making grocery lists)
- play games that involve specific directions (such as "Simon Says")
- have conversations with children during mealtimes and throughout the day

Phase 3: Early reading and writing (goals for first grade)

Children begin to read simple stories and can write about a topic that is meaningful to them.

First graders can

- read and retell familiar stories

(continued)

- use strategies (rereading, predicting, questioning, contextualizing) when comprehension breaks down
- use reading and writing for various purposes on their own initiative
- orally read with reasonable fluency
- use letter-sound associations, word parts, and context to identify new words
- identify an increasing number [of] words by sight
- sound out and represent all substantial sounds in spelling a word
- write about topics that are personally meaningful
- attempt to use some punctuation and capitalization

What teachers do

- support the development of vocabulary by reading daily to the children, transcribing their language, and selecting materials that expand children's knowledge and language development
- model strategies and provide practice for identifying unknown words
- give children opportunities for independent reading and writing practice
- read, write, and discuss a range of different text types (poems, informational books)
- introduce new words and teach strategies for learning to spell new words
- demonstrate and model strategies to use when comprehension breaks down
- help children build lists of commonly used words from their writing

What parents and family members can do

- talk about favorite storybooks
- read to children and encourage them to read to you
- suggest that children write to friends and relatives
- bring to a parent-teacher conference evidence of what your child can do in writing and reading
- encourage children to share what they have learned about their writing and reading

Phase 4: Transitional reading and writing (goals for second grade)

Children begin to read more fluently and write various text forms using simple and more complex sentences.

Second graders can

- read with greater fluency
- use strategies more efficiently (rereading, questioning, and so on) when comprehension breaks down

- use word identification strategies with greater facility to unlock unknown words
- identify an increasing number of words by sight
- write about a range of topics to suit different audiences
- use common letter patterns and critical features to spell words
- punctuate simple sentences correctly and proofread their own work
- spend time reading daily and use reading to research topics

What teachers do

- create a climate that fosters analytic, evaluative, and reflective thinking
- teach children to write in multiple forms (stories, information, poems)
- ensure that children read a range of texts for a variety of purposes
- teach revising, editing, and proofreading skills
- teach strategies for spelling new and difficult words
- model enjoyment of reading

What parents and family members can do

- continue to read to children and encourage them to read to you
- engage children in activities that require reading and writing
- become involved in school activities
- show children your interest in their learning by displaying their written work
- visit the library regularly
- support your child's specific hobby or interest with reading materials and references

Phase 5: Independent and productive reading and writing (goals for third grade)

Children continue to extend and refine their reading and writing to suit varying purposes and audiences.

Third graders can

- read fluently and enjoy reading
- use a range of strategies when drawing meaning from the text
- use word identification strategies appropriately and automatically when encountering unknown words
- recognize and discuss elements of different text structures
- make critical connections between texts
- write expressively in many different forms (stories, poems, reports)
- use a rich variety of vocabulary and sentences appropriate to text forms

(continued)

- revise and edit their own writing during and after composing
- spell words correctly in final writing drafts

What teachers do

- provide opportunities daily for children to read, examine, and critically evaluate narrative and expository texts
- continue to create a climate that fosters critical reading and personal response
- teach children to examine ideas in texts
- encourage children to use writing as a tool for thinking and learning
- extend children's knowledge of the correct use of writing conventions
- emphasize the importance of correct spelling in finished written products

- create a climate that engages all children as a community of literacy learners

What parents and family members can do

- continue to support children's learning and interest by visiting the library and bookstores with them
- find ways to highlight children's progress in reading and writing
- stay in regular contact with your child's teachers about activities and progress in reading and writing
- encourage children to use and enjoy print for many purposes (such as recipes, directions, games, and sports)
- build a love of language in all its forms and engage children in conversation

rect spellings, the process encouraged them to think actively about letter-sound relations. As children engage in writing, they are learning to segment the words they wish to spell into constituent sounds.

Classrooms that provide children with regular opportunities to express themselves on paper, without feeling too constrained for correct spelling and proper handwriting, also help children understand that writing has real purpose (Dyson, 1988; Graves, 1983; Sulzby, 1985). Teachers can organize situations that both demonstrate the writing process and get children actively involved in it. Some teachers serve as scribes and help children write down their ideas, keeping in mind the balance between children doing it themselves and asking for help. In the beginning these products likely emphasize pictures with few attempts at writing letters or words. With encouragement, children begin to label their pictures, tell stories, and attempt to write stories about the pictures they have drawn. Such novice writing activity sends the important message that writing is not just handwriting practice—children are using their own words to compose a message to communicate with others.

Thus the picture that emerges from research in these first years of children's reading and writing is one that emphasizes wide exposure to print and to developing concepts about its forms and functions. Classrooms filled with print, language and literacy play, storybook reading, and writing allow children to experience the joy and power associated with reading and writing while mastering basic concepts about print that research has shown are strong predictors of achievement.

In kindergarten

Knowledge of the forms and functions of print serves as a foundation from which children become increasingly sensitive to letter shapes, names, sounds, and words. However, not all children typically come to kindergarten with similar levels of knowledge about printed language. Estimating where each child is developmentally and building on that base, a key feature of all good teaching, is particularly important for the kindergarten teacher. Instruction will need to be adapted to account for children's differences. For those children with lots of print experiences, instruction will extend their knowledge as they learn more about the formal features of letters and their sound correspondences. For other children with fewer prior experiences, initiating them to the alphabetic principle, that the alphabet comprises a limited set of letters and that these letters stand for the sounds that make up spoken words, will require more focused and direct instruction. In all cases, however, children need to interact with a rich variety of print (Morrow, Strickland, & Woo, 1998).

In this critical year kindergarten teachers need to capitalize on every opportunity for enhancing children's *vocabulary development*. One approach is through listening to stories (Elley, 1989; Feitelson, Kita, & Goldstein,

1986). Children need to be exposed to vocabulary from a wide variety of genres, including informational texts as well as narratives. The learning of vocabulary, however, is not necessarily simply a byproduct of reading stories (Leung & Pikulski, 1990). Some explanation of vocabulary words prior to listening to a story is related significantly to children's learning of new words (Elley, 1989). Dickinson and Smith (1994), for example, found that asking predictive and analytic questions before and after the readings produced positive effects on vocabulary and comprehension.

Repeated readings appear to further reinforce the language of the text as well as to familiarize children with the way different genres are structured (Eller, Pappas, & Brown, 1988; Morrow, 1988). Understanding the forms of informational and narrative texts seems to distinguish those children who have been well read to from those who have not (Pappas, 1991). In one study, for example, Pappas found that with multiple exposures to a story (three readings), children's retelling became increasing rich, integrating what they knew about the world, the language of the book, and the message of the author. Thus, considering the benefits for vocabulary development and comprehension, the case is strong for interactive storybook reading (Anderson, 1995). Increasing the volume of children's playful, stimulating experiences with good books is associated with accelerated growth in reading competence.

Activities that help children clarify the *concept of word* are also worthy of time and attention in the kindergarten curriculum (Juel, 1991). Language experience charts that let teachers demonstrate how talk can be written down provide a natural medium for children's developing word awareness in meaningful contexts. Transposing children's spoken words into written symbols through dictation provides a concrete demonstration that strings of letters between spaces are words and that not all words are the same length. Studies by Clay (1979) and Bissex (1980) confirm the value of what many teachers have known and done for years: Teacher dictations of children's stories help develop word awareness, spelling, and the conventions of written language.

Many children enter kindergarten with at least some perfunctory knowledge of the alphabet letters. An important goal for the kindergarten teacher is to reinforce this skill by ensuring that children can recognize and discriminate these letter shapes with increasing ease and fluency (Mason, 1980; Snow, Burns, & Griffin, 1998). Children's proficiency in *letter naming* is a well-established predictor of their end-of-year achievement (Bond & Dykstra, 1967; Riley, 1996), probably because it mediates the ability to remember sounds. Generally a good rule according to current learning theory (Adams, 1990) is to start with the more easily visualized uppercase letters, to be followed by identifying lowercase letters. In each case, introducing just a few letters at a time, rather than many, enhances mastery.

At about the time children are readily able to identify letter names, they begin to connect the letters with the sounds they hear. A fundamental insight in this phase of learning is that a letter and letter sequences map onto phonological forms. Phonemic awareness, however, is not merely a solitary insight or an instant ability (Juel, 1991). It takes time and practice.

Children who are phonemically aware can think about and manipulate sounds in words. They know when words rhyme or do not; they know when words begin or end with the same sound; and they know that a word like *bat* is composed of three sounds /b/ /a/ /t/ and that these sounds can be blended into a spoken word. Popular rhyming books, for example, may draw children's attention to rhyming patterns, serving as a basis for extending vocabulary (Ehri & Robbins, 1992). Using initial letter cues, children can learn many new words through analogy, taking the familiar word *bake* as a strategy for figuring out a new word, *lake*.

Further, as teachers engage children in shared writing, they can pause before writing a word, say it slowly, and stretch out the sounds as they write it. Such activities in the context of real reading and writing help children attend to the features of print and the alphabetic nature of English.

There is accumulated evidence that instructing children in phonemic awareness activities in kindergarten (and first grade) enhances reading achievement (Bryne & Fielding-Barnsley, 1991, 1993, 1995; Lundberg, Frost, & Petersen, 1988; Stanovich, 1986). Although a large number of children will acquire phonemic awareness skills as they learn to read, an estimated 20% will not without additional training. A statement by the IRA (1998) indicates that "the likelihood of these students becoming successful as readers is slim to none. . . . This figure [20%], however, can be substantially reduced through more systematic attention to engagement with language early on in the child's home, preschool and kindergarten classes." A study by Hanson and Farrell (1995), for example, examined the long-term benefits of a carefully developed kindergarten curriculum that focused on word study and decoding skills, along with sets of stories so that children would be able to practice these skills in meaningful contexts. High school seniors who early on had received this type of instruction outperformed their counterparts on reading achievement, attitude toward schooling, grades, and attendance.

In kindergarten many children will begin to read some words through recognition or by processing letter-sound relations. Studies by Domico (1993) and Richgels (1995) suggest that children's ability to read words is tied to their ability to write words in a somewhat reciprocal relationship. The more opportunities children have to write, the greater the likelihood that they will reproduce spellings of words they have seen and heard. Though not conventional, these spellings likely show greater letter-sound correspondences and partial encoding of some parts of words, like *SWM* for *swim*, than do the inventions of preschoolers (Clay, 1975).

To provide more intensive and extensive practice, some teachers try to integrate writing in other areas of the curriculum like literacy-related play (Neuman & Roskos, 1992), and other project activities (Katz & Chard, 1989). These types of projects engage children in using reading and writing for multiple purposes while they are learning about topics meaningful to them.

Early literacy activities teach children a great deal about writing and reading but often in ways that do not look much like traditional elementary school instruction. Capitalizing on the active and social nature of children's learning, early instruction must provide rich demonstrations, interactions, and models of literacy in the course of activities that make sense to young children. Children must also learn about the relation between oral and written language and the relation between letters, sounds, and words. In classrooms built around a wide variety of print activities, and in talking, reading, writing, playing, and listening to one another, children will want to read and write and feel capable that they can do so.

The primary grades

Instruction takes on a more formal nature as children move into the elementary grades. Here it is virtually certain that children will receive at least some instruction from a commercially published product, like a basal or literature anthology series.

Although research has clearly established that no one method is superior for all children (Bond & Dykstra, 1967; Snow, Burns, & Griffin, 1998), approaches that favor some type of *systematic code instruction along with meaningful connected reading* report children's superior progress in reading. Instruction should aim to teach the important letter-sound relationships, which once learned are practiced through having many opportunities to read. Most likely these research findings are a positive result of the Matthew Effect, the rich-get-richer effects that are embedded in such instruction; that is, children who acquire alphabetic coding skills begin to recognize many words (Stanovich, 1986). As word recognition processes become more automatic, children are likely to allocate more attention to higher level processes of comprehension. Since these reading experiences tend to be rewarding for children, they may read more often; thus reading achievement may be a byproduct of reading enjoyment.

One of the hallmarks of skilled reading is *fluent, accurate word identification* (Juel, Griffith, & Gough, 1986). Yet instruction in simply word calling with flashcards is not reading. Real reading is comprehension. Children need to read a wide variety of interesting, comprehensible materials, which they can read orally with about 90 to 95% accuracy (Durrell & Catterson, 1980). In the beginning children are likely to read slowly and deliberately as they focus on exactly what's on the page. In fact they may seem "glued to print" (Chall, 1983), figuring out the fine points of form at the word level. However, children's reading expression, fluency, and comprehension generally improve when they read familiar texts. Some authorities have found the practice of repeated rereadings in which children reread short selections significantly enhances their confidence, fluency, and comprehension in reading (Moyer, 1982; Samuels, 1979).

Children not only use their increasing knowledge of letter-sound patterns to read unfamiliar texts. They also use a variety of strategies. Studies reveal that early readers are capable of being intentional in their use of *metacognitive strategies* (Brown & DeLoache, 1978; Rowe, 1994). Even in these early grades, children makes predictions about what they are to read, self-correct, reread, and question if necessary, giving evidence that they are able to adjust their reading when understanding breaks down. Teacher practices, such as the Directed Reading-Thinking Activity (DRTA), effectively model these strategies by helping children set purposes for reading, ask questions, and summarize ideas through the text (Stauffer, 1970).

But children also need time for *independent practice.* These activities may take on numerous forms. Some research, for example, has demonstrated the powerful effects that children's reading to their caregivers has on promoting confidence as well as reading proficiency (Hannon, 1995). Visiting the library and scheduling independent reading and writing periods in literacy-rich classrooms also provide children with opportunities to select books of their own choosing. They may engage in the social activities of reading with their peers, asking questions, and writing stories (Morrow & Weinstein, 1986), all of which may nurture interest and appreciation for reading and writing.

Supportive relationships between these communication processes lead many teachers to *integrate reading and writing* in classroom instruction (Tierney & Shanahan, 1991). After all, writing challenges children to actively think about print. As young authors struggle to express themselves, they come to grips with different written forms, syntactic patterns, and themes. They use writing for multiple purposes: to write descriptions, lists, and stories to communicate with others. It is important for teachers to expose children to a range of text forms, including stories, reports, and informational texts, and to help children select vocabulary and punctuate simple sentences that meet the demands of audience and purpose. Since handwriting instruction helps children communicate effectively, it should also be part of the writing process (McGee & Richgels, 1996). Short lessons demonstrating certain letter formations tied to the publication of writing provide an ideal time for instruction. Reading and writing workshops, in which teachers provide small-group and individual instruction, may help children to develop the skills they need for communicating with others.

Although children's initial writing drafts will contain invented spellings, learning about spelling will take on increasing importance in these years (Henderson & Beers, 1980; Richgels, 1986). *Spelling instruction* should be an important component of the reading and writing program since it directly affects reading ability. Some teachers create their own spelling lists, focusing on words with common patterns and high-frequency words, as well as some personally meaningful words from the children's writing. Research indicates that seeing a word in print, imagining how it is spelled, and copying new words is an effective way of acquiring spellings (Barron, 1980). Nevertheless, even though the teacher's goal is to foster more conventionalized forms, it is important to recognize that there is more to writing than just spelling and grammatically correct sentences. Rather, writing has been characterized by Applebee (1977) as "thinking with a pencil." It is true that children will need adult help to master the complexities of the writing process. But they also will need to learn that the power of writing is expressing one's own ideas in ways that can be understood by others.

As children's capabilities develop and become more fluent, instruction will turn from a central focus on helping children learn to read and write to helping them read and write to learn. Increasingly the emphasis for teachers will be on encouraging children to become *independent and productive readers*, helping them to extend their reasoning and comprehension abilities in learning about their world. Teachers will need to provide challenging materials that require children to analyze and think creatively and from different points of view. They also will need to ensure that children have practice in reading and writing (both in and out of school) and many opportunities to analyze topics, generate questions, and organize written responses for different purposes in meaningful activities.

Throughout these critical years *accurate assessment* of children's knowledge, skills, and dispositions in reading and writing will help teachers better match instruction with how and what children are learning. However, early reading and writing cannot simply be measured as a set of narrowly defined skills on standardized tests. These measures often are not reliable or valid indicators of what children can do in typical practice, nor are they sensitive to language variation, culture, or the experiences of young children (Johnston, 1997; Shepard, 1994; Shepard & Smith, 1988). Rather, a sound assessment should be anchored in real-life writing and reading tasks and continuously chronicle a wide range of children's literacy activities in different situations. Good assessment is essential to help teachers tailor appropriate instruction to young children and to know when and how much intensive instruction on any particular skill or strategy might be needed.

By the end of the third grade, children will still have much to learn about literacy. Clearly some will be further along the path to independent reading and writing than others. Yet with high-quality instruction, the majority of children will be able to decode words with a fair degree of facility, use a variety of strategies to adapt to different types of text, and be able to communicate effectively for multiple purposes using conventionalized spelling and punctuation. Most of all they will have come to see themselves as capable readers and writers, having mastered the complex set of attitudes, expectations, behaviors, and skills related to written language.

Statement of position

IRA and NAEYC believe that achieving high standards of literacy for every child in the U.S. is a shared responsibility of schools, early childhood programs, families, and communities. But teachers of young children, whether employed in preschools, child care programs, or elementary schools, have a unique responsibility to promote children's literacy development, based on the most current professional knowledge and research.

A review of research along with the collective wisdom and experience of members has led IRA and NAEYC to conclude that learning to read and write is a complex, multifaceted process that requires a wide variety of instructional approaches, a conclusion similar to that reached by an esteemed panel of experts for the National Academy of Sciences (Snow, Burns, & Griffin, 1998).

Similarly, this review of research leads to a theoretical model of literacy learning and development as an interactive process. Research supports the view of the child as an active constructor of his or her own learning, while at the same time studies emphasize the critical role of the supportive, interested, engaged adult (e.g., teacher, parent, or tutor) who provides scaffolding for the child's development of greater skill and understanding (Mason & Sinha, 1993; Riley, 1996). The principle of learning is that "children are active learners, drawing on direct social and physical experience as well as culturally transmitted knowledge to construct their own understanding of the world around them" (Bredekamp & Copple, 1997, p. 13).

IRA and NAEYC believe that goals and expectations for young children's achievement in reading and writing should be developmentally appropriate, that is, *challenging but achievable*, with sufficient adult support. A continuum of reading and writing development is generally accepted and useful for teachers in understanding the goals of literacy instruction and in assessing children's progress toward those goals. (An abbreviated continuum of reading and writing development appears on pp. 200–201; for more detailed examples, see Chall, 1983; Education Department of Western Australia, 1994; Snow, Burns, & Griffin, 1998; Whitmore & Goodman, 1995.) Good teachers understand that children do not progress along this developmental continuum in rigid sequence. Rather, each child exhibits a unique pattern and timing in acquiring skills and understanding related to reading and writing.

Like other complex skills, reading and writing are outcomes that result from the continual interplay of development and learning, and therefore a range of individual variation is to be expected in the rate and pace at which children gain literacy skills. Given exposure to appropriate literacy experiences and good teaching during early childhood, most children learn to read at age 6 or 7, a few learn at 4, some learn at 5, and others need intensive individualized support to learn to read at 8 or 9. Some children who do not explore books and other print during their early years are likely to need more focused support for literacy development when they enter an educational program, whether at preschool, kindergarten, or first grade (since preschool and even kindergarten attendance is not universal). Other children who enter school speaking little or no English are likely to need instructional strategies in their home language (Snow, Burns, & Griffin, 1998).

Given the range within which children typically master reading, even with exposure to print-rich environments and good teaching, a developmentally appropriate expectation is for most children to achieve beginning conventional reading (also called early reading) by age 7. For children with disabilities or special learning needs, achievable but challenging goals for their individual reading and writing development in an inclusive environment are established by teachers, families, and specialists working in collaboration (Division for Early Childhood Task Force on Recommended Practices, 1993; Division for Early Childhood of the Council for Exceptional Children, 1994).

IRA and NAEYC believe that early childhood teachers need to understand the developmental continuum of reading and writing and be skilled in a variety of strategies to assess and support individual children's development and learning across the continuum. At the same time teachers must set developmentally appropriate literacy goals for young children and then adapt instructional strategies for children whose learning and development are advanced or lag behind those goals. Good teachers make instructional decisions based on their knowledge of reading and writing, current research, appropriate expectations, and their knowledge of individual children's strengths and needs.

A continuum of reading and writing development is useful for identifying challenging but achievable goals or benchmarks for children's literacy learning, remembering that individual variation is to be expected and supported. Using a developmental continuum enables teachers to assess individual children's progress against realistic goals and then adapt instruction to ensure that children continue to progress. During the preschool years most children can be expected to function in phase 1 of the developmental continuum, Awareness and Exploration. In kindergarten an appropriate expectation is that most children will be at phase 2, Experimental Reading and Writing. By the end of first grade, most children will function in phase 3, Early Reading and Writing. An appropriate expectation for second grade is Transitional Reading and Writing (phase 4), while the goal for third grade is Independent and Productive Reading and Writing (phase 5). Advanced Reading is the goal for fourth grade and above.

As fundamental as the principle of individual variation is the principle that human development and learning occur in and are influenced by social and cultural contexts. Language, reading, and writing are strongly shaped by culture. Children enter early childhood programs or schools having learned to communicate and make sense of their experiences at home and in their communities. When the ways of making and communicating meaning are similar at home and in school, children's transitions are eased. However, when the language and culture of the home and school are not congruent, teachers and parents must work together to help children strengthen and preserve their home language and culture while acquiring skills needed to participate in the shared culture of the school (NAEYC, 1996a).

Most important, teachers must understand how children learn a second language and how this process applies to young children's literacy development. Teachers need to respect the child's home language and culture and use it as a base on which to build and extend children's language and literacy experiences. Unfortunately teachers too often react negatively to children's linguistic and cultural diversity, equating difference with deficit. Such situations hurt children whose abilities within their own cultural context are not recognized because they do not match the cultural expectations of the school. Failing to recognize children's strengths or capabilities, teachers may underestimate their competence. Competence is not tied to any particular language, dialect, or culture. Teachers should never use a child's dialect, language, or culture as a basis for making judgments about the child's intellect or capability. Linguistically and culturally diverse children bring multiple perspectives and impressive skills, such as code-switching (the ability to go back and forth between two languages to deepen conceptual understanding), to the tasks of learning to speak, read, and write a second language. These self-motivated, self-initiating, constructive thinking processes should be celebrated and used as rich teaching and learning resources for all children.

Recommended teaching practices

During the infant and toddler years. Children need relationships with caring adults who engage in many one-on-one, face-to-face interactions with them to support their oral language development and lay the foundation for later literacy learning. Important experiences and teaching behaviors include but are not limited to

• talking to babies and toddlers with simple language, frequent eye contact, and responsiveness to children's cues and language attempts;

• frequently playing with, talking to, singing to, and doing fingerplays with very young children;

- sharing cardboard books with babies and frequently reading to toddlers on the adult's lap or together with one or two other children; and

- providing simple art materials such as crayons, markers, and large paper for toddlers to explore and manipulate.

During the preschool years. Young children need developmentally appropriate experiences and teaching to support literacy learning. These include but are not limited to

- positive, nurturing relationships with adults who engage in responsive conversations with individual children, model reading and writing behavior, and foster children's interest in and enjoyment of reading and writing;

- print-rich environments that provide opportunities and tools for children to see and use written language for a variety of purposes, with teachers' drawing children's attention to specific letters and words;

- adults' daily reading of high-quality books to individual children or small groups, including books that positively reflect children's identity, home language, and culture;

- opportunities for children to talk about what is read and to focus on the sounds and parts of language as well as the meaning;

- teaching strategies and experiences that develop phonemic awareness, such as songs, fingerplays, games, poems, and stories in which phonemic patterns such as rhyme and alliteration are salient;

- opportunities to engage in play that incorporates literacy tools, such as writing grocery lists in dramatic play, making signs in block building, and using icons and words in exploring a computer game; and

- firsthand experiences that expand children's vocabulary, such as trips in the community and exposure to various tools, objects and materials.

In kindergarten and primary grades. Teachers should continue many of these same good practices with the goal of continually advancing children's learning and development (see the continuum of children's development in early reading and writing for appropriate grade-level expectations). In addition every child is entitled to excellent instruction in reading and writing that includes but is not limited to

- daily experiences of being read to and independently reading meaningful and engaging stories and informational texts;

- a balanced instructional program that includes systematic code instruction along with meaningful reading and writing activities;

- daily opportunities and teacher support to write many kinds of texts for different purposes, including stories, lists, messages to others, poems, reports, and responses to literature;

- writing experiences that allow the flexibility to use nonconventional forms of writing at first (invented or phonic spelling) and over time move to conventional forms;

- opportunities to work in small groups for focused instruction and collaboration with other children;

- an intellectually engaging and challenging curriculum that expands knowledge of the world and vocabulary; and

- adaptation of instructional strategies or more individualized instruction if the child fails to make expected progress in reading or when literacy skills are advanced.

Although experiences during the earliest years of life can have powerful long-term consequences, human beings are amazingly resilient and incredibly capable of learning throughout life. We should strengthen our resolve to ensure that every child has the benefit of positive early childhood experiences that support literacy development. At the same time, regardless of children's prior learning, schools have the responsibility to educate every child and to never give up even if later interventions must be more intensive and costly.

Recommended policies essential for achieving developmentally appropriate literacy experiences

Early childhood programs and elementary schools in the U.S. operate in widely differing contexts with varying levels of funding and resources. Regardless of the resources available, professionals have an ethical responsibility to teach, to the best of their ability, according to the standards of the profession. Nevertheless the kinds of practices advocated here are more likely to be implemented within an infrastructure of supportive policies and resources. IRA and NAEYC strongly recommend that the following policies be developed and adequately funded at the appropriate state or local levels:

1. A comprehensive, consistent system of early childhood professional preparation and ongoing professional development (see Darling-Hammond, 1997; Kagan & Cohen, 1997). Such a professional preparation system is badly needed in every state to ensure that

staff in early childhood programs and teachers in primary schools obtain specialized, college-level education that informs them about developmental patterns in early literacy learning and about research-based ways of teaching reading and writing during the early childhood years. Ongoing professional development is essential for teachers to stay current in an ever-expanding research base and to continually improve their teaching skills and the learning outcomes for children.

2. Sufficient resources to ensure adequate ratios of qualified teachers to children and small groups for individualizing instruction.

For 4- and 5-year-olds, adult-child ratios should be one adult for no more than 8 to 10 children, with a maximum group size of 20 (Cost, Quality, and Child Outcomes Study Team 1995; Howes, Phillips, & Whitebook, 1992). Optimum class size in the early grades is 15 to 18 with one teacher (Nye, Boyd-Zaharias, & Fulton, 1994; Nye, Boyd-Zaharis, Fulton, & Wallenhurst, 1992). Young children benefit most from being taught in small groups or as individuals. There will always be a wide range of individual differences among children. Small class size increases the likelihood that teachers will be able to accommodate children's diverse abilities and interests, strengths and needs.

3. Sufficient resources to ensure classroom, school, and public libraries that include a wide range of high-quality children's books, computer software, and multimedia resources at various levels of difficulty and reflecting various cultural and family backgrounds.

Studies have found that a minimum of five books per child is necessary to provide even the most basic print-rich environment (Neuman, in press-b). Computers and developmentally appropriate software should also be available to provide alternative, engaging, enriching literacy experiences (NAEYC, 1996b).

4. Policies that promote children's continuous learning progress.

When individual children do not make expected progress in literacy development, resources should be available to provide more individualized instruction, focused time, tutoring by trained and qualified tutors, or other individualized intervention strategies. These instructional strategies are used to accelerate children's learning instead of either grade retention or social promotion, neither of which has been proven effective in improving children's achievement (Shepard & Smith, 1988).

5. Appropriate assessment strategies that promote children's learning and development.

Teachers need to regularly and systematically use multiple indicators—observation of children's oral language, evaluation of children's work, and performance at authentic reading and writing tasks—to assess and monitor children's progress in reading and writing development, plan and adapt instruction, and communicate with parents (Shepard, Kagan, & Wurtz, 1998). Group-administered, multiple-choice standardized achievement tests in reading and writing skills should not be used before third grade or preferably even before fourth grade. The younger the child, the more difficult it is to obtain valid and reliable indices of his or her development and learning using one-time test administrations. Standardized testing has a legitimate function, but on its own it tends to lead to standardized teaching—one approach fits all—the opposite of the kind of individualized diagnosis and teaching that is needed to help young children continue to progress in reading and writing.

6. Access to regular, ongoing health care for every child.

Every young child needs to have a regular health care provider as well as screening for early diagnosis and treatment of vision and hearing problems. Chronic untreated middle-ear infections in the earliest years of life may delay language development, which in turn may delay reading development (Vernon-Feagans, Emanuel, & Blood, 1992). Similarly, vision problems should never be allowed to go uncorrected, causing a child difficulty with reading and writing.

7. Increased public investment to ensure access to high-quality preschool and child care programs for all children who need them.

The National Academy of Sciences (Snow, Burns, & Griffin, 1998) and decades of longitudinal research (see, for example, Barnett, 1995) demonstrate the benefits of preschool education for literacy learning. Unfortunately, these is no system to ensure accessible, affordable, high-quality early childhood education programs for all families who choose to use them (Kagan & Cohen, 1997). As a result, preschool attendance varies considerably by family income; for example, 80% of 4-year-olds whose families earn more than US$50,000 per year attend preschool compared to approximately 50% of 4-year-olds attending preschool from families earning less than $20,000 (National Center for Education Statistics, 1996). In addition, due primarily to inadequate funding, the quality of preschool and child care programs varies considerably, with studies finding that the majority of programs provide only mediocre quality and that only about 15% rate as good quality (Cost, Quality, & Child Outcomes Study Team, 1995; Galinsky, Howes, Kontos, & Shinn, 1994; Layzer, Goodson, & Moss 1993).

Conclusion

Collaboration between IRA and NAEYC is symbolic of the coming together of the two essential bodies of knowledge necessary to support literacy development of young children: knowledge about the processes of reading and writing and knowledge of child development and learning. Developmentally appropriate practices (Bredekamp & Copple, 1997) in reading and writing are ways of teaching that consider

1. what is generally known about children's development and learning to set achievable but challenging goals for literacy learning and to plan learning experiences and teaching strategies that vary with the age and experience of the learners;

2. results of ongoing assessment of individual children's progress in reading and writing to plan next steps or to adapt instruction when children fail to make expected progress or are at advanced levels; and

3. social and cultural contexts in which children live so as to help them make sense of their learning experiences in relation to what they already know and are able to do.

To teach in developmentally appropriate ways, teachers must understand *both* the continuum of reading and writing development *and* children's individual and cultural variations. Teachers must recognize when variation is within the typical range and when intervention is necessary, because early intervention is more effective and less costly than later remediation.

Learning to read and write is one of the most important and powerful achievements in life. Its value is clearly seen in the faces of young children—the proud, confident smile of the capable reader contrasts sharply with the furrowed brow and sullen frown of the discouraged nonreader. Ensuring that all young children reach their potentials as readers and writers is the shared responsibility of teachers, administrators, families, and communities. Educators have a special responsi-

bility to teach every child and not to blame children, families, or each other when the task is difficult. All responsible adults need to work together to help children become competent readers and writers.

References

Adams, M. (1990). *Beginning to read.* Cambridge, MA: MIT Press.

Anbar, A. (1986). Reading acquisition of preschool children without systematic instruction. *Early Childhood Research Quarterly, 1,* 69–83.

Anderson, R. C. (1995). *Research foundations for wide reading.* Paper presented at invitational conference on the impact of Wide Reading, Center for the Study of Reading, Urbana, IL.

Applebee, A. N. (1977). Long-term effects of early childhood programs on cognitive and school outcomes. *The Future of Children, 5,* 25–50.

Barron, R. W. (1980). Visual and phonological strategies in reading and spelling. In U. Frith (Ed.), *Cognitive processes in spelling* (pp. 339–353). New York: Academic.

Berk, L. (1996). *Infants and children: Prenatal through middle childhood* (2nd ed.). Boston: Allyn & Bacon.

Bissex, G. (1980). *GNYS at work: A child learns to write and read.* Cambridge, MA: Harvard University Press.

Bond, G., & Dykstra, R. (1967). The cooperative research program in first-grade reading instruction. *Reading Research Quarterly, 2,* 5–142.

Bradley, L., & Bryant, P. E. (1983). Categorizing sounds and learning to read—A causal connection. *Nature, 301,* 419–421.

Bredekamp, S., & Copple, C. (Eds.). (1997). *Developmentally appropriate practice in early childhood programs* (Rev. ed.). Washington, DC: NAEYC.

Brown, A. L., & DeLoache, J. S. (1978). Skills, plans and self-regulation. In R. Siegler (Ed.), *Children's thinking: What develops?* (pp. 3–36). Hillsdale, NJ: Erlbaum.

Bryant, P. E., MacLean, M., Bradley, L., & Crossland, J. (1990). Rhyme and alliteration, phoneme detection, and learning to read. *Developmental Psychology, 26,* 429–438.

Bryne, B., & Fielding-Barnsley, R. (1991). Evaluation of a program to teach phonemic awareness to young children. *Journal of Educational Psychology, 83,* 451–455.

Bryne, B., & Fielding-Barnsley, R. (1993). Evaluation of a program to teach phonemic awareness to young children: a 1-year follow-up. *Journal of Educational Psychology, 85,* 104–111.

Bryne, B., & Fielding-Barnsley, R. (1995). Evaluation of a program to teach phonemic awareness to young children: A 2- and 3-year follow-up and a new preschool trial. *Journal of Educational Psychology, 87,* 488–503.

Bus, A., Belsky, J., van IJzendoorn, M. H., & Crnic, K. (1997). Attachment and book-reading patterns: A study of mothers, fathers, and their toddlers. *Early Childhood Research Quarterly, 12,* 81–98.

Bus, A., & Van IJzendoorn, M. (1995). Mothers reading to their 3-year-olds: The role of mother-child attachment security in becoming literate. *Reading Research Quarterly, 30,* 998–1015.

Bus, A., Van IJzendoorn, M., & Pellegrini, A. (1995). Joint book reading makes for success in learning to read: A meta-analysis on intergenerational transmission of literacy. *Review of Educational Research, 65,* 1–21.

Chomsky, C. (1979). Approaching reading through invented spelling. In L. B. Resnick & P. A. Weaver (Eds.), *Theory and practice of early reading* (Vol. 2, pp. 43–65). Hillsdale, NJ: Erlbaum.

Clarke, L. (1988). Invented versus traditional spelling in first graders' writings: Effects on learning to spell and read. *Research in the Teaching of English, 22,* 281–309.

Clay, M. (1975). *What did I write?* Portsmouth, NH: Heinemann.

Clay, M. (1979). *The early detection of reading difficulties.* Portsmouth, NH: Heinemann.

Clay, M. (1991). *Becoming literate.* Portsmouth, NH: Heinemann.

Cost, Quality, and Child Outcomes Study Team. (1995). *Cost, quality, and child outcomes in child care centers* (Public report, 2nd ed.). Denver, CO: Economics Department, University of Colorado.

Cummins, J. (1979). Linguistic interdependence and the educational development of bilingual children. *Review of Educational Research, 49,* 222–251.

Cunningham, A. (1990). Explicit versus implicit instruction in phonemic awareness. *Journal of Experimental Child Psychology, 50,* 429–444.

Darling-Hammond, L. (1997). *Doing what matters most: Investing in quality teaching.* New York: National Commission on Teaching and America's Future.

Division for Early Childhood of the Council for Exceptional Children. (1994). Position on inclusion. *Young Children, 49*(5), 78.

Division for Early Childhood Task Force on Recommended Practices. (1993). *DEC recommended practices: Indicators of quality in programs for infants and young children with special needs and their families.* Reston, VA: Council for Exceptional Children.

Dickinson, D., & Smith, M. (1994). Long-term effects of preschool teachers' book readings on low-income children's vocabulary and story comprehension. *Reading Research Quarterly, 29,* 104–122.

Domico, M. A. (1993). Patterns of development in narrative stories of emergent writers. In C. Kinzer & D. Leu (Eds.), *Examining central issues in literacy research, theory, and practice* (pp. 391–404). Chicago: National Reading Conference.

Durkin, D. (1966). *Children who read early.* New York: Teachers College Press.

Durrell, D. D., & Catterson, J. H. (1980). *Durrell analysis of reading difficulty* (Rev. ed). New York: Psychological Corp.

Dyson, A. H. (1988). Appreciate the drawing and dictating of young children. *Young Children 43*(3), 25–32.

Education Department of Western Australia. (1994). *Reading, writing, spelling, verbal language developmental continuum.* Portsmouth, NH: Heinemann.

Ehri, L. (1994). Development of the ability to read words: Update. In R. Ruddell, M. R. Ruddell, & H. Singer (Eds.), *Theoretical models and processes of reading* (pp. 323–358). Newark, DE: International Reading Association.

Ehri, L. C., & Robbins, C. (1992). Beginners need some decoding skill to read words by analogy. *Reading Research Quarterly, 27,* 13–26.

Ehri, L., & Sweet, J. (1991). Finger-point reading of memorized text: What enables beginners to process the print? *Reading Research Quarterly, 26,* 442–461.

Elkonin, D. B. (1973). USSR. In J. Downing (Ed.), *Comparative reading* (pp. 551–580). New York: Macmillian.

Eller, R., Pappas, C., & Brown, E. (1988). The lexical development of kindergartners: Learning from written context. *Journal of Reading Behavior, 20,* 5–24.

Elley, W. (1989). Vocabulary acquisition from listening to stories. *Reading Research Quarterly, 24,* 174–187.

Feitelson, D., Kita, B., & Goldstein, Z. (1986). Effects of listening to series stories on first graders' comprehension and use of language. *Research in the Teaching of English, 20,* 339–355.

Foorman, B., Novy, D., Francis, D., & Liberman, D. (1991). How letter-sound instruction mediates progress in first-grade reading and spelling. *Journal of Educational Psychology 83,* 456–469.

Galinsky, E., Howes, C., Kontos, S., & Shinn, M. (1994). *The study of children in family child care and relative care: Highlights of findings.* New York: Families and Work Institute.

Gibson, E., & Levin, E. (1975). *The psychology of reading.* Cambridge, MA: MIT Press.

Graves, D. (1983). *Writing: Teachers and children at work.* Portsmouth, NH: Heinemann.

Hannon, P. (1995). *Literacy, home and school.* London: Falmer.

Hanson, R., & Farrell, D. (1995). The long-term effects on high school seniors of learning to read in kindergarten. *Reading Research Quarterly, 30,* 908–933.

Hart, B., & Risley, T. (1995). *Meaningful differences.* Baltimore, MD: Paul Brookes.

Henderson, E. H., & Beers, J. W. (1980). *Developmental and cognitive aspects of learning to spell.* Newark, DE: International Reading Association.

Holdaway, D. (1979). *The foundations of literacy.* Portsmouth, NH: Heinemann.

Howes, C., Phillips, D. A., & Whitebook, M. (1992). Thresholds of quality: Implications for the social development of children in center-based child care. *Child Development, 63,* 449–460.

International Reading Association. (1998). *Phonics in the early reading program: A position statement.* Newark, DE: Author.

Johnston, P. (1997). *Knowing literacy: Constructive literacy assessment.* York, ME: Stenhouse.

Juel, C. (1991). Beginning reading. In R. Barr, M. Kamil, P. Mosenthal, & P. D. Pearson (Eds.), *Handbook of reading research* (Vol. 2, pp. 759–788). New York: Longman.

Juel, C., Griffith, P. L., & Gough, P. (1986). Acquisition of literacy: A longitudinal study of children in first and second grade. *Journal of Educational Psychology, 78,* 243–255.

Kagan, S. L., & Cohen, N. (1997). *Not by chance: Creating an early care and education system for America's children.* New Haven, CT: Bush Center in Child Development and Social Policy, Yale University.

Karweit, N., & Wasik, B. (1996). The effects of story reading programs on literacy and language development of disadvantaged pre-schoolers. *Journal of Education for Students Placed At-Risk, 4,* 319–348.

Katz, L., & Chard, C. (1989). *Engaging children's minds.* Norwood, NJ: Ablex.

Layzer, J., Goodson, B., & Moss, M. (1993). *Life in preschool: Volume one of an observational study of early childhood programs for disadvantaged four-year-olds.* Cambridge, MA: Abt Associates.

Leung, C. B., & Pikulski, J. J. (1990). Incidental learning of word meanings by kindergarten and first grade children through repeated read aloud events. In J. Zutell & S. McCormick (Eds.), *Literacy theory and research: Analyses from multiple paradigms* (pp. 231–240). Chicago: National Reading Conference.

Lundberg, I., Frost, J., & Petersen, O. P. (1988). Effects of an extensive program for stimulating phonological awareness in preschool children. *Reading Research Quarterly, 23,* 263–284.

MacLean, M., Bryant, P., & Bradley, L. (1987). Rhymes, nursery rhymes, and reading in early childhood. *Merrill-Palmer Quarterly, 33,* 255–281.

Mason, J., & Sinha, S. (1993). Emerging literacy in the early childhood years: Applying a Vygotskian model of learning and development. In B. Spodek (Ed.), *Handbook of research on the education of young children* (pp. 137–150). New York: Macmillian.

McGee, L., Lomax, R., & Head, M. (1988). Young children's written language knowledge: What environmental and functional print reading reveals. *Journal of Reading Behavior, 20,* 99–118.

McGee, L., & Richgels, D. (1996). *Literacy's beginnings.* Boston: Allyn & Bacon.

McGill-Franzen, A., & Lanford, C. (1994). Exposing the edge of the preschool curriculum: Teachers' talk about text and children's literary understandings. *Language Arts, 71,* 264–273.

Morrow, L. M. (1988). Young children's responses to one-to-one readings in school settings. *Reading Research Quarterly, 23,* 89–107.

Morrow, L. M. (1990). Preparing the classroom environment to promote literacy during play. *Early Childhood Research Quarterly, 5,* 537–554.

Morrow, L. M., Strickland, D., & Woo, D. G. (1998). *Literacy instruction in half-and whole-day kindergarten.* Newark, DE: International Reading Association.

Morrow, L. M., & Weinstein, C. (1986). Encouraging voluntary reading: The impact of a literature program on children's use of library centers. *Reading Research Quarterly, 21,* 300–346.

Moyer, S. B. (1982). Repeated reading. *Journal of Learning Disabilities, 15,* 619–623.

National Association for the Education of Young Children. (1996a). NAEYC position statement: Responding to linguistic and cultural diversity—Recommendations for effective early childhood education. *Young Children, 51*(2), 4–12.

National Association for the Education of Young Children. (1996b). NAEYC position statement: Technology and young children—Ages three through eight. *Young Children, 51*(6), 11–16.

National Center for Education Statistics. (1996). *The condition of education.* Washington, DC: U.S. Department of Education.

Neuman, S. B. (in press-a). How can we enable all children to achieve? In S. B. Neuman & K. Roskos (Eds.), *Children achieving: Best practices in early literacy.* Newark, DE: International Reading Association.

Neuman, S. B. (in press-b). Books make a difference: A study of access to literacy. *Reading Research Quarterly.*

Neuman, S. B., & Roskos, K. (1992). Literacy objects as cultural tools: Effects on children's literacy behaviors in play. *Reading Research Quarterly, 27,* 202–225.

Neuman, S. B., & Roskos, K. (1993). Access to print for children of poverty: Differential effects of adult mediation and literacy-enriched play settings on environmental and functional print tasks. *American Educational Research Journal, 30,* 95–122.

Neuman, S. B., & Roskos, K. (1997). Literacy knowledge in practice: Contexts of participation for young writers and readers. *Reading Research Quarterly, 32,* 10–32.

Nye, B. A., Boyd-Zaharias, J., & Fulton, B. D. (1994). *The lasting benefits study: A continuing analysis of the effect of small class size in kindergarten through third grade on student achievement test scores in subsequent grade levels—seventh grade (1992–93)* (Tech. Rep.). Nashville, TN: Center of Excellence for Research in Basic Skills, Tennessee State University.

Nye, B. A., Boyd-Zaharias, J., Fulton, B. D., & Wallenhorst, M. P. (1992). Smaller classes really are better. *The American School Board Journal, 179*(5), 31–33.

Pappas, C. (1991). Young children's strategies in learning the "book language" of information books. *Discourse Processes, 14,* 203–225.

Read, C. (1971). Pre-school children's knowledge of English phonology. *Harvard Educational Review, 41,* 1–34.

Richgels, D. J. (1986). Beginning first graders' "invented spelling" ability and their performance in functional classroom writing activities. *Early Childhood Research Quarterly, 1,* 85–97.

Richgels, D. J. (1995). Invented spelling ability and printed word learning in kindergarten. *Reading Research Quarterly, 30,* 96–109.

Riley, J. (1996). *The teaching of reading.* London: Paul Chapman.

Roberts, B. (in press). "I No EverethENGe": What skills are essential in early literacy? In S. B. Neuman & K. Roskos (Eds.), *Children achieving: Best practices in early literacy.* Newark, DE: International Reading Association.

Rowe, D. W. (1994). *Preschoolers as authors.* Cresskill, NJ: Hampton.

Samuels, S. J. (1979). The method of repeated readings. *The Reading Teacher, 32,* 403–408.

Shepard, L. (1994). The challenges of assessing young children appropriately. *Phi Delta Kappan, 76,* 206–213.

Shepard, L., Kagan, S. L., & Wurtz, E. (Eds.). (1998). *Principles and recommendations for early childhood assessments.* Washington, DC: National Education Goals Panel.

Shepard, L., & Smith, M. L. (1988). Escalating academic demand in kindergarten: Some nonsolutions. *Elementary School Journal, 89,* 135–146.

Snow, C. (1991). The theoretical basis for relationships between language and literacy in development. *Journal of Research in Childhood Education, 6,* 5–10.

Snow, C., Burns, M. S., & Griffin, P. (1998). *Preventing reading difficulties in young children.* Washington, DC: National Academy Press.

Snow, C., Tabors, P., Nicholson, P., & Kurland, B. (1995). SHELL: Oral language and early literacy skills in kindergarten and first-grade children. *Journal of Research in Childhood Education, 10,* 37–48.

Stanovich, K. E. (1986). Matthew effects in reading: Some consequences of individual differences in the acquisition of literacy. *Reading Research Quarterly, 21,* 360–406.

Stanovich, K. E., & West, R. F. (1989). Exposure to print and orthographic processing. *Reading Research Quarterly, 24,* 402–433.

Stauffer, R. (1970). *The language experience approach to the teaching of reading.* New York: Harper & Row.

Strickland, D. (1994). Educating African American learners at risk: Finding a better way. *Language Arts, 71,* 328–336.

Sulzby, E. (1985). Kindergartners as writers and readers. In M. Farr (Ed.), *Advances in writing research* (pp. 127–199). Norwood, NJ: Ablex.

Teale, W. (1984). Reading to young children: Its significance for literacy development in H. Goelman, A. Oberg, & F. Smith (Eds.), *Awakening to literacy* (pp. 110–121). Portsmouth, NH: Heinemann.

Tierney, R., & Shanahan, T. (1991). Research on the reading-writing relationship: Interactions, transactions, and outcomes. In R. Barr, M. Kamil, P. Mosenthal, & P. D. Pearson (Eds.), *Handbook on reading research* (Vol. 2, pp. 246–280). New York: Longman.

Vernon-Feagans, L., Emanuel, D., & Blood, I. (1992). About middle ear problems: The effect of otitis media and quality of day care on children's language development. *Journal of Applied Developmental Psychology, 18,* 395–409.

Vukelich, C. (1994). Effects of play interventions on young children's reading of environmental print. *Early Childhood Research Quarterly, 9,* 153–170.

Wagner, R., & Torgesen, J. (1987). The nature of phonological processing and its causal role in the acquisition of reading skills. *Psychological Bulletin, 101,* 192–212.

Wells, G. (1985). *The meaning makers.* Portsmouth, NH: Heinemann.

Whitehurst, G., Arnold, D., Epstein, J., Angell, A., Smith, M., & Fischel, J. (1994). A picture book reading intervention in day care and home for children from low-income families. *Developmental Psychology, 30,* 679–689.

Whitmore, K., & Goodman, Y. (1995). Transforming curriculum in language and literacy. In S. Bredekamp & T. Rosengrant (Eds.), *Reaching potentials: Transforming early childhood curriculum and assessment* (Vol. 2). Washington, DC: National Association for the Education of Young Children.

Wong Fillmore, L. (1991). When learning a second language means losing the first. *Early Childhood Research Quarterly, 6,* 323–346....

NAEYC Position Statement: Responding to Linguistic and Cultural Diversity—Recommendations for Effective Early Childhood Education

Adopted November 1995

Linguistically and culturally diverse *is an educational term used by the U.S. Department of Education to define children enrolled in educational programs who are either non-English-proficient (NEP) or limited-English-proficient (LEP). Educators use this phrase, linguistically and culturally diverse, to identify children from homes and communities where English is not the primary language of communication (Garciá 1991). For the purposes of this statement, the phrase will be used in a similar manner.*

This document primarily describes linguistically and culturally diverse children who speak languages other than English. However, the recommendations of this position statement can also apply to children who, although they speak only English, are also linguistically and culturally diverse.

Introduction

The children and families served in early childhood programs reflect the ethnic, cultural, and linguistic diversity of the nation. The nation's children all deserve an early childhood education that is responsive to their families, communities, and racial, ethnic, and cultural backgrounds. For young children to develop and learn optimally, the early childhood professional must be prepared to meet their diverse developmental, cultural, linguistic, and educational needs. Early childhood educators face the challenge of how best to respond to these needs.

The acquisition of language is essential to children's cognitive and social development. Regardless of what language children speak, they still develop and learn. Educators recognize that linguistically and culturally diverse children come to early childhood programs with previously acquired knowledge and learning based upon the language used in their home. For young children, the language of the home is the language they have used since birth, the language they use to make and establish meaningful communicative relationships, and the language they use to begin to construct their knowledge and test their learning. The home language is tied to children's culture, and culture and language communicate traditions, values, and attitudes (Chang 1993). Parents should be encouraged to use and develop children's home language; early childhood educators should respect children's linguistic and cultural backgrounds and their diverse learning styles. In so doing, adults will enhance children's learning and development.

From *Young Children*, January 1996, pp. 4-12. © 1996 by the National Association for the Education of Young Children. Reprinted by permission.

Just as children learn and develop at different rates, individual differences exist in how children whose home language is not English acquire English. For example, some children may experience a silent period (of six or more months) while they acquire English; other children may practice their knowledge by mixing or combining languages (for example, "Mi mamá me put on mi coat"); still other children may seem to have acquired English-language skills (appropriate accent, use of vernacular, vocabulary, and grammatical rules) but are not truly proficient; yet some children will quickly acquire English-language proficiency. Each child's way of learning a new language should be viewed as acceptable, logical, and part of the ongoing development and learning of any new language.

Defining the problem

At younger and younger ages, children are negotiating difficult transitions between their home and educational settings, requiring an adaptation to two or more diverse sets of rules, values, expectations, and behaviors. Educational programs and families must *respect* and *reinforce* each other as they work together to achieve the greatest benefit for all children. For some young children, entering any new environment—including early childhood programs—can be intimidating. The lives of many young children today are further complicated by having to communicate and learn in a language that may be unfamiliar. In the past, children entering U.S. schools from families whose home language is not English were expected to immerse themselves in the mainstream of schools, primarily through the use of English (Soto 1991; Wong Fillmore 1991). Sometimes the negative attitudes conveyed or expressed toward certain languages lead children to "give up" their home language. Early childhood professionals must recognize the feeling of loneliness,

fear, and abandonment children may feel when they are thrust into settings that isolate them from their home community and language. The loss of children's home language may result in the disruption of family communication patterns, which may lead to the loss of intergenerational wisdom; damage to individual and community esteem; and children's potential nonmastery of their home language or English.

NAEYC's position

NAEYC's goal is to build support for equal access to high-quality educational programs that recognize and promote all aspects of children's development and learning, enabling all children to become competent, successful, and socially responsible adults. Children's educational experiences should afford them the opportunity to learn and to become effective, functioning members of society. Language development is essential for learning, and the development of children's home language does not interfere with their ability to learn English. Because knowing more than one language is a cognitive asset Wakuta & García 1989), early education programs should encourage the development of children's home language while fostering the acquisition of English.

> For the optimal development and learning of all children, educators must **accept** the legitimacy of children's home language, **respect** (hold in high regard) and **value** (esteem, appreciate) the home culture, and **promote** and **encourage** the active involvement and support of all families, including extended and nontraditional family units.

When early childhood educators acknowledge and respect children's home language and culture, ties between the family and programs are strengthened. This atmosphere provides increased opportunity for learning because young children feel

supported, nurtured, and connected not only to their home communities and families but also to teachers and the educational setting.

The challenges

The United States is a nation of great cultural diversity, and our diversity creates opportunities to learn and share both similar and different experiences. There are opportunities to learn about people from different backgrounds; the opportunity to foster a bilingual citizenry with skills necessary to succeed in a global economy; and opportunities to share one's own cherished heritage and traditions with others.

Historically, our nation has tended to regard differences, especially language differences, as cultural handicaps rather than cultural resources (Meier & Cazden 1982). "Although most Americans are reluctant to say it publicly, many are anxious about the changing racial and ethnic composition of the country" (Sharry 1994). As the early childhood profession transforms its thinking,

> the challenge for early childhood educators is to become more knowledgeable about how to relate to children and families whose linguistic or cultural background is different from their own.

Between 1979 and 1989 the number of children in the United States from culturally and linguistically diverse backgrounds increased considerably (NCES 1993), and, according to a report released by the Center for the Study of Social Policy (1992), that diversity is even more pronounced among children younger than age 6. Contrary to popular belief, many of these children are neither foreign born nor immigrants but were born in the United States (Waggoner 1993). Approximately 9.9 million of the estimated 45 million school-age children, more than one in five, live in households in which languages other than English are spoken (Waggoner 1994). In some communities, however, the number of children living in a family in which a language other than English is spoken is likely to be much larger. Head Start reports that the largest number of linguistically and culturally diverse children served through Head Start are Spanish speakers, with other language groups representing smaller but growing percentages (Head Start Bureau 1995).

The challenge for teachers is to provide high-quality care and education for the increasing number of children who are likely to be linguistically and culturally diverse.

Families and communities are faced with increasingly complex responsibilities. Children used to be cared for by parents and family members who typically spoke the home language of their family, be it English or another language. With the increasing need of family members to work, even while children are very young, more and more children are placed in care and educational settings with adults who may not speak the child's home language or share their cultural background. Even so, children will spend an ever increasing amount of their waking lives with these teachers. What happens in care will have a tremendous impact on the child's social, emotional, and cognitive development. These interactions will influence the child's values, view of the world, perspectives on family, and connections to community. This places a tremendous responsibility in the hands of the early childhood community.

Responding to linguistic and cultural diversity can be challenging. At times the challenges can be complicated further by the specific needs or issues of the child, the family, or the educational program. Solutions may not be evident. Individual circumstances can affect each situation differently There are no easy answers, and often myths and misin-

formation may flourish. The challenges may even seem to be too numerous for any one teacher or provider to manage. Nonetheless, despite the complexity, it is the responsibility of all educators to assume the tasks and meet the challenges. Once a situation occurs, the early childhood educator should enter into a dialogue with colleagues, parents, and others in an effort to arrive at a negotiated agreement that will meet the best interest of the child. For example,

• A mother, father, and primary caregiver each have different cultural and linguistic backgrounds and do not speak English. Should the language of one of these persons be affirmed or respected above the others? How can the teacher affirm and respect the backgrounds of each of these individuals?

• The principal is concerned that all children learn English and, therefore, does not want any language other than English spoken in the early childhood setting. In the interest of the child, how should the educator respond?

• An educator questions whether a child will ever learn English if the home language is used as the primary language in the early childhood setting. How is this concern best addressed?

Solutions exist for each of these linguistic and cultural challenges, just as they do for the many other issues that early childhood educators confront within the early childhood setting. These challenges must be viewed as opportunities for the early childhood educator to reflect, question, and effectively respond to the needs of linguistically and culturally diverse children. Although appropriate responses to every linguistically and culturally diverse situation cannot be addressed through this document, early childhood educators should consider the following recommendations.

Recommendations for a responsive learning environment

Early childhood educators should stop and reflect on the best ways to ensure appropriate educational and developmental experiences for all young children. The unique qualities and characteristics of each individual child must be acknowledged. Just as each child is different, methods and strategies to work with young children must vary.

The issue of home language and its importance to young children is also relevant for children who speak English but come from different cultural backgrounds, for example, speakers of English who have dialects, such as people from Appalachia or other regions having distinct patterns of speech, speakers of Black English, or second- and third-generation speakers of English who maintain the dominant accent of their heritage language. While this position statement basically responds to children who are from homes in which English is not the dominant language, the recommendations provided may be helpful when working with children who come from diverse cultural backgrounds, even when they only speak English. The overall goal for early childhood professionals, however, is to provide every child, including children who are linguistically and culturally diverse, with a responsive learning environment. The following recommendations help achieve this goal.

A. Recommendations for working with children

Recognize that all children are cognitively, linguistically, and emotionally connected to the language and culture of their home.

When program settings acknowledge and support children's home language and culture, ties between the family and school are strengthened. In a supportive atmosphere young children's home language is less likely to atrophy (Chang 1993), a situation that could threaten the children's important ties to family and community.

Acknowledge that children can demonstrate their knowledge and capabilities in many ways.

In response to linguistic and cultural diversity, the goal for early childhood educators should be to make the most of children's potential, strengthening and building upon the skills they bring when they enter programs. Education, as Cummins states, implies "drawing out children's potential and making them more than they were" (1989, vii). Educational programs and practices must recognize the strengths that children possess. Whatever language children speak, they should be able to demonstrate their capabilities and also feel the success of being appreciated and valued. Teachers must build upon children's diversity of gifts and skills and provide young children opportunities to exhibit these skills in early childhood programs.

The learning environment must focus on the learner and allow opportunities for children to express themselves across the curriculum, including art, music, dramatization, and even block building. By using a nondeficit approach (tapping and recognizing children's strengths rather than focusing the child's home environment on skills yet unlearned) in their teaching, teachers should take the time to observe and engage children in a variety of learning activities. Children's strengths should be celebrated, and they should be given numerous ways to express their interests and talents. In doing this, teachers will provide children an opportunity to display their intellect and knowledge that may far exceed the boundaries of language.

Understand that without comprehensible input, second-language learning can be difficult.

It takes time to become linguistically proficient and competent in any language. Linguistically and culturally diverse children may be able to master basic communication skills; however, mastery of the more cognitively complex language skills needed for academic learning (Cummins 1989) is more dependent on the learning environment. Academic learning relies on significant amounts of information presented in decontextualized learning situations. Success in school becomes more and more difficult as children are required to learn, to be tested and evaluated based on ever-increasing amounts of information, consistently presented in a decontextualized manner. Children learn best when they are given a context in which to learn, and the knowledge that children acquire in "their first language can make second-language input much more comprehensible" (Krashen 1992, 37). Young children can gain knowledge more easily when they obtain quality instruction through their first language. Children can acquire the necessary language and cognitive skills required to succeed in school when given an appropriate learning environment, one that is tailored to meet their needs (NAEYC & NAECS/SDE 1991; Bredekamp & Rosegrant 1992).

Although verbal proficiency in a second language can be accomplished within two to three years, the skills necessary to achieve the higher level educational skills of understanding academic content through reading and writing may require four or more years (Cummins 1981; Corner 1989). Young children may seem to be fluent and at ease with English but may not be capable of understanding or expressing themselves as competently as their English-speaking peers. Although children seem to be speaking a second language with ease, *speaking* a

language does not equate to being proficient in that language. Full proficiency in the first language, including complex uses of the language, contributes to the development of the second language. Children who do not become *proficient* in their second language after two or three years of regular use probably are not proficient in their first language either.

Young children may seem to be fluent and at ease speaking a second language, but they may not be fully capable of understanding or expressing themselves in the more complex aspects of language and may demonstrate weaknesses in language-learning skills, including vocabulary skills, auditory memory and discrimination skills, simple problem-solving tasks, and the ability to follow sequenced directions. Language difficulties such as these often can result in the linguistically and culturally diverse child being overreferred to special education, classified as learning disabled, or perceived as developmentally delayed.

B. Recommendations for working with families

Actively involve parents and families in the early learning program and setting.

Parents and families should be actively involved in the learning and development of their children. Teachers should actively seek parental involvement and pursue establishing a partnership with children's families. When possible, teachers should visit the child's community (for example, shops, churches, and playgrounds); read and learn about the community through the use of books, pictures, observations, and conversations with community members; and visit the home and meet with other family members.

Parents and families should be invited to share, participate, and engage in activities with their children. Parent involvement can be accomplished in a number of ways, including asking parents to share stories, songs, drawings, and experiences of their linguistic and cultural background and asking parents to serve as monitors or field trip organizers. Families and parents should be invited to share activities that are developmentally appropriate and meaningful within their culture. These opportunities demonstrate to the parent what their child is learning; increase the knowledge, information, and understanding of all children regarding people of different cultures and linguistic backgrounds; and establish a meaningful relationship with the parent. The early childhood educator should ensure that parents are informed and engaged with their child in meaningful activities that promote linkages between the home and the early care setting.

Encourage and assist all parents in becoming knowledgeable about the cognitive value for children of knowing more than one language, and provide them with strategies to support, maintain, and preserve home-language learning.

In an early childhood setting and atmosphere in which home language is preserved, acknowledged, and respected, all parents can learn the value of home-language development and the strength it provides children as they add to their existing knowledge and understanding. Parents and teachers can learn how to become advocates regarding the long-term benefits that result from bilingualism.

Parents and teachers recognize the acquisition of English as an intellectual accomplishment, an opportunity for economic growth and development, and a means for achieving academic success. There are even times when parents may wish for the ability, or have been mistakenly encouraged, to speak to their children only in English, a language of which the parents themselves may not have command. The educator should understand the effects that speaking only in English can have upon the child, the family, and the child's learning. The teacher must be able to explain that speaking to the child only in English can often result in communications being significantly hindered and verbal interactions being limited and unnatural between the parent and the child. In using limited English, parents may communicate to children using simple phrases and commands (for example, "Sit down" or "Stop"); modeling grammatically incorrect phrases (for example, "We no go store"); or demonstrating other incorrect usages of language that are common when persons acquire a second language. From these limited and incorrect verbal interactions, the amount of language the child is hearing is reduced, and the child's vocabulary growth is restricted, contributing to an overall decrease in verbal expression. When parents do not master the second language yet use the second language to communicate with their child, there is an increased likelihood that the child will not hear complex ideas or abstract thoughts—important skills needed for cognitive and language development. The teacher must explain that language is developed through natural language interactions. These natural interactions occur within the day-to-day setting, through radio and television, when using public transportation, and in play with children whose dominant language is English. The parent and the teacher must work collaboratively to achieve the goal of children's learning English.

Through the home language and culture, families transmit to their children a sense of identity, an understanding of how to relate to other people, and, a sense of belonging. When parents and children cannot communicate with one another, family and community destabilization can occur. Children who are proficient in their home language are able to maintain a connectedness to their histories, their stories, and the day-to-day events shared by parents, grandparents, and other family members who may speak only the home language. Without the ability to communicate, parents are not able to socialize their children, share beliefs and value systems, and directly influence, coach, and model with their children.

Recognize that parents and families must rely on caregivers and educators to honor and support their children in the cultural values and norms of the home.

Parents depend on high-quality early childhood programs to assist them with their children's development and learning. Early childhood programs should make provisions to communicate with families in their home language and to provide parent-teacher encounters that both welcome and accommodate families. Partnerships between the home and the early childhood setting must be developed to ensure that practices of the home and expectations of the program are complementary. Linguistic and cultural continuity between the home and the early childhood program supports children's social and emotional development. By working together, parents and teachers have the opportunity to influence the understanding of language and culture and to encourage multicultural learning and acceptance in a positive way.

C. Recommendations for professional preparation

Provide early childhood educators with professional preparation and development in the areas of culture, language, and diversity.

Efforts to understand the languages and cultural backgrounds of young children are essential in helping children to learn. Uncertainty can exist when educators are unsure of how to relate to children and families of linguistic and cultural backgrounds different from their own. Early childhood educators need to understand and appreciate their own cultural and linguistic backgrounds. Adults' cultural background affects how they interact with and/or teach young children. The educator's background influences how children are taught, reinforced, and disciplined. The child's background influences how the child constructs knowledge, responds to discipline and praise, and interacts in the early childhood setting.

Preservice and inservice training opportunities in early childhood education programs assist educators in overcoming some of the linguistic and cultural challenges they may face in working with young children. Training institutions and programs can consider providing specific courses in the following topic areas or include these issues in current courses: language acquisition; second-language learning; use of translators; working with diverse families; sociolinguistics; cross-cultural communication; issues pertaining to the politics of race, language, and culture; and community involvement.

Recruit and support early childhood educators who are trained in languages other than English.

Within the field of early childhood education, there is a need for knowledgeable, trained, competent, and sensitive multilingual multicultural early childhood educators. Early childhood educators who speak more than one language and are culturally knowledgeable are an invaluable resource in the early childhood setting. In some instances the educator may speak multiple languages or may be able to communicate using various linguistic re-

gionalisms or dialects spoken by the child or the family. The educator may have an understanding of sociocultural and economic issues relevant within the local linguistically and culturally diverse community and can help support the family in the use and development of the child's home language and in the acquisition of English. The early childhood teacher who is trained in linguistic and cultural diversity can be a much-needed resource for information about the community and can assist in the inservice cultural orientation and awareness training for the early childhood program. The bilingual educator also can be a strong advocate for family and community members.

Too often, however, bilingual early childhood professionals are called upon to provide numerous other services, some of which they may not be equipped to provide. For example, the bilingual professional, although a fluent speaker, may not have the vocabulary needed to effectively communicate with other adults or, in some instances, may be able to read and write only in English, not in the second language. In addition, bilingual teachers should not be expected to meet the needs of *all* linguistically and culturally diverse children and families in the program, especially those whose language they do not speak. Bilingual providers should not be asked to translate forms, particularly at a moment's notice, nor should they be required to stop their work in order to serve as interpreters. Bilingual teachers should not serve in roles, such as advising or counseling, in which they may lack professional training. These assignments may seem simple but often can be burdensome and must be viewed as added duties placed upon the bilingual teacher.

Preservice and inservice training programs are needed to support bilingual early childhood educators in furthering educators' knowledge and mastery of the language(s) other than English that they speak, and

training should also credit content-based courses offered in languages other than English. Professional preparation instructors must urge all teachers to support multilingual/multicultural professionals in their role as advocates for linguistically and culturally diverse children. Early childhood professionals should be trained to work collaboratively with the bilingual early childhood teacher and should be informed of the vital role of the bilingual educator. Additionally, there is a need for continued research in the area of linguistic and cultural diversity of young children.

D. Recommendations for programs and practice

Recognize that children can and will acquire the use of English even when their home language is used and respected.

Children should build upon their current skills as they acquire new skills. While children maintain and build upon their home language skills and culture, children can organize and develop proficiency and knowledge in English. Bilingualism has been associated with higher levels of cognitive attainment (Hakuta & García 1989) and does not interfere with either language proficiency or cognitive development. Consistent learning opportunities to read, be read to, and see print messages should be given to linguistically and culturally diverse children. Literacy developed in the home language will transfer to the second language (Krashen 1992). Bilingualism should be viewed as an asset and an educational achievement.

Support and preserve home language usage.

If the early childhood teacher *speaks* the child's home language, then the teacher can comfortably use this language around the child, thereby providing the child with opportunities to hear and use the home language within the early childhood setting. Use of the language should be clearly evident throughout the learning environment (e.g., in meeting charts, tape recordings, the library corner). Educators should develop a parent information board, using a language and reading level appropriate for the parents. Teachers should involve parents and community members in the early childhood program. Parents and community members can assist children in hearing the home language from many different adults, in addition to the teacher who speaks the home language. Parents and community members can assist other parents who may be unable to read, or they can assist the teacher in communicating with families whose home language may not have a written form.

If the early childhood educator *does not speak* the language, he or she should make efforts to provide visible signs of the home language throughout the learning environment through books and other relevant reading material in the child's language and with a parent bulletin board (get a bilingual colleague to help review for accuracy of written messages). The teacher can learn a few selected words in the child's language, thus demonstrating a willingness to take risks similar to the risks asked of children as they learn a second language. This effort by the teacher also helps to validate and affirm the child's language and culture, further demonstrating the teacher's esteem and respect for the child's linguistic and cultural background. The teacher should model appropriate use of English and provide the child with opportunities to use newly acquired vocabulary and language. The teacher also must actively involve the parent and the community in the program.

If the teacher is *faced with many different languages* in the program or classroom, the suggestions listed above are still relevant. Often teachers feel overwhelmed if more than one language is spoken in the program; however, they should remember that the goal is for children to learn, and that learning is made easier when children can build on knowledge in their home language. The teacher should consider grouping together at specific times during the day children who speak the same or similar languages so that the children can construct knowledge with others who speak their home language. The early childhood educator should ensure that these children do not become socially isolated as efforts are made to optimize their learning. Care should be taken to continually create an environment that provides for high learning expectations.

Develop and provide alternative and creative strategies for young children's learning.

Early childhood educators are encouraged to rely on their creative skills in working with children to infuse cultural and linguistic diversity in their programs. They should provide children with multiple opportunities to learn and ways for them to demonstrate their learning, participate in program activities, and work interactively with other children.

To learn more about working with linguistically and culturally diverse children, early childhood educators should collaborate with each other and with colleagues from other professions. To guide the implementation of a developmentally, linguistically, and culturally appropriate program, collaborative parent and teacher workgroups should be developed. These committees should discuss activities and strategies that would be effective for use with linguistically and culturally diverse children. Such committees promote good practices for children and shared learning between teachers and parents.

Summary

Early childhood educators can best help linguistic and culturally diverse children and their families by acknowledging and responding to the importance of the child's home language and culture. Administrative support for bilingualism as a goal is necessary within the educational setting. Educational practices should focus on educating children toward the "school culture" while preserving and respecting the diversity of the home language and culture that each child brings to the early learning setting. Early childhood professionals and families must work together to achieve high-quality care and education for *all* children.

References

Bredekamp, S., & T. Rosegrant, eds. 1992. *Reaching potentials: Appropriate curriculum and assessment for young children.* Vol. 1. Washington, DC: NAEYC.

Center for the Study of Social Policy. 1992. *The challenge of change: What the 1990 census tells us about children.* Washington, DC: Author.

Chang, H.N.-L. 1993. *Affirming children's roots: Cultural and linguistic diversity in early care and education.* San Francisco: California Tomorrow.

Collier, V. 1989. How long: A synthesis of research on academic achievement in second language. *TESOL Quarterly* 23: 509–31.

Cummins, J. 1981. The role of primary language development in promoting educational success for language minority students. In *Schooling and language minority students: A theoretical framework,* eds. M. Ortiz, D. Parker, & F. Tempes. Office of Bilingual Bicultural Education, California State Department of Education. Los Angeles: Evaluation, Dissemination, and Assessment Center, California State University.

Cummins, J. 1989. *Empowering minority students.* Sacramento: California Association for Bilingual Education.

García, E. 1991. *The education of linguistically and culturally diverse students: Effective instructional practices.* Santa Cruz: National Center for Research on Cultural Diversity and Second Language Learning, University of California.

Hakuta, K., & E. Garciá. 1989. Bilingualism and education. *American Psychologist* 44 (2): 374–79.

Head Start Bureau, Administration on Children, Youth, and Families, Department of Health and Human Services. 1995. *Program information report*. Washington, DC: Author.

Krashen, 5. 1992. *Fundamentals of language education*. Torrance, CA: Laredo Publishing.

Meier, T.R., & C.B. Cazden. 1982. A focus on oral language and writing from a multicultural perspective. *Language Arts* 59: 504–12.

National Association for the Education of Young Children (NAEYC) and National Association of Early Childhood Specialists in State Departments of Education (NAECS/SDE). 1991. Guidelines for appropriate curriculum content and assessment in programs serving children ages 3 through 8. *Young Children* 46 (3): 21–38.

National Center for Education Statistics (NCES). 1993. *Language characteristics and schooling in the United States, a changing picture: 1979 and 1989*. NCES 93-699. Washington, DC: U.S. Department of Education, Office of Educational Research and Improvement.

Sharry, F. 1994. *The rise of nativism in the United States and how to respond to it*. Washington, DC: National Education Forum.

Soto, L.D. 1991. Understanding bilingual/bicultural children. *Young Children* 46 (2): 30–36.

Waggoner, D., ed. 1993. *Numbers and needs: ethnic and linguistic minorities in the United States* 3 (6).

Waggoner, D. 1994. Language minority school age population now totals 9.9 million. *NABE News* 18(1): 1, 24–26.

Wong Fillmore, L. 1991. When learning a second language means losing the first. *Early Childhood Research Quarterly* 6: 323–46.

Resources

Banks, J. 1993. Multicultural education for young children: Racial and ethnic attitudes and their modification. In *Handbook of research on the education of young children*, ed. B. Spodek, 236–51. New York: Macmillan.

Collier, V. 1989. How long: A synthesis of research on academic achievement in second language. *TESOL Quarterly* 23: 509–31.

Collier, V., & C. Twyford. 1988. The effect of age on acquisition of a second language for school. *National Clearinghouse for Bilingual Education* 2 (Winter): 1–12.

Derman-Sparks, L., & the A.B.C. Task Force. 1989. *Anti-bias curriculum: Tools for empowering young children*. Washington, DC: NAEYC.

McLaughlin, B. 1992. *Myths and misconceptions about second language learning: What every teacher needs to unlearn*. Santa Cruz: National Center for Research on Cultural Diversity and Second Language Learning, University of California.

Neugebauer, B., ed. 1992. *Alike and different: Exploring our humanity with young children*. Redmond, WA: Exchange Press, 1987. Reprint, Washington, DC: NAEYC.

Ogbu, J.U. 1978. *Minority education and caste: The American system in cross cultural perspective*. New York: Academic.

Phillips, C.B. 1988. Nurturing diversity for today's children and tomorrow's leaders. *Young Children* 43 (2): 42–47.

Tharp, R.G. 1989. Psychocultural variables and constants: Effects on teaching and learning in schools. *American Psychologist* 44: 349–59.

RETHINKING WHAT WE DO

Beginning to Implement the Reggio Philosophy

Lynn Staley

As an early childhood teacher educator and staff development professional, I find that the Reggio Approach, from Reggio Emilia, Italy, is by far the most requested topic for discussion. Following almost every workshop or inservice session I conduct on the subject, however, caregivers, preschool teachers, and kindergarten teachers all make the same plea for help: "I love what I hear about Reggio Emilia. It's everything I believe about young children, but it all seems so overwhelming. Where do I start? How do I begin?"

Hoping to encourage others, our university preschool teachers agreed to carefully and candidly document their own first steps toward implementation. In Reggio the teacher is not only a practitioner, but also a co-leader, researcher, and risk-taker as

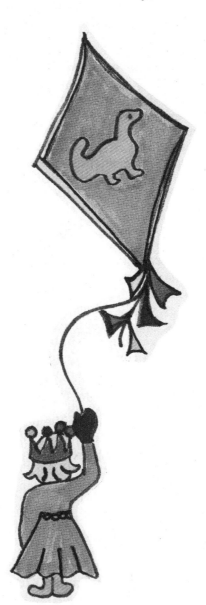

Lynn Staley, Ed.D., *is an assistant professor of early childhood education at Ball State University in Muncie, Indiana. She was a member of the 1995 Spring Study Tour to Reggio Emilia and is now serving as the director of the Indiana Reggio Network.*

adults and children experiment together. Our teachers too were taking risks as they stepped away from the traditional, very secure, teacher-directed curriculum and began asking serious questions about how young children learn best. Getting started was scary, but the results were well worth it!

Our Story

While the Reggio Approach does not represent a new philosophy, it is the rare and remarkable synergy that exists in Reggio Emilia between theory and practice that inspired us to reflect upon our own philosophies, beliefs, and practices. As our teachers prepared to implement the Reggio Approach, they too were overwhelmed and asked, "Where do we start? How do we begin?"

The parent-teacher partnership

The first step was to develop a renewed partnership with parents. The staff wanted to elicit parental enthusiasm, involvement, and participation in this new adventure, so

The Reggio Approach

Who is the young child?

Children are seen as capable, competent, curious, and creative (Rinaldi 1993). They are natural researchers as they question what they see, hypothesize solutions, predict outcomes, experiment, and reflect on their discoveries. Children are not passive, empty vessels waiting to be filled; rather, they are self-motivated learners actively seeking to understand the complex world in which they live. They are intrinsically motivated to learn and can be trusted as partners in curriculum development.

How do young children learn best?

Loris Malaguzzi founded the Reggio schools within the context of educational theorists such as Montessori, Dewey, Piaget, and Vygotsky (Malaguzzi 1993). Reggio's eclectic philosophy is highlighted by the Italian tradition of Maria Montessori, who respected children as capable and competent learners in need of an environment carefully prepared to stimulate curiosity, exploration, inquiry, and self-learning (Montessori 1965). Dewey's emphasis on designing curriculum based on children's interests (Archambault 1964) is evident in Reggio as one observes children pursuing their own projects.

Piaget's appreciation for children's cognitive development as a process of ongoing adaptation to one's environment (Forman & Kuschner 1983) contributes to the Reggio school's emphasis on "active education" (Malaguzzi 1993, 52). Malaguzzi referred to the schools as "amiable" schools that allow "maximum movement, interdependence, and interaction" (p. 56). Consistent with Vygotsky's sociocultural philosophy is an emphasis on relationships in which adults and children come together in an active process of education.

Value should be placed on contexts, communicative processes, and the construction of a wide network of reciprocal exchanges among children and between children and adults. (p. 62)

Thus, children acquire knowledge best by construction rather than instruction (DeVries & Kohlberg 1990). Children need many opportunities for hands-on, multisensory experiences and active exploration (Bredekamp 1987; Bredekamp & Copple 1997). It is only as children search for answers to their own questions via discussion, investigation, and experimentation that they begin to grasp and understand complex concepts that are foundational to later learning. Rather than use teacher-directed thematic units, teachers integrate curriculum goals carefully within open-ended projects of inquiry chosen by the children (Katz & Chard 1989). Learning is therefore an ongoing, flexible, open-ended process wherein children construct their own understanding. Teaching is not telling; teaching is guiding discovery.

In Reggio, learning often takes place within the structure of small-group projects. Opportunities for discussion with other children and adults is essential if children are to construct and reconstruct ideas for themselves (Rosa & Montero 1990; Berk & Winsler 1995). Only as children articulate to others that which they believe to be true do they come face-to-face with errors in their thinking. As children find it necessary to explain, support, or defend their position, they must define and redefine what they know. Children learn best by doing and talking.

Curriculum planning is understood in Reggio Emilia as a "sense of preparation and organization of space, materials, thoughts, situations, and occasions for learning" (Rinaldi 1993, 102). Vea Vecchi, *atelierista* (art specialist) from Reggio

---

they planned a meeting to introduce the Reggio Approach to parents.

In addition to sharing the key concepts, staff warned parents not to expect the familiar "refrigerator art"; rather, they encouraged parents to appreciate their children's first steps in contributing to an emerging curriculum and using authentic art materials to represent what they had learned.

The teacher-teacher partnership

A very important ingredient in the Reggio Approach is a sense of collegiality and support. The staff is open to comments, suggestions, questions, and criticisms as everyone seeks the best ways to ignite children's in-

terests, provoke questions, and sustain learning.

Based on trust and mutual respect, teacher interaction is positive and supportive. To facilitate such collegiality, we scheduled a weekly staff meeting to reflect together on daily observations of the children as the basis for curriculum design.

The teacher-child partnership

The next step was to move away from preplanned, teacher-directed, thematic units and whole-group, structured activities. Preplanned lessons had fostered a sense of security and control for the staff; they knew what to expect.

Letting go of thematic units made them feel anxious, nervous, uneasy, and insecure. Even at the close of the year, one teacher recalled, "The hardest things to learn were to be flexible and to let go of themes. The 'negotiated curriculum' [Fyfe & Forman 1996] seemed so unpredictable at first." (For those teachers already familiar with project-based emergent curriculum, incorporating the Reggio Approach should prove to be much easier.)

Project #1—Dinosaurs

After listening to children's conversations and observing their play, the teachers pursued the topic of dinosaurs. Needing a little structure to

Emilia, tells a story about shadows that illustrates well how teachers thoughtfully prepare the environment to provoke interest and ignite inquiry:

> Once I noticed that the sun, shining behind one of the trees outside the window, cast a shadow of the leaves onto the glass. I taped a sheet of translucent white paper onto the glass. As children came in that morning, they exclaimed with surprise and pleasure at the sight of the shadow of leaves on the paper. Many things followed. The children even came to use the shadow as a clock. One said, "It's time to go to lunch. Look at the design on the paper." (Vecchi 1993, 126–27)

Something as simple as taping paper to the window provoked incredible learning of complex concepts. What a patient teacher and keen observer!

How do young children express what they know?

While young children socially construct knowledge as they communicate their understandings to others, spoken language is sometimes inadequate for such expression. Young children often have images and understandings of complex concepts in their minds, but they can't put them into words. Young children in particular need alternative languages to express themselves. Whether they use the language of paint, clay, wire, pen and ink, mosaic, collage, puppetry, music, or dance, the children of Reggio Emilia demonstrate an eagerness to create visual and symbolic representations of what they know and understand. How appropriate that the Italian educators speak of this expression as *The Hundred Languages of Children* (Department of Education 1987; Edwards, Gandini, & Forman 1993).

How do young children benefit from documentation?

Along the children's journey of cognitive development, the teacher must record or document the learning process.

Much like recording a personal vacation, the teacher compiles photographs, videotapes, audio recordings, models, and notes of children's conversations and accomplishments. Documentation of children's learning abounds in the Reggio schools. Visitors view mobiles, photo stories, wind machines, mosaics, sculptures, and much more as a tribute to children's learning. When children's creations are displayed in the school, there is a clear message to those who visit that children do indeed pursue intelligent and important work.

In addition to serving as a historical record, documentation is a tool for assessing children's understanding in order to design effective curriculum. Upon observing, listening, and recording children's interests, questions, and hypotheses, the parents and teachers in Reggio can carefully structure learning environments that assist children in their quest for further understanding.

Who are the partners in learning?

Much attention is given in the Reggio Approach to facilitating an effective partnership with families. The parent is considered the child's first teacher and therefore worthy of respect, inclusion, involvement, consultation, and contribution to curriculum design.

Summary

The teachers in Reggio Emilia consider children to be active, competent, and capable of directing their own learning. Teaching strategies include (a) providing time and materials for children to explore their own topics, (b) supporting small group projects in which children coconstruct knowledge, (c) incorporating the use of authentic art materials, (d) documenting children's journeys of discovery, and (e) including parents as part of the education team.

guide their first steps, the teachers chose to adapt the KWL method (Ogle 1986; Carr & Ogle 1987). They hoped that by asking the children three questions,

K—What do you **know** about dinosaurs?

W—What do you **want** to know about dinosaurs?

L—What did you **learn** about dinosaurs?

this method would help build a framework of questions from which the project would develop.

The children loved sharing what they "knew" about dinosaurs; however, when the teachers asked them what they wanted to know, the children had no idea. We understood later that children need a substantial knowledge base for a topic before they can contemplate further questions. They didn't know enough about dinosaurs to ask questions!

Following a field trip, teachers and children incorporated dinosaurs into the computer center, block center, literacy center, and math center.

The children lost interest in the topic of dinosaurs after a few weeks. They had been very dependent upon the adults, who were always there and were familiar with previous conversations, discussions, and explorations related to the topic. Inconsistent staffing and peer-group attendance may have contributed to the lack of sustained interest.

Reflections on project #1

Asking good questions. The teachers were very frustrated with their perceived inability to ask effective, engaging, provoking questions that would ignite children's discoveries. They understood that good teachers ask questions that motivate children (Kramer 1994, 32), good questions help children find words for their thinking (Schifter 1996), and good questions help children solve problems (Berk & Winsler 1995).

A student teacher said, "It's hard to ask questions. . . . I sort of listen and don't know what to say next. I want to encourage [the children] to think, but I don't know how. How do I keep them going?"

Teachers work with each child to deepen and extend understanding and effort.

Drawing the costume on paper.

Making a pattern the right size.

Admiring a gown fit for a princess.

Further investigation revealed that leading children to a higher level of thinking depends upon

• asking questions that help children relate prior experiences to present learning;

• asking for literal details to assess understanding;

• helping children draw relationships;

• asking children for further clarification (Why? How? What if . . . ?), requiring children to rethink their beliefs and test their understanding;

• asking open-ended questions without any hint of appropriate or expected responses;

• asking open-ended questions that pose problems, contradictions, comparisons, alternatives; and

• waiting for responses (Sigel & Saunders 1977; Isbell 1979; Finkelstein & Ritter 1980; Berk & Winsler 1995).

Open-ended questions demand "active cognitive engagement" (Fowell & Lawton 1992, 419). Asking questions is like playing tennis. The "ball" (question) is served into the children's court, and they are expected to respond. By waiting, the teacher silently communicates a confidence in the children's ability to respond; the teacher validates the

learner and gives the children time to organize their thoughts.

One teacher stated,

I believe it is imperative that, as teachers, we listen to children intently and only interject ideas very occasionally that will assist each child in further construction of his or her knowledge. It is so tempting to lead a child to new understandings. It is difficult to wait for children to lead themselves. It is tempting to jump in with information that seems important and obvious to us. It is difficult to facilitate situations that allow the child to discover without directing the discovery.

Could it be that effective questioning depends first on our patient listening?

Project #2—Kites

After the dinosaur project a boy shared a book about kites. The class was so captivated with the topic that they decided to design, build, and test their own kite creations. Seeing design flaws, the teachers were silent and allowed some kites to fail. Surprisingly, this motivated the children to redesign and retest until they finally experienced success.

Reflections on project #2

This was the best project of the year. The staff noted that short-term projects might be the easiest way to begin using the Reggio Approach.

Project #3—Castles, princes, princesses

During the second half of the year, the children become interested in castles, princes, and princesses. The boys were primarily interested in how castles were built, and the girls were interested in the clothes the princesses wore. One little girl brought in several child-size princess gowns that generated great excitement in the dress-up corner.

The children wrote stories, researched books, and built catapults for complex block structures. A small group of girls decided to sew their own costumes. They drew designs on paper and prepared paper tube models from the designs. They then drew life-size patterns from the models, made adjustments, and cut out the patterns. They pinned the patterns to the fabric, cut them out, and sewed the pieces together. (The girls had difficulty pinning and cutting, so the teachers intervened to help the girls continue.)

Upon completion, a teacher reported, "One girl tried her outfit on, and she was really proud. She walked around and showed it to everybody. And one boy ... said, 'Wow, that's really neat!' ... She looked in the mirror. I wish you could have seen her face.... It got the other children excited too." One boy also became interested in sewing and made a long shirtlike costume.

Reflections on project #3

Who is our atelierista? An *atelierista* resides in each of the Reggio schools helping children and teachers continue the connection between art and learning. Our teachers longed for someone who could help the children use authentic art materials (for example, clay, wire, watercolors) to represent what they know. A university student with an art background volunteered to be our *atelierista*. As a result, the children began to incorporate clay into their thinking about castles.

Why do children revisit their work? The teachers observed that when children had repeated opportunities to revisit their ideas, they constructed more complex, detailed, and accurate representations than before. Commented one teacher, "For many of [the children], it's usually a one-time shot. A project is over in ten minutes, and then we go on to something else. This [project was] something special they revisited over and over and over."

What is the role of the teacher? Struggling to find the balance between child-directed and teacher-directed learning, the teachers were hesitant to instruct. If children learn best by discovery and exploration, then what is the role of the teacher?

Lella Gandini, Reggio Emilia liaison to the United States, visited our campus and explained that at times children depend on us to teach them a skill needed to pursue their goal. Without teacher intervention at points of frustration, children might be tempted to give up and never experience the joys of fruitful discovery. Teachers must still teach!

Closing reflections

What did the children learn?

"More than anything else, the children are learning to solve their own problems," concluded one teacher. "They are learning to negotiate with their friends. They are learning to work together. They are learning that they are competent learners."

> **Children are natural researchers as they question what they see, hypothesize, predict, experiment, and reflect.**

The children used to come to school and say, "What are we learning today?" As the year progressed, they came prepared to direct their own course and make their own decisions about what they wanted to learn.

Adults valued their questions and suggestions for solutions; children were learning to be decisionmakers, thinkers, problem seekers, and problem solvers. Some parents noticed greater self-confidence in their child!

Topic selection

Reflecting further on the dinosaur and castles/princes/princesses projects, we teachers agreed that the topics were not the best choices. Topics should (a) be relevant to children's lives, (b) contribute to a balanced curriculum, (c) have the potential for artistic and expressive representation, and (d) prepare children for later life (Katz & Chard 1989; Chard 1996).

There are no universally successful project topics. Topics depend on careful observation and consideration of a particular group of children as well as the interests of the teacher. (In the second year of implementation, two topics, butterflies and mixtures, were very successful. The teachers attributed the success of these topics to the fact that they were real and, as they said, "the children could touch them.")

Documentation

The teachers took lots of pictures and the parents raved about the display panels, but the extensive time required to prepare scripted photos for formal display continued to frustrate the staff throughout the year.

"Following children and listening and interacting at the same time is frustrating," a teacher explained. "Even taping requires transcribing. We can't do everything ... We want to stay involved, not with our heads in the paper all the time."

While taking quick notes was faster and more effective than taping and transcribing children's comments and conversations, the staff suggested that educators implementing the Reggio Approach for the first time might consider delaying the emphasis on formal documentation and instead focus on listening. Without undervaluing the importance of documentation to guide curriculum design and inform families, the teachers felt that learning to prepare documentation for formal display is a process that occurs over time and with much trial and error.

Learning what to document and how to document can easily distract a teacher from the most important component of the Reggio Approach—listening to the children.

Supportive collaboration

At the end of the year, successful implementation of the Reggio Approach appeared to be very dependent on the weekly staff meetings. The group generated many more exciting and creative curriculum ideas than any one individual could have initiated. The meetings also contributed to a greater sense of collegiality and mutual respect among teachers than ever before. When teachers needed to talk through times of unknowing, insecurity, and confusion, the emotional support staff gave to one another fostered the confidence necessary to pursue new strategies.

Suggestions for future implementation

After a year of successes, failures, triumphs, and defeats, we offer the following advice to those interested in trying the Reggio Approach:

• study three key textbooks—*Engaging Children's Minds: The Project Approach* (Katz & Chard 1989), *First Steps Toward Teaching the Reggio Way* (Hendrick 1997), and *The Hundred Languages of Children* (Edwards, Gandini, & Forman 1993)—prior to implementation;

• include parents;

• find a teacher-partner willing to give professional support during curriculum experimentation and implementation;

• find an art specialist willing to serve as a resource person;

• begin with short-term small-group projects;

• choose topics that are real and relevant;

• experiment with effective questioning techniques;

• allow children time to revisit their work;

• delay emphasis on formal documentation, but continue to observe and record; and

• continue to teach, but perhaps teach differently.

With all that's been said, our best advice is to *listen* to your children, and there you will find the wonder and beauty of teaching the young child.

References

Archambault, R., ed. 1964. *John Dewey on education—Selected writings.* New York: Random House.

Berk, L. E., & A. Winsler. 1995. *Scaffolding children's learning: Vygotsky and early childhood education.* Washington, DC: NAEYC.

Bredekamp, S., ed. 1987. *Developmentally appropriate practice in early childhood programs serving children from birth through age 8.* Washington, DC: NAEYC.

Bredekamp, S., & C. Copple, eds. 1997. *Developmentally appropriate practice in early childhood programs.* Washington, DC: NAEYC.

Carr, E., & D. Ogle. 1987. K-W-L plus: A strategy for comprehension and summarization. *Journal of Reading* 30 (7): 626–31.

Chard. S. 1996. Highlights from the Reggio e-mail bulletin board. *Innovations* 4 (1): 4.

Department of Education. 1987. *The hundred languages of children.* Reggio Emilia, Italy: Author.

DeVries, R., & L. Kohlberg. 1990. *Constructivist early education: Overview and comparison with other programs.* Washington, DC: NAEYC.

Edwards, C., L. Gandini, & G. Forman, eds. 1993. *The hundred languages of children: The Reggio Emilia approach to early childhood education.* Norwood, NJ: Ablex.

Finkelstein, J., & V. Ritter. 1980. *Does anyone have any questions?* ERIC, ED 188768.

Forman, G., & D. Kuschner. 1983. *The child's construction of knowledge: Piaget for teaching children.* Washington, DC: NAEYC.

Fowell, N., & J. Lawton. 1992. Dependencies between questions and responses during small-group instruction in two preschool programs. *Early Childhood Research Quarterly* 7: 415–39.

Fyfe, B., & G. Forman. 1996. The negotiated curriculum. *Innovations* 3 (4): 4–7.

Hendrick, J. 1997. *First steps toward teaching the Reggio way.* Upper Saddle River, NJ: Prentice-Hall.

Isbell, C. 1979. Developing levels of thinking in young children. In *Collected papers: International Seminar in Childhood Education,* ed. R. Gardner. Ogden, UT: Weber State College. ERIC, ED 184690.

Katz, L. G., & S. C. Chard. 1989. *Engaging children's minds: The project approach.* Norwood, NJ: Ablex.

Kramer, J. F. 1994. Defining competence as readiness to learn. In *New perspectives in early childhood teacher education: Bringing practitioners into the debate,* eds. S. G. Goffin & D. E. Day, 29–36. New York: Teachers College Press.

Malaguzzi, L. 1993. History, ideas, and basic philosophy: An interview with Lella Gandini. In *The hundred languages of children: The Reggio Emilia approach to early childhood education,* eds. C. Edwards, L. Gandini, & G. Forman, 41–89. Norwood, NJ: Ablex.

Montessori, M. 1965. *Dr. Montessori's own handbook.* New York: Schocken.

Ogle, D. M. 1986. K-W-L: A teaching model that develops active reading of expository text. *The Reading Teacher* 39 (6): 564–70.

Rinaldi, C. 1993. The emergent curriculum and social constructivism. In *The hundred languages of children: The Reggio Emilia approach to early childhood education,* eds. C. Edwards, L. Gandini, & G. Forman, 101–12. Norwood, NJ: Ablex.

Rosa, A., & I. Montero. 1990. The historical context of Vygotsky's work: A sociohistorical approach. In *Vygotsky and education,* ed. L. C. Moll, 59–88. Cambridge, UK: Cambridge University Press.

Schifter, D. 1996. A constructivist perspective on teaching and learning mathematics. *Phi Delta Kappan* 77 (7): 492–99.

Sigel, I., & R. Saunders. 1977. *An inquiry into inquiry: Question-asking as an instructional model.* Urbana, IL: ERIC Clearinghouse on Early Childhood Education. ERIC. ED 158871.

Vecchi, V. 1993. The role of the *atelierista.* In *The hundred languages of children: The Reggio Emilia approach to early childhood education,* eds. C. Edwards, L. Gandini, & G. Forman, 119–27. Norwood, NJ: Ablex.

Supporting Math Thinking

Fred Bell

BY ALICE P. WAKEFIELD

When children solve their own problems and are accountable for the consequences, they become more confident about their problem solving and more autonomous as well, Ms. Wakefield points out. So let the games begin!

Just as children's disposition and ability to read benefit immeasurably from having had nursery rhymes and picture books read to them, so do children acquire a sense of number when they have early opportunities to think about "number in action." Families that provide opportunities for children to share a treat equally, to make intelligent guesses, and to play simple board and card games that require the players to count, add, subtract, and match are giving their children thinking challenges that develop their number sense. Children who come to school

without this kind of previous experience encounter problems when math programs assume that mathematical relationships can be taught directly by the teacher in accordance with the curriculum rather than being constructed by each child according to his or her level of previous knowledge.

Sometimes parents and teachers think that they are teaching children only when they are telling them directly how to do something, as with the rote learning of letters and numbers. However, children learn much more when they use letters and numbers to accomplish what they themselves want

to do. The normal interactions of children at play (e.g., figuring out how many spaces to move a game piece according to the roll of the dice, what combination of cards adds up to 15, or what a "Chance" card requires) provide

ALICE P. WAKEFIELD is an associate professor of early childhood education at the Darden College of Education, Old Dominion University, Norfolk, Va. An expanded version of this article is included in her book Early Childhood Number Games: Teachers Reinvent Math Instruction, Pre-K Through Third Grade *(Allyn and Bacon, 1997).*

natural challenges that involve reading and numbers.

The Role of Active Thinking

Adults formed their understanding of counting and of adding and subtracting so long ago that it is hard to identify with the internal struggle young children face as they attempt to form these relationships for themselves. Many of us have experienced the difficulty of directing a young child to count the spaces around the game board—"peck, peck, peck." It seems so simple to us. But if the child has not formed a one-to-one correspondence of number to space, we might as well save our breath.

I've heard educators say, "Problem solving and thinking may be fine, but certain things, such as math facts and multiplication tables, must be memorized." Unfortunately, some teachers and parents take this to mean only one thing: drill and practice through the use of worksheets, flash cards, and other rote activities. These people seem to have a "no pain, no gain" mentality about learning math facts. The very name "math facts" implies that these "facts" are simply external data to be memorized through practice rather than relationships to be constructed by a thinking individual.

In workshops on creating supportive math environments, I ask teachers to think back to how they felt as children when they were asked to complete worksheets. Occasionally, someone will say that he or she *liked* doing worksheets. At first, that response shocked me, for I have no such fond memories of the dreary task. But, I suppose, if you were among the students who could get the answers and if you got a bang out of gold stars and teacher praise, you might remember them more fondly than I. There is a profound dilemma inherent in the drill-and-practice mentality of teaching early math relationships. Since children have to *know* these relationships in order to *do* the worksheets, what possible purpose do the worksheets serve? If you already know your "math facts," you surely don't need them. If you don't know them, the worksheet does nothing to teach them; it simply reminds you that you are a failure in math.

Children *do* benefit by committing to memory what have come to be known as "math facts." However, passively learning them by rote is not only unpleasant, it may also be counterproductive. When memorizing prevents children from actively thinking about and figuring out number solutions for themselves, there is little, if any, mental growth. The children's knowledge base will not develop without thinking and, therefore, will not support the ever more complex number challenges to come.

Let us consider what teachers and parents can do to replace the traditional drill-and-practice approach to memorizing "math facts." When children confront problems involving numbers in their lives outside of school, they use their natural ability to think. When they add two numbers less than 10, they count off the first number and then continue their count until they arrive at the total. It is the classic counting-on-your-fingers method. Repetition of this process does contribute to remembering, but the passive, rote practice of worksheets is boring and usually bypasses active thought. And thinking must accompany repetition so that the double payoff of constructing a knowledge base *and* remembering a math fact can be realized.

Dice, cards, and board games offer perfect opportunities for children to practice adding small numbers together repeatedly without growing bored. Children will play these games over and over and still beg for "just one more." In fact, one principal invited me into his office to talk about the math game fever that had "invaded" his elementary school. He couldn't believe that the children preferred playing math games to going out for recess! He had never seen such interest in math in more than 30 years in education.

Very young children can match the spots on cards or the dots on dice to similar configurations on their game boards in bingo-type games. (We call them "cover-up" games.) When game boards with numerals are added, children will stretch to meet the new demand of matching spots or dots to a number. Remember playing war, that perennial favorite among children's card games? It is a perfect game for young children as they consider which card has the higher number. Children can play this game whether they know the number value or not. If they don't know, they can count the card markings for themselves. Games can become more complex as children match, compare, or add the cards or dice. For example, double war, with only the lower-numbered cards from two decks, offers young children many addition problems to solve as they figure out which player has the higher sum. Typically, children play these games happily time and time again until they no longer have to "figure out" that 6 plus 3 equals 9 or that 5 plus 3 equals 8; they simply know it. Repetition, coupled with active thinking, leads to remembering—and, more important, helps them construct their number sense.

The Role of Social Interaction

Children learn and improve their understanding of number as they encounter new and varied number experiences that challenge their previous understanding. Logical ideas about number are formed gradually, often over long periods of time. Illogical or less efficient ideas are changed as new experiences challenge previously held notions. The debate and exchange of views that occur quite naturally during dice, card, and board games encourage children to examine their own thinking.

Let me give an example. Two kindergartners, Jimmy and Kyle, were playing a simple board game. A spinner was spun to indicate how many moves to make on the board. Jimmy continually counted the space of his present location, which he had reached on his last turn, as the first space of his present turn.

At first, Kyle did not notice this, but eventually he saw what was happening. Recognizing that this was not the way counting worked, Kyle endeavored to give Jimmy a quick "lesson" on how to "count on" from his present location. Kyle's first explanation consisted of directions to "do it like this: one, two, three, four, five." But Jimmy could not make the mental connection. There was too big a gap between his level of understanding of counting and what Kyle was showing him. As far as he was concerned, "one, two, three, four, five" was exactly the way he *was* doing it.

Finally, in exasperation, Kyle said, "No, do it like this: um, one, two, three, four, five." Even though Kyle did not have the word for zero, he could conceptualize that the space your game marker was on came before "one." He didn't have the word, so he created a new one instead. And Jimmy counted his turn starting with "um" for the place where his game marker already was.

It is likely that Kyle learned more from his own "lesson" by forming it than Jimmy did by observing it. Jimmy may or may not be executing Kyle's directions by rote, without reflection. On the other hand, Kyle took on the task of explaining an important concept about counting that was barely within his ability to conceptualize. This requires intensely focused thinking. And it is precisely this kind of thinking that leads to better understanding, which then supports ever more complex mental structures. The question parents and teachers need to be asking is, "What kind of learning environment fosters and supports this kind of focused thinking?" The answer to this question, in part, is "one that provides the opportunity for children to interact and thus to exchange views."

The Role of Previous Knowledge

Piaget said that children cannot see, hear, or remember that which they cannot understand. If the mental structures are not in place to support what is seen or heard, there will be no mental connection, and consequently it will not be remembered. I am reminded of this phenomenon each time I hear a new word that I am sure I have never heard before and then am amazed to hear that same word three times in the following week. Had I never heard the word before or had I just never noticed it because it had no meaning for me?

The level of a learner's previous knowledge plays a critical role as the learner struggles to figure out how to reconcile new information with old. If the gap between what is understood and the new information is too great, there will be no mental "wrestling" and no new understanding will be constructed. If there is not enough challenge to previous knowledge, students lose interest, and their attention wanders. If new learning does not "hook into" the understanding of what has been learned previously, it will not last. That is one of the reasons that the spelling words memorized for last Friday's test are misspelled on Monday's creative writing project.

The Role of Choice

Child-initiated choice plays another important role in learning. When children have real opportunities to choose (e.g., which book to read, what to build or pretend, which game to play), they do things because they want to. When the choice is freely made, it is driven by interest. And that interest presents distinct opportunities to practice the important dispositions of initiative and curiosity. Children with initiative and curiosity are in a good position to de-

velop other positive dispositions, such as persistence and industry. As all teachers know well, developing or not developing these dispositions will profoundly affect children for rest of their lives.

Of course, interest is very much related to what children already know. Children tend to be interested in something that varies "moderately" from what they already understand. A new twist on a familiar game will often captivate a child's attention. For the most part, teachers are very good at determining what is "age appropriate" for the children in their classes. However, it is more difficult to understand the fine-tuning of what makes something "individually appropriate." Constructivist teachers know that to understand what is individually appropriate for young children, they must observe them as they make choices for themselves.

A second-grade teacher told me about Mayla, a little girl in her class who was very weak in math. The only math game Mayla would play was a version of Go Fish. Instead of matching pairs of cards, as in the original version, the objective of this game was to make pairs that added to 10. Mayla had played the game with everyone in the class several times and was having a hard time trying to find someone who would play it yet again. The game was no longer "moderately novel" to her classmates. They had moved on to play more challenging games. Because children choose their own games and their own partners, Mayla would have to learn a new game if she wanted to play. Ultimately, her desire to play overcame her reluctance to try something new. An alert teacher helped her along by introducing her to a "moderately novel" game. That was all she needed, and she was ready for another round of play. Slowly, Mayla's repertoire of games increased. She never became a math whiz, but she enjoyed some of the math games and continued to build her mathematical knowledge base.

Mayla continued to choose the same game over and over for a very good reason. Children usually do not choose to do that which they are unable to do. Mayla was still getting as much challenge from repeating Go Fish as she could comfortably handle. If the teacher had assigned game partners and games or produced a worksheet, Mayla might well have experienced even less success than she did. When children have trouble working math problems assigned to them, they tend to focus on their failure and mistakes

rather than on what they are doing correctly. When this scenario is repeated frequently enough, children come to see themselves as being "dumb" in math.

Because children rarely choose to do what they can't, giving them a choice almost always ensures success. When children are successful, they feel confident about what they can do. They see themselves as being "smart," and self-esteem rises. This sense of success and competence helps create an optimal environment for further learning.

Thus a constructive, positive learning cycle is likely to occur when teachers allow for child-initiated choice in their classrooms. When children can choose something that varies moderately from what they already know, the choice reflects their interest and allows the success that leads to increased self-confidence. This in turn creates a classroom climate that is ideal for making more challenging choices that then lead to further interest, success, and confidence—and finally to higher competence. Consequently, teachers who provide opportunities for choice in the classroom ensure that their students have "individually appropriate" challenges available to them throughout the day.

Accepting Developmental Errors

It has always baffled me that some teachers work so hard to promote self-esteem in children yet simultaneously give them inappropriate academic tasks to perform. Some teachers fail to recognize and acknowledge that a child's response may be "on the way to being right." Children develop self-confidence from experiencing success. Teacher praise, sticker awards, and "all about me" theme projects will not alter the perception children have of themselves if failure dominates their day.

I am reminded of a kindergartner who would not show me the sentence he had just written on the computer because not all the words were spelled correctly. I was delighted that he had phonemic awareness and could work independently at the computer. However, even though he was obviously very advanced, instead of being pleased with his accomplishment, he was anxious about his lack of perfection and felt inadequate. He felt far less satisfaction with his efforts than another child who busily and thoughtfully wrote sentence after sentence in his journal using a less advanced level of invented spelling. All other characteristics of these two 5-year-olds being equal, who is more likely to develop the disposition to be a writer?

Recognizing what is "right" about a young child's work or response in math requires teachers to have a more complete understanding of logico/mathematical thinking. For example, when children count to 10, what do they actually know about the numbers? Can they count 10 items with one-to-one correspondence of number to item? When the teacher says, "Show me eight chips," do they point to the eighth chip or to a collection of eight chips? When children add two collections together, can they "count on" from the first collection, or must they start over from one? Which dice do the children choose to use, the dice with dots or those with numerals? What do they do when they have one of each? Little Amy proudly showed me three fingers in response to her daddy's request to tell me how old she was. "So Amy's this many," I replied, smiling and holding up one finger on one hand and two on the other. "Oh, no," Amy responded and showed me again her one-handed version of three fingers.

Teachers observe young children all day as they reveal their incomplete understanding of their world. What purpose does it serve to point out that the child's level of understanding is wrong according to our adult standard? Can Amy's daddy show her all the different ways to represent three with her fingers? Of course. But the real issue here is *should* he do this, or will Amy figure it out for herself in time? Could teaching Amy directly have a negative effect on her disposition to figure things out for herself?. Does it unnaturally emphasize to her what she does wrong rather than accept what is "on the way" to being right?

What teachers and parents alike *should* be doing is providing environments that encourage children to think and figure things out for themselves. And part of providing such an environment involves accepting developmental errors as "on the way to being right."

Where to Start

So what's a teacher to do? Try beginning with a familiar game that can be adapted to support your math objectives. For example, double war can be used to practice addition, subtraction, or multiplication. Strip out the cards you do not need from two decks and begin. Let the children "invent" their own ways of keeping score, or tell them a way you saw other children keeping score that they could try. The point is to have the children assume responsibility for as much of the activity as possible. Older children can even make their own number cards on the computer and color in the spots. You can laminate them so they will last longer. In addition to the satisfaction, there are some other advantages to making your own cards. You can eliminate the "extra" spot under the number on the corners. These spots invariably confuse the youngest children, who meticulously count them along with those representing the number. Also, the ace can be replaced with a 1, and the face cards can be dropped altogether. Sometimes it is useful to have a zero. Because some parents feel that playing cards have no place in school, we call our creations "counting cards" instead.

You may also begin by asking the children to suggest solutions to a real problem in the class. One teacher told me that their math time at the end of the school day was always being interrupted by fire drills, school announcements, or assemblies. The children were upset about this because they really enjoyed their math time. (You may be skeptical, but I hear this quite a lot.) They had a class meeting and voted to exchange math time with an earlier recess slot.

When children solve their own problems and are accountable for the consequences, they become more confident about their problem solving and more autonomous as well. And as your students become more autonomous, your classroom will become a more supportive environment for thinking and learning. Let the games begin!

Documenting Children's Learning

Judy Harris Helm, Sallee Beneke and Kathy Steinheimer

*Judy Harris Helm is an Early Childhood Specialist, Brimfield, Illinois.
Sallee Beneke is a Master Teacher, Oglesby, Illinois.
Kathy Steinheimer is a Preprimary Teacher, Peoria, Illinois.*

doc·u·ment, -ment·ed, -ment·ing, -ments (dŏk'-ye-mènt')

2. To support (an assertion or a claim, for example) with evidence or decisive information.

The American Heritage Dictionary of the English Language, Third Edition

Documenting children's learning may be one of the most valuable skills a teacher can learn. When teachers carefully collect, analyze, interpret and display evidence of learning, they are better able to understand how children learn and to help others recognize that learning. Regular and consistent documentation of children's work can benefit teachers in five ways.

1. Teachers who can document children's learning in a variety of ways are able to respond to demands for accountability.
An increased demand for accountability and program evaluation is a strong trend in edu-

cation. Schools and other early childhood programs must prove their effectiveness to their constituencies. In an effort to meet these demands for accountability, some programs have turned to increased use of standardized tests. Such group administered tests, however, are especially inappropriate for assessing children younger than 3rd grade (Meisels, 1993). The Association for Childhood Education International's official position is that standardized testing should not occur earlier than Grade 3 (ACEI/Perrone, 1991). In contrast to achievement tests, comprehensive and quality documentation can:

- provide evidence of children's learning in all areas of their development: physical, emotional, social and cognitive
- provide insight into complex learning experiences when teachers use an integrated approach
- provide a framework for organizing teachers' observations and recording each child's special interests and developmental progress
- emphasize learning as an interactive process by documenting what children learn through active exploration and interaction with adults, other children and materials
- show the advantages of activities and materials that are concrete, real and relevant to young children, as opposed to abstract and artificial events such as group testing situations
- enable the teacher to assess children's knowledge and abilities in order to increase activities' difficulty, complexity and challenge as children develop understanding and skills.

From *Childhood Education*, Summer 1997, pp. 200-205. © 1997 by the Association for Childhood Education International, 17904 Georgia Avenue, Suite 215, Olney, MD. Reprinted by permission.

2. Teachers who document are more often able to teach children through direct, firsthand, interactive experiences that enhance brain development.

Documentation enables the teacher to provide evidence that children are learning as a result of firsthand experiences. Recent research on brain development (Sylwester, 1995) suggests that children learn better when they are active, engaged and involved. Learning is related to children's feelings and emotions; therefore, their dispositions towards learning are important (Katz, 1995). How a child feels about reading, and whether or not the child wants to learn to read, will affect that child's reading achievement over the long term. Traditional methods for monitoring children's progress, such as standardized tests, do not reveal such attitudes.

Brain research also shows that learning is interconnected and cannot be isolated or compartmentalized into subject areas (Howard, 1994). Subject matter tests and standardized achievement tests do not provide information about how children integrate their learning and apply content knowledge to real life challenges. A systematic collection of children's work documents how children integrate and apply what they learn. Teachers can then assess that integration and provide more meaningful experiences.

Sylwester also showed that the brain adapts and develops by exposure to continuously changing and challenging environments. Children learn from hands-on, thought-provoking experiences that challenge them to think and stimulate their brain's growth and development. Such experiences cannot be assessed easily by conventional methods.

As teachers strive to develop curricula that is brain enhancing, they must also be mindful of assessing students' growth, development and intellectual and social learning. The two circles in Figure 1 represent these simultaneous challenges.

3. Teachers are more effective when they document.

Perhaps the greatest value of comprehensive documentation is its power to inform teaching. Teachers who have good documentation skills will make more productive planning decisions, including how to set up the classroom, what to do next, what questions to ask, what resources to provide and how to stimulate each child's development. The more information a teacher can gather when making these decisions, the more effective a teacher is likely to be.

Lev Vygotsky's sociocultural theory explains the importance of teachers' decisions in maximizing learning. According to Vygotsky (1978), the teacher is most effective when teaching is directed towards a *zone of proximal development* for each child. Children learn best when learning experiences are within their zone of development. The teacher needs to assess a child's development, probe the child's thinking on the topic and provide learning experiences that will build a bridge, or "scaffold," to higher level thought processes (Berk & Winsler, 1995). Data that reveal what the child partially understands, what the child is beginning to be able to do, or what the child is trying to integrate are often the most helpful pieces of information for teachers. Standardized tests primarily provide a limited sample of what the student has already mastered. By focusing only on what children already know, teachers cannot be as effective in helping them reach the next learning steps.

Documentation can also help the teacher decide if and when a child needs additional support systems. If the teacher collects a child's work over a period of time, the teacher can see if the child is progressing as expected or if mastery of a skill is just around the corner. When the teacher does not see mastery or emerging skills, she can seek additional help, such as early special assistance.

4. Teachers who can document children's work are better able to meet special needs.

Because of changing demographics early childhood teachers need even more skills than ever. Children with special needs are now part of many prekindergarten and primary classrooms. Some of these special needs include giftedness, physical disabilities, learning problems requiring individualized education plans, and challenges resulting from growing up in poverty. Teachers who know how to gather information and assess children's development are better able to identify the appropriate

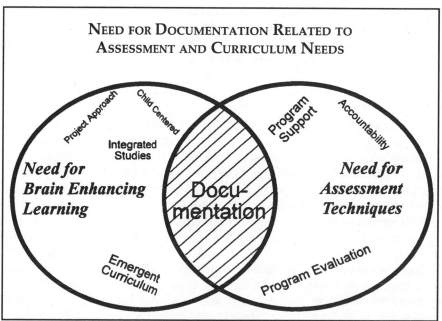

Figure 1

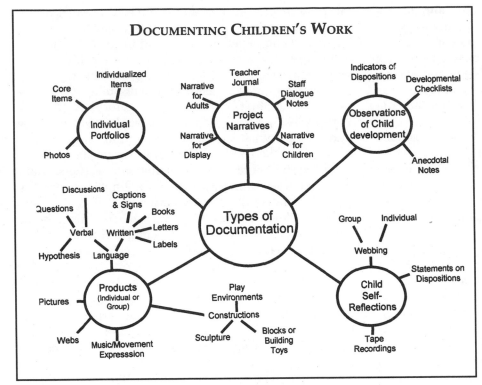

DOCUMENTING CHILDREN'S WORK

Figure 2

learning experiences for these children as well as for more typically developing children.

5. Children perceive learning to be important and worthwhile when teachers document their learning.

Extensive documentation communicates to children that their efforts to learn are important and valued. As teachers pay more attention to documentation, they find their students become more careful about their work and more evaluative. By documenting children's first, second and even third attempts at a task, teachers encourage children to reflect upon their own skill development. Children also understand how tangible evidence of their learning, through documentation, affects their parents.

The Documentation Web and the Valeska Hinton Center

Most teachers have some familiarity with documenting children's learning. They may use a developmental checklist, take anecdotal notes or systematically collect some of children's work, such as self-portraits done at the beginning and the end of the year. Many teachers may not recognize, however, all the options for assessing and demonstrating children's learning. Greater familiarity with these methods helps teachers document meaningfully.

To be most effective, teachers should vary their documentation to match children's learning experiences and to meet the needs of the intended audience. A teacher who wants to discover what a child knows about a topic might collect the child's drawings and writings about

that topic, but may not consider asking the child to help construct a beginning web about what he knows. The teacher may assemble a photographic display, but not think to have the child dictate an accompanying narrative. With a variety of ways to document at hand, the teacher will be able to obtain more accurate information about a particular child. A child who has not developed extensive language skills, for example, may not be able to dictate a narrative but may be able to draw a picture, or construct a block play environment, that shows his depth of understanding.

When teachers at the Valeska Hinton Early Childhood Education Center in Peoria, Illinois, introduced the project approach in their classrooms of children ages 3 through 6 they wanted to increase their documentation. The Professional Development Coordinator and Lead Teacher developed a web to illustrate the variety of ways that documentation could occur (see Figure 2). Teachers and other staff added to the web as they identified more ways to document. The resulting web classifies documentation methods into five clusters: Individual Portfolios, Project Narratives, Observations of Child Development, Products (both individual and group) and Self-reflections. Each of these types of documentation provides a way to view and understand children's work.

There are as many different ways to document learning as there are ways that active, engaged children try to make sense of their world. Therefore, the web is neither an exhaustive list nor an exclusive classification system. The documentation web informs and reminds teachers of the variety of ways they can document and provides a vocabulary and a structure for teachers to communicate with each other about documentation.

Project Narratives

A narrative statement, which tells the story or history of a learning experience or project, is the most traditional method of documentation. Stories are a powerful way of understanding other people's events and experiences. Such narratives can take the form of stories for and by children, records of conversations with other teachers, teacher journals, narratives for adults in the form of books and letters, or visual displays. They are usually created over a period of time, marking change and growth in knowledge, skills and dispositions.

To take advantage of the interest that comes from an evolving project, teachers can write narratives that are continuously updated as the children's work proceeds. Kathy Steinheimer's pre-kindergarten class of 3- and 4-year-olds at the Valeska Hinton Center became engaged in constructing a mail system, for example. Kathy accompanied a photo display that illustrated the mailbag design process with the following narrative:

> Karissa and Tim took on the job of creating a mailbag out of paper. This led to a lengthy interchange about the handle. Karissa drew a short handle using a picture on the cover of a book as her reference. Tim told her that it had to be bigger. Karissa drew a handle that was a little longer and wider. Tim told her that the handle was too fat. Karissa insisted that it would work and kept on cutting. Tim tried to convince Karissa that he needed the long strip on the edge of her paper. She did not agree and finished her cutting. Then, he showed her the picture on the book cover. Karissa kept on cutting. Next, she tried her handle on for size and discovered that it would not work. Therefore, she asked Tim to draw the handle. She cut out the long and narrow handle that he drew. It tore as she cut it out. However, they still thought that it would work after they cut it out. It did not. I gave them a yardstick and showed the pair how to draw a straight line with it. They made a long and wide handle for the bag, which they attached to the bag with tape. After a trial run without mail, they were satisfied with their accomplishment.

The problem-solving skills that the children developed through this experience would not be evident to others without the teacher's narrative.

mastered a particular skill, some checklists, when systematically combined with anecdotal notes and children's work samples, enable a teacher to reliably identify skills, knowledge, behaviors, dispositions and accomplishments as they emerge and become consistent. For example, Beth Crider-Olcott, a preprimary teacher at Valeska Hinton Center, recorded the following observation to document the growth in 4-year-old Thea's writing skills:

> Our project has really encouraged Thea's writing development. She had been writing her name consistently, but with the drawing of the cages, Thea attempted to copy the word "cages." With her success, Thea began to copy any word put in front of her! She copied the words "shampoo" and "alcohol" to make labels for bottles in the clinic.

Figure 3

Crider-Olcott was able to record on the developmental checklist that Thea was able to complete the skill, "Copies or writes words needed for work or play" (Jablon, Marsden, Meisels & Dichtelmiller, 1994). (See Figure 3.)

Observations of Child Development

Observing and recording development is a familiar practice for many teachers of young children. In general, child development observations may be recorded as items on a developmental checklist, anecdotal notes or indicators of dispositions. These practices have been used primarily to report on mastery of discrete skills, to assess children's progress in school, or to indicate the frequency, duration and nature of a behavior at a particular point in time.

In recent years, observation systems such as the Work Sampling System have expanded the practical uses of checklists to document growth and skill development over time. Rather than focusing on whether a child has

Individual Portfolios

Collection of children's work is another familiar type of documentation. For years, teachers have saved children's work to share with parents and to use when evaluating a child's progress at the end of the year. Teachers often collect children's self-portraits or writing samples.

Teachers can observe and document growth by systematically collecting children's work over time. This documentation is more significant when it is linked to a "comprehensive and developmentally appropriate picture of what children can be expected to know and do across all domains of growth and learning" (Meisels et al., 1994, p. 8). Portfolio items are evidence of a child's progress, as measured on a checklist that is based on such a picture. Beth Crider-Olcott, for example, saved Thea's attempts to copy words, including a map that Thea labeled by copying names of vegetables (see Figure 4).

Child Self-reflections

Self-reflections provide the most accurate assessment of a child's emotional involvement with a project's content area. The teacher can assess whether an experience is developmentally appropriate and the extent to which it will contribute to the child's disposition to learn. Observations of child self-reflections provide the most direct evidence of appropriate classroom experiences.

As part of a water project, some children in Pam Scranton's multi-age pre-kindergarten class at Valeska Hinton made foil boats. Scranton recorded 4-year-old Antonio's self-reflections:

Antonio has shown an increased disposition towards sticking with something. During the foil-boat activity, he struggled with his boat and how to connect the sides. He was beginning to become frustrated when he observed Rommel's boat and the way he pinched the sides closed. Antonio tried this and it worked. He exclaimed, "Look, Teacher, now my sides is gonna work good!" He manipulated both of his sides in this way and spent nearly 20 minutes perfecting the shape. Antonio's comments on his own progress and the length of his involvement with the boat indicate that Antonio was appropriately challenged and engaged.

Products

Products, the manifestations of children's learning, are the most obvious means of documenting learning. Adults probably consider writing samples to be the most visible signs of children's learning. Pictures, webs, musical expressions, constructions, and collections of data and oral language samples also produce significant documentation. These products can be produced either individually or by a group of children. Occasionally, the product speaks for itself; in general, however, this usefulness can be augmented by carefully selecting products for display and including an explanation of the product's significance. When displaying group work, a teacher may choose to select those products that are significant

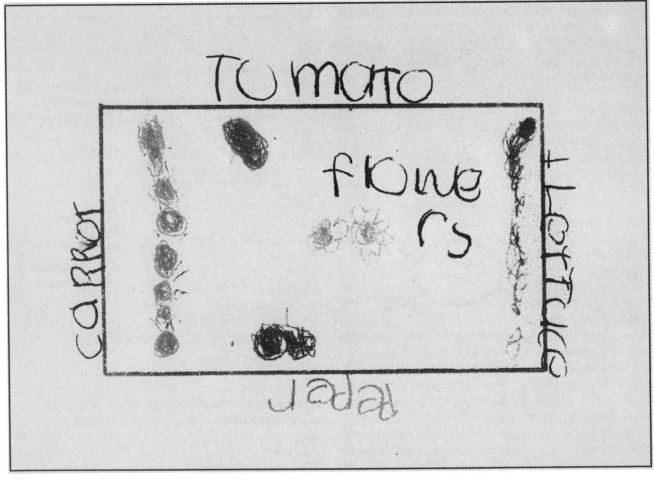

Figure 4

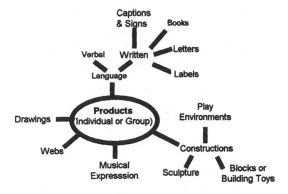

in telling the story of the project or in documenting an individual child's development through participation in the project. It is not usually necessary to display all of the children's pictures.

Group-constructed play environments are one of the most effective products to use when documenting children's knowledge and skills. What the children build reflects what they know, and the workmanship of the construction reflects their skills. Val Timmes' multi-age kindergarten/1st-grade class constructed a grocery store in their classroom, for example, as an outgrowth of their investigation of fruits and vegetables.

The children visited the grocery story, made sketches of what they saw, and then drew and refined floor plans for their store. They made lists and diagrams. They measured, cut and created, forming teams to construct the store's various departments. The resulting play environment was rich with examples of the children's knowledge of the grocery store and their ability to measure, read, write, problem-solve, work with number concepts and create. By documenting this play environment with written explanations of the various constructions, and by displaying photographs of the children in the process of constructing, Val Timmes was able to share the significance of these products with parents, children and other visitors.

Conclusion

Documentation is a powerful skill for the teacher. A letter from a parent at Valeska Hinton Center shows the effect that high quality documentation can have on parents' perceptions of a school. This parent was in the process of choosing a preschool program for her child and first encountered the project approach when she visited the center.

> My first actual encounter with projects occurred in late spring at an open house for prospective parents . . . I was skeptical—the so-called traditional approaches had worked for me, so why wouldn't it also provide success for our child? . . . Walking around the school that night, I began to be impressed. I studied [the documentation on] a project on reflections. I marveled at the insights shared by the children. The critical thinking skills [that] their work exhibited was phenomenal. Direct quotations included sentences of greater length and complexity than I would have expected. Their vocabulary was very specific. I went home and attempted to describe what I had seen to my husband . . . After our discussion, we became convinced that this was the place for our daughter to learn.
>
> —*Nancy Higgins, parent*

Ultimately, the teacher's skill and the time and effort spent in documentation benefited the children, the parents and the school.

References

Association for Childhood Education International/Perrone, V. (1991). On standardized testing. A position paper. *Childhood Education, 67,* 132–142.

Berk, L., & Winsler, A. (1995). *Scaffolding children's learning: Vygotsky and early childhood education.* Washington, DC: National Association for the Education of Young Children.

Howard, P. (1994). *The owner's manual for the brain.* Austin, TX: Leornian Press.

Jablon, J. R., Marsden, D., Meisels, S., & Dichtelmiller, M. (1994). *Omnibus guidelines: Preschool through third grade* (3rd ed.) Ann Arbor, MI: Rebus Planning Associates.

Katz, L. (1995). *Talks with teachers of young children: A collection.* Norwood, NJ: Albex Publishing.

Meisels, S. (1993). Remaking classroom assessment with the work sampling system. *Young Children, 48,* 34–40.

Meisels, S., Jablon, J., Marsden, D., Dichtelmiller, M., Dorfman, A., & Steele, D. (1994). *An overview* (3rd ed.) Ann Arbor, MI: Rebus Planning Associates.

Sylwester, R. (1995). *A celebration of neurons: An educator's guide to the human brain.* Alexandria, VA: Association for Supervision and Curriculum Development.

Vygotsky, L. S., edited and translated by M. Cole, V. John-Steiner, S. Scribner, & E. Souberman. (1978). *Mind in society: The development of higher mental processes.* Cambridge, MA: Harvard University Press.

Unit 6

Key Points to Consider

❖ Make a list of predictions about childhood in the new millennium.

❖ How will teaching change in the new millennium?

❖ How close to "life on the outside" is " life on the inside" of child care?

❖ Predict your future as a teacher. What will be required of you? How will your knowledge have to expand?

❖ What role do the diverse lifestyles of the children in a classroom play in the development of the curriculum?

 **Links**

www.dushkin.com/online/

These sites are annotated on pages 4 and 5.

An intriguing look at childhood in the future is the lead article of this unit on trends. "Tomorrow's Child" by Jerry Adler is a forecast of the challenges and opportunities facing children who will grow up in the new millennium. Depending on social forces and advances in technology, tomorrow's child may be "enhanced" intellectually or physically. The author predicts, however, that the most significant change for children may be universal adoption of pre–K programs. This would mean that all children, not just those of middle-class families, would have access to early childhood programs and that free preschools may be commonplace. Important landmarks in family life are described throughout the article as a backdrop for forecasting. One of the most significant landmarks is certainly the invention of color TV, which changed the way many preschool children were first introduced to letters and words. Perhaps equally significant is the more recent landmark—the widespread use of Ritalin, the drug used for attention deficit hyperactivity disorder, which also changes the way children approach learning.

As a profession, early childhood education is relatively new. Teachers are still experiencing the growing pains always associated with the emergence of new institutions. We are creating our own traditions as a profession and in the process, we are discovering "authentic practice." Lyn Fasoli

and Janet Gonzalez-Mena ask us to consider how authentic we are in teaching young children. Their article, "Let's Be Real!" is packed with interesting vignettes of teachers engaging in authentic practices. They invite us to create first-hand experiences for children and to be honest in all our dealings with children and colleagues. This is the way we, as early childhood educators, can be our real selves. Even more significant, it is the way the profession will match beliefs with actions.

"What Matters Most: A Competent Teacher for Every Child" is Linda Darling-Hammond's discussion of the report of the National Commission on Teaching and America's Future. The report calls for all children to have competent, caring, and qualified teachers by the year 2006. More than 2 million teachers will be hired during the next decade, many for early childhood classrooms. These teachers will be faced with the challenge of higher expectations. They will need more training and in-depth knowledge of content. The commission calls for tougher standards for both students and teachers. They recommend that teacher preparation be reorganized to be more rigorous and that continuing professional development be required. For early childhood teachers, the challenge will be to remain true to active learning and developmentally appropriate practice, while becoming an effective teacher for the twenty-first century.

Amazing medical advances, great economic opportunities, earlier schooling and many new kinds of Barbie dolls are among the wonders in store for the first Americans of a new century. BY JERRY ADLER

TOMORROW'S CHILD

SHE WILL BE CONCEIVED, ALMOST CERtainly, sometime in the next six months, and will tumble headfirst into the world nine months later, wholly unconscious of her uniqueness as the first American of the millennium. Escaping by a stroke of the clock the awful burden of the present century, she (or he) will never hear the screams at Dachau or see the sky burst into flames over Hiroshima; the cold war will be as remote as the epic of Gilgamesh. For that matter, even the re-runs of "Barney" will bear the musty reek of the classics. Some things are eternal, though, and present trends indicate that sometime in the next century the average American girl could have more Barbie dolls than she has classmates. Grandchild of baby boomers! The very phrase boggles the mind—although not so much, perhaps, as the fact that of the 8.9 million American children who will be born in the year 2000, at least 70,000 of them are expected to still be alive in 2100.

First, though, they'll survive being dropped on their heads in the delivery room when the Y2K computer bug shuts off the electricity. To each century belongs its own terrors, and also its own pleasures. The child born in the year 2000 may face epidemics of previously unknown tropical diseases, but he also may be able to eat broccoli Jell-O instead of broccoli. And the toy industry may come to the rescue of lonely kids with a doll designed to remind them of their mothers. "We have so many latchkey children in search of a human connection," muses marketing consultant Faith Popcorn. "They'll be able to carry their mother around in doll form!" A lot has been written lately about the future as the venue for abstract breakthroughs in science, technology and medicine, but much less on the concrete questions of how Americans will actually live in it.

The millennium baby will be born into a nation of approximately 275 million, the third largest in the world, and still growing; the midrange estimate of the Census Bureau is that the population will reach 323 million by 2020 and 394 million by midcentury. Where will all those people live? Mostly in California, Texas and Florida, which among them will account for almost three out of 10 Americans by 2025. They will be squeezed onto proportionately less land: the median lot size of a new single-family house will almost certainly continue the slow, steady drop of the last 20 years. Children born in the year 2000 will live, on average, twice as long as those born in 1900 But they will live in bigger houses; the median floor area will reach 2,000 square feet any year now, a 25 percent increase since 1977. "The 800-square-foot Levittown house—that's a big family room now," says Columbia University historian Kenneth T. Jackson.

The cohort born circa 2000 should also benefit from what some economists are calling "the great asset sell-off" of the 21st century—the liquidation of family homes as the baby boomers start retiring in the second and third decades. "Younger Americans will get some great deals" on real estate, says Teresa Ghilarducci, a specialist in economic forecasting at Notre Dame. And, she adds, "it will be a great time to look for and get great jobs." But boomers will also be liquidating their investments, so stock-market values will stagnate. Except in some favored sunbelt locales, families moving out will create what Ghilarducci ominously calls "suburban wastelands." Downtown neighborhoods that haven't gentrified by then will be just out of luck.

The salient economic fact in the child's life may be the growing gap between the haves and have-nots, says Robert Litan, director of economic studies at the Brookings Institution. As disparities of wealth and income continue to widen, he says, "we could find ourselves living in a winner-take-all society. If people don't see economic opportunity, they drop out" of civil society. These trends will play themselves out in an America increasingly populated by minorities. By 2050, the Census Bureau projects an American population that is one-quarter black, Asian or Native American and one-quarter Hispanic. How the nation fares in the next century will depend on whether those changes widen the socioeconomic gap between races or help close it. And meanwhile, which of the children born in the year 2000 will be chosen for the Harvard class of 2022—bearing in mind that by the time they enroll, the projected cost of a Harvard education will be more than $320,000?

There are a few things we can say with some assurance. Millennium babies will be about the same size as their parents. The long-term trend among Caucasians toward greater size is a factor of better nutrition, but as everyone knows, Americans are already maxed out when it comes to food consumption. Children born in the year 2000 will, however; live longer than ever: 73 years, on average, for a boy, and almost 80 for a girl—approximately double the average life expectancy of a newborn at the turn of the last century. And the figures are expected to rise steadily throughout the first half of the century. Those averages, though, conceal a wide disparity among different races. Whites, interestingly, are about in the middle; the category of Asians and Pacific Islanders will live the longest; blacks the shortest. It is a depressing statistic that a black male born in 2000 will have a life expectancy of 64.6 years—actually *less* than for an older brother born in 1995.

Some of the improvement in life span will come from reducing already low rates

The reading wars will continue, with increasing reliance on computers, but kids will still be put to bed with 'Goodnight Moon'

of infant death. Dr. James Marks of the Centers for Disease Control estimates that the mortality rate for newborns, around eight per 1,000 live births, could drop to as little as one per 1,000. Premature births account for many newborn deaths, but in the next decade, says bioethicist Arthur Caplan of the University of Pennsylvania, doctors will perform the astonishing feat of keeping alive babies born as early as 19 or 20 weeks after conception, weighing only eight ounces. Preemies younger than about 24 weeks now almost invariably succumb to the failure of their underdeveloped lungs, but techniques are now being developed to allow them to breathe oxygen from a liquid solution until they can sustain themselves in the air.

Even more impressive are advances forecast for in utero surgery. Already doctors can remove fetal tumors and correct conditions such as diaphragmatic hernia—a hole in the diaphragm that can cause serious lung problems. But standard open surgery on a living fetus is a very high-risk procedure. Within the next decade, surgeons will be performing these operations with the help of tiny cameras mounted on needle-like probes, according to Dr. Michael Harrison, head of the Fetal Treatment Center at the University of California, San Francisco. Ultimately, he expects, doctors will be able to do anything on a fetus that can be done after birth. "Heart repairs? We're working on them day and night [in animals]," Harrison says. "It hasn't been done in humans yet, but we will be there in the next century."

The road map to the 21st century is being written now in the Human Genome Project, the monumentally ambitious attempt to catalog the entire complement of a normal person's DNA. When it's completed, in about 2003, researchers will be able to identify the genes responsible for many of mankind's most intractable afflictions—such as cystic fibrosis, muscular dystrophy and congenital immune deficiency. As a first step, doctors will be able to diagnose these diseases in utero, and parents will have the chance—and, consequently, the burden—of deciding whether to end the pregnancy. (Some of these tests are already in use.) But by the early years of the next century doctors will

perform the equivalent of alchemy, curing disease by directly tinkering with patients' DNA. They will synthesize normal copies of the defective gene, or altered genes that counteract it, and attach them to a "vector" such as a benign virus to carry them into the patient's cells. In combination with Harrison's fetal-surgery techniques, it may be possible to cure congenital conditions even before birth.

For most babies born in the year 2000, smoking and overeating obviously will be a bigger threat to health than birth defects. Childhood obesity "is up dramatically since the '80s," says Marks of the CDC, and is expected to increase among kids who lift a finger only to click a mouse button. But routine genetic screening early in the next century will make a difference there, too, by identifying the health risks specific to each individual. The public-health lesson of this century is that people generally change their lifestyles only under the threat of death, which is why those born in the future will probably not have to sit through so many public-service exhortations about fitness from Arnold Schwarzenegger. Instead, doctors will tell them which particular risks they run, and what they have to do to stay alive—including, for example, the nutritional supplements that will do them the most good. On smoking, diet and exercise the advice is probably going to be pretty much the same as it is now—except that there are always people who will live a long time no matter what they eat. One of the great pleasures of living in the next century may be finding out you're one of them.

A new theory will change our attitudes about child rearing— we don't know what it is yet, but there always is one

In terms of psychological health, a new theory will revolutionize parents' attitudes toward child rearing. No one knows what the new theory will be, but there always is one. The 20th century's succession of mutually contradictory panaceas (more structure; more freedom; it doesn't make a difference) shouldn't obscure the point that until about the 1940s, "most parents didn't give much thought to child development at all," says Jerome Singer, a Yale child psychologist. "From a parenting point of view, children are better off today, and will be better off in

the next few decades. Parents realize children need attention and oversight of what's going on in their lives, and those beliefs are penetrating into the lower socioeconomic groups."

And if kids persist in being maladjusted, there will be lots more ways to treat them. Caplan foresees radical new therapies that will rely on virtual-reality simulators (so the patient can practice, say, controlling his aggression in a mock situation) and brain scans that will tell the therapist on the spot whether the patient was learning. With this technique, he says, "you could look for change in real time," a boon to patients and insurance companies alike. There also will be many more problems to treat. The frontier of therapy in the next century will be "sub-syndromal" conditions such as mild depression, social phobias and anxieties. "We'll be treating emotional disabilities that we don't even label today," says Dr. Solomon H. Snyder, who heads the department of neuroscience at Johns Hopkins University. The debates over Prozac and Ritalin, which some authorities suspect are being prescribed indiscriminately, prefigure what will be two of the most important questions in 21st-century medical ethics: How far should we go in "enhancing" people who are essentially normal? And who will pay for it?

And periodically someone will invent the one and only best method to teach reading, rendering all other techniques hopelessly obsolete. It might well involve computers; there is already a burgeoning market for what's called "lapware," software aimed at children under a year old, who do their computing while sitting on Mommy's lap. "I've seen some that attempt to teach kids to associate letters and sounds with colors," says a very dubious David Elkind, a professor of child development at Tufts University. "That's a skill most children don't have until they're 4 or 5." Whatever the new movement is, it will provoke an equally strong reaction as soon as parents discover that it doesn't automatically turn their toddlers into John Updike. "The reading wars"—basically pitting old-fashioned phonics against everything else—"have been going on for a century and a half, so what chance do we have of ending them by the year 2000?" says Timothy Shanahan, a professor of education at the University of Illinois-Chicago.

The truth, well known to researchers, is that most kids can learn to read with almost any method, and will do it by themselves if left alone with a pile of books. And there will still be books in the next century. As births increased in the 1980s, the number of new children's titles published annually doubled, even as families started buying computers for the first time. Paula Quint, president of the Children's Book Council, expects that as births level off over the next few years the number of new titles will hold steady at about 5,000 a year. A few of these may even turn into classics, but it's safe to say that in the next century and beyond, kids will still be put to bed with "Goodnight Moon."

The change that is likely to make a real difference in the lives of millennium kids is a mundane one: the slow adoption of universal pre-K education. Most of the kids who attend preschool now are from relatively well-off families, even though research shows that the programs most benefit poor children. A few states, in search of a morally unassailable use of gambling proceeds, are dedicating them to providing free programs for 4-year-olds. "In 10 years," predicts Anne Mitchell, a consultant on early-childhood programs, "free preschool will be commonplace."

And in so many other ways, the year 2000 will be a great time to be born. Kids will have terrifically cool ethnic names like Pilar, Selena or Kai—although there may also be a countertrend, fueled by millennial religious fervor, for Biblical names like Isaiah and Elijah. Their mothers are more likely to breast-feed them than has been true for a generation (a quarter of all mothers nursed their children for at least six months last year, up from about 5 percent in 1971). And they will be able, if their parents don't mind, to run around in diapers until they're almost 4. Recognizing a trend toward later toilet training (and bigger kids), Procter & Gamble recently introduced Pampers in size 6, for toddlers 35 pounds and over. Of course, kids who are kept in diapers until

Babies born as early as 19 weeks after conception may survive, thanks to a technology enabling them to breathe through a liquid

the age of 4 can only help drive up the cost of raising them, which, according to U.S. Department of Agriculture statistics, will amount to approximately $250,000 for the first 18 years of a millennium baby's life.

Inevitably, part of that sum will go toward the purchase of Barbie dolls. In the early 1980s, most girls were content with one Barbie; the average collection is now up to 10 and likely to rise in the future as Mattel expands the line into infinity—adding just this year, for example, Chilean, Thai, Polish and Native American Barbies. Last year Mattel added a wheelchair Barbie, and a spokeswoman suggests "there may be more dolls with other disabilities in the future."

Yes, the kid of the future will be, if anything, even more pampered and catered to than the fabled baby boomers themselves, at least in part because there's so much money to be made off them. Leaving the house at 7:30 in the morning for 12-hour days of school, restaurants and shopping, they will require ever-more-elaborate "urban survival clothes," like the currently popular cargo pants in whose capacious pockets one can stow a meatball grinder, a palmtop computer and a jar of The Limited's most exciting new cosmetic product, fruit-scented antibacterial glitter gel. In what marketing guru Popcorn regards as one of the most significant social trends of the next millennium, "cross-aging," kids will be more like adults (and vice versa): "We're going to see health clubs for kids, kids as experts on things like the Internet, and new businesses, like Kinko's for Kids, to provide professional quality project presentations." The travel market of the future will increasingly be geared to kids, and not just at theme parks—24 million business trips included children in 1996, up 160 percent from 1991. So, to anyone who may have wondered whether it was right to bring a child into the uncertain world of the 21st century, it's fair to say, your fears are groundless.

The next millennium is going to be great for kids.

It's the adults who will miss the 1990s.

With PAT WINGERT, KAREN SPRINGEN, ELIZABETH ANGELL *and* MICHAEL MEYER

Let's Be Real!

Authenticity in Child Care

by Lyn Fasoli and Janet Gonzalez-Mena

Do you ever catch yourself speaking pleasantly when you don't feel pleasant at all? Do you sometimes feel that you are acting a part, and that the real you is left at home? Are you being your version of a professional, but you don't feel professional? Perhaps you are having an authenticity crisis.

Jim Greenman (1992) talks about how children spend their childhoods in child care. It's a sobering thought, a childhood in child care.

What kinds of childhoods are we professionals creating for children? How authentic are they? How honest are the emotional exchanges children see and experience? How rich and authentic are the conversations? How close to "life on the outside" is "life on the inside" of child care? How often do real events, real objects, real people from the outside world have a real impact on the child-centered world in which children spend up to five years of their lives?

How influenced are we by the kinds of packaged environments, curricula, materials, and toys available on the market? Do we understand what happens if a child never has a chance to wander, rummage around in a shed, barn, attic, basement, or other clutter-gathering space? When we protect children from the real world, do we inadvertently discourage the very qualities we say we value in children: curiosity, inquisitiveness, initiative, risk taking, and persistence?

What about opportunities to investigate and explore what exists in the home? Old things such as broken radios, sewing machines, screwdrivers, strips of material to make into dress up, real kitchen bowls, spoons, and stuff for concoctions. Do we rely too much on pretend tool kits, toy construction kits, store-bought play dough? Toys are not the same as real things that adults use. Children deserve the chance to learn firsthand about their culture through playing with real things that come from their culture.

The child care center is a relatively new institution still in the process of formation. We are at the precedent setting stage in developing places where childhoods do indeed happen. Unlike schools, child care centers are not encumbered by centuries of tradition. In our short history, we have acquired few impediments to creating a new institution. What kinds of tradition will we create? Can we dream a healthy vision of what can be or will we today produce baggage that those who follow us will have to carry?

We are making strides. We, as a profession, have established codes of eth-

ics and developmentally appropriate practices to guide us in examining the experience we provide for young children in care. Ever since the groundbreaking document by the NAEYC in 1987 (Bredekamp, 1987) defined nationally agreed upon guidelines for practice (known as developmentally appropriate practices, or DAP), we have focused our attention increasingly on the issue of what is appropriate.

We continue to make strides. DAP is not a static concept. It has been expanded in the brand new edition to include more cultural sensitivity. We would like to suggest that appropriate practice must also be examined in terms of authenticity. We ask the question—is it truly appropriate if it isn't also authentic?

Authenticity is a dimension sometimes neglected in discussions of practices with young children. Thinking in terms of authenticity of experience may help identify the feelings of discontent reflected in the questions we asked in the first paragraph.

Here are some examples of teachers engaging in small samples of what we consider authentic practice.

Three toddlers and two four year olds are sitting in front of the TV at 5:40 PM. They are the last to go and there is still 20 minutes to wait. Jean, their caregiver, looks at them and asks, "Do you want to count money?" Without hesitation, they shout, "Yes!" They know and love "counting money." Jean takes them out to the front office and asks the director if she has any money that needs counting. The director tips out the change drawer, spilling hundreds of coins onto the carpeted floor. The children settle down happily to count the money, which means making piles of coins that go together. The 20 minutes fly by.

A seven year old is allowed to spend several hours combining parts of several old ball-point pens into a new creation of his own that is short and stubby, doesn't look like a pen, but writes like one. He shows more pride in this creation than any of the craft projects presented him in his after-school care program.

A teacher looking for a way to lock the new trike shed discovers an abandoned box full of locks and keys, but doesn't have time to pick through and find one that works. A four year old who has a notably short attention span happens along and shows interest in the jumble in the box. He spends the rest of the morning matching keys to padlocks, and proudly presents the box of keys in locks to the teacher right before lunch.

A tired, filthy three year old remarks while showing off a hole out in the back corner of the play yard, "That's the best thing I ever did in nursery school." His teachers tell his mother when she comes to pick him up and confirm that he worked hours digging the hole with a small adult shovel. It was his own idea. Nobody suggested it to him. The next day he filled the hole back in without being asked.

Tom, a caregiver of three year olds, decides he will bring his motorbike to work to fix it. Why not? He used to help his dad when he was a little fellow. Soon he is surrounded by small bits of motorcycle, tools, and rags. Off to the right there is a line of small mechanics also tinkering with their tricycles.

What is authentic to one person, place, or situation will not necessarily hold for another. However, we all seem to recognize an authentic experience when we have one. It feels right. It sounds right. When we only consider appropriateness, is there a danger that we leave out this personal check point of authenticity? Authenticity is a useful word. Authenticity wears its association with personal value judgments on its sleeve. Appropriateness, on the other hand, depends on what some group somewhere considers to be acceptable in some general sense. Appropriateness is arrived at by consensus decision making. When we try to decide what is appropriate, invariably we refer to higher, broader, and more remote authorities than ourselves and our immediate community. We often forget to consult our own beliefs and gut feelings and consider the requirements of the contexts we work in. It is when we trust ourselves and what we, as the local "expert," know that we access authenticity.

Here are some examples of familiar practices that cause many of us to feel that something inauthentic is happening.

Sam: It's a box I got from my Nan and my brother got one, too, but his is already broken when my dog got it.

Sarah: So, what shape would you call that box, Sam?

Sam: A box.

Sarah: But what shape is it?

Sam: A box shape?

Sarah: It's a square shape, isn't it?

Sam: Uh huh.

Sarah: Actually there are lots of square shapes on your box, aren't there? Can you show the children a square on your box?

Sam: (Holds the box aloft for the children to see.)

How authentic is it to talk about shapes when the dog ate your brother's box?

Marie is asked by another caregiver to take over in the sleep room. Marie groans inwardly. She absolutely hates patting children to sleep. It is boring. She always falls asleep herself and, besides, she's no good at it. They never go to sleep when she does it because she just doesn't believe in it. It's no good for children to be patted to sleep. It just makes them dependent on adults to get them to sleep. They should learn to do it themselves. There's no point in thinking such thoughts, though. The policy at this center is to pat, so pat she will.

Is authentic to do something you don't like, don't feel is effective, and don't want to do?

Wendy is an assistant teacher in the toddler room. She is also the mother of four. She has been assigned to supervise finger painting with chocolate pudding. She watches several children hold back, and is told to encourage them because it is important for young children to have sensory experiences. She is repulsed by the activity and wonders how this practice might conflict with what the children are being taught at home about touching food (or feces). She wonders if, at this age, they can distinguish between a sensory activity and a "no, no." How authentic is it to carry out a practice that disgusts you—one you don't believe in?

These next examples push the issue of authenticity a bit further.

Dawn uses the saying "You capture more flies with honey than with vinegar" to guide her interactions with children and co-workers. She has a 100% positive approach to everything and can twist children around her finger with sweet talk. She manages to waylay most behavior problems by distracting offenders with new activities or promises of "surprises." Her techniques work. Are her manipulations appropriate? Are they authentic? How would you know?

On the contrary, Lilly, is gruff and stern with children. She confronts behavior head on. Nobody gets away with anything around her and she uses no sweet talk. She's always got an eye out for misbehavior and issues regular warnings when she sees something coming. As stern as she is in the face of misbehavior, that's how warm and loving she is at other times. She handles the children a lot. Some are in awe of her sternness, but melt in her warmth.

Is Lilly appropriate? Is she authentic? How would you know?

Samantha has been working with Jim for a week now. He is great with the kids, but he does get them stirred up. For instance, this morning he was horsing about with them pretending to be a lion and one of the children actually started crying. He cuddled her

and got her screaming with laughter again soon after but Samantha doesn't really think this is appropriate behavior for a teacher.

Is Jim's behavior authentic? Is it appropriate? Does it have to be both?

Research in early childhood education has begun to recognize that personal as well as formal knowledge has a place in teachers' and caregivers' decision making. In studies of teachers' and caregivers' thinking about their practice, researchers highlight stories of practice that "ring true" or sound authentic (Jalongo and Isenberg, 1995). These studies emphasize the knowledge that teachers and caregivers themselves generate. Authentic, personal, and contextualized knowledge can be found in stories that teachers tell about their own practice. More formal knowledge sources tend to eliminate this kind of knowledge as being too specific and context bound.

It is the formal, principled knowledge that we find in curriculum guides, textbooks, directives from higher authorities, and indeed the NAEYC *Developmentally Appropriate Practice* document. Principled knowledge is what it sounds like—knowledge that is expressed in terms of principles or generalities and, as such, it is perceived to be context free (Mclean, 1993).

As early childhood educators, we are trained, in-serviced, and pressured by others to value principled knowledge more than the personal, practical, context-specific knowledge we generate ourselves, know on an intuitive level, and accumulate through our everyday experiences with young children. The stories of practice we tell each other and the practical knowledge embodied within them connect with what we know to be true, with what we believe.

This is not an argument to discard or denigrate principled knowledge. Both kinds of knowledge are important. But one always needs to be examined

in light of the other. Some who work in child care only operate out of personal knowledge and experience and miss the broader view of principled knowledge that comes from research and formal study. They are one sided. On the other hand, some neglect to examine their principled knowledge in the light of personal feelings and experience. They fail to go beyond what they've been taught. They lack trust in their own ability to determine what is authentic for the circumstances and setting (Stonehouse, 1993).

Those who operate as professionals but fail to balance principled knowledge with personal knowledge and authenticity may have some of the feelings alluded to in the opening paragraph.

Some professionals who are also parents may operate authentically at home and feel guilty that they don't act more "professional" with their own children. How many of us yell in anger and frustration at our own children, but would never raise our voices or show anger around the children with whom we work? How many of us feel guilty at the inconsistency? (Gonzalez-Mena, 1995)

We suggest that perhaps child care teachers should balance principled knowledge with gut knowledge and aim for increased authenticity. This kind of balance may change both their teacher roles and their parent roles to some extent. That is not to say that we propose teachers and parents should act alike. Teachers, after all, must be more thoughtful, plan more for learning, not become overly attached, and be concerned about fairness to all children.

Parents, on the other hand, should accept the fact that parenting is a passionate job. Parents are, and should be, more attached, more spontaneous, more emotional, and a champion for their own child. It's not that they shouldn't be thoughtful about what they are doing, but too much analysis creates "analysis paralysis" and gets in the way of healthy parenting (Katz, 1977). Both teachers and parents should operate out of principled knowledge and personal, practical knowledge. Both parents and teachers should be authentic. How do we know and recognize authentic experiences, objects, interactions, conversations? Where does what is developmentally appropriate fit with what is authentic? Like everything else in life, there are many diverse ideas about what constitutes authenticity in child care. If authentic is that which reflects reality, one common definition, then the question is "whose reality?" Do we know what constitutes an authentic experience for the children we work with—for their families as well? How do we find out? There are likely to be many authentic ways to work with children and they won't all look the same.

Like "quality," authenticity is a complex and elusive characteristic and best understood as occurring along a continuum. Most experience can probably be located somewhere between entirely authentic and entirely unauthentic rather than at either end of the spectrum. Perhaps thinking along these continua will help in evaluating the authenticity of an experience.

An authentic experience is one that:

• is closer to being true than false in nature;

• is the real thing more often than a replica;

• is characterized more by honesty than deception;

• is richer, wider, deeper than its synthetic counterpart;

• feels more right than wrong

• is more evocative than evoking no feeling at all.

The key is to avoid dichotomies of right and wrong, appropriate and inappropriate, but consider that almost every situation is potentially both. We must tap into our personal knowledge base and that of others with whom we work and live to discover the knowledge held in the variety of beliefs and views. That knowledge must work in conjunction with principled knowledge in determining what is appropriate and authentic. We can't use books or sets of guidelines alone, but must use our gut reactions as well.

We must bring our "real selves" to work with us. Consider the caregiver who is angry and frustrated about a child who continually hits other children. For the tenth time, she hustles over to intervene when Matthew and Tommy are struggling over the red-handled shovel. She arrives just in time to stop Matthew from whapping Tommy in the head with a blue-handled shovel. She squats down next to Matthew and says in a calm, even tone, "Matthew, use your words. Tell Tommy what you want." She's well trained. She hides her true feelings about the situation.

How authentic is it to speak as if you were ordering a cappuccino when, in fact, you are completely fed up? Shouldn't children perhaps know when an adult is feeling something deeply?

How bad would it be for children to see adults being natural in a child care setting? Consider this scene. The director glances up and sees the new caregiver, Miriam, talking and laughing once again with another caregiver while they're both sitting on the edge of the sand pit. Miriam is almost weeping with the hilarity of some incident. So is the other caregiver. A few children approach them and stand watching them laugh. Soon there is a circle of children all standing around the two women laughing. They, have big smiles on their faces. They start giggling. In no time, the whole group is laughing.

Why shouldn't children see adults enjoying themselves, having a good laugh? At home, children are likely to see adults expressing all sorts of feelings. If they are to have a childhood in child care, shouldn't they see adults being more authentic than they are when acting in an unemotional "professional" manner?

We must not miss the opportunity we have today to expand our definitions of good quality care and education to include not only what we, as a profession, believe is appropriate, but what we, as professional individuals, know is authentic. This is not going to be an easy process. It will require much discussion, argument, and compromise as groups of early childhood professionals and parents determine what they mean by "authentic" for the children who spend their childhoods in child care. In doing this, we won't be generating new sets of guidelines for others to follow. Accommodating the principle of personal authenticity will always remain within the domain of the personal and local. Nevertheless, determining a process for distinguishing what is authentic from what is not provides a growth point for the profession.

References

Bredekamp, S. (editor). *Developmentally Appropriate Practice in Early Childhood Programs Serving Children From Birth through Age 8.* Washington, DC: National Association for the Education of Young Children, 1987.

Gonzalez-Mena, J. *Dragon Mom: Confessions of a Child Development Expert.* Napa, CA: Rattle OK Publications, 1995. Greenman, J. "Living in the Real World." *Child Care Information Exchange,* July 1992, pp. 21–23. Jalongo, M. R. and J. P. Isenberg. *Teachers' Stories: From Personal Narrative to Professional Insight.* San Francisco: Jossey-Bass, 1995.

Katz, L. G. *Talks with Teachers.* Washington, DC: National Association for the Education of Young Children, 1977.

Mclean, V. "Learning from Teachers' Stories." *Childhood Education.* Annual Theme Issue, 1993, pp. 265–268.

Stonehouse, A. "Is Appropriate Practice the Same Whatever the Setting?" Symposium address given at the Creche and Kindergarten Association of Queensland National Early Childhood Conference, Brisbane, June 1993.

What Matters Most

A Competent Teacher for Every Child

BY LINDA DARLING-HAMMOND

The report of the National Commission on Teaching and America's Future offers a blueprint for recruiting, preparing, supporting, and rewarding excellent educators in all of America's schools, according to Ms. Darling-Hammond. For the details, read on.

We propose an audacious goal . . . by the year 2006, America will provide all students with what should be their educational birthright: access to competent, caring, and qualified teachers.[1]

WITH THESE words, the National Commission on Teaching and America's Future summarized its challenge to the American public. After two years of intense study and discussion, the commission—a 26-member bipartisan blue-ribbon panel supported by the Rockefeller Foundation and the Carnegie Corporation of New York—concluded that the reform of elementary and secondary education depends first and foremost on restructuring its foundation, the teaching profession. The restructuring, the commission made clear, must go in two directions: toward increasing teachers' knowledge to meet the demands they face and toward redesigning schools to support high-quality teaching and learning.

The commission found a profession that has suffered from decades of ne-

glect. By the standards of other professions and other countries, U.S. teacher education has historically been thin, uneven, and poorly financed. Teacher recruitment is distressingly ad hoc, and teacher salaries lag significantly behind those of other professions. This produces chronic shortages of qualified teachers in fields like mathematics and science and the continual hiring

Kay Salem

LINDA DARLING-HAMMOND is William F. Russell Professor of Education at Teachers College, Columbia University, New York, N.Y., and executive director of the National Commission on Teaching and America's Future. She is a member of the Kappan Board of Editorial Consultants.

of large numbers of "teachers" who are unprepared for their jobs.

Furthermore, in contrast to other countries that invest most of their education dollars in well-prepared and well-supported teachers, half of the education dollars in the United States are spent on personnel and activities outside the classroom. A lack of standards for students and teachers, coupled with schools that are organized for 19th-century learning, leaves educators without an adequate foundation for constructing good teaching. Under these conditions, excellence is hard to achieve.

The commission is clear about what needs to change. No more hiring unqualified teachers on the sly. No more nods and winks at teacher education programs that fail to prepare teachers properly. No more tolerance for incompetence in the classroom. Children are compelled to attend school. Every state guarantees them equal protection under the law, and most promise them a sound education. In the face of these obligations, students have a right to competent, caring teachers who work in schools organized for success.

The commission is also clear about what needs to be done. Like the Flexner report that led to the transformation of the medical profession in 1910, this report, *What Matters Most: Teaching for America's Future,* examines successful practices within and outside the United States to describe what works. The commission concludes that children can reap the benefits of current knowledge about teaching and learning only if schools and schools of education are dramatically redesigned.

The report offers a blueprint for recruiting, preparing, supporting, and rewarding excellent educators in all of America's schools. The plan is aimed at ensuring that all schools have teachers with the knowledge and skills they need to enable all children to learn. If a caring, qualified teacher for every child is the most important ingredient in education reform, then it should no longer be the factor most frequently overlooked.

At the same time, such teachers must have available to them schools and school systems that are well designed to achieve their key academic mission: they must be focused on clear, high standards for students; organized to provide a coherent, high-quality curriculum across the grades; and designed to support teachers' collective work and learning.

We note that this challenge is accompanied by an equally great opportunity; over the next decade we will recruit and hire more than two million teachers for America's schools. More than half of the teachers who will be teaching 10 years from now will be hired during the next decade. If we can focus our energies on providing this generation of teachers with the kinds of knowledge and skills they need to help students succeed, we will have made an enormous contribution to America's future.

The Nature of the Problem

The education challenge facing the U.S. is not that its schools are not as good as they once were. It is that schools must help the vast majority of young people reach levels of skill and competence that were once thought to be within the reach of only a few.

After more than a decade of school reform, America is still a very long way from achieving its educational goals. Instead of all children coming to school ready to learn, more are living in poverty and without health care than a decade ago.[2] Graduation rates and student achievement in most subjects have remained flat or have increased only slightly.[3] Fewer than 10% of high school students can read, write, compute, and manage scientific material at the high levels required for today's "knowledge work" jobs.[4]

This distance between our stated goals and current realities is not due to lack of effort. Many initiatives have been launched in local communities with positive effects. Nonetheless, we have reached an impasse in spreading these promising efforts to the system as a whole. It is now clear that most schools and teachers cannot produce the kind of learning demanded by the new reforms—not because they do not want to, but because they do not know how, and the systems they work in do not support their efforts to do so.

The Challenge for Teaching

A more complex, knowledge-based, and multicultural society creates new expectations for teaching. To help diverse learners master more challenging content, teachers must go far beyond dispensing information, giving a test, and giving a grade. They must themselves know their subject areas deeply, and they must understand how students think, if they are to create experiences that actually work to produce learning.

Developing the kind of teaching that is needed will require much greater clarity about what students need to learn in order to succeed in the world that awaits them and what teachers need to know and do in order to help students learn it. Standards that reflect these imperatives for student learning and for teaching are largely absent in our nation today. States are just now beginning to establish standards for student learning.

Standards for teaching are equally haphazard. Although most parents might assume that teachers, like other professionals, are educated in similar ways so that they acquire common knowledge before they are admitted to practice, this is not the case. Unlike doctors, lawyers, accountants, or architects, all teachers do not have the same training. Some teachers have very high levels of skills—particularly in states that require a bachelor's degree in the discipline to be taught—along with coursework in teaching, learning, curriculum, and child development; extensive practice teaching; and a master's degree in education. Others learn little about their subject matter or about teaching, learning, and child development—particularly in states that have low requirements for licensing.

And while states have recently begun to require some form of testing for a teaching license, most licensing exams are little more than multiple-choice tests of basic skills and general knowledge, widely criticized by educators and experts as woefully inadequate to measure teaching skill.[5] Furthermore, in many states the cutoff scores are so low that there is no effective standard for entry.

These difficulties are barely known to the public. The schools' most closely held secret amounts to a great national shame: roughly one-quarter of newly hired American teachers lack the qualifications for their jobs. More than 12% of new hires enter the classroom without any formal training at all, and another 14% arrive without fully meeting state standards.

Although no state will permit a person to write wills, practice medicine, fix plumbing, or style hair without completing training and passing an examination, more than 40 states allow districts to hire teachers who have not met basic requirements. States pay more attention to the qualifications of the veterinarians treating America's pets than to those of the people educating the nation's youngsters. Consider the following facts:

- In recent years, more than 50,000 people who lack the training required for their jobs have entered teaching annually on emergency or substandard licenses.[6]

- Nearly one-fourth (23%) of all secondary teachers do not have even a minor in their main teaching field. This is true for more than 30% of mathematics teachers.[7]
- Among teachers who teach a second subject, 36% are unlicensed in that field, and 50% lack a minor in it.[8]
- Fifty-six percent of high school students taking physical science are taught by out-of-field teachers, as are 27% of those taking mathematics and 21% of those taking English.[9] The proportions are much greater in high-poverty schools and lower-track classes.
- In schools with the highest minority enrollments, students have less than a 50% chance of getting a science or mathematics teacher who holds a license and a degree in the field in which he or she teaches.[10]

In the nation's poorest schools, where hiring is most lax and teacher turnover is constant, the results are disastrous. Thousands of children are taught throughout their school careers by a parade of teachers without preparation in the fields in which they teach, inexperienced beginners with little training and no mentoring, and short-term substitutes trying to cope with constant staff disruptions.[11] It is more surprising that some of these children manage to learn than that so many fail to do so.

Current Barriers

Unequal resources and inadequate investments in teacher recruitment are major problems. Other industrialized countries fund their schools equally and make sure there are qualified teachers for all of them by underwriting teacher preparation and salaries. However, teachers in the U.S. must go into substantial debt to become prepared for a field that in most states pays less than any other occupation requiring a college degree.

This situation is not necessary or inevitable. The hiring of unprepared teachers was almost eliminated during the 1970s with scholarships and loans for college students preparing to teach, Urban Teacher Corps initiatives, and master of arts in teaching (MAT) programs, coupled with wage increases. However, the cancellation of most of these recruitment incentives in the 1980s led to renewed shortages when student enrollments started to climb once again, especially in cities. Be-

tween 1987 and 1991, the proportion of well-qualified new teachers—those entering teaching with a college major or minor and a license in their fields—actually declined from about 74% to 67%.[12]

There is no real system for recruiting, preparing, and developing America's teachers. Major problems include:

Inadequate teacher education. Because accreditation is not required of teacher education programs, their quality varies widely, with excellent programs standing alongside shoddy ones that are allowed to operate even when they do an utterly inadequate job. Too many American universities still treat their schools of education as "cash cows" whose excess revenues are spent on the training of doctors, lawyers, accountants, and almost any students other than prospective teachers themselves.

Slipshod recruitment. Although the share of academically able young people entering teaching has been increasing, there are still too few in some parts of the country and in critical subjects like mathematics and science. Federal incentives that once existed to induce talented people into high-need fields and locations have largely been eliminated.

Haphazard hiring and induction. School districts often lose the best candidates because of inefficient and cumbersome hiring practices, barriers to teacher mobility, and inattention to teacher qualifications. Those who do get hired are typically given the most difficult assignments and left to sink or swim, without the kind of help provided by internships and residencies in other professions. Isolated behind classroom doors with little feedback or help, as many as 30% leave in the first few years, while others learn merely to cope rather than to teach well.

Lack of professional development and rewards for knowledge and skill. In addition to the lack of support for beginning teachers, most school districts invest little in ongoing professional development for experienced teachers and spend much of these limited resources on unproductive "hit-and-run" workshops. Furthermore, most U.S. teachers have only three to five hours each week for planning. This leaves them with almost no regular time to consult together or to learn about new teaching strategies, unlike their peers in many European and Asian countries who spend between 15 and 20 hours per week working jointly on refining lessons and learning about new methods.

The teaching career does not encourage teachers to develop or use growing expertise. Evaluation and tenure decisions often lack a tangible connection to a clear vision of high-quality teaching, important skills are rarely rewarded, and—when budgets must be cut—professional development is often the first item sacrificed. Historically, the only route to advancement in teaching has been to leave the classroom for administration.

In contrast, many European and Asian countries hire a greater number of better-paid teachers, provide them with more extensive preparation, give them time to work together, and structure schools so that teachers can focus on teaching and can come to know their students well. Teachers share decision making and take on a range of professional responsibilities without leaving teaching. This is possible because these other countries invest their resources in many more classroom teachers—typically constituting 60% to 80% of staff, as compared to only 43% in the United States—and many fewer nonteaching employees.[13]

Schools structured for failure. Today's schools are organized in ways that support neither student learning nor teacher learning well. Teachers are isolated from one another so that they cannot share knowledge or take responsibility for overall student learning. Technologies that could enable alternative uses of personnel and time are not yet readily available in schools, and few staff members are prepared to use them. Moreover, too many people and resources are allocated to jobs and activities outside of classrooms, on the sidelines rather than at the front lines of teaching and learning.

High-performance businesses are abandoning the organizational assumptions that led to this way of managing work. They are flattening hierarchies, creating teams, and training employees to take on wide responsibilities using technologies that allow them to perform their work more efficiently. Schools that have restructured their work in these ways have been able to provide more time for teachers to work together and more time for students to work closely with teachers around more clearly defined standards for learning.[14]

Goals for the Nation

To address these problems, the commission challenges the nation to embrace a set of goals that will put us on the path to serious, long-term improvements in teaching and learning for America. The commission has six goals for the year 2006.

- All children will be taught by teachers who have the knowledge, skills, and commitment to teach children well.
- All teacher education programs will meet professional standards, or they will be closed.
- All teachers will have access to high-quality professional development, and they will have regularly scheduled time for collegial work and planning.
- Both teachers and principals will be hired and retained based on their ability to meet professional standards of practice.
- Teachers' salaries will be based on their knowledge and skills.
- High-quality teaching will be the central investment of schools. Most education dollars will be spent on classroom teaching.

The Commission's Recommendations

The commission's proposals provide a vision and a blueprint for the development of a 21st-century teaching profession that can make good on the nation's educational goals. The recommendations are systemic in scope—not a recipe for more short-lived pilot and demonstration projects. They describe a new infrastructure for professional learning and an accountability system that ensures attention to standards for educators as well as for students at every level: national, state, district, school, and classroom.

The commission urges a complete overhaul in the systems of teacher preparation and professional development to ensure that they reflect current knowledge and practice. This redesign should create a continuum of teacher learning based on compatible standards that operate from recruitment and preservice education through licensing, hiring, and induction into the profession, to advanced certification and ongoing professional development.

The commission also proposes a comprehensive set of changes in school organization and management. And finally, it recommends a set of measures for ensuring that only those who are competent to teach or to lead schools are allowed to enter or to continue in the profession—a starting point for creating professional accountability. The specific recommendations are enumerated below.

1. Get serious about standards for both students and teachers. "The Commission recommends that we renew the national promise to bring every American child up to world-class standards in core academic areas and to develop and enforce rigorous standards for teacher preparation, initial licensing, and continuing development."

With respect to student standards, the commission believes that every state should work on incorporating challenging standards for learning—such as those developed by professional bodies like the National Council of Teachers of Mathematics—into curriculum frameworks and new assessments of student performance. Implementation must go beyond the tautology that "all children can learn" to examine what they should learn and how much they need to know.

Standards should be accompanied by benchmarks of performance—from "acceptable" to "highly accomplished"—so that students and teachers know how to direct their efforts toward greater excellence.

Clearly, if students are to achieve high standards, we can expect no less from teachers and other educators. Our highest priority must be to reach agreement on what teachers should know and be able to do in order to help students succeed. Unaddressed for decades, this task has recently been completed by three professional bodies: the National Council for Accreditation of Teacher Education (NCATE), the Interstate New Teacher Assessment and Support Consortium (INTASC), and the National Board for Professional Teaching Standards (the National Board). Their combined efforts to set standards for teacher education, beginning teacher licensing, and advanced certification outline a continuum of teacher development throughout the career and offer the most powerful tools we have for reaching and rejuvenating the soul of the profession.

These standards and the assessments that grow out of them identify what it takes to be an effective teacher: subject-matter expertise coupled with an understanding of how children learn and develop; skill in using a range of teaching strategies and technologies; sensitivity and effectiveness in working with students from diverse backgrounds; the ability to work well with parents and other teachers; and assessment expertise capable of discerning how well children are doing, what they are learning, and what needs to be done next to move them along.

The standards reflect a teaching role in which the teacher is an instructional leader who orchestrates learning experiences in response to curriculum goals and student needs and who coaches students to high levels of independent performance. To advance standards, the commission recommends that states:

- establish their own professional standards boards;
- insist on professional accreditation for all schools of education;
- close inadequate schools of education;
- license teachers based on demonstrated performance, including tests of subject-matter knowledge, teaching knowledge, and teaching skill; and
- use National Board standards as the benchmark for accomplished teaching.

2. Reinvent teacher preparation and professional development. "The Commission recommends that colleges and schools work with states to redesign teacher education so that the two million teachers to be hired in the next decade are adequately prepared and so that all teachers have access to high-quality learning opportunities."

For this to occur, states, school districts, and education schools should:

- organize teacher education and professional development around standards for students and teachers;
- institute extended, graduate-level teacher preparation programs that provide yearlong internships in a professional development school;
- create and fund mentoring programs for beginning teachers, along with evaluation of teaching skills;
- create stable, high-quality sources of professional development—and then allocate 1% of state and local spending to support them, along with additional matching funds to school districts;
- organize new sources of professional development, such as teacher academies, school/university partnerships, and learning networks that transcend school boundaries; and
- make professional development an ongoing part of teachers' daily work.

If teachers are to be ready to help their students meet the new standards that are now being set for them, teacher preparation and professional development programs must consciously examine the expectations embodied in new curriculum frameworks and assessments and understand what they imply for teaching and for learning to teach. Then they must develop effective strategies for preparing teachers to teach in these much more demanding ways.

Over the past decade, many schools of education have changed their programs to incorporate new knowledge. More than 300 have developed extended programs that add a fifth (and occasionally a sixth) year of undergraduate training. These programs allow beginning teachers to complete a degree in their subject area as well as to acquire a firmer grounding in teaching skills. They allow coursework to be connected to extended practice teaching in schools—ideally, in professional development schools that, like teaching hospitals in medicine, have a special mission to support research and training. Recent studies show that graduates of extended programs are rated as better-prepared and more effective teachers and are far more likely to enter and remain in teaching than are their peers from traditional four-year programs.[15]

New teachers should have support from an expert mentor during the first year of teaching. Research shows that such support improves both teacher effectiveness and retention.[16] In the system we propose, teachers will have completed initial tests of subject-matter and basic teaching knowledge before entry and will be ready to undertake the second stage—a performance assessment of teaching skills—during this first year.

Throughout their careers, teachers should have ongoing opportunities to update their skills. In addition to time for joint planning and problem solving with in-school colleagues, teachers should have access to networks, school/university partnerships, and academies where they can connect with other educators to study subject-matter teaching, new pedagogies, and school change. The benefit of these opportunities is that they offer sustained work on problems of practice that are directly connected to teachers' work and student learning.

3. Overhaul teacher recruitment and put qualified teachers in every classroom. "The Commission recommends that states and school districts pursue aggressive policies to put qualified teachers in every classroom by providing financial incentives to correct shortages, streamlining hiring procedures, and reducing barriers to teacher mobility."

Although each year the U.S. produces more new teachers than it needs, shortages of qualified candidates in particular fields (e.g., mathematics and science) and particular locations (primarily inner city and rural) are chronic.

In large districts, logistics can overwhelm everything else. It is sometimes the case that central offices cannot find out about classroom vacancies, principals are left in the dark about applicants, and candidates cannot get any information at all.

Finally, it should be stressed that large pools of potential mid-career teacher entrants—former employees of downsizing corporations, military and government retirees, and teacher aides already in the schools—are for the most part untapped.

To remedy these situations, the commission suggests the following actions:

- increase the ability of financially disadvantaged districts to pay for qualified teachers and insist that school districts hire only qualified teachers;
- redesign and streamline hiring at the district level—principally by creating a central "electronic hiring hall" for all qualified candidates and establishing cooperative relationships with universities to encourage early hiring of teachers;
- eliminate barriers to teacher mobility by promoting reciprocal interstate licensing and by working across states to develop portable pensions;
- provide incentives (including scholarships and premium pay) to recruit teachers for high-need subjects and locations; and
- develop high-quality pathways to teaching for recent graduates, mid-career changers, paraprofessionals already in the classroom, and military and government retirees.

4. Encourage and reward knowledge and skill. "The Commission recommends that school districts, states, and professional associations cooperate to make teaching a true profession, with a career continuum that places teaching at the top and rewards teachers for their knowledge and skills."

Schools have few ways of encouraging outstanding teaching, supporting teachers who take on the most challenging work, or rewarding increases in knowledge and skill. Newcomers who enter teaching without adequate preparation are paid at the same levels as those who enter with highly developed skills. Novices take on exactly

the same kind of work as 30-year veterans, with little differentiation based on expertise. Mediocre teachers receive the same rewards as outstanding ones. And unlicensed "teachers" are placed on the same salary schedule as licensed teachers in high-demand fields such as mathematics and science or as teachers licensed in two or more subjects.

One testament to the inability of the existing system to understand what it is doing is that it rewards experience with easier work instead of encouraging senior teachers to deal with difficult learning problems and tough learning situations. As teachers gain experience, they can look forward to teaching in more affluent schools, working with easier schedules, dealing with "better" classes, or moving out of the classroom into administration. Teachers are rarely rewarded for applying their expertise to the most challenging learning problems or major needs of the system.

To address these issues, the commission recommends that state and local education agencies:

- develop a career continuum linked to assessments and compensation systems that reward knowledge and skill (e.g., the ability to teach expertly in two or more subjects, as demonstrated by additional licenses, or the ability to pass examinations of teaching skill, such as those offered by INTASC and the National Board);
- remove incompetent teachers through peer review programs that provide necessary assistance and due process; and
- set goals and enact incentives for National Board certification in every district, with the aim of certifying 105,000 teachers during the next 10 years.

If teaching is organized as are other professions that have set consistent licensing requirements, standards of practice, and assessment methods, then advancement can be tied to professional growth and development. A career continuum that places teaching at the top and supports growing expertise should 1) recognize accomplishment, 2) anticipate that teachers will continue to teach while taking on other roles that allow them to share their knowledge, and 3) promote continued skill development related to clear standards.

Some districts, such as Cincinnati and Rochester, New York, have already begun to develop career pathways that tie evaluations to salary increments at key stages as teachers move from their *initial license* to *resident teacher* (under the supervision of a mentor) to the designation of *professional teacher*. The major decision to grant *tenure* is made after rigorous evaluation of performance (including both administrator and peer review) in the first several years of teaching. Advanced certification from the National Board for Professional Teaching Standards may qualify teachers for another salary step and/or for the position of lead teacher—a role that is awarded to those who have demonstrated high levels of competence and want to serve as mentors or consulting teachers.

One other feature of a new compensation system is key. The central importance of teaching to the mission of schools should be acknowledged by having the highest-paid professional in a school system be an experienced, National Board-certified teacher. As in other professions, roles should become less distinct. The jobs of teacher, consultant, supervisor, principal, curriculum developer, researcher, mentor, and professor should be hyphenated roles, allowing many ways for individuals to use their talents and expertise without abandoning the core work of the profession.

5. Create schools that are organized for student and teacher success. "The Commission recommends that schools be restructured to become genuine learning organizations for both students and teachers: organizations that respect learning, honor teaching, and teach for understanding."

Many experts have observed that the demands of serious teaching and learning bear little relationship to the organization of the typical American school. Nothing more clearly reveals this problem than how we allocate the principal resources of school—time, money, and people. Far too many sit in offices on the sidelines of the school's core work, managing routines rather than improving learning. Our schools are bureaucratic inheritances from the 19th century, not the kinds of learning organizations required for the 21st century.

Across the United States, the ratio of school staff to students is 1 to 9 (with "staff" including district employees, school administrators, teachers, instructional aides, guidance counselors, librarians, and support staff). However, actual class size averages about 24 and reaches 35 or more in some cities. Teaching loads for high school teachers generally exceed 100 students per day. Yet many schools have proved that it is possible to restructure adults' use of time so that more teachers and administrators actually work in the classroom, face-to-face with students on a daily basis, thus reducing class sizes while creating more time for teacher collaboration. They do this by creating teams of teachers who share students; engaging almost all adults in the school in these teaching teams, where they can share expertise directly with one another; and reducing pullouts and nonteaching jobs.

Schools must be freed from the tyrannies of time and tradition to permit more powerful student and teacher learning. To accomplish this the commission recommends that state and local boards work to:

- flatten hierarchies and reallocate resources to invest more in teachers and technology and less in nonteaching personnel;
- provide venture capital in the form of challenge grants that will promote learning linked to school improvement and will reward effective team efforts; and
- select, prepare, and retain principals who understand teaching and learning and who can lead high-performing schools.

If students have an inalienable right to be taught by a qualified teacher, teachers have a right to be supervised by a highly qualified principal. The job began as that of a "principal teacher," and this conception is ever more relevant as the focus of the school recenters on academic achievement for students. Principals should teach at least part of the time (as do most European, Asian, and private school directors), and they should be well prepared as instructional leaders, with a solid understanding of teaching and learning.

Next Steps

Developing recommendations is easy. Implementing them is hard work. The first step is to recognize that these ideas must be pursued together—as an entire tapestry that is tightly interwoven.

The second step is to build on the substantial work of education reform undertaken in the last decade. All across the country, successful programs for recruiting, educating, and mentoring new teachers have sprung up. Professional networks and teacher academies have been launched, many teacher preparation programs have been redesigned, higher standards for licensing teachers and accrediting education schools have been developed, and, of course, the National Board for Professional Teaching Standards is now fully established and beginning to define and reward accomplished teaching.

While much of what the commission proposes can and should be accomplished by reallocating resources that are currently used unproductively, there will be new costs. The estimated additional annual costs of the commission's key recommendations are as follows: scholarships for teaching recruits, $500 million; teacher education reforms, $875 million; mentoring supports and new licensing assessments, $750 million; and state funds for professional development, $2.75 billion. The total is just under $5 billion annually—less than 1% of the amount spent on the federal savings-and-loan bailout. This is not too much, we believe, to bail out our schools and to secure our future.

A Call to Action

Setting the commission's agenda in motion and carrying it to completion will demand the best of us all. The commission calls on governors and legislators to create state professional boards to govern teacher licensing standards and to issue annual report cards on the status of teaching. It asks state legislators and governors to set aside at least 1% of funds for standards-based teacher training. It urges Congress to put money behind the professional development programs it has already approved but never funded.

Moreover, the commission asks the profession to take seriously its responsibilities to children and the American future. Among other measures, the commission insists that state educators close the loopholes that permit administrators to put unqualified "teachers" in the classroom. It calls on university officials to take up the hard work of improving the preparation and skills of new and practicing teachers. It asks administrators and teachers to take on the difficult task of guaranteeing teaching competence in the classroom. And it asks local school boards and superintendents to play their vital role by streamlining hiring procedures, upgrading quality, and putting more staff and resources into the front lines of teaching.

If all of these things are accomplished, the teaching profession of the 21st century will look much different from the one we have today. Indeed, someone entering the profession might expect to advance along a continuum that unfolds much like this:

For as long as she could remember, Elena had wanted to teach. As a peer tutor in middle school, she loved the feeling she got whenever her partner learned something new. In high school, she served as a teacher's aide for her community service project. She linked up with other students through an Internet group started by Future Educators of America.

When she arrived at college she knew she wanted to prepare to teach, so she began taking courses in developmental and cognitive psychology early in her sophomore year. She chose mathematics as a major and applied in her junior year for the university's five-year course of study leading to a master of arts in teaching. After a round of interviews and a review of her record thus far, Elena was admitted into the highly selective teacher education program.

The theories Elena studied in her courses came to life before her eyes as she conducted a case study of John, a 7-year-old whom she tutored in a nearby school. She was struck by John's amazing ability to build things, in contrast with his struggles to learn to read. She carried these puzzles back to her seminar and on into her other courses as she tried to understand learning.

Over time, she examined other cases, some of them available on a multimedia computer system that allowed her to see videotapes of children, samples of their work, and documentation from their teachers about their learning strategies, problems, and progress. From these data, Elena and her classmates developed a concrete sense of different learning approaches. She began to think about how she could use John's strengths to create productive pathways into other areas of learning.

Elena's teachers modeled the kinds of strategies she herself would be using as a teacher. Instead of lecturing from texts, they enabled students to develop and apply knowledge in the context of real teaching situations. These frequently occurred in the professional development school (PDS) where Elena was engaged in a yearlong internship, guided by a faculty of university- and school-based teacher educators.

In the PDS, Elena was placed with a team of student teachers who worked with a team of expert veteran teachers. Her team included teachers of art, language arts, and science, as well as mathematics. They discussed learning within and across these domains in many of their assignments and constructed interdisciplinary curricula together.

Most of the school- and university-based teacher educators who made up the PDS faculty had been certified as accomplished practitioners by the National Board for Professional Teaching Standards, having completed a portfolio of evidence about their teaching along with a set of rigorous performance assessments. The faculty members created courses, internship experiences, and seminars that allowed them to integrate theory and practice, pose fundamental dilemmas of teaching, and address specific aspects of learning to teach.

Elena's classroom work included observing and documenting the learning and behavior of specific children, evaluating lessons that illustrated important concepts and strategies, tutoring and working with small groups, sitting in on family conferences, engaging in school and team planning meetings, visiting homes and community agencies to learn about their resources, planning field trips and curriculum segments, teaching lessons and short units, and ultimately taking major responsibility for the class for a month at the end of the year. This work was supplemented by readings and discussions grounded in case studies of teaching.

A team of PDS teachers videotaped all their classes over the course of the year to serve as the basis for discussions of teaching decisions and outcomes. These teachers' lesson plans, student work, audiotaped planning journals, and reflections on lessons were also available in a multimedia database. This allowed student teachers to look at practice from many angles, examine how classroom situations arose from things that had happened in the past, see how various strategies turned out, and understand a teacher's thinking about students, subjects, and curriculum goals as he or she made decisions. Because the PDS was also wired for video and computer communication with the school of education, master teachers could hold conversations with student teachers by teleconference or e-mail when on-site visits were impossible.

When Elena finished her rich, exhausting internship year, she was ready to try her hand at what she knew would be a demanding first year of teaching. She submitted her portfolio for review by the state professional standards board and sat for the examination of subject-matter and teaching knowledge that was required for an initial teaching license. She was both exhilarated and anxious when she received

a job offer, but she felt she was ready to try her hand at teaching.

Elena spent that summer eagerly developing curriculum ideas for her new class. She had the benefit of advice from the district mentor teacher already assigned to work with her in her first year of teaching, and she had access to an on-line database of teaching materials developed by teachers across the country and organized around the curriculum standards of the National Council of Teachers of Mathematics, of which she had become a member.

Elena's mentor teacher worked with her and several other new middle school mathematics and science teachers throughout the year, meeting with them individually and in groups to examine their teaching and provide support. The mentors and their first-year colleagues also met in groups once a month at the PDS to discuss specific problems of practice.

Elena met weekly with the other math and science teachers in the school to discuss curriculum plans and share demonstration lessons. This extended lunch meeting occurred while her students were in a Project Adventure/physical education course that taught them teamwork and cooperation skills. She also met with the four other members of her teaching team for three hours each week while their students were at community-service placements. The team used this time to discuss cross-disciplinary teaching plans and the progress of the 80 students they shared.

In addition to these built-in opportunities for daily learning, Elena and her colleagues benefited from the study groups they had developed at their school and the professional development offerings at the local university and the Teachers Academy.

At the Teachers Academy, school- and university-based faculty members taught extended courses in areas ranging from advances in learning theory to all kinds of teaching methods, from elementary science to advanced calculus. These courses usually featured case studies and teaching demonstrations as well as follow-up work in teachers' own classrooms. The academy provided the technologies needed for multimedia conferencing, which allowed teachers to "meet" with one another across their schools and to see one another's classroom work. They could also connect to courses and study groups at the university, including a popular master's degree program that helped teachers prepare for National Board certification.

With the strength of a preparation that had helped her put theory and practice together and with the support of so many colleagues, Elena felt confident that she could succeed at her life's goal: becoming—and, as she now understood, always *becoming—a teacher.*

1. *What Matters Most: Teaching for America's Future* (New York: National Commission on Teaching and America's Future, 1996.) Copies of this report can be obtained from the National Commission on Teaching and America's Future, P.O. Box 5239, Woodbridge, VA 22194-5239. Prices, including postage and handling, are $18 for the full report, $5 for the summary report, and $20 for both reports. Orders must be prepaid.

2. *Income, Poverty, and Valuation of Non-Cash Benefits: 1993* (Washington, D.C.: U.S. Bureau of the Census, Current Population Reports, Series P-60, No. 188, 1995). Table D-5, p. D-17. See also *Current Population Survey: March 1988/March 1995* (Washington, D.C.: U.S. Bureau of the Census, 1995).

3. *National Education Goals Report: Executive Summary* (Washington, D.C.: National Education Goals Panel, 1995).

4. National Center for Education Statistics, *Report in Brief: National Assessment of Education Progress (NAEP) 1992 Trends in Academic Progress* (Washington, D.C.: U.S. Department of Education, 1994).

5. For reviews of teacher licensing tests, see Linda Darling-Hammond, "Teaching Knowledge: How Do We Test It?," *American Educator,* Fall 1986, pp. 18–21, 46; Lee Shulman, "Knowledge and Teaching: Foundations of the New Reform," *Harvard Educational Review,* January 1987, pp. 1–22; C. J. MacMillan and Shirley Pendlebury, "The Florida Performance Measurement System; A Consideration," *Teachers College Record,* Fall 1985, pp. 67–78; Walter Haney, George Madaus, and Amelia Kreitzer, "Charms Talismanic: Testing Teachers for the Improvement of American Education," in Ernest Z. Rothkopf, ed., *Review of Research in Education, Vol. 14* (Washington, D.C.: American Educational Research Association, 1987), pp. 169–238; and Edward H. Haertel, "New Forms of Teacher Assessment," in Gerald Grant, ed., *Review of Research in Education, Vol. 17* (Washington, D.C.: American Educational Research Association, 1991), pp. 3–29.

6. C. Emily Feistritzer and David T. Chester, *Alternative Teacher Certification: A State-by-State Analysis* (Washington, D.C.: National Center for Education Information, 1996).

7. Marilyn M. McMillen, Sharon A. Bobbitt, and Hilda F. Lynch, "Teacher Training, Certification, and Assignment in Public Schools: 1990–91," paper presented at the annual meeting of the American Educational Research Association, New Orleans, April 1994.

8. National Center for Education Statistics, *The Condition of Education 1995* (Washington, D.C.: U.S. Department of Education, 1995), p. x.

9. Richard M. Ingersoll, *Schools and Staffing Survey: Teacher Supply, Teacher Qualifications, and Teacher Turnover, 1990–1991* (Washington, D.C.: National Center for Education Statistics, 1995), p. 28.

10. Jeannie Oakes, *Multiplying Inequalities: The Effects of Race, Social Class, and Tracking on Opportunities to Learn Mathematics and Science* (Santa Monica, Calif.: RAND Corporation, 1990).

11. *Who Will Teach Our Children?* (Sacramento: California Commission on Teaching, 1985); and Linda Darling-Hammond, "Inequality and Access to Knowledge," in James Banks, ed., *Handbook of Research on Multicultural Education* (New York: Macmillan, 1995), pp. 465–83.

12. Mary Rollefson, *Teacher Supply in the United States: Sources of Newly Hired Teachers in Public and Private Schools* (Washington, D.C.: National Center for Education Statistics, 1993).

13. *Education Indicators at a Glance* (Paris: Organisation for Economic Cooperation and Development, 1995).

14. Linda Darling-Hammond, "Beyond Bureaucracy: Restructuring Schools for High Performance," in Susan Fuhrman and Jennifer O'Day, eds., *Rewards and Reform* (San Francisco: Jossey-Bass, 1996), pp. 144–94; Linda Darling-Hammond, Jacqueline Ancess, and Beverly Falk, *Authentic Assessment in Action: Studies of Schools and Students at Work* (New York: Teachers College Press, 1995); Fred Newman and Gary Wehlage, *Successful School Restructuring: A Report to the Public and Educators by the Center on Organization and Restructuring of Schools* (Madison: Board of Regents of the University of Wisconsin System, 1995); and Ann Lieberman, ed., *The Work of Restructuring Schools: Building from the Ground Up* (New York: Teachers College Press, 1995).

15. For data on effectiveness and retention, see Michael Andrew, "The Differences Between Graduates of Four-Year and Five-Year Teacher Preparation Programs," *Journal of Teacher Education,* vol. 41, 1990, pp. 45–51; Thomas Baker, "A Survey of Four-Year and Five-Year Program Graduates and Their Principals," *Southeastern Regional Association of Teacher Educators (SRATE) Journal,* Summer 1993, pp. 28–33; Michael Andrew and Richard L. Schwab, "Has Reform in Teacher Education Influenced Teacher Performance? An Outcome Assessment of Graduates of Eleven Teacher Education Programs," *Action in Teacher Education,* Fall 1995, pp. 43–53; Jon J. Denton and William H. Peters, "Program Assessment Report: Curriculum Evaluation of a Nontraditional Program for Certifying Teachers," unpublished report, Texas A & M University, College Station, 1988; and Hyun-Seok Shin, "Estimating Future Teacher Supply: An Application of Survival Analysis," paper presented at the annual meeting of the American Educational Research Association, New Orleans, April 1994.

16. Leslie Huling-Austin, ed., *Assisting the Beginning Teacher* (Reston, Va.: Association of Teacher Educators, 1989); Mark A. Smylie, "Redesigning Teachers' Work: Connections to the Classroom," in Linda Darling-Hammond, ed., *Review of Research in Education, Vol. 20* (Washington, D.C.: American Educational Research Association, 1994); and Linda Darling-Hammond, ed., *Professional Development Schools: Schools for Developing a Profession* (New York: Teachers College Press, 1994).

AE Article Review Form

We encourage you to photocopy and use this page as a tool to assess how the articles in **Annual Editions** expand on the information in your textbook. By reflecting on the articles you will gain enhanced text information. You can also access this useful form on a product's book support Web site at **http://www.dushkin.com/online/.**

NAME: DATE:

TITLE AND NUMBER OF ARTICLE:

BRIEFLY STATE THE MAIN IDEA OF THIS ARTICLE:

LIST THREE IMPORTANT FACTS THAT THE AUTHOR USES TO SUPPORT THE MAIN IDEA:

WHAT INFORMATION OR IDEAS DISCUSSED IN THIS ARTICLE ARE ALSO DISCUSSED IN YOUR TEXTBOOK OR OTHER READINGS THAT YOU HAVE DONE? LIST THE TEXTBOOK CHAPTERS AND PAGE NUMBERS:

LIST ANY EXAMPLES OF BIAS OR FAULTY REASONING THAT YOU FOUND IN THE ARTICLE:

LIST ANY NEW TERMS/CONCEPTS THAT WERE DISCUSSED IN THE ARTICLE, AND WRITE A SHORT DEFINITION:

ANNUAL EDITIONS revisions depend on two major opinion sources: one is our Advisory Board, listed in the front of this volume, which works with us in scanning the thousands of articles published in the public press each year; the other is you—the person actually using the book. Please help us and the users of the next edition by completing the prepaid article rating form on this page and returning it to us. Thank you for your help!

ANNUAL EDITIONS: Early Childhood Education 99/00

ARTICLE RATING FORM

Here is an opportunity for you to have direct input into the next revision of this volume. We would like you to rate each of the 36 articles listed below, using the following scale:

1. **Excellent: should definitely be retained**
2. **Above average: should probably be retained**
3. **Below average: should probably be deleted**
4. **Poor: should definitely be deleted**

Your ratings will play a vital part in the next revision. So please mail this prepaid form to us just as soon as you complete it. Thanks for your help!

We Want Your Advice

RATING / ARTICLE

1. Preschoolers' Education Takes Center Stage
2. New Brain Development Research—A Wonderful Window of Opportunity to Build Public Support for Early Childhood Education!
3. Highlights of the Quality 2000 Initiative: Not by Chance
4. A Child Shall Lead Us
5. Child Care: How Does Your State Rate?
6. Can Education Reduce Social Inequity?
7. Fetal Psychology
8. Children's Prenatal Exposure to Drugs: Implications for Early Childhood Educators
9. A Bundle of Emotions
10. Baby Talk
11. Boys Will Be Boys
12. The Education of Hispanics in Early Childhood: Of Roots and Wings
13. It May Cause Anxiety, but Day Care Can Benefit Kids
14. Meeting Basic Needs: Health and Safety Practices in Feeding and Diapering Infants
15. Simply Sensational Spaces: A Multi-"S" Approach to Toddler Environments
16. Homework Doesn't Help
17. Don't Shut Fathers Out
18. From Philosophy to Practice in Inclusive Early Childhood Programs
19. Together Is Better: Specific Tips on How to Include Children with Various Types of Disabilities

RATING / ARTICLE

20. Inclusion of Young Children with Special Needs in Early Childhood Education: The Research Base
21. Challenges to Family Involvement
22. Beyond Discipline to Guidance
23. Teaching Peace Concepts to Children
24. Creating a Community of Learning for Homeless Children
25. Fostering Intrinsic Motivation in Early Childhood Classrooms
26. Why Curriculum Matters in Early Childhood Education
27. Fostering Creativity in the Early Childhood Classroom
28. Challenging Movement Experiences for Young Children
29. Learning to Read and Write: Developmentally Appropriate Practices for Young Children
30. NAEYC Position Statement: Responding to Linguistic and Cultural Diversity—Recommendations for Effective Early Childhood Education
31. Beginning to Implement the Reggio Philosophy
32. Supporting Math Thinking
33. Documenting Children's Learning
34. Tomorrow's Child
35. Let's Be Real!
36. What Matters Most: A Competent Teacher for Every Child

(Continued on next page)

BUSINESS REPLY MAIL
FIRST-CLASS MAIL PERMIT NO. 84 GUILFORD CT

POSTAGE WILL BE PAID BY ADDRESSEE

Dushkin/McGraw-Hill
Sluice Dock
Guilford, CT 06437-9989

ABOUT YOU

Name   Date

Are you a teacher? ☐   A student? ☐
Your school's name

Department

Address   City   State   Zip

School telephone #

YOUR COMMENTS ARE IMPORTANT TO US !

Please fill in the following information:
For which course did you use this book?

Did you use a text with this *ANNUAL EDITION*? ☐ yes ☐ no
What was the title of the text?

What are your general reactions to the *Annual Editions* concept?

Have you read any particular articles recently that you think should be included in the next edition?

Are there any articles you feel should be replaced in the next edition? Why?

Are there any World Wide Web sites you feel should be included in the next edition? Please annotate.

May we contact you for editorial input? ☐ yes ☐ no
May we quote your comments? ☐ yes ☐ no